Care, Control and COVID-19

Care, Control and COVID-19

Health and Biopolitics in Philosophy and Literature

Edited by
Raili Marling and Marko Pajević

DE GRUYTER

ISBN 978-3-11-162778-6
e-ISBN (PDF) 978-3-11-079936-1
e-ISBN (EPUB) 978-3-11-079944-6

Library of Congress Control Number: 2023933355

Bibliographic information published by the Deutsche Nationalbibliothek
The Deutsche Nationalbibliothek lists this publication in the Deutsche Nationalbibliografie;
detailed bibliographic data are available on the internet at http://dnb.dnb.de.

© 2024 Walter de Gruyter GmbH, Berlin/Boston
This volume is text- and page-identical with the hardback published in 2023.
Cover image: Photo courtesy of St Albans Cathedral, Hertfordshire (GB) / Tim Bull
Typesetting: Integra Software Services Pvt. Ltd.

www.degruyter.com

Acknowledgements

This book was made possible, first and foremost, by the intellectual curiosity and social nerve of the scholars who gathered for a conference on health biopolitics at the University of Tartu, Estonia, on 17–18 September 2021, after the lifting of sanctions made international travel possible. The stimulating papers and informal discussions helped to shape the chapters that are gathered in the volume here.

The event and the research were made possible by different funders. Raili Marling's research and part of the conference were supported by the Estonian Research Council grant PRG934 "Imagining Crisis Ordinariness". Marko Pajević's research and part of the conference were supported by the University of Tartu ASTRA Project PER ASPERA, financed by the (European Union) European Regional Development Fund. The conference also received support from Marko Pajević's baseline funding from the University of Tartu.

We also want to thank our editor, Myrto Aspioti, for her guidance and William Marling for his language editing advice.

Contents

Acknowledgements —— V

Marko Pajević and Raili Marling
Introduction: Health and Biopolitics in COVID-19 Times – What Constitutes a Healthy Society? —— 1

Daniele Monticelli
Preliminary Remarks for a Biopolitical History of Western Plague Narratives —— 25

Meelis Friedenthal
How to Manage Plague and COVID-19: Parallels and Differences Between Today and Premodern and Early-Modern Medical Theories —— 47

Thomas Crew
"Civilization is Sterilization": Utopia, Biopolitics and the Total Society in Horkheimer and Adorno's *Dialectic of Enlightenment* **and Aldous Huxley's** *Brave New World* **—— 59**

Timothy Campbell
COVID-19 as Event: Mythology and Ritual in Agamben's Pandemic Dispatches —— 91

Sherryl Vint
Biopolitics, Form-of-Life, A New Use of Bodies —— 111

Raili Marling
The Relationality and Representability of Biopolitical Crises —— 133

Marko Pajević
State Control Versus Humanity: Biopolitics and Health in Juli Zeh's *The METHOD* **(***Corpus Delicti***, 2009) —— 155**

Betiel Wasihun
The Quantified Self: Surveillance, Biopolitics and Literary Resistance —— 183

Frank Kraushaar
When "Total War" Joins "People's War": China's Recent Surge of Biopolitics and Its Repercussions in Internet Poetry —— 205

Marge Käsper
Inside in Immunity, Outside in Community? Discussing Esposito and Framing Pandemic Polemics in France —— 233

Michael Eskin
Needful Facts, Big and Small: On Bodies, Equality, and Treatment —— 251

About the Authors —— 265

Index —— 271

Marko Pajević and Raili Marling

Introduction: Health and Biopolitics in COVID-19 Times – What Constitutes a Healthy Society?

1 The Lost Balance of Care and Control in COVID-19 Times

The term "biopolitics" usually designates the strategies that states use to organize the lives of their citizens through the control of reproduction, welfare and health. In biopolitics, human life and human health become something to be monitored and optimized, to ensure the smooth reproduction of the population as a potential work force. This ordering of life may seem benign, but it imposes considerable controls on human action. This is why the term has been productively used in the analysis of areas where issues of control have major resonance, for example gender, the body, environment, politics, law, social media and surveillance. Biopolitics has become more relevant than ever in the context of the global COVID-19 pandemic: societies confronted with a novel virus mobilized to protect public health, and considerable state power was unleashed to achieve this aim. It is thus timely to return to the meaning of this often employed, but equally often poorly understood notion.

The term "biopolitics" is often used to designate some kind of a repressive and controlling power. However, this is not all: the control is imposed to provide care and to achieve desirable outcomes: we all want to enjoy the benefits of a functioning social infrastructure with reliable healthcare, welfare and benefits. There is no doubt that the state providing such services is a major achievement of modern times and few would want to be deprived of these blessings. Nonetheless, there is always the question of the right balance between a paternalizing state and the freedom of the citizens to decide about their lives, that is, the balance between care and control.

It is this balance that has become a matter of intense public debate during the global mobilization in response to the COVID-19 virus. Several world leaders, for example the French president Emmanuel Macron and, before him, the Chinese leader Xi Jinping, explicitly declared war on the virus, stressing both danger and the need for collective solidarity in response to the threat. This mobilization has led to biopolitical measures previously unheard of in liberal Western societies,[1] resulting in

---

[1] There is ample research on how the pandemic increased surveillance measures in countries with fewer human rights protections like China where the use of these coercive measures was

https://doi.org/10.1515/9783110799361-001

deep and potentially lasting transformations of our societies. In the past three years, we have come to accept controls on our freedom of movement and assembly, limitations to freedom of movement across national boundaries and the reinforcement of what could be called biological citizenship (Rose and Novas 2005, 440). We are still in the midst of it as of this writing and it is not possible to predict which of the new rules will persist and in what forms.

The positions concerning the "right reaction" to what has been presented as the greatest threat to society since World War II by major figures such as then German chancellor Angela Merkel[2] seem irreconcilable. In most countries, the different biopolitical measures have been met by vocal responses from a diverse coalition of voices from very different ends of the political spectrum. In many countries, opposing camps have become increasingly extreme in their rejection of opinions diverging from their own, to the extent that it seems almost impossible to have a cultivated conversation on this topic. One either believes that only vaccination (or, now, booster vaccination) can solve the problem and that the unvaccinated represent the obstacle for a return to a normal functioning of society, or that politicians, supported by mainstream media and scientists, have been led into a cul-de-sac by a non-controllable strategy of fear, if not by some evil conspiracy.[3]

This radical split clearly is not a sign of a healthy society. Health can be defined in different ways and even major national and international institutions are far from pursuing the same ideas in this respect (see Pajević in this volume). Health should not be reduced, however, particularly when applied to society, to an absence of illness or pain. The health of a society cannot be exclusively measured by a narrow physical conceptualization of health. Beyond physical health, there is first of all mental health, which has infinite repercussions on all aspects of individual and social life. In order to evaluate the "health" of a society, we would need not only virologists or internists, but also other medical specialists, including psychologists. We would also need sociologists, historians, political scientists, economists, legal scholars, philosophers, cultural theorists and representatives of arts and humanities and, basically, of all fields of social life. The philosopher of ethics Andreas Brenner calls the COVID-19 times' focus on one highly specialized discipline of science, presented usually only from one perspective, an example of "tunnel vision" and criticizes the push for homogeneity under the label

---

credited with containing the virus by the Chinese authorities (see e.g., Liu and Zhao 2021). The very success of these measures in non-liberal societies increases their appeal elsewhere.

2 Angela Merkel in an address to the German nation on 18 March 2020: https://www.bundesregierung.de/resource/blob/975232/1732182/d4af29ba76f62f61f1320c32d39a7383/fernsehansprache-von-bundeskanzlerin-angela-merkel-data.pdf. Last accessed 18 December 2021.

3 There is increasing research on the confluence of conspiracy theories and the pandemic (e.g. Morelock and Narita 2022).

"science" while ignoring the core of the scientific method.[4] This loss of the habits of debate, both in public discourse and in the sciences, derives from the common use of war rhetoric by politicians and media alike (Brenner 2020, 36–37).

The period of the pandemic has seen the deluge of different statistics: on infections, hospitalizations, deaths, and vaccinations, to list the most obvious. Numbers and statistics always require interpretation. Even more: they need to be interpreted in a specific context; on their own, they do not mean much. In the context of today's information disorder (Hansson et al. 2021), it seems difficult to have a reasonable debate on how to interpret the data we have. However, we have to face the complexity of life and believe in the power of an exchange of ideas in order to maintain an open society and the principles of Enlightenment. In view of the rise of different forms of authoritarianism and wide public support for them even in old democracies, Enlightenment principles should not be thrown out carelessly. After two years of the pandemic, we need to get out of the emergency mode and consider the long-term consequences of the crisis in a more global manner. We need a real debate that includes all aspects of social life, since giving life the absolute status of mere survival carries the risk of totalitarianism. Instead, we should strive for the dignity of life as well as the openness of societies as goals (cf. Brenner 2020, 91).

This discussion requires, perhaps, some distance. This volume proposes an approach coming from the study of cultural representations. Literature has for centuries suggested scenarios for responding to and recovering from pandemics as well as models of society where health policy shapes political structures and common life. While it might be too early to have a clear perspective on the present crisis, we can learn from the previous ones to understand how people respond to fear of death and how they retain or regain full dignity of life. We can also see examples of biopolitical measures established to protect health and their impact on humans as individuals and members of societies. Literary works, we argue, allow us to see something that remains invisible to policy documents and health guidelines: the ambiguity and complexity of human beings, their contradictory wishes and behaviours. The biopolitical management of the present crisis has lacked imagination and we want to provide examples of imaginaries where richer responses to biopolitical crises are modelled.[5] This richness comes from fiction and poetic voices in different cultures of the world, but also from in-depth

---

[4] The presence of misinformation and conspiracy theories on social media has indeed created the situation where scientists do not want to be misunderstood or misused – and this hinders scholarly exchange on the pandemic or its origins, as acknowledged in leading medical journals like *The Lancet* (van Helden et al. 2021).
[5] For example, Sherryl Vint (2021) has shown how speculative fiction can shed light on biotechnological commodification of life and its effects on human personhood.

philosophical reflection. It also comes from lived experience. The editors lived in the USA, Estonia, Germany and Cyprus during the pandemic and thus were able to observe very different practices and to appreciate the difference specific locatedness makes in our conceptualization of issues. Our authors' experiences further expand this range.

Some contributions to this volume focus on different aspects and interpretations of what biopolitics conceptually means and implies, to better circumscribe and seize the issues at stake. Others discuss culturally divergent literary representations that help us to better understand what our societies currently undergo. The volume deliberately does not aim to establish one normative position. The contributions build an ensemble of varying, at times perhaps even contradictory, perspectives. Such a wide range of disciplinary, methodological, historical, geographical and political approaches reflects the complexity of the range of issues raised by the pandemic and the diversity of ways in which people responded to them. The volume does not want to reduce this complexity but to illuminate it, against all tendencies of simplification that are all too common in today's society. This approach enables us to take a step back and to observe the issue with some distance, the distance of philosophical reflection and of fictional imaginaries, to consider the stakes of the events and of the political decisions taken or still ahead. This distance, we hope, also allows us to tackle issues that the toxic public debate has made harder to discuss because of fear of misunderstanding or misinterpretation.

2 What Is Biopolitics?

But what do we actually mean by "biopolitics"? The term is used in various ways, contexts and disciplines, and is far from being clearly defined. The notion was first employed at the start of the twentieth century in the context of the philosophy of life, inspired by thinkers such as Friedrich Nietzsche and Henri Bergson. Several authors adapted the idea of life as a basic category to thinking about the state. The Swedish political scientist Rudolf Kjellén (1924) developed an organicist conception of the state as a living organism. In this vision, the state exists before individuals or communities and all social relations are built on a somewhat mystic living whole that is outside of rational decision-making. Unsurprisingly, such approaches appealed to racists, and the Nazis used them amply to develop their ideology of the *Volkskörper* (the body of the people) and a world completely based on biological causes. The Nazis were not alone, however. Stalin's communism also wanted to build what was called the "new human being" in Soviet propaganda (Prozorov 2016) and in early post-imperial China of the 1920s–1960s eugenicists like Quentin

Pan (1898–1967) shared the common, almost sacrosanct, goal of building a strong, modern Chinese nation. In the USA, as well as in many Western European countries, sterilization programmes and other eugenic practices from the first half of the twentieth century share some of these ideas (Allen 2001). In 1938, the English writer Morley Roberts referred to biopolitics to describe the relevance of concepts from evolutionary theory for explaining political behaviour. Even after World War II, biopoliticians developed various theories based on the idea of innate qualities, and these in turn led to the potential of using genetic engineering for social intervention, however benign (Kay 1993).

Another strand of biopolitics emerged in the 1960s on the basis of ecological processes and looming environmental disaster. The growing global population also invited mostly right-wing thinkers to use the term biopolitics to develop strategies against what was then called "overpopulation" and "mixing of races". Starting from the 1970s, technological innovations such as the invention of genetic engineering both created the temptation of biopolitical tinkering and also called for a regulation of such scientific progress.[6] Such policies are still being pursued in China against ethnic Uighurs, for example.

As this brief introduction already shows, biopolitics is historically not a clearly defined term and has been used to designate quite different ideas. For what is at stake here, Michel Foucault's influential – but vague enough – reflections created a whole line of argument relevant for today's humanities and political theorists. Most chapters in this volume, in one way or another, proceed from Foucault or scholars who developed his ideas. Foucault pursued this idea throughout his life. The term "biopolitics" as such is defined in the first volume of *The History of Sexuality*, published in 1976, where Foucault views biopolitics as something that "exerts a positive influence on life, that endeavors to administer, optimize, and multiply it, subjecting it to precise controls and comprehensive regulations" (Foucault 1978, 137). Such power seeks to put life "in order" (Foucault 1978, 138). In his later work, Foucault's definition is situated in the context of his 1978–1979 reflections on governmentality (Foucault 2008). He sees biopolitics as the way the modern state manages demographic phenomena such as health, hygiene, birth rates, life expectancy and race, and he points to their growing importance since the nineteenth century. Foucault defines biopolitics as a specific strategy of power, which is very different from all of the theories mentioned above. Two years prior, he had employed the term to describe a shift in the eighteenth century from a sovereign power, directed at the

---

6 See for an introduction to these aspects of the notion Lemke 2011 (German original 2007). Lemke also presents a good survey and commentary on Foucault and Agamben's relevant writings as well as on later biologically oriented positions. Also see the substantial introduction by Campbell and Sitze in their anthology *Biopolitics. A Reader* from 2013.

human body, that makes die and lets live, towards the processes that make live and let die (Foucault 2003, 241). In other words, according to Foucault, as the new liberal economic system develops, more and more attention is directed at the population and at methods of regulating and making use of the life of the people. The interest is obvious: in order to prosper, the state and economy need people to function well.

The background for Foucault's reflections on biopolitics can be found in his engagement with early English utilitarianism as a way of dealing with the emerging neoliberal society and the rise of the *homo oeconomicus*. Of particular interest are his observations on the panopticon in the fascinating chapter 3 in part III of *Discipline and Punish* from 1975 (in English 1977). Jeremy Bentham's architectural model, created to allow one person to surveil an entire prison or factory without the inmates or workers being able to see their guard, leads to them disciplining themselves since they are *potentially* always being surveilled. This is based on Hobbes's vision of humankind, in which man is a wolf to man, *homo homini lupus*, and that consequently the state, in order to provide freedom for the highest possible number, must discipline and monitor everybody. What Foucault calls disciplinary society is based on the feeling of the population that they could be controlled, disciplined and punished at any moment, so that the exercise of that power becomes superfluous; no coercion is needed since the population subjects itself to this potential control. Power becomes automatized and de-individualized, which promotes the production of docile subjects, obedient and productive.

Foucault's concept of "disciplinary society" (as analysed in his work on the hospital (1961), the psychiatric clinic (1963) and the prison (1975) (in English respectively in 1965, 1973 and 1977) implies a positive suppression, a care system based on "rational evidence". This analysis of the disciplinary society does not stay in the past: in his 1978–1979 lectures on biopolitics he also talks about how contemporary forms of governmentality govern people through the use of the illusion of freedom and choice. The neoliberal subject is supposed to be free but only free to compete and to maximize itself as human capital. Paradoxically, for Foucault (2008, 270), this makes the neoliberal subject "eminently governable".[7] At this point it is important to add that Foucault's work is not normative and that he does not present this vision of society as a model or as an object of explicit criticism. He merely observes the emergent social formations. *Power* generally in Foucault's *oeuvre* is not negative in itself, and thus it is not unambiguously so in the case of biopolitics or biopower. Foucault's successors like Deleuze and Agamben insist on the double character of biopolitics:

---

7 Wendy Brown (2015) links neoliberal technologies of the self to a de-democratization of the subject and the hollowing out of democracy. This issue is also relevant in connection with the COVID-19 pandemic.

biopolitical measures can be both emancipating for the individual and totalizing (Deleuze 1992, 4; Agamben 1998). Who would want to oppose the State as a provider of health care, education and infrastructure of all kinds? The benefits of a regulating state are evident, and many societies provide an exceptional level of justice and wellbeing for a majority of the population.

The question that Foucault raises is how biopolitics, developed to promote and to care for life, could become oppressive or even destructive. This danger emerges when states make a distinction between those deserving care and protection and those who are excluded. One of his sharpest criticisms is of racism, in the lectures from 1975–1976 when his attention shifts to "what must live and what must die" (Foucault 2003, 254). His argument operates with a very broad notion of racism, which, he contends, is used to fragment the continuum of humanity so that the state can, on the premises of biopower, fight what is defined as "lower life" in the interest of a healthier and purer life in general. Looking at life in such a biological manner paves the ideological path to killing some individuals in the interest of the population as a whole: an individual deemed racially or otherwise inferior is a threat to the population and needs to be eradicated. This extreme version of biopolitics has been put into practice, and not only by National Socialism, not only as the result of a lack of reason, but rather as one possible logical consequence of Enlightenment when it takes the form of instrumentalized reason (cf. Horkheimer and Adorno 1947, Bauman 1989). Eugenic thinking was popular across the Western world in early twentieth century resulting in the sterilization of people deemed to be mentally deficient or deviant. For example, Sweden practiced compulsory sterilizations until the 1970s. Compulsory sterilization, forced abortion, social and legal sanctions became the new norm in China during the implementation of the "One-Child-Policy" since the 1980s. Its abolishment in 2021 coincides with the forced implementation of radical measures such as birth-control, forced abortion and sterilization against "minority" populations in China whose cultural and historical difference from the majority of Han Chinese is officially considered a threat to the prosperity of the nation. These examples show that biopower and biopolitics can be used to subdue the body politic and to control the population in the interest of inhumane goals that seemed perfectly rational at the time. Foucault (1978, 149–150) also mentions biopower as such a technique for suppression in the first volume of *The History of Sexuality*. In the present volume, Crew takes a closer look at the effects of instrumentalized reason.

Giorgio Agamben builds on this aspect of Foucault's work but takes a more radical position. By looking at life reductively from a biological or functional perspective, politics (at the time of his writing, in 1995) had become completely biopolitical and therefore also totalitarian in Agamben's view. He develops this thesis via the notion of the *homo sacer*, a figure of Roman law, a person placed outside divine and human law. A *homo sacer* can therefore be killed but not sacrificed for religious purposes. Such a being becomes, according to Agamben, "bare life", reduced to a merely biological being, to a physical body, deprived of all aspects of "good life" available to citizens who are incorporated into the body politic. Agamben compares the reduced existence of *homo sacer* with (concentration) camps, which, in his view, have become the global biopolitical paradigm (Agamben 1998, 166). After all, the twenty-first century seems to be lived in the shadow of cataclysmic events like the 9/11 terrorist attacks or the present pandemic, which call for what Agamben, referring to Carl Schmitt, designates as *states of exception*, in which normal laws and rules are suspended in even liberal democracies and where the value of human life is radically revalued or, more precisely, where the decisions about whose lives are valued are being made.[8] Biopolitics thus always has a flip side, the politics of death for which Agamben uses the term "thanatopolitics" (2015, 24). Achille Mbembe (2003), in turn, has coined the term "necropolitics", the power to dictate who may live and who must die, applied to the colonial and post-colonial situation.[9] The government of life is for Agamben – more than for Foucault – the government of death.

Agamben refers to the supposed ancient Greek difference between *zoē* and *bios*, that is, the bare fact of life as opposed to life as a *form of life* (Agamben 1998, 11). This latter term implies for him a life that is impossible to separate from its form, and which is thus possibilities and potentialities and never simply facts.[10] It is only when we fuse biological and political existence that we can disarm the more menacing aspect of biopolitics (Agamben 2000, Mills 2018, 49–55). The following chapters are interested in both the threat and the potentiality: for example, Eskin critically interrogates Agamben's core terms, while Vint examines Agamben's notion of forms of life to probe for a possibility of community building.

Agamben has applied these ideas himself to the current COVID-19 crisis in his native Italy (2021, a collection of public interventions from February to November 2020). Observing that Italians are willing to sacrifice practically everything when faced with the risk of illness and death, he deplores that bare life has become the sole criterion in today's society (Agamben 2021, 17–18). He points out that this has become the norm in a purely biological state. As in his previous *oeuvre*, Agamben does not shy away from stating the similarities to the National Socialist state of exception that lasted for

---

[8] For a relevant engagement with whose lives are grievable, see Butler (2016).
[9] Mbembe refers to Carl Schmitt's right-wing political ideas, stating that sovereignty is defined by the power to declare the state of exception and applies it to colonialism.
[10] Agamben develops the idea of a happy life that erases the biopolitical separation of *zoē* and *bios* as a form of life in his later work (Agamben 2000). Michael Eskin explains in this volume that Agamben's distinction between the two Greek terms is not precise (cf. Finlayson 2010).

twelve years (2021, 8). He points to the new devices of monitoring and surveillance, security cameras and cell phones that allow for a level of control that far exceeds any former totalitarian forms.

To people familiar with Agamben's earlier work, these comments do not come as a surprise, but they acquired a new political meaning in the context of the early pandemic. The wording is provocative, as 2020 lockdowns are not comparable to the horrors of the camps, as was pointed out by several leading thinkers like Jean-Luc Nancy and Roberto Esposito.[11] Sergei Prozorov (2021) shows how the comments reveal certain central inconsistencies in Agamben's work. In our volume, Monticelli and Pajević return to these interventions from different angles. Yet the seemingly unideological medicalization of politics is a long-term political process, now accompanied by the politicization of medicine, as Esposito argues.[12] We do not have to agree with Agamben's alarmist wording to see several concerns converging in the global pandemic response, especially when we add the presence of what Shoshana Zuboff (2019) has called surveillance capitalism, with its pervasive but invisible systems of control.

3 Towards a Society of Control?

Gilles Deleuze saw this tendency as early as 1992, when he stated that, with new digital technologies, Foucault's disciplinary society transforms into a control society in which the citizens, by measuring their life data, constantly control themselves (Deleuze 1992). As is now widely known, practical innovations such as using a debit card, a mobile phone or a smart watch make us leave a big data trail. We leave a similar trail when we shop online, stream music or videos or leave comments on a Facebook posting. This exposes us to the depredations of data-mining and algorithmic prediction, in addition to enabling biopolitical surveillance and control over "the transparent citizen" (Reidenberg 2015). This is perfected in techno-optimistic societies like Estonia where citizens' health data is amassed into national databases and gene banks without any public protest, as technology is assumed to be value free and neutral. Today, the early British utilitarianism that Foucault based his ideas on, coupled with American pragmatism, has been infinitely empowered by digitalization and makes possible near-absolute monitoring and control.

---

[11] Cf. for both reactions the Facebook post of Newcastle University: https://www.facebook.com/NewcastleUniversityPhilosophy/posts/568958693708583. Last accessed 17 February 2023.
[12] Christiaens and De Cauwer's interview with Roberto Esposito from 16 June 2020 (https://antipodeonline.org/2020/06/16/interview-with-roberto-esposito/). Last accessed 10 April 2022.

In 2010 Mark Zuckerberg, with his Facebook platform, famously declared the end of privacy.[13] Dave Eggers already in 2013 successfully demonstrated the potential consequences of this end of privacy in his novel *The Circle*, wherein a social media empire manages to gain complete control over every aspect of life, including political life, under the label of sharing and responsibility. But in the final instance it completely destroys human dignity and freedom.[14] Wasihun tackles this range of issues in her chapter in this volume.

Roberto Simanowski, a media studies researcher, argues that the events related to COVID-19 have resulted in an enormous acceleration of digitalization. This convergence of trends needs close attention. Social media are more opaque than traditional media in that their mediating effect largely remains invisible. This invisibility or lack of transparency represents a danger for the cohesiveness of societies; their power over reception, their cultural and political consequences, and their economic reasons need closer scrutiny (Simanowski 2021, 14–15).[15] Already in 1964, Marshall McLuhan, the father of media studies, said: "the medium is the message". Simanowski warns that the pandemic was an opportunity for the break-through of a new digitalization politics, and that history books will consider 2021 not the year of the virus but the year of the crisis of democracy (Simanowski 2021, 15–16). The same idea is also echoed by other media scholars, like Benjamin Bratton (2021), even if he in the end embraces technology as an inevitable option. The dangers of big data, much discussed before the pandemic, especially after the manipulations of the 2016 elections in the UK and US, seem all of a sudden negligible in the face of fear induced by the virus.

We should, however, remember that the fight for the new key resource of power, information and data, is a mighty driver in the presentation of the pandemic. With COVID passports, tracking apps and QR codes, the state could gain back some of the data now largely in the hands of social media and IT companies. Yet state control might be illusory: the state mostly outsources this data-gathering to private enterprises. Their economic interests are clearly visible: already in October 2020, a QR-code entrepreneur sold the contact data of the COVID-19 QR codes routinely shown in restaurants across Europe.[16] Simanowski also points to the possibilities of big data

---

[13] https://www.theguardian.com/technology/2010/jan/11/facebook-privacy. Last accessed 18 December 2021.
[14] It is also turned into a film by James Ponsoldt, with Emma Watson and Tom Hanks, in 2017, which, however, turns the ending completely around, mitigating the position. The book has a sequel, *The Every*, 2021.
[15] Cf. also his book *The Death Algorithm and Other Digital Dilemmas*, 2018.
[16] Simanowski gives a reference to *The Times*, 11 October 2020, in his footnote 27: https://www.thetimes.co.uk/article/contact-tracing-data-harvested-from-pubs-and-restaurants-being-sold-on-s0d85mkrr.

mining in Zoom recordings and other channels widely used for interpersonal communication. Software for facial recognition and for analysing facial expressions is already available, for instance the app *Affectiva* that enthusiastically promises to interpret 90 percent of non-verbal communication. While Facebook's 2014 manipulation of emotions on its news feed was met with academic commentary and critique (Selinger and Hartzog 2016), *Affectiva* has been fatalistically accepted as inevitable.[17] Still, Zuckerberg and Facebook helped to pave the way for today's emotional manipulation and control. Such technology detects what we do not want our conversation partners to know; this is the end of diplomacy, and it grants those with the power over such technologies enormous leverage over everybody else (Simanowski 2021, 61–62). It is no coincidence that in the recent blockbuster *Don't Look Up* (2021) by Adam McKay, the CEO of the leading social media company pulls the strings and considers himself to be not an entrepreneur, but a creator of societies and of the future. The dystopia of *The Circle* is not far.

Biopolitics thus navigates between rendering life more prosperous, safe and pleasant on the one hand, and more controlled and modelled to benefit mostly economic interest groups on the other. While at the start of the COVID-19 measures people said that nobody can be interested in a lockdown and blocking the economy, by now it has become evident that some sectors of the economy – already the biggest before the pandemic, like IT service providers, e-commerce and pharmaceutical companies – not only were not blocked by the measures, but made gigantic profits. On 20 July 2020, Amazon founder Jeff Bezos, for instance, increased his wealth by 20 billion US dollars due to a re-evaluation of Amazon stock; eleven days later he made another seven billion. Bezos was not alone. Billionaires globally increased their wealth by 4 trillion US dollars in 2020–2021, while over 100 million people fell under the poverty line (Stiglitz 2022). This is not only an unheard-of increase in private fortunes, but a question of power in and over society. Political reports recommending the dissolution of IT giants who have market monopolies have not led anywhere, even in the EU where such policies have been aggressively pursued, and soon these big enterprises will be too powerful to be controlled by politics at all (cf. Simanowski 2021, 73–74). Although measures like the EU General Data Protection Regulation (GDPR) and Digital Markets Act (DMA) have been designed to establish tough privacy laws and to foster competition, this might be coming too late. The fact that Twitter, one of these giants, could deny Donald Trump access to this platform, as did other social networks, might be a reason to rejoice for some of us.

---

[17] The ubiquity of surveillance leads to the emergence of new products: there are designers who offer clothes designed to mask the wearer from facial recognition in streets (Seabrook 2020).

However, such "deplatforming"[18] is also a troublesome sign of the rapidly increasing power of such private enterprises that are reshaping the public sphere without any democratic legitimation or oversight (cf. Simanowski 2021, 77–78).

This control of the population by private entrepreneurs (Facebook, now rebranded as Meta,[19] for instance is largely controlled by one person, Mark Zuckerberg) is undermining the principles of democracy (Schmidt 2021, 57). The digitalization of education has now largely been realized due to the lockdowns and other isolation measures necessitating online teaching. For example, Salesforce, a major cloud-based software company that sells customer relationship management software, has also branched into education. In the USA, there already are examples of a school cloud, in which every student will have a digital learning biography, which can be potentially consulted by any employer later on (Schmitt 2021, 86–89).[20]

The European Union's General Data Protection Regulation (GDPR) is supposed to make this type of data use illegal, but research shows that there are many loopholes that make data surveillance a normality even in the EU (Alier et al 2021). Many public voices lament the strong data protection laws in Germany. When a German school buys Microsoft software, Microsoft as an American enterprise is obliged to give, if asked, information to the US government. Microsoft Europe has its headquarters in Ireland and must give information to the Irish authorities, too, if asked, but not to the German ones. German students have no control over their data at all (Schmitt 2021, 86–89). Other scholars have criticized the GDPR for not requiring clearer informed consent (van Ooijen and Vrabec 2019). In the context of information overload, we are used to clicking through forms without reading them and might disregard important privacy information if the language is opaque. As a result, students and teachers might be giving consent to uses that they do not comprehend. The long-term consequences of datafied childhood (Mascheroni 2020) can only be imagined at this point. These processes were well under way before the pandemic, but the pandemic reduced the amount of debate and cemented the use of many of these practices.

This new media situation creates infinite possibilities for control and completely changes the biopolitical situation. This has been grasped by the German writer

---

[18] The effect of deplatforming and its effect on radicalization has been studied by, for example, Richard Rogers (2020).
[19] It has been argued that the rebranding was a result of the intense criticism of Facebook for its role in the spread of misinformation, but also that it is part of a broader strategy of expanding beyond being just a social media platform (Stokel-Walker 2021).
[20] In the USA, privacy issues at school are covered by the Family Educational Rights and Privacy Act (FERPA) that protects the privacy of students' education records and that applies to all schools that receive funding from the U.S. Department of Education.

Timur Vermes. In his 2012 novel *Look Who's Back* (*Er ist wieder da*) he imagines the return of Hitler to contemporary Germany. Hitler immediately sizes up the manipulative dimension of the Internet and is enthused: with this, he says, it will be so easy to manipulate and subdue the masses and to secure power.

This is not, however, just the stuff of fiction. Viral logic, used so casually in the case of social media, and its addictive quality, has acquired a new meaning in the context of the present pandemic. The notion of the virus itself requires theoretical inquiry. The initial logic of protection against the virus and of immunity implies first of all an introduction to the lethal threat within oneself and then a turning against the other and the foreign. The desire for security has been examined by Roberto Esposito, who uses the language of immunity to speak about the body politic.[21] On a theoretical level, the immunitary logic leads to an obsession with security and exclusion, the creation of borders and protections against perceived threats. Desire for immunity characterizes communities that struggle to maintain a sense of control in a chaotic situation like the present one. The challenge is to avoid the logic of immunitary exclusion and to reach a community logic.

Ingo Reuter (2020) has applied similar ideas to the COVID-19 times and studied the social dangers and consequences of this viral logic with respect to the Other/stranger. He stresses the importance, both medically and socially, of a positive infection and of being touched (in the concrete and the figurative senses of the expression). Life without the other is impossible; the contact with the other must be constructively considered and cautiously dealt with.[22] Marling and Käsper return to this range of questions in this volume, from different angles.

4 Biopolitics and Health

This brings us back to *health* in biopolitics. It is no coincidence that Foucault develops his concept of biopolitics from the example of a city in times of the plague (e.g. *Discipline and Punish* as well as in his lectures on the Abnormal from 1974–1975). He never fully develops the health dimension of the notion, but the ways in which a society deals with health is central throughout his work. He develops three models of government centred around different forms of health measures. The first is the model of leprosy in his first important book from 1961,

---

[21] Cf. Esposito 2011 (Italian original 2002).
[22] The poet and performer Kae Tempest stresses the importance of contact in presence, not on screen, in her reflections on the key importance of connection for human life and creativity (2020).

Madness and Civilization (Foucault 1965). It actually starts with the statement that leprosy disappears from the Occident in the Middle Ages. Leper colonies are gradually transformed into asylums for the poor and the mad. Foucault's thesis is that in this first medieval model the power separates the healthy from the sick, preferably banning the sick from urban centres to leave them to their own devices. The second model is based on the plague that preoccupied early modern times. Foucault declares in chapter 3 of part III of his 1975 work, *Discipline and Punish*, that, starting in the seventeenth century, a disciplinary power develops which does not simply ban the deviant but subjects everybody to a rigorous disciplinarization for the sake of increasing the productivity of their bodies. Foucault paints the image of a society in which the authorities impose strict and complete regulations that in the time of the plague confine all citizens to their houses. This represents, according to Foucault, the political dream of disciplinarization, and the plague city is the utopia of a completely governed and surveilled society.

However, Foucault then relativizes this gloomy vision of government in his lectures on governmentality from 1977 to 1979. His third model for government strategies in modern times is based on smallpox and vaccination. It grants the individual a fundamental freedom, albeit primarily an economic one. Now governing is not primarily concerned with disciplinarization, but more with the regulation of the population. The government favours a liberal flow of activities, and vaccinations allow this flow to remain unrestricted – this is the model of a liberal market society. For this, everything has to be subjected to a norm. Before, sovereign power wanted to surveil every single action of all citizens. Foucault describes this in the example of Bentham's panopticon (*Discipline and Punish*, chapter 3, part III) discussed above. The disciplinarization functions automatically and without the need of coercion since individuals, knowing that they can be seen and punished, will obediently subject themselves. This principle forms the disciplinary society and produces docile individuals. In modern times, the life of the population, by contrast, is looked at in statistics about birth and death rates, health, alimentation, work and living conditions. This power does not deal with the individual, but with statistics. For Foucault, this liberal system grounds biopolitics. The danger of biopolitics is to go back to the plague model and to adopt its totalitarian features.[23]

---

[23] Philipp Sarasin (2020) described these three phases to refute early on the militant (ab)use of Foucault's notion of biopolitics for the COVID-19 situation. In his view from March 2020, in spite of the danger of the plague model and some voices tempted by the leprosy model, the smallpox model is in force and needs to be enforced to avoid the other models. Sebastian Krach (2021) criticizes Agamben and Esposito's neglect of resistance to biopolitical measures and reproaches them for following a too simple binary logic in their version of biopolitics. Krach considers

5 Biopolitical Shifts and Consequences of COVID-19

One could argue that biopolitics in COVID-19 times constantly fails, as people flaunt regulations without much punishment, policies are inconsistent and ineffective, and governments seem not to know what they are doing and simply try to show action to prevent criticism. In any case, they cannot provide health. Early on many commentators, including famous thinkers such as Slavoj Žižek (2020, 16), suggested that authoritarian states could deal better with such a crisis and looked almost with envy at China. The temptation of totalitarianism becomes quite prominent when people are ruled by fear. The signs of the rise of authoritarianism across Europe are finding their first academic analyses (e.g. Hesham 2020). Biopolitics always implies an entire set of strategies, and fear continues to be a powerful lever to regulate the way people think, especially in societies where disease and death have become invisible in public discourse. Using words like "strategies" does not suggest conspiratorial thinking,[24] but calls attention to the broader logic of the biopolitical state.

The spread of conspiracy theories, however, is also fueled by the increase in inequality during the present crisis: deepening immiseration side by side with the profits of global technology platforms and pharmaceutical companies. These differences create very different access to political decision-making and to impacting funding priorities, be it in social policy or medical research. People who have lost faith in the public institutions increasingly turn to alternative sources and also to alternative medical solutions. Regardless of how problematic some of these sources are, we should note the troubling loss of faith in shared public sphere and shared knowledge.

The world of COVID-19 has created its own universe of discourse. Existing research on representative populations across social media shows that there is no single static discourse, but rather a series of fluctuating discourses in which, in addition to the anticipated anger and fear, we also get anticipation and even trust (see e.g. Schweinberger et al. 2021). In the official messaging, there is also a great degree of inconsistency about rules, masked by the use of linguistic certainty.

---

biopolitics a useful term but prefers to focus on the notion of governmentality as specific practices of government.

24 Conspiracy theories and paranoia have been characteristic of contemporary capitalism even before the COVID-19 outbreak. However, conspiracy thinking has proliferated during the pandemic, fuelled by the easy spreadability of such content via social media echo chambers (see e.g. Ferreira et al. 2022). Conspiratorial thinking is also exploited politically, as can be seen in the spread of the QAnon conspiracy in the USA (and increasingly elsewhere).

Before COVID-19 in several European countries, like France and Switzerland, there were laws or debates about bans on wearing veils and masks, mostly directed against leftist demonstrators and Islamic women. Only weeks later an *obligation* to wear masks was introduced. What was declared to be either criminal or against dignity came to be presented as ethical and responsible. What used to be a sign of danger, became suddenly a means of salvation. Being a hero meant doing nothing and staying home on the couch.

The discourse of COVID-19 has strangely blended with the neoliberal discourse of individual productivity and responsibility. We are supposed to maintain our productive roles when working from home – of course, this applies only to those of us lucky to work in the knowledge economy, differently from underpaid delivery people and service workers. The language of remote work already hides inequalities. Moreover, the current discourse of responsibility in the name of a healthy society is actually reducing social cohesion. There is the so-called 'responsibility paradox': something that in isolation seems responsible can be, in its context and with knock-on effects, an irresponsible act that causes more damage than it prevents (cf. Brenner 2020, 15 and 39–40). Particularly in Germany, it was remarkable how politicians granted one scientist, virologist Christian Drosten, a near monopoly on explaining the situation. Consequently, having given exclusive authority to one scientist, politicians had to take responsibility for scientific claims without having the competence to evaluate them. This led them into a spiral of defensive message control, without proper attention to the human beings who were the targets of the messages. Another problem is that the more the state prescribes what the population has to do, the more people develop the feeling that everything else is unproblematic – as a consequence, the state takes over more responsibility, even without prescribing anything. Everything that is not regulated, in this logic, is allowed and right.

Strong and widespread biopolitical measures, ironically, lead thus to a lessening of a responsible mindset in the population. In the COVID-19 crisis, at least in Germany, the political establishment has fuelled fear by purposefully spreading worst-case scenarios through traditional media to justify strong measures.[25] This cultivation of catastrophe scenarios, however, initiates a landslide of actionism that, with its pathos of responsibility, loses sight of the overall consequences of

---

[25] There is a leaked internal government paper in which politicians in Germany at the start of the crisis urged the media and scientists to present the virus in dramatic terms to reach consent regarding the measures. Cf. *Die Welt*, 8 February 2021, "Wenn der Staatssekretär Wissenschaftler zu 'maximaler Kollaboration' aufruft", https://www.welt.de/politik/deutschland/plus225868061/Corona-Politik-Wie-das-Innenministerium-Wissenschaftler-einspannte.html, cf. also a follow-up article on 9 February 2021.

actions. The fear created in the population then drives the media to serve this dynamic even further and forces politicians to act accordingly, so that the principle of prospective care can tip over into irresponsible decisions (Brenner 2020, 58–59). Similar scenarios can also be seen on a global scale in the case of COVID-19. The flip side of the strict regulations is their violation: while many managed to maintain a middle ground, some people were consumed by an often-irrational fear caused by the pervasive spread of disaster scenarios in public discourse, others flaunt the rules without any public sanction. Even in countries with massive biopolitical data sets (like Estonia's national health database) and public surveillance, failure to comply with vaccination recommendation or mask wearing has not, at the time of this writing, resulted in massive legal sanctions. This creates further scepticism about the disaster messaging and leads to further uncertainty in the population.

Solidarity has been one of the main arguments in favour of strict measures, but at the same time these economic measures led to a hundred million more children suffering from hunger and poverty, according to UNICEF. While this suffering is presented as being caused by the virus,[26] the cause is actually the anti-virus-measures imposed by rich countries (Brenner 2020, 61). Double standards could be seen all through the pandemic, with developed Western countries prioritizing their own citizens and re-imposing strict borders. The pandemic has been characterized by the use of partial morals mixed with a moralism that challenges established truth-finding processes. The moralistic dynamic of the COVID-19 crisis has led to politicians making decisions that they possibly did not want (Brenner 2020, 76–79). The emotionally charged topic of health and the way it has been dealt with, by the discourse in social media as well as by the state and the traditional media, accelerated the polarization of society and the public sphere which had already begun by debates about digitalization. It further challenges health and the public sphere. Our societies have been strained by the pandemic, not just in numbers of hospital beds and respirators, but also in the sphere of public trust. The medicalization of public discourse is not going to help to resuscitate public trust or to generate narratives of care in already fractured societies.

Such a critique of the medicalization of society is nothing new. In 1975 philosopher Ivan Illich wrote a detailed and, for that time, well-researched attack on the ill effects of modern Western medicine in his book *Medical Nemesis*, criticizing a system which makes people into life-long patients with its drug-induced

---

26 See for instance *Die Welt*, 9 December 2021 "Pandemie gefährdet Kinder laut Unicef in 'nie dagewesenem Maß'", or also the *Süddeutsche Zeitung* of the same day: "Corona-Pandemie hat zusätzlich 100 Mio Kinder in Armut gestürzt".

illness and side effects. A wealth of statistics demonstrates that the supposed success of modern medicine has resulted more from the improvement of general living conditions, while medicalization has created multiple new health problems and particularly an attitude in which people give up the responsibility for their wellbeing and believe in a doctor who will repair them when needed. Health care, Illich argues, has become an illness-producing enterprise and the fear induced in the population leads instead to an ever-increasing proliferation. For him, health means the degree to which people cope with their inner states and their environmental conditions. Consequently, health would be the best where people are allowed to cope with life in a personal, autonomous and responsible manner (Illich 1975, 7). The mass of medical expenses has no positive effect on health, while a considerable part of these funds is used to cure medicine-induced harm (Illich 1975, 228). Illich demands that nobody "be seized, imprisoned, hospitalised, treated, or otherwise molested in the name of health" without their consent, and that "no services are to be forcibly imposed on an individual against his will" (Illich 1975, 243).

This is not, however, an argument against all aspects of Western medicine. There is no doubt that in some respects, particularly when it comes to accident surgery and treatment, Western medicine does miracles. However, today medicine is also an industry, most obviously in the United States, that creates the patients it needs. People stop being agents and become patients. Today's medicine has made people dependent on ever more medications that often work to counteract previous medications. The influence of Big Pharma on the medical establishment has been widely documented; its abuses have been often sanctioned, most famously in the case of the opiate-use epidemic (most famously in the case of Purdue Pharma), but to little avail. Today the medical system is harshly criticized for being driven by profit which works against the interest of health and creates a mentality of consumerism and an abandonment of responsibility for one own's health.[27] Profit-driven medical systems, like those in the US, leave many needy people without proper care. This failure of commercialized medicine has opened the way for an equally commercialized wellness industry that lets people down, especially the underprivileged, with its frequent propagation of pseudo-science and the co-optation of language of resistance (McBain 2020).

Health is the key factor in biopolitics: a healthy person is functional in the economy or in war, today as in the past. In our time, the health-care industry has

---

[27] See for instance the German bestseller *Der verlorene Patient. Wie uns das Geschäft mit der Gesundheit krank macht* by the surgeon Umes Arunagirinathan together with Doris Mendlewitsch (2020). Even though the health care systems are very different in different countries, the ill effects of the for-profit system will be comparable everywhere.

become a major economic power. Health – or rather fear of illness, pain and death – is a very powerful tool of manipulation in today's society, in which many people have bought into the ideal of life as painless and death as something that takes place in far-away places and invisibly to the majority of wealthy Westerners. We are currently experiencing how the state, via biopolitics, fights a virus to protect the citizens, but also how the virus is transforming society: there is an economic transformation towards much greater inequality and a political transformation, powered by digitalization, towards what is, in biopolitical terms, a far more controlling state and invisible media corporations. It is very questionable whether this serves health and a healthy society.

But there is some hope in the apparent confusion of liberal Western societies in handling the crisis. Despite the biopolitical control available to states and corporations, even major economies and their advanced medical systems have staggered under the pandemic, unable to create a unified response to the proliferating variants. States have neither become more effective nor more aligned in the third year of the pandemic: some have relaxed all rules, some have scaled them down, while others have imposed draconian sanctions. As argued before, it seems that states rather desperately performed a mimicry of "doing something", as opposed to control. Meanwhile, in most countries we have seen the rise of authoritarianism and populism that feed on both popular fear and state ineffectiveness. This has contributed even more to polarization in our societies. The virus has not only damaged human bodies but the public understanding that social existence is a complex ecosystem of actors that cannot be reduced to a black-and-white caricature or a zero-sum game. We need to come back to recognizing our shared vulnerability and shared humanity. The balance between control and care is at stake.

6 Negotiating Biopolitics

It is this need to acknowledge the complexity of the world and of human beings that makes us turn to philosophy and literature in this volume to look for ways of returning our attention to care. Literature depends on human complexity and ambiguity. Thus, in the heated public sphere of today where people scream at each other not to engage in an exchange of opinions, but just to prove they are right, we should slow down, read and reflect. This might be the best antidote to today's crisis, although it does not promise quick fixes.

Our volume builds on three types of analysis. In the first part, we turn to historical narratives and imaginaries. Because we are still in the middle of the pandemic and have no way of telling what the ultimate result might be, we can benefit from critically looking at biopolitical crises whose resolution we know. Daniele Monticelli discusses plague narratives ranging from Sophocles to Defoe and Manzoni to show how they represent different biopolitical management strategies. This allows him to compare the views of Foucault and Agamben, and to apply them to our present situation. Meelis Friedenthal reflects on the parallels between early-modern responses to the plague and today's measures against COVID-19 and, in contrast to the caricatures often trotted out in the media, shows surprising parallels and continuities. Thomas Crew investigates Aldous Huxley's *Brave New World* and Max Horkheimer and Theodor Adorno's *Dialectics of Enlightenment* as well as the political and intellectual debates of their times in terms of biopolitics as a means of interrogating our present crisis, demonstrating that these works are valuable canonical texts for our debates on biopolitics.

The second type of reflection builds largely on philosophical ideas about biopolitics, proposing new readings and offering fresh insights, often illustrating the conceptual analysis with literary examples. Timothy Campbell builds on Italian philosopher Carlo Diano's work on the eventic form of the present pandemic, its myths and rituals. Sherryl Vint continues the discussion of inequalities by focusing on Giorgio Agamben's notions of form-of-life and use-of-bodies. She asks whether the pandemic can help us reimagine community beyond the anthropogenic machine imagined by Agamben, elaborating this on the example of Nicola Griffith's speculative fiction novel *Ammonite* (2002). Raili Marling also proceeds from the question of whether we can imagine new forms of community, rooted in vulnerability and relationality, combining the work of Rosi Braidotti and Judith Butler with critical affect theory. Her chapter is illustrated by an interpretation of two novels written during the pandemic, Gary Shteyngart's *Our Country Friends* (2021) and Sarah Moss's *The Fell* (2021).

Finally, we turn to the already existing representations of COVID-19 or books that provide eerie parallels to today. For this, we consider examples from major Western nations, the USA, Germany, France, but also China, to take a look at how an authoritarian country responded to COVID-19. Marko Pajević focuses on German writer and public intellectual Juli Zeh's novel *The Method* (*Corpus Delicti* 2009) and the companion commentary that Zeh added in 2020 to show the dystopian nature of the biopolitical state, with its restriction of individual liberties in the name of public health. Betiel Wasihun turns to another central issue in today's biopolitics, quantification, through reading German writer Marc-Uwe Kling's novel *QualityLand* (2017) as a warning against algorithmic control. Frank Kraushaar's object of interest is a very different cultural space, contemporary China. He reflects on bio-ethical thought in pre-modern China and the use of classical poetry to subvert the biopolitical mandates of the state in cyberpoetry. Marge Käsper looks at the French reception of Roberto Esposito's *Immunitas* (published in Italian in 2002, but translated into French in 2021) and its echoes in French public discourse. Finally, Michael Eskin dissects the question of what exactly is biopolitics's object: lives and bodies or actual human beings. His discussion is illustrated by references to African-American writers who have pointed to gaps and inequalities in contemporary biopower.

These diverse investigations, we believe, show that literary and philosophical works provide us with the nuance and complexity that we need if we are to understand other people around us and to imagine new forms of community beyond the calming notions of medico-political control. It has become habitual to state that COVID-19 hit the world as a shock. Although COVID-19 has emerged as an unprecedented event, it is apparent that we can very well imagine disasters and their human effects before they occur. However, these imaginaries have not been taken sufficiently seriously as spaces for modelling social crises and potential responses, be they individual or social. We hope that by providing a range of different points of view and types of imaginaries we can also help our readers to imagine better, to think beyond the simplified caricatures that are thrown around on social media and in government messaging. It is only with these expanded imaginaries that we can help ourselves out of the vicious circle of coercion and resistance. As human societies, we need new ways of thinking, and this is where the humanities are invaluable. We can look at how people have imagined biopolitical crises in the past to show patterns and outlines and perhaps point to novel imaginaries that have not surfaced in policy analysis.

References

Agamben, Giorgio. *Homo Sacer. Sovereign Power and Bare Life*. Trans. Daniel Heller-Roazen. Stanford: Stanford University Press, 1998.

Agamben, Giorgio. *Means without End: Notes on Politics*. Trans. Vincenzo Binetti and Cesare Casarino. Minneapolis University of Minnesota Press, 2000.

Agamben, Giorgio. *Stasis. Civil War as a Political Paradigm (Homo Sacer II, 2)*. Trans. Nicholas Heron. Stanford: Stanford University Press, 2015.

Agamben, Giorgio. *Where Are We Now? The Pandemic as Politics*. Trans. Valeria Dani. London: Urtext Ltd., 2021.

Alier, Marc, Maria Jose Casañ Guerrero, Daniel Amo, Charles Severance, and David Fonseca. "Privacy and E-Learning: A Pending Task." *Sustainability* 13 (2021). https://doi.org/10.3390/su13169206.

Allen, Garland. "Eugenics as an International Movement." *International Encyclopedia of the Social & Behavioral Sciences*. Eds. Neil J. Smelser and Paul B. Baltes. 1st ed. Amsterdam: Elsevier, 2001. 4882–4889.

Arunagirinathan, Umes and Doris Mendlewitsch. *Der verlorene Patient. Wie uns das Geschäft mit der Gesundheit krank macht*. Hamburg: Rowohlt Polaris, 2020.

Bauman, Zygmunt. *Modernity and the Holocaust*. Cambridge: Polity, 1989.

Brenner, Andreas. *Corona-Ethik. Ein Fall von Global-Verantwortung?* Würzburg: Königshausen & Neumann, 2020.
Brown, Wendy. *Undoing the Demos: Neoliberalism's Stealth Revolution*. New York: Zone Books, 2015.
Butler, Judith. *Frames of War. When is Life Grievable?* London: Verso, 2016.
Campbell, Timothy, and Adam Sitze. "Biopolitics: An Encounter." *Biopolitics. A Reader*. Eds. Timothy Campbell and Adam Sitze. Durham: Duke University Press, 2013. 1–40.
Christiaens, Tim, and Stijn De Cauwer. "The Biopolitics of Immunity in Times of COVID-19: An Interview with Roberto Esposito." *Antipode Online*, 16 June 2020. https://antipodeonline.org/2020/06/16/interview-with-roberto-esposito/. Last accessed 10 April 2022.
Deleuze, Gilles. "Postscript on the Societies of Control." *October* 59 (Winter, 1992): 3–7.
Don't Look Up. Dir. Adam McKay, 2021.
Eggers, Dave. *The Circle: A Novel*. New York: Alfred A. Knopf, 2013.
Eggers, Dave. *The Every*. New York: Vintage Books, Penguin, 2021.
Ferreira, Simao, Carlos Campos, Beatriz Marinho, Susana Rocha, Eduardo Fonseca-Pedreiro, and Nuno Barbosa Rocha. "What Drives Beliefs in COVID-19 Conspiracy Theories? The Role of Psychotic-Like Experiences and Confinement-Related Factors." *Social Science & Medicine* 292 (January 2022).
Finlayson, James Gordon. "'Bare Life' and Politics in Agamben's Reading of Aristotle." *The Review of Politics* 72.1 (2010): 97–126.
Foucault, Michel. *Madness and Civilization. A History of Insanity in the Age of Reason*. Trans. Richard Howard. New York: Pantheon Books, 1965.
Foucault, Michel. *The Birth of the Clinic. An Archaeology of Medical Perception*. Trans. A. M. Sheridan Smith. New York: Pantheon Books, 1973.
Foucault, Michel. *Discipline and Punish. The Birth of the Prison*. Trans. Alan Sheridan. New York: Pantheon Books, 1977.
Foucault, Michel. *The History of Sexuality*, vol I. Trans. Robert Hurley. New York: Pantheon Books, 1978.
Foucault, Michel. *"Society Must Be Defended": Lectures at the Collège de France, 1975–76*. Trans. David Macey. New York. Picador, 2003.
Foucault, Michel. *Abnormal: Lectures at the Collège de France, 1974–75*. Trans. Graham Burchell. New York: Picador, 2004.
Foucault, Michel. *The Birth of Biopolitics. Lectures at the Collège de France, 1978–79*. Trans. Graham Burchell. New York: Picador, 2008.
Hansson, Sten et al. "COVID-19 Information Disorder: Six Types of Harmful Information During the Pandemic in Europe." *Journal of Risk Research* 24. 3–4 (2021): 380–393.
Helden, Jacques van et al. "An Appeal for an Objective, Open, and Transparent Scientific Debate about the Origin of SARS-CoV-2." *The Lancet* 388. 10309 (2021): 1402–1404.
Hesham, Angie. "Authoritarianism in the Time of COVID." *Cambridge Open Engage*, 2020. doi:10.33774/coe-2020-pmh32.
Horkheimer, Max, and Theodor W. Adorno. *Dialektik der Aufklärung*. Amsterdam: Querido, 1947.
Illich, Ivan. *Medical Nemesis. The Expropriation of Health*. London: Calder & Boyars, 1975.
Kay, Lily E. *The Molecular Vision of Life: Caltech, the Rockefeller Foundation, and the Rise of the New Biology*. New York: Oxford University Press, 1993.
Kjellén, Rudolf. *Der Staat als Lebensform*. Berlin: Kurt Vowinckel Verlag, 1924.
Krach, Sebastian. "Kritik der Biopolitik. Überlegungen zur biopolitischen Gouvernementalität in Zeiten des Coronavirus und die Möglichkeit ihrer Kritik." *Zeitschrift für Praktische Philosophie* 8.1 (2021): 149–180.
Lemke, Thomas. *Biopolitics. An Advanced Introduction*. NY: NYU Press, 2011.

Liu, Jun and Hui Zhao. "Privacy Lost: Appropriating Surveillance Technology in China's Fight Against COVID-19." *Business Horizons* 64 (2021): 743–756.
Mbembe, Achille. "Necropolitics." *Public Culture* 15.1 (2003): 11–40.
McLuhan, Marshall. *Understanding Media: The Extensions of Man*. New York: McGraw Hill, 1964.
Mascheroni, Giovanna. "Datafied Childhoods. Contextualising Datafication in Everyday Life." *Current Sociology* 68.6 (2020): 798–813.
McBain, Sophie. "The Dark Side of the Wellness Industry." *New Statesman*. 17 June 2002. https://www.newstatesman.com/uncategorized/2020/06/dark-side-wellness-industry. Last accessed 10 April 2022.
Mills, Catherine. *Biopolitics*. London: Routledge, 2018.
Morelock, Jeremiah, and Felipe Ziotti Narita. "The Nexus of QAnon and COVID-19: Legitimation Crisis and Epistemic Crisis." *Critical Sociology* (2022): 1–22.
Newcastle University, Facebook blog, 6 March 2020: https://www.facebook.com/NewcastleUniversityPhilosophy/posts/568958693708583. Last accessed 17 February 2023.
Ooijen, I. van, and Helena U. Vrabec. "Does the GDPR Enhance Consumers' Control over Personal Data? An Analysis from a Behavioural Perspective." *Journal of Consumer Policy* 42 (2019): 91–107.
Prozorov, Sergei. *The Biopolitics of Stalinism*. Edinburgh: Edinburgh University Press, 2016.
Prozorov, Sergei. "A Farewell to Homo Sacer? Sovereign Power and Bare Life in Agamben's Coronavirus Commentary." *Law and Critique* 2021. https://doi.org/10.1007/s10978-021-09314-x.
Reidenberg, Joel R. "The Transparent Citizen." *Loyola University of Chicago Law Journal* 47.2 (2015): 437–463.
Reuter, Ingo. *Ansteckung. Das Fremde in viralen Zeiten*. Würzburg: Königshausen & Neumann, 2020.
Rogers, Richard. "Deplatforming: Following Extreme Internet Celebrities to Telegram and Alternative Social Media." *European Journal of Communication* 35.3 (2020): 213–229.
Rose, Nikolas, and Carlos Novas. "Biological Citizenship." *Global Assemblages: Technology, Politics and Ethics as Anthropological Problems*. Eds. Aihwa Ong and Stephen Collier. Malden, MA: Blackwell, 2005. 439–463.
Sarasin, Philipp. "Mit Foucault die Pandemie verstehen?" Geschichte der Gegenwart, 25 March 2020. https://geschichtedergegenwart.ch/mit-foucault-die-pandemie-verstehen/. Last accessed 9 April 2022.
Schmitt, Peter. *Postdigital. Medienkritik im 21. Jahrhundert*. Hamburg: Meiner, 2021.
Schweinberger, Martin, Michael Haugh, and Sam Hames. "Analysing Discourse Around COVID-19 in the Australian Twittersphere: A Real-Time Corpus-Based Analysis." *Big Data & Society* (2021). https://doi.org/10.1177/20539517211021437.
Seabrook, John. "Dressing for the Surveillance Age." *New Yorker*, 20 March 2020. https://www.newyorker.com/magazine/2020/03/16/dressing-for-the-surveillance-age. Last accessed 9 April 2022.
Selinger, Evan, and Woodrow Hartzog. "Facebook's Emotional Contagion Study and the Ethical Problem of Co-Opted Identity in Mediated Environments Where Users Lack Control." *Research Ethics* 12.1 (2016): 35–43.
Simanowski, Roberto. *The Death Algorithms and Other Virtual Dilemmas*. Cambridge: MIT Press, 2018.
Simanowski, Roberto. *Das Virus und das Digitale*. Vienna: Passagen-Verlag, 2021.
Stiglitz, Joseph E. "COVID Has Made Global Inequality Much Worse." *Scientific American*, March 1, 2022. https://www.scientificamerican.com/article/covid-has-made-global-inequality-much-worse/. Last accessed 9 April 2022.
Stokel-Walker, Chris. "Why Has Facebook Changed Its Name to Meta and What Is the Metaverse." *New Scientist*, October 29, 2021. https://www.newscientist.com/article/2295438-why-has-facebook-changed-its-name-to-meta-and-what-is-the-metaverse/. Last accessed 9 April 2022.

Tempest, Kae. *On Connection*. London: Faber & Faber, 2020.
The Circle. Dir. James Ponsoldt, 2017.
Vermes, Timur. *Er ist wieder da*. Köln: Eichborn, 2012.
Vint, Sherryl. *Biopolitical Futures in Twenty-First-Century Speculative Fiction*. Cambridge: Cambridge University Press, 2021.
Žižek, Slavoj. *PANdemIC! Covid-19 Shakes the World*. London: Polity Press, 2020.
Zuboff, Shoshana. *Surveillance Capitalism*. New York: Public Affairs, 2019.

Daniele Monticelli
Preliminary Remarks for a Biopolitical History of Western Plague Narratives

Abstract: Plague narratives have been from the beginning of Western literature a way of reflecting on the behaviours of sovereign powers and the people in a state of emergency, where life as such becomes the main object of individual concern and public interventions. Such narratives are in this respect a privileged place to test the different definitions and genealogies of biopolitics in the works of Michel Foucault and Giorgio Agamben: is biopolitics a modern invention, in which the "government of men" replaces the old sovereign power over life and death of the subjects or is the creation of a "biopolitical body" the essential activity of Western political power that originates in the Greek *polis*? This chapter considers from this perspective a series of plague narratives spanning from Homer's *Iliad* and Sophocles' *Oedipus Rex* to Daniel Defoe's *Journal of the Plague Year* and Alessandro Manzoni's *The Betrothed*. I argue that explicitly biopolitical elements of plague management emerge only in modern plague narratives, confirming Michel Foucault's vision of the modern age as the time in which issues such as health and hygiene first become a matter of government. Nevertheless, older narratives present interesting elements that point to the more distinctive aspects of Agamben's understanding of biopolitics as it diverges from Foucault's. The chapter thus analyses the plague as a materialization of the dissolution of society in Thucydides and Boccaccio and of the sovereign exception in Homer and Sophocles. Manzoni's and Defoe's plague narratives are also considered on the background of Agamben's critical remarks on "social distancing" and lockdowns during the COVID-19 pandemic.

1 Introduction

Since the beginning of the COVID-19 pandemic, countless references to past literary accounts of epidemics have appeared in the media all over the world with a quite limited range of uses and approaches. Sometimes the intent is simply to show the public that there is nothing new under the sun, sometimes how unprecedented our pandemic is in comparison with epidemics of the past. Sometimes past plague narratives are employed as sources of warning and knowledge to be employed in coming to terms with the present situation.

    This chapter reads Western plague narratives from antiquity to the late-modern age in order to see whether, when and how biopolitical motifs enter the literary representation of epidemics and what they can tell us about current discussions on health and biopolitics. As Hunter H. Gardner (2019, 17) claimed, "the potency of the plague metaphor is its function as an extension of the persistent analogy between human bodies and social units", i.e. the physiological disorder provoked by disease becomes a figure of the disorder of the body politic, of social and political crisis (Turner 1996). Biopolitics can be considered as the point at which the "persistent analogy" between the human body and society becomes a reality, with politics administering society as a body that needs to be grown, exercised, cured.

Let us first of all consider a well-known divergence in the understanding of the genesis of biopolitics and its relationship with sovereignty in the Western political tradition.[1] For Michel Foucault the birth of biopolitics coincides with the shift that took place in the classical age (the eighteenth and nineteenth centuries) from the old, absolutist sovereign and his unlimited power over the life and death of his subjects to the new "biopower" that "exerts a positive influence on life, that endeavours to administer, optimize, and multiply it, subjecting it to precise controls and comprehensive regulations" (Foucault 1998, 137). The aforementioned equivalence between the human body and society is thus realized in biopolitics by what Foucault refers to as the "population", which becomes the object of a series of interventions and regulatory controls focused on the "species body, the body imbued with the mechanics of life and serving as the basis of the biological processes: propagation, births and mortality, the level of health, life expectancy and longevity, with all the conditions that can cause these to vary" (Foucault 1998, 139). At the threshold of modernity, sovereign power is thus transformed into a "government of men" which takes as its object society as population, a body which must be disciplined and defended (Foucault 2003) with all the necessary means.

In his *Homo Sacer: Sovereign Power and Bare Life*, Giorgio Agamben (1998, 3) introduces biopolitics through Foucault, but he drastically widens the notion to include the totality of Western politics, thus conflating the Foucauldian distinction between the deadly power of the pre-modern sovereign and the "positive influence" of the new biopower on the life of the population. The "sovereign exception" is the key notion through which Agamben intersects the juridico-institutional and the biopolitical models of power that Foucault had disjoined. For Agamben Western politics coincides from the beginning with the inclusion of simple natural life (the Aristotelian *zoé*) in the political realm of qualified life (the Aristotelian *bíos*). According to Agamben this inclusion is possible only through the "sovereign ability to transcend the rule of law" (1998, 6), which articulates *zoé*

---

[1] See the introduction to this volume for a contextualizing geneology of the concept of biopolitics.

and *bíos* by opening of a space of indeterminacy at the margins of the political sphere: so much included for the sovereign to have power over it, but so much excluded for this power to exceed the limits otherwise imposed on it by the politico-juridical order. This space of "exception" is inhabited by what Agamben calls "bare life", which is the real political object of sovereign power. Agamben thus argues that

> the inclusion of bare life in the political realm constitutes the original – if concealed – *nucleus* of sovereign power. *It can even be said that the production of a biopolitical body is the original activity of sovereign power*. In this sense, biopolitics is at least as old as the sovereign exception. (1998, 6)

This is how Agamben comes to the radical conclusion that the "state of exception" is the paradigmatic figure of the constitutive and permanent exceptionality and unconditionality of sovereign power. This means that biopolitics is always about to turn into "thanatopolitics" as "the sole form in which life as such can be politicized is its unconditioned exposure to death – that is, bare life" (Agamben 2015, 24). Agamben illustrates this with a long series of historical embodiments of bare life, from the *homo sacer* of Roman law and the bandit of ancient Germanic law to the refugee in the national State, the Jew in the Nazi regime and the immigrant in contemporary democracies.[2]

From our perspective it is important to stress that the issues of medicine, health and illness play an important role in the understanding of biopolitics in Foucault as well as in Agamben. As for the former, it has been argued (Gougelet 2008) that the very origin of the Foucauldian notion of biopolitics, which is commonly situated in the philosopher's writings of the 1970s, should be dated back to *The Birth of the Clinic* of 1963, in which Foucault reconstructed the genealogy of modern medicine and the modern hospital as its core institution. The "medicalization of human life" and the "institutionalization of illness" can be considered as founding events in biopolitics, because they provoked a shift of attention from individual health to "the health of the social body as a whole" (Gougelet 2008, 50). According to Foucault, the notion of epidemic as a massive illness played a pivotal role in this shift to a "medicine of the collective", the main (biopolitical) aim of which becomes the protection of the population through its medicalization (Gougelet 2008, 51). Such an approach to epidemics clearly required the centralized support of a state "police" as an administrative body in charge not only of the practice of medicine, but also of "the control of other aspects of life bearing

---

[2] Michael Eskin's chapter also starts with a critical appraisal of Agamben's "debunking of Foucault's biopolitical argument". Eskin claims there that Agamben's misunderstands the Aristotelian distinction of *zoé* and *bíos*.

directly upon the health of the social body" (Gougelet 2008, 53). Mechanisms of power are thus extended over the entire social body in the name of its wellbeing, which is the core characteristic of biopolitics.

Agamben related biopolitics to medicine, health and illness already in the first volume of his *Homo Sacer* project, where in a chapter titled "Politicizing Death" he describes coma patients in contemporary hospitals as the most extreme form of bare life. His most heatedly discussed intervention on the political implication of medicine is the recent *A che punto siamo?* (2020), which gathers his critical essays and interviews on the Italian government's management of the COVID-19 pandemic and is significantly subtitled "The Epidemic as Politics". Following the lines of his general theory, according to which modernity has progressively turned the exception into a permanent condition, Agamben argues that the pandemic has become an excuse for a transformation of governmental paradigms based on the idea of "biosecurity". The threat to health thus becomes a sufficient reason not only for a state of emergency with unprecedented limitations to freedom, but also for the transformation of bare life into the only social value to be defended. "Social distancing" is for Agamben the pivotal means of such transformation, in which the preservation of bare life turns into a new model of (anti-)society and every public space is abolished. "People", concludes Agamben (2021, 27), "have become so used to living in a state of perennial crisis and emergency that they seem not to realise that their lives have been reduced to a purely biological state. Life is losing not only its social and political dimensions, but also its human and affective ones." I will not enter here into Agamben's dubious understanding of the nature of the COVID-19 pandemic, but I will take more seriously his reflection on epidemic as politics, its relations with sovereign power, the state of exception and social distancing.[3]

2 Plague Narratives

In Western literature plague narratives have been a way of reflecting on the behaviours of sovereign powers and the people during states of emergency, when mere survival and life as such become the main object of individual choices and

---

[3] The tenability and usefulness of Agamben's positions are considered in several chapters of this volume. Marko Pajević applies Agamben's critique of biosecurity to the analysis of a fictional, but uncannily familiar, "health dictatorship". Raili Marling rather starts from the "failure of the dream of biopolitical control" in the COVID-19 pademic and sets aside Foucault and Agamben, rather turning to Butler and Braidotti, in order to explore "biopolitical relationality" as a potential source of political agency. Timothy Campbell develops a thorough critical discussion of Agamben's perspective on the pandemic.

public interventions. In what follows I will read those narratives in order to test Foucault's and Agamben's different understandings of biopolitics. In order to do that I will consider similarities and divergences in the attention that these narratives pay to the biopolitical aspects of the epidemics they describe.

The literary works I will analyse present different degrees of fictionality and facticity. When they narrate real epidemics they differ in the relations of the authors with the narrated facts. Thucydides and Giovanni Boccaccio were eyewitnesses to the epidemics they describe: the Athens' plague of 430 BC, narrated in the second book of the *History of the Peloponnesian War* (early fifth century BC), and the Black Death epidemics of 1348 in Florence, narrated in the introduction of the *Decameron* (1348–1353). Thucydides himself became sick with plague and recovered. Daniel Defoe and Alessandro Manzoni took real seventeenth-century pestilences as a basis for their fiction. *A Journal of the Plague Year* (1722) describes, through the first-person narrative of the fictional saddler H. F., the 1665 Great Plague of London, while Chapters 31–32 of *The Betrothed* (1840) narrate Milan's plague of 1630 in the third person. Although their narratives are not based on personal experience, Defoe and Manzoni make extensive use of historical documents and chronicles covering the two epidemics. Their plague narratives are characterized by a documentary style that privileges the narrator's voice and opinions. Finally, Homer and Sophocles use fictional epidemics as an expedient way to set their narrative in motion at the beginning of the *Iliad* (eighth century BC), and in the prologue of *Oedipus Rex* (presumably first performed in 429 BC).[4]

When referring to the mentioned works as "plague narratives", I use the word plague in the very generic sense of "a variety of ills that affect the community as a whole and threaten [. . .] the very existence of social life" (Girard 1974, 834) in the shape of a contagious epidemic. From a medical perspective Boccaccio's as well as Defoe's and Manzoni's epidemics can be clearly identified as the bubonic plague, Thucydides's "plague" may possibly have been an epidemic of measles (Cunha 2004) and Sophocles's plague an epidemic of brucellosis (Kousoulis et al. 2012). The real nature of these epidemics is not relevant for my analysis, which rather focuses on the biopolitical aspects of their management. The plague narratives mentioned above will be considered in a chronological order, but not for chronological reasons. The chronology, rather, allows me to cluster the narratives on a thematic basis, which brings out different biopolitical layers and authorial attitudes toward them.

---

[4] According to some researchers the plague in *Oedipus Rex* might have been based on a real epidemic in Thebes (see Kousoulis et al. 2012).

2.1 In the Beginning was Discord: Plague, Sovereign Exception and Stasis in Book I of the *Iliad*

It is a noteworthy, though often overlooked, fact that Homer's *Iliad* as well as Sophocles's *Oedipus Rex*, two pillars of Western epic and dramatic literature, both start with descriptions of an epidemic. As has been observed (Michelakis 2019, 383), the representation of the plague in both books blurs the boundary between the literary and the figurative, thus creating narratives of crisis and disorder. More specifically, the plague is represented in the *Iliad* and *Oedipus Rex* as a political issue related to the destiny of the people and the city, an issue that requires a sovereign decision on a state of emergency. In both works the plague narrative establishes an equivalence between the biological body, the political body and sovereignty. The plague thus functions as the symptomatic embodiment of a political crisis that sets into motion a process of repair, although interestingly the cures that Homer and Sophocles suggest diverge.

The *Iliad* begins with a "foul pestilence" (*νόσος κακός* I, 10), which hits the camp of the Achaeans for ten days. The pestilence is caused by the god Apollo and "comes as night comes down" (I, 47) to take revenge on the Greek sovereign, king Agamemnon or "the lord of men" (*ἄναξ ἀνδρῶν*), as Homer describes him in I, 6 of the *Iliad*. Agamemnon had dishonoured the Trojan priest of Apollo, Chryses, refusing to release his daughter Chryseis, caught as a spoil of war and made into the king's slave.

The plague is therefore the means by which a supernatural force punishes the whole community for the trespasses of its sovereign, who violated family bonds and religious customs. The end of the "shameful plague" (I, 97) requires the conciliation of the angry god by returning the daughter to her father and setting the wrong right, as the Greek priest Kalchas explains to Achilles. Homer's plague thus embodies a political crisis in the literal medical sense of the word. It is both the decisive moment and the moment for decisions. It is, of course, the sovereign Agamemnon who finally decides to return the daughter to his father. But Agamemnon's decision can be considered a limited sovereign decision because the circumstances force it on him under pressure from Achilles, who behaves as a judge in this situation, finding out the truth and imposing the consequences of this truth on Agamemnon. The plague provokes a state of emergency, although this is not the Agambenian "free and juridically empty space" (Agamben 1998, 36) of the exception in which sovereign power no longer knows the limits fixed by the *nomos*. On the contrary, the epidemic state of emergency (provoked by the god) comes as an interruption to the sovereign exception, i.e. Agamemnon's unlimited right to violence. The epidemic is the symptom of a political crisis, forcing the sovereign to recognize the limits of his power as a condition for the return to normality.

It is interesting to observe that the Homeric pestilence is thoroughly represented in military terms. The divine archer Apollo spread the disease by attacking the Achaeans with his arrows and, at the start of his quest for the reason for this assault, Achilles explicitly couples war (πόλεμος) and plague (λοιμός) as forces overpowering the Achaeans (I: 60–61).[5] This coupling of war and plague is not resolved by Agamemnon's belated decision to return Chryseis to her father, because this decision opens up a conflict within the political body of the Achaeans. As a matter of fact, Agamemnon takes immediate revenge on Achilles, claiming for himself Achilles' slave Briseis and thus reaffirming the violence and arbitrariness of sovereign power. This causes the proverbial anger of Achilles "and its devastation, which put pains thousandfold upon the Achaeans" (I, 2). When the truth is disclosed, the plague thus turns into an internal struggle between Agamemnon and Achilles that Homer defines as a bitter collision and a conflict tearing the two apart (διαστήτην ἐρίσαντε: I, 6). Homer's διαστήτην is closely related to στάσις (both originating from ἵστημι), that Greek political thought will later use to define a dysfunction of the *polis* provoked by civic strife, i.e. internal struggle between different political factions (Serafim 2020, 674; Näripä 2019, 73–124).[6] In his book on civil war as a political paradigm, Agamben (2015, 22) states that *stasis* "forms part of a device that functions in a manner similar to the state of exception" as in *stasis* the *polis* is considered from the perspective of the state of nature, i.e. "as if it were dissolved" (2015, 53). Thus, after Agamemnon's revenge by taking Briseis, Achilles calls him, significantly, a "King who feeds on his own people" (δημοβόρος βασιλεὺς) since he "rules over nonentities" or a "worthless sum" (ἐπεὶ οὐτιδανοῖσιν ἀνάσσεις: I, 231), that is, exactly the kind of dissolved multitude that characterizes *stasis* according to Agamben.

Summing up, Homer's plague narrative offers us a complex representation of sovereign power, the exception it opens in the political field, and its consequences. Plague, on the one hand, points to the limit of Agamemnon's exceptional power in front of a more powerful "divine sovereign" and it provokes a reestablishment of the *nomos* (religious cult and familiar ties), which Agamemnon had violated. On the other hand, when the divine epidemic is appeased through

---

[5] The use of war metaphors in the description of epidemics has been criticized by Susan Sontag (1989, 94–95), according to whom illness, war, and politics are perversely entangled in our imagery with nefarious consequences for our ways of understanding and treating medical as well as social issues.

[6] The intimate relationship between the Homeric "division in conflict", which devours the Greek army, and the στάσις of Greek philosophers, which dissolves the political unity of the Greek *polis*, is revealed by Plato, when in 545d–e of the *Politeia*, he quotes the first lines of the *Iliad*, inadvertently replacing Homer's διαστήτην with στάσις.

Agamemnon's apparent capitulation, it breaks out again as *stasis*, this time not caused by an external intervention but stemming from within the Achaeans. The price paid by Agamemnon for re-imposing sovereign exception on the Greek camp is civic war with Achilles, which proves that the Greek political body is actually a dissolved multitude in a state of exception.

In his philological analysis of *Iliad*'s Book I, Daniel Blickman (1987) stresses the pervasive relation between discord and plague as expressed in the central motif of wrath (μῆνις), which characterizes the external sovereign enemy (Apollo) as well as the internal sovereign adversary (Achilles). It follows from this that the looming defeat of the Greeks, due to Achilles' refusal to fight, is described "with the same term as is used for the destruction brought by the plague" (Blickman 1987, 4). Homer consequently describes the fight between the two kings as ἀντιβίοσ that is "lethal to life" and Blickman concludes his analysis with the claim that "the breach among the Achaeans could almost be described as a secular plague. The *Iliad* foreshadows later connections made between *stasis* and plague" (Blickman 1987, 9). The Homeric plague thus mobilizes different elements of the Agambenian conception of biopolitics, helping to thematize and problematize the lawlessness of sovereign power and its relations with the state of exception as *stasis*.

2.2 Purifying the Miasma: Plague and the "Sacrification" of the Sovereign in *Oedipus Rex*

At the beginning of Sophocles's *Oedipus Rex*, the "God of Plague" raids the city of Thebes (Prologue, 30–31). But instead of following Homer in the description of the plague as an attack by a specific God, Sophocles focuses on the relations between the sovereign and his suffering people, defined in the tragedy as "children" (παῖδες). Through the voice of the priest, the people describe the cruel suffering inflicted by the plague, while the chorus introduces the dissolving effects of the epidemic on the social body: "fear unjoints me, the roots of my heart tremble" (Parados, 4). The people seek "safety" (44) from the king and significantly stress, in a Foucauldian fashion, the sovereign's responsibility for the security of his people and the good administration of their lives as a fundamental aim of sovereign power: "No man questions your power to rule the land: But rule over men, not over a dead city! Ships are only hulls, high walls are nothing, when no life moves in the empty passageways!" (Prologue, 57–59). Contrary to Agamemnon, Oedipus is immediately eager to fulfil all the conditions to relieve the suffering of the city as his spirit groans not only for himself but for the whole people (66). However, Oedipus's "ruling over men" does not translate into biopolitical measures for the administration of the diseased population, but rather into a quest for the truth, i.e. the hidden cause of the plague, as the only solution to the epidemic. Just as in Homer, the plague situates itself within a politico-juridical paradigm rather than in a medical one.

Apollo plays an important role here too, not as the plague carrier of the *Iliad*, but as a source of knowledge (the oracle of Delphi) and, in the words of the priest and the chorus, as a potential "healer" (153). When Creon, sent by Oedipus to ask the oracle how to end the epidemic, returns to Thebes, Oedipus orders him to give the oracle's verdict not to him separately, but to repeat it in front of the gathered people. Then Creon announces that the god commands the city to "expel from the land of Thebes an old defilement we are sheltering. It is a deathly thing, beyond cure. We must not let it feed upon us longer" (98–102). The word "defilement" is a translation of *μίασμα*, a word used in Ancient Greek and later medicine meaning "bad air" rising from the decomposition of organic matter and considered responsible for epidemics (Kannadan 2018). In Greek mythology miasma was represented as a contagious power produced by unnatural deeds which needed to be purged by the sacrifice of the wrongdoer responsible for those deeds. In the case of a sovereign the contamination produced by his wrongdoing extended to the social body as a whole, taking the form of a plague epidemic (Armstrong 2006, 55).

In Sophocles's tragedy, Creon reveals that the cause of the miasma provoking the epidemic is the unpunished murder of the previous king, Laios. The plague thus rises as a symptom of the hidden secret at the heart of the city, i.e. the moral and political contamination of the city is the real cause of decay, which hits the individual as well as the social body. Oedipus wishes to "bring what is dark to light" (134) and "be rid of evil" (140), that is, to re-establish the order of the *nomos* violated by the murder of Laios, and in this way to put an end to the pestilence. Thus, Oedipus initially takes care of the suffering people as well as of his own personal interests, because a sovereign cannot tolerate regicide. But when he is found to be the murderer of Laios, the violent foundation of his sovereign power is revealed instead. The king is identified as the origin of the miasma and the plague. From that moment sovereign exception turns into mere lawlessness, revealing, in a very Agambenian fashion, the secret solidarity between the sovereign and the *homo sacer*, the one who must be banned from the city in order to restore the wellbeing of the people.[7] At the end of the tragedy the sovereign thus

---

7 As Michelakis (2019, 383) remarks, the metaphorical identification of "plague" (*λοιμός*) as a political enemy harmful to society and scapegoat was a strongly established rhetorical weapon in Ancient-Greek politics.

expels himself from the city as an outlaw in order to clean the political body of the miasma which contaminated it.

If in the *Iliad* it was an issue of placating the rage of the divine carrier of the plague, while rage itself carried on as *stasis*, the dissolving working of the plague on the social body of the Achaeans, in *Oedipus Rex* it is only with the final expulsion of the contamination source at the very heart of sovereign power that the epidemic can be beaten. Sophocles' description of the plague also abounds in military metaphors and the end of Thebes's epidemic coincides with a violent act (the blinding and expulsion of Oedipus). But this act is intended as an act of justice in the name of the safety of the social body, unlike the rage of Agamemnon and Achilles, which perpetuates the destructiveness of the plague as political *stasis*.[8]

In conclusion, both the *Iliad*'s plague, which falls upon the people as a dark night, and *Oedipus*'s plague, which rises from the people as a contaminating miasma, expose the Agambenian biopolitical mechanism by working as a sort of exception to the sovereign exception and pointing to the limits of sovereign power and the ruin which awaits the trespassers. The plague as exception to the sovereign exception is provoked in both texts by the intervention of a higher authority identified in the *Iliad* with the god Apollo and more vaguely compared in *Oedipus Rex* with various types of non-human agency such as gods, monsters and weapons (Michelakis 2019, 388). However, something has clearly changed in the relationship between sovereign power and exception from the Homeric period to Pericles's Athens where Sophocles's tragedy was performed. While in the *Iliad* the end of the pestilence provokes an immediate return of the sovereign μῆνις, in Oedipus the sovereign/outlaw amends the violent and immoral foundation of his power by expelling himself permanently from the city.

2.3 *Societas tam quam dissoluta* in Thucydides's and Boccaccio's Plague Narratives

In Homer and Sophocles the plague is the story of sovereign exception, its excesses and their consequences. The biopolitical body of the people is present only as the passive place of sufferance for the mischiefs of its sovereign. In Thucydides's and Boccaccio's plague narratives, this body becomes the protagonist of the narration, while the figure of the sovereign disappears from the scene. In these

---

8 It is nevertheless interesting to observe that if we consider the Theban Cycle as a whole, here too the expulsion of king Oedipus and the end of the pestilence becomes civic war between the two sons of Oedipus, Eteocles and Polynices, narrated by Aeschylus in his tragedy *Seven against Thebes*.

narratives the plague is truly a state and space of exception inhabited by bare life. Thucydides's "hardly alive" people[9] who "wallowed the streets and crawled about every fountain" (II.52.2) of plagued Athens evoke the uncanny threshold figure of the Agambenian "living dead" in Nazi concentration camps. The fundamental difference is that in Thucydides and Boccaccio there is apparently no one to decide on the state of exception and the bare life it generates.

At the centre of Thucydides's and Boccaccio's reflection on the plague is rather what Agamben calls "the idea of contagion" (2021, 21). Agamben observes that the notion was unknown to Hippocratic medicine, while it emerged in the context of modern (sixteenth–seventeenth century) plague epidemics when it started to function as a means of blame and scapegoating against supposed plague spreaders. The idea of contagion is, according to Agamben, also at the basis of the exceptional decrees issued by governments for the management of the COVID-19 pandemic, which "transform, in effect, every individual into a potential plague-spreader, just as the orders against terrorism considered every citizen as a de facto and de jure potential terrorist" (Agamben 2021, 23). Despite the absence of the notion of contagion in Greek medicine, the "idea of contagion" is clearly described in Thucydides (Longrigg 1992, 33–34) and, more clearly, in Boccaccio:

> what made this pestilence even more severe was that whenever those suffering from it mixed with people who were still unaffected, it would rush upon these with the speed of a fire racing through dry or oily substances that happened to come within its reach. Nor was this the full extent of its evil, for not only did it infect healthy persons who conversed or had any dealings with the sick, making them ill or visiting an equally horrible death upon them, but it also seemed to transfer the sickness to anyone touching the clothes or other objects which had been handled or used by its victims. (2003, 331–332)

While, as observed above, there is no sovereign to decree here on the state of emergency through measures (social distancing) banning humans from "intercourse" and "association", the effects of the idea of contagion are still represented by both Thucydides and Boccaccio as the dissolution of even the closest social bonds. A horrified Boccaccio describes this as a kind of voluntary social distancing provoked by the fear of contagion:

> It was not merely a question of one citizen avoiding another, and of people almost invariably neglecting their neighbours and rarely or never visiting their relatives, addressing them only from a distance; this scourge had implanted so great a terror in the hearts of men and women that brothers abandoned brothers, uncles their nephews, sisters their

---

[9] In his retelling of Thucydides's text in *De Rerum Natura*, Lucretius coins the Latin word *semanimo* (half-alive/animated) as an adequate description of plagued people.

> brothers, and in many cases wives deserted their husbands. But even worse, and almost incredible, was the fact that fathers and mothers refused to nurse and assist their own children, as though they did not belong to them. (2003, 337–338)

Thucydides interestingly represents this issue as a kind of unresolvable dilemma: "When they were afraid to visit one another, the sufferers died in their solitude, so that many houses were empty because there had been no one left to take care of the sick; or if they ventured they perished, especially those who aspired to heroism." (II, 51, 4–5).

What interests us here is that the "social distancing" provoked by the idea of contagion rescinds the social ties and provokes the dissolution of the political relationship that held the city together. For Thucydides the plague thus turns into "lawlessness" (ἀνομία, II, 53, 1) as "those who saw all perishing alike, thought that the worship or neglect of the Gods made no difference. For offences against human law no punishment was to be feared" (II, 53, 4). Boccaccio similarly writes that "in the face of so much affliction and misery, all respect for the laws of God and man had virtually broken down and been extinguished (*dissoluta*) in our city. [. . .] Hence everyone was free to behave as he pleased" (2003, 335–336). We encounter here the terrifying idea of a human condition freed from the constraints of sovereign power, the Hobbesian representation of the state of nature as a paradoxical society *ut tanquam dissoluta consideretur* – "considered as if it were dissolved" (Hobbes 1983, 79–80), where freedom corresponds with a natural right unlimited by social norms. Agamben uses exactly this Hobbesian passage on the state of nature as a "dissolved society" in order to make his point on the state of exception as the essential though hidden core of sovereign power. Thus, he comments that "the state of nature did not necessarily have to be conceived as a real epoch, but rather could be understood as a principle internal to the State revealed in the moment in which the State is considered 'as if it were dissolved'" (Agamben 1998, 36). But what then appears, Agamben continues, "is in fact not the state of nature (as an earlier stage into which men would fall back) but the state of exception." (1998, 37) This uncanny coincidence of the fantasized state of nature and the hidden state of exception brings Agamben to the conclusion that "the principle of the preservation of one's own life is truly the innermost center of the political system." (1998, 36).

In his analysis of the famous frontispiece image of Hobbes' *Leviathan*, Agamben turns his attention to the few tiny figures represented in the otherwise empty city topped by the huge body of the sovereign: the armed guards and two characters wearing the characteristic beaked masks of plague doctors (2015, 47–48). Indeed, the dissolved multitude that "dwells in the city, but only as the object of the duties and concerns of those who exercise the sovereignty" is similar to "the mass of plague victims", who can be represented "only through the guards who monitor its obedience and the doctors who treat it" (Agamben 2015, 48). Through this comparison between the plague and the sovereign exception, Agamben concludes that the co-presence of the sovereign Leviathan and the plague doctors in Hobbes' frontispiece image is an index of the biopolitical nature of sovereign power.

It is on this last point that Agamben's interpretation of Hobbes' *civitas ut tanquam dissoluta consideretur* ceases to fit Thucydides's and Boccaccio's plague narratives. Both authors describe in great detail the decay of the diseased physiological body and draw the parallel with the dissolution of the body politic. The plague does not punish the community for the mischief of the sovereign, as in Homer and Sophocles, but provokes the decomposition of society and the return of the citizens to the disorder and chaos of the state of nature, where there are no limits to people's freedom and they live "in wild disorder" (Thucydides II, 52.2). However, this disordered condition is only partially driven by "the principle of preservation of one's own life", while Thucydides and Boccaccio actually describe a series of (self-)destructive behaviours in their plague narratives. Instead what seems to impress them most is the new regime of death established by the wild disorder of the epidemic, in which the customary funeral rituals are "universally violated" (Thucydides II, 52.4) and "disappeared" (Boccaccio 2003, 340) and people die like animals – "sheep" in Thucydides's narrative (II, 51.4), which is closely echoed by Boccaccio: "folk recked no more of men that died than nowadays they would of goats" (Boccaccio 2003, 24).[10]

So, if in Thucydides and Boccaccio as well as in Agamben the preservation of one's own life, through fear of contagion and social distancing, is the cause of the dissolution of the social bond, this dissolution provokes in its turn, in Thucydides's and Boccaccio's plague narratives, a progressive indifference toward life as well as death. The most striking difference with Agamben's analysis lies, therefore, in the fact that the epidemic state of exception in Thucydides and Boccaccio does not reveal the "hidden principle internal to the state" as the biopolitical grip upon the bare life of "the mass of plague victims" secured through the sovereign decisions and emergency measures. Thucydides and Boccaccio only briefly refer

---

10 If in Homer's plague narrative we find a passing reference to funeral rites – "constantly the pyres of the dead burned thick" (Iliad, I, 52) –, Sophocles shares Thucydides's and Boccaccio's horror at the interruption of funeral rites during the epidemic through the lament of the chorus: "pallid children laden with death / lie unwept in the stony ways" (Parados, 28–29). These observations contradict Agamben's claim about the unprecedented, i.e. "something that, from Antigone to the present day, has never happened" (Agamben 2021, 52), and "barbaric" disposal of the bodies of the dead burned without a funeral during the COVID-19 pandemic, "purely in the name of an indeterminable risk" (Agamben 2021, 52). Contrary to Agamben's claim of "unprecedentedness", plague narratives of the past recurrently bring to the fore the interruption of funeral rites and the merely animal quality of death as the results of the dissolution of social bonds brought about by the epidemic state of exception.

to the biopolitical management of contagion: the latter mentioning the cleansing of the city by officials appointed for the purpose, the refusal of entrance to all sick people, and the adoption of other precautions for the preservation of health (Boccaccio 2003, 329). This seems just a premise to the conclusion that no remedy had any effect on the spread of the epidemic. Instead of the resolving sovereign decision on the epidemic state of exception of the *Iliad* and *Oedipus Rex*, Thucydides and Boccaccio represent many individual, chaotic and contradictory decisions of Athens's and Florence's citizens, which all help to accelerate the dissolution of society.

An interesting alternative reading of Boccaccio has been presented by Shona Kelly Wray (2004), who considers the argument in the introduction of the *Decameron* to be an implicit condemnation of medical advice (*consilia*) on the containment of the plague of 1348. The behaviours of Florentines, and particularly their attempt to banish the sick, would be a direct application of such advice, which Boccaccio calls a "very inhuman precaution" (Boccaccio 2003, 335) as it ends with the worst of all diseases: the destruction of society. According to Wray's argument, Boccaccio would oppose the uncompassionate and society-corroding advice of doctors, with a call for human compassion: "The doctors counsel self-protection, but compassion towards others in need is more important. Compassion is fundamentally human, as made clear in the first words of the Proem, immediately following the title of the *Decameron*: *Umana cosa e' aver compassione degli afflitti*" (Wray 2004, 312). In his COVID-19 volume, Agamben similarly opposes "social distancing" with the imperative of "love of one's neighbour" [*amore del prossimo*].

While Wray's argument is suggestive and interesting for a critical assessment of biosecurity and social distancing, it is a fact that the plague narrative in the introduction to the *Decameron* is immediately followed by the decision of the ten young storytellers to leave the plagued city. The decision is prompted by the speech of one of the ladies of the company, Pampinea, who, most importantly for us, bases her argument on the natural right of every human being "to sustain, preserve, and defend his own life to the best of his ability" (Boccaccio 2003, 350). This right which, as Pampinea explains, exonerates even those who killed others in self-defence, completely legitimizes an action that does not directly harm anyone, as with the storytellers' decision to leave the plagued city. Here compassion turns into self-compassion and the duty to stay in the city into the right to flee it. The voluntary golden exile of the ten young Florentine storytellers of the *Decameron* to a countryside villa can in this respect be considered an escapist Utopia that restores human bonds, and a kind of order only at the expense of abandoning the decomposing political body and the "wild disorder" of the plagued city.

2.4 Modern Plagues and Biopolitics in Defoe and Manzoni

While ancient and medieval plague narratives functioned as a symptom of the sovereign exception and as an allegory of civil strife or the dissolution of the body politic, and are therefore considered here mainly according to an Agambenian understanding of biopolitics, it is not surprising that modern plague narratives bring to the fore quite a few aspects of the Foucauldian version of biopolitics.[11] Daniel Defoe's and Alessandro Manzoni's plague narratives focus on what Defoe (2008, 105) calls "the whole Body of the People", that is, Foucault's "population", and on the exceptional biosecurity "measures for managing the people" (Defoe 2008, 170) employed during the epidemics they describe. This is also the reason for the documentary nature of their narratives, in which they mention or directly quote the historical chronicles of the epidemics and original orders of the authorities, which contain a long list of extraordinary institutions, officers and measures for the containment of the epidemics in London and Milan (see Table 1).

Table 1: The biopolitical management of the epidemic in Defoe's and Manzoni's plague narratives.

	Institutions	Officers	Measures
Defoe's *Journal of the Plague Year*	Pest houses	examiners, searchers, watchmen, nurse keepers, etc.	shutting up the houses of the sick, certificates of health to move around, bills of mortality, mass graves, prohibition of assemblies of people and public feasting, execution of dogs and cats, 'death carts', etc.
Manzoni's *Betrothed*	Commission of Health (*Tribunale della salute*), lazaretto	*monatti* (liquidate dead bodies), *apparitori* (warn people of passing funeral carriages), *commissari* (preside over monatti and apparitori)	prescription of quarantine, shutting of houses, confiscation and burning of infected goods, etc.

The function of such special institutions, officers and measures is to govern the "wild disorder" brought about by epidemics through the establishment of a new, exceptional order, fundamentally based on the separation of the sick from the healthy part of the "Body of the People". In Manzoni's narrative the central institution for the separation and management of the sick part of the body of the people is Milan's lazaretto (*lazzaretto*), where infected citizens are confined. From a

---

11 See the remarks on Foucault's "plague city" in the introduction of this volume.

Foucauldian perspective it is interesting to observe that for Manzoni the administration of the lazaretto is a matter of government, as he makes clear when he writes about the Commission of Health looking for "someone capable of taking on the government of that unhappy realm (the lazaretto)" (Manzoni 1983, 1185). Moreover, Manzoni later defines the "government" of the lazaretto as a "dictatorship" (*dittatura*) and describes it as "a most extraordinary device for the magistrates to adopt – as extraordinary as that calamitous emergency, as the times themselves" (Manzoni 1983, 1187). The lazaretto's "dictator", the Capuchin friar Felice Casati, is "in charge of the place, with the fullest authority over everybody there" (Manzoni 1983, 1186), an authority that Manzoni describes as follows:

> Father Felice was always on the move [. . .] He inspired and controlled everything; he calmed riots, solved disputes, threatened, punished, reproved and comforted; he dried the tears of others and shed tears of his own (Manzoni 1983, 1186–1187).

Social distancing is not, as in Thucydides and Boccaccio, the chaotic reaction of a horrified people to the spread of contagion. It is a proper biopolitical mechanism based on the paradigm of biosecurity (lockdown, isolation, reclusion) decided upon by a basically unlimited sovereign power – a dictatorship. However, the description of Father Felice's power in the passage above reminds us rather of what Foucault defined as "pastoral power", as it successfully reunites the opposites of Boccaccio's plague narrative: the medical (biopolitical) measures for the separation of the sick from the healthy (the lazaretto) and human compassion (the Capuchin caretakers).

The epidemic disorder is thus governed through the exceptional establishment of a stricter order, control, surveillance for the administration of the whole body of the people through the segregation of the sick, which is aimed at avoiding the dissolution of the social body: the "destruction of the City" as Manzoni observes, quoting a chronicle of the time. The risk of such destruction is represented in Manzoni's plague narrative by irrational reactions to the epidemic based on the "vague suspicion" of a plot to spread the disease by poisoning city places, a conspiracy against the biosecurity of the people; such suspicion gradually becomes a "blind, uncontrolled panic" (1983, 1192), sending the already "agitated city" into an "utter turmoil" (1983, 1996), a madness propagating itself as fast as the plague (1983, 1210).[12] What in Thucydides and Boccaccio was the spontaneous reaction to the idea of contagion that pushed the healthy to avoid the sick, thus

---

[12] The plague narrative of chapters 31–32 has been in this respect compared by scholars (see for example Grendene 2017) with the revolt narrative of chapters 11–13, where the so-called "riot of San Martin" in 1628 Milan is described. In both cases Manzoni illustrates and criticizes the irrational and destructive behaviour of a disordered "multitude" (*moltitudine*). In the present volume Meelis Friedenthal shows that the seventeenth century's medical understandings of the plague

becomes in Manzoni's narrative an active witch hunt for the "anointers" (*untori*), people accused of voluntarily spreading the plague, by applying infected mixtures to objects in the city's public places. The dark fear of the epidemic, fed by old prejudices and superstitious beliefs, is thus channelled by the people at presumed public enemies to be persecuted and eliminated; "anointers" naturally come to be embodied by the foreigners who, as Manzoni writes, "were suspect as such; and as they were easily recognizable by their dress in those days, they were often arrested in the streets by the people and taken to the police" (1983, 1196).

It is therefore not by chance that Giorgio Agamben begins his essay on contagion (2021, 21) with a quote from Manzoni: "The anointer! Catch him! Catch him! Catch the anointer!". However, Agamben misrepresents Manzoni's intention when he relates the witch-hunt for the anointers with the government decrees for the containment of the contagion. Manzoni sorely criticizes the inadequate and backward authorities who governed Milan during the 1630 epidemic, but his enlightened critique focuses on the initial denialism and later impotence and inertness of the city powers, who instead of rationally analysing the situation and managing the epidemic, flirted dangerously with the disordered and irrational reaction of the confused people.[13] In contrast, as we have seen, Manzoni praises the good and rational emergency measures taken to govern the plagued population that were implemented through the efficient, though dictatorial, management of the Milan lazaretto. This was closely reminiscent of the new rationality of the Foucauldian "government of men" and the kind of emergency measures which Agamben criticizes in his book on the COVID-19 pandemic. Moreover, Manzoni states that this kind of management should have been extended to the government of the whole city during the plague epidemic.

Daniel Defoe's *Journal* is more ambivalent about the biopolitical management of the London epidemic of 1665. Its protagonist expresses concerns about the exceptional measures for the administration of the social body that to a certain degree resemble Agamben's critique of the biosecurity paradigm. On the one hand, Defoe praises the public and private "measures" and "managements" (2010, 105) "taken by the magistrate for the general Safety" (2010, 33), particularly as they managed to

---

actually contained some of the believes that Manzoni attributes to the ignorance and superstition of the populace in those time.

13 In a separate historical essay titled *Storia della colonna infame*, Manzoni narrates in detail the infamous trial of two supposed anointers who were sentenced to death during the 1630 plague in Milan. Adriano Prosperi (2018) interestingly suggests that Manzoni's description of the trial was actually thought of as a critical allegory of the tribunals of terror during the French Revolution: in both cases the minds of the people were infected by the conspiracist obsession with a hidden enemy to be revealed and destroyed.

"preserve the good order" (2010, 33) and prevented "the Rage and Desperation of the People from breaking out in Rabbles and Tumults, / . . . / from the Poor plundering the Rich" (2010, 111). The medical management of the situation is thus directly related to the political management, the former avoiding the degeneration of the epidemic into *stasis* and the dissolution of society as described by Thucydides and Boccaccio. Not only a writer but also a trader and journalist, Defoe admits the negative, coercive character of the measures on individual freedom, although he, like Manzoni, reaches the conclusion that, in the exceptional circumstances of the epidemic, such coercion "was a public Good that justified the private Mischief" (2010, 43).

Nevertheless, Defoe's protagonist also expresses a critical view of the dangerous and unnecessary impact of specific measures on the "whole body of the people", and it is here that Defoe's observation reminds us most closely of the biopolitical management of the COVID-19 pandemic and Agamben's critique of social distancing and the biosecurity paradigm. Indeed, while the protagonist of the *Journal* praises the biopolitical containment of the epidemic to maintain order, he criticizes the most extreme forms of coercion in the division of the body of the people into a healthy or, as Defoe also writes, "sound" part to be preserved and a sick one to be confined. For instance, the protagonist and narrator of the *Journal* comments that shutting sick people into their houses "does not answer the end at all" (2010, 47), because instead of overruling private mischief in the name of the public good, it actually drives people to "extremities" (2010, 47) in the attempt to escape seclusion. Containment measures thus risk increasing, rather than moderating, public disorder. The protagonist sums this up as follows:

> I believ'd then, and do believe still, that the shutting up Houses thus by Force, and restraining, or rather imprisoning People in their own Houses, as is said above, was of little or no Service in the Whole; nay, I am of Opinion, it was rather hurtful, having forc'd those desperate People to wander abroad with the Plague upon them. (2010, 62)

Moreover, Defoe is aware of the risk that management of the epidemic might turn into a biosecurity apparatus that transforms every potentially infected person into a threat and an enemy. In a very Agambenian fashion, the protagonist of the *Journal* targets the progressive expansion of containment measures from the sick to potentially the whole population. In the first step in his argument Defoe's protagonist adds to the categories of the "sound" (healthy) people and the "sick" (symptomatic plague victims), the third category of the "well":

> By the Well, I mean such as had received the Contagion, and had it really upon them, and in their Blood, yet did not show the Consequences of it in their Countenances, nay even were not sensible of it themselves, as many were not for several Days: These breathed Death in every Place [. . .] Men went about apparently well, many Days after they had the taint of

> the Disease in their Vitals, and after their Spirits were so seiz'd, as that they could never escape it; and that all the while they did so, they were dangerous to others. (2010, 164)

Defoe identifies here what we call today the "asymptomatic carriers" of the plague and describes them as the most insidious invisible threats – "walking destroyers" (2010, 164) – within the whole body of the people. Nevertheless, his argument actually ends up as a warning against the risks and nonsense of extending the measure of isolation to all potential "well", following the principle that, in the context of the COVID-19 pandemic, has been called of "close contact". This would in fact eventually make every person a potential bearer of the plague to be confined:

> shutting up the WELL or removing the SICK will not do it, unless they can go back and shut up all those that the Sick had Convers'd with, even before they knew themselves to be sick, and none knows how far to carry that back, or where to stop; for none knows when, or where, or how they may have received the Infection, or from whom (2010, 164).

Every "potentially infected person" thus coincides with every person, the whole body of the people coming consequently to coincide with its sick part. Defoe's protagonist warns us that the final result of the fear against an invisible internal enemy (the "Well") is the potential extension of surveillance and seclusion to the body of the people as a whole, something which, according to Agamben, has really happened in that universalization of the state of exception brought about by the total lockdowns and social distancing measures of the COVID-19 pandemic.

Summing up, there is a general similarity, as well as an important difference, between the two modern plague narratives considered above. Like Manzoni, Defoe closely analyses the combined effects of the epidemic and of its biopolitical containment on the social body. However, contrary to Manzoni, who attributed the invention of the anointers to popular superstition and fear, Defoe reveals the solidarity between the most extreme measures for the management of the epidemic and the stigmatization of potentially every single member of society. The uncanny figure of the "well" is the point at which the biosecurity paradigm fails (as Defoe's protagonist notes), but, at the same time, it is the means by which biopower can eventually extend its grip on the whole of society. What has to be defended (the healthy) becomes indistinguishable from what it has to be defended from and, consequently, is chased and persecuted (the sick). The "none knows how far" in Defoe's quote above mirrors the question in the title of Agamben's COVID-19 booklet: Where are we now? This is how far we have gone, and where shall we stop?

3 Conclusion

This preliminary analysis of plague narratives shows that they contain a lot of elements for a reflection on epidemics and biopolitics, particularly if we integrate Foucault's understanding of biopolitical governmentality with Agamben's observations on sovereign power and bare life.

Explicitly biopolitical elements of epidemic management occupy a central position only in modern plague narratives, confirming Michel Foucault's vision of the modern age as the time in which people's health first became a matter for government. In Defoe's *Journal of the Plague Year* and Manzoni's *The Betrothed*, social distancing, isolation and seclusion are represented as necessary measures for the administration of life during an epidemic state of emergency, though the more sinister potential of Agamben's sovereign exception in its biosecurity version also shines through in Defoe's critical remarks. The effectiveness as well as the legitimacy of biopolitical measures thus become issues for discussion, challenging the all too easy dismissal of the violation of fundamental human rights and values in the name of the "public good".

In older narratives, there is almost no trace of biopower in the Foucauldian sense. Rather these narratives present interesting elements that point to the more distinct aspects of Agamben's understanding of biopolitics and its relationship with the state of exception. We find there two different or perhaps complementary ways of understanding the epidemic state of exception. In Thucydides's and Boccaccio's plague narratives, we have a state of exception – the plague as a materialization of "society as if it would be dissolved" – and bare life, i.e. people living and dying in a zone of indistinction between proper human life and mere biological survival/death. But the sovereign is absent, there is neither administration of nor decision on the epidemic state of exception. Social distancing and the terror which provokes it are the *trait d'union* between the individual and the social side of the epidemic state of exception, which devours the physiological as well as the political body of Athens's and Florence's citizenry.

While René Girard (1974) has identified the idea of social disorder, reversal and undifferentiation of social statuses as a common denominator of all plague narratives, I have shown that such disorder is the bearer of importantly different biopolitical meanings in different plague narratives. Contrary to Thucydides and Boccaccio, the sovereign is the protagonist of Homer's and Sophocles's plague narratives. The epidemic does not constitute there an excuse for the magnification of sovereign power, as Agamben argues in the case of COVID-19. The *Iliad*'s and *Oedipus*'s plagues are, rather, a trial to the excesses of sovereign power, they work as an exception to the sovereign exception. A sovereign decision on the epidemic state of exception is thus required to re-affirm in a more or less stable manner the validity of the *nomos* that the sovereign himself violated. The outcomes of such a decision differ interestingly in the *Iliad* and *Oedipus Rex*. If Oedipus's decision transforms the sovereign into an outlaw, Agamemnon's turns the plague into civic strife.

Thus, plague narratives offer us an interesting reflection on society and power when they are driven to extremes, where the preservation of life as such becomes the main issue for sovereign power as well as for individuals. The most interesting result in the analysis of the plague narratives considered here is, I think, the wide range of biopolitical issues that emerge and the different outcomes of the articulation of the physical and the social, the individual and the public, people and power, illness and health, exception and rule. The next steps in the research could, on the one hand, deepen the analysis of the single plague narratives and, on the other, widen the scope of the analysis to other plague narratives excluded from my preliminary choice.

References

Agamben, Giorgio. *Homo Sacer. Sovereign Power and Bare Life*. Trans. Daniele Heller-Roazen. Stanford: Stanford University Press, 1998.

Agamben, Giorgio. *Stasis. Civil War as a Political Paradigm (Homo Sacer II, 2)*. Trans. Nicholas Heron. Stanford: Stanford University Press, 2015.

Agamben, Giorgio. *Where Are We Now? The Epidemic as Politics*. Trans. Valeria Dani. London: Eris, 2021.

Armstrong, Karen. *The Great Transformation: The Beginning of Our Religious Traditions*. New York: Random House, 2006.

Blickman, Daniel R. "The Role of the Plague in the 'Iliad'." *Classical Antiquity* 6.1 (1987): 1–10.

Girard, René. "The Plague in Literature and Myth." *Texas Studies in Literature and Language* 15.5, *A Special Classics Issue on Myth and Interpretation* (1974): 833–850.

Boccaccio, Giovanni. *The Decameron*. Trans. G. H. McWilliam. London: Penguin Classics, 2003 (e-book).

Cunha, Burke A. "The Cause of the Plague of Athens: Plague, Typhoid, Typhus, Smallpox, or Measles?" *Infectious Disease Clinics of North America* 18 (2004): 29–43.

Defoe, Daniel. *A Journal of the Plague Year*. Oxford: Oxford University Press, 2008.

Foucault, Michel. *The Will to Knowledge: The History of Sexuality, Volume 1*. Trans. Robert Hurley. New York: Pantheon Books, 1998.

Foucault, Michel. *"Society Must Be Defended": Lectures at the Collège de France, 1975–1976*. Trans. David Macey. New York: Picador, 2003.

Gardner, Hunter H. *Pestilence and the Body Politic in Latin Literature*. Oxford: Oxford University Press, 2019.

Gougelet, David-Olivier. "The World is One Great Hospital." *Journal of French and Francophone Philosophy* XVIII.1 (2008): 43–66.

Grendene, Filippo. "Rivolta peste carnevale: carsismi manzoniani." *Allegoria* 76 *Teoria e Critica* (2017): 25–45.

Hobbes, Thomas. *De cive: The Latin Version*. Ed. Howard Warrender. Oxford: Clarendon Press, 1983.
Homer, *The Iliad*. Trans. Richmond Lattimore. Chicago: The University of Chicago Press, 2011.
Kannadan, Ajesh. "History of the Miasma Theory of Disease." *ESSAI* 16 (2018): 41–43.
Kousoulis, Antonis A., P. Konstantinos, Effie Economopoulos, Effie Poulakou-Rebelakou, George Androutsos, and Sotirios Tsiodras. "The Plague of Thebes, a Historical Epidemic in Sophocles' Oedipus Rex." *Emerging Infectious Diseases* 18.1 (2012): 153–157.
Longrigg, James. "Epidemic, Ideas and Classical Athenian society." *Epidemics and Ideas. Essays on the Historical Perception of Pestilence*. Eds. Terence Ranger and Paul Slack. Cambridge: Cambridge University Press, 1992. 21–44.
Manzoni, Alessandro. *The Betrothed*. Trans. Bruce Penman. London: Penguin Classics, 1983 (e-book).
Michelakis, Pantelis. "Naming the Plague in Homer, Sophocles, and Thucydides." *American Journal of Philology* 14.3 (2019): 381–414.
Näripä, Neeme. *Stasis. Ein antikes Konzept*. Dissertationes studiorum graecorum et latinorum Universitatis Tartuensis 9. Tartu: Tartu University Press, 2019.
Prosperi, Adriano. "Manzoni, the Plague, and the Terror. Conspiracy and History in Chapter XXXI of Promessi sposi." *Studi Storici* 59.1 (2018): 23–45.
Serafim, Andreas. "Sicking Bodies: Stasis as Disease in the Human Body and the Body Politic." *A Volume in Honour of Professor Katerina Synodinou*. Ed. Helen Gasti. Ioannina: Carpe Diem Publications, 2020. 673–695.
Sontag, Susan. *AIDS and Its Metaphors*. New York: Farrar, Straus and Giroux, 1989.
Sophocles. *Oedipus Rex*. Trans. Dudley Fitts and Robert Fitzgerald. San Diego, CA: Harcourt, 1977.
Thucydides. *History of the Peloponnesian War*. Trans. Benjamin Jowett. London: Folio Society, 1994.
Turner, Bryan. *The Body and Society. Explorations in Social Theories*. New York: SAGE Publications, 1996.
Wray, Shona Kelly. "Boccaccio and the Doctors: Medicine and Compassion in the Face of Plague." *Journal of Medieval History* 30 (2004): 301–322.

Meelis Friedenthal
How to Manage Plague and COVID-19: Parallels and Differences Between Today and Premodern and Early-Modern Medical Theories

Abstract: During the COVID-19 pandemic, there has been growing interest in outbreaks of epidemic diseases that occurred earlier on in history. One of the recurring themes in such treatments seems be a desire to highlight how modern perceptions have advanced enormously compared to the past, at least in the Estonian press, to which this essay reacts. The aim of this piece is, on the contrary, to provide a brief overview of some of such past ideas about the causes of the infectious diseases (especially the plague), with an emphasis on how, despite the undoubtedly remarkable development of medical science, perceptions of such diseases and the methods used to combat them have remained surprisingly similar in many respects over the centuries.

The article looks at some of the early modern understandings of the plague, drawing mainly on the English physician John Allen (ca. 1660–1741) and the Austrian physician and writer Adam von Lebenwaldt (1624–1696). Both of them were personally engaged as plague doctors and drew on their own experience, comparing it with views from antiquity and contemporary literature. Early modern authors had introduced many new theories compared to the Middle Ages and as Europe was struck by several plague epidemics in the sixteenth and seventeenth centuries, the amount of material to draw on increased substantially.

Probably one of the most important lessons from the history of epidemics is the realization that uncertainties and a degree of panic have been a feature of both historical and modern pandemics. Uncertainties can arise from a variety of circumstances. For example, historical outbreaks are often linked to environmental changes, such as natural disasters, deforestation or urbanization, which create new opportunities for disease transmission along with psychological stress and anxieties. As such, epidemic diseases have been and still are a complex phenomenon and a study of the strategies and tactics used in the past to combat the disease can help us understand not only the effectiveness of different methods but also the possible societal reactions. During the COVID-19 pandemic, it became common to ridicule historical practices, or simply to portray them as a curiosity, but at the same time, a number of historical practices were reproduced, starting from isolation and quarantine and extending to apocalyptic doomsday fears and hostility towards

https://doi.org/10.1515/9783110799361-003

minority groups (Jedwab et al. 2021). In the following, I will look at some of the themes related to responses to epidemics mainly during the early modern period.

Often the stories about historical reaction to epidemics, which at first sight may indeed seem and thus often are presented as unscientific and ridiculous, on closer inspection turn out to be astonishingly perceptive and have a remarkable explanatory power. For example, much irony has been deployed in connection with the observation of earlier authors that comets and earthquakes could be harbingers of an approaching plague epidemic. Although there is indeed no straightforward causal link between these events, it has been often the case that deteriorating sanitary conditions and population displacement as a result of natural disasters have proved to be a contributing factor in the outbreak of epidemics (Watson, Gayer, and Connolly 2007; Tsiamis, Poulakou-Rebelakou, and Marketos 2013). Similarly, it has recently been pointed out that one of the contributors to the "Justinian plague" of the sixth century may have been a comet that hit the Earth in 536, creating a cloud of dust in the atmosphere that caused a short-term global temperature drop. Alternatively, the authors mention volcanic eruptions as possible causes (cf. Rigby, Symonds, and Ward-Thompson 2004, 536). So it is perhaps not entirely unreasonable to expect such unusual natural phenomena to have bad consequences, and it is not entirely unreasonable to see a link between them, regardless of whether we consider them to be God-given signs or global climate change.

The press also regularly mentions the story that cats were thought to be Satan's animals in the Middle Ages and during the plague people were encouraged to kill them *en masse*, allowing the rodents to run free and thereby contributing to the spread of the plague.[1] Although the story is not entirely true, it is not a complete lie either, as is often the case with such reports. One element of the story is probably based on an interpretation of the papal bull *Vox in Rama*, issued by Pope Gregory IX in 1233, which tells of the worship of the great black cat by the Luciferians in Germany (Russell 1972, 159–161). Although there is no doubt about the existence of such a document, its influence was local (it was not incorporated into the body of canon law) and there are no known medieval injunctions to destroy cats because of this association. There are, however, reports of cats, dogs and other domestic animals being killed in later times during the plague, not because they were considered to be satanic, but because they were suspected of spreading the plague. Such an accusation is not entirely unfounded, as cats can indeed transmit plague to humans. In addition, the view has recently emerged in scientific literature that the main vector of medieval plague may not have been

---

[1] In the Estonian press, e.g. Jürgen Rooste referring to the book "Rutto" ("Plague") by Lena and Larry Huldén and Kari Heliövaara. Rooste 2020.

fleas from rats at all (Yang and Anisimov 2016, 20; Hufthammer and Walløe 2013; Ell 1980). While the role of rats as a possible vector is not entirely denied, the main cause of the plague epidemic appears to have been the human flea (*Pulex irritans*) or direct human-to-human infection. There is therefore reason to question both the cat-killing story itself and its possible consequences – it is unlikely that large-scale culling of cats, which could theoretically have affected the rat population, took place at all and, secondly, it is questionable how large the role of rats was in spreading the plague.

To look at history in such a way – to console ourselves that we are now much better off and much wiser than our ancestors – is maybe excusable, but perhaps it is also possible to learn from history and not necessarily twist the facts to our advantage. In some ways, we have lived in an unusual time – we have not had a major epidemic, famine or war in the West for almost eighty years.[2] The claim that the plague, war and famine usually occur together has been of little importance or completely forgotten, but again, it seems that as a result of current political developments we are being reminded of these historical observations. Can history teach us something here?

Historically epidemics and infectious diseases have been common rather than exceptional, in contrast to today. Of course, one could challenge this statement and ask: is AIDS not an epidemic? It is known that a total of about 32 million people have died from AIDS and its complications.[3] However, the slow progression of the disease and the mechanisms of infection give AIDS a somewhat different character than plague. We could argue that the coronavirus outbreak is clearly an epidemic in the etymological sense of the word, which means that it is "among the people" (*epi demos* in Greek), and as we move among the people and talk with people we can also become infected.

Perhaps it is precisely because we in Europe have been untouched by such epidemics for so long that the current outbreak is being spoken of as something completely unprecedented and exceptional. However, the flu pandemic a century ago, for example, was just as global an event, killing many times more people than COVID-19 has done up until today – an estimated fifty million died of flu a century ago.[4] Estonia was also not immune to the "Spanish flu", as it was called at the time

---

[2] There are of course many counter-arguments that could be made here – the Yugoslav war, the Falklands conflict, the 1957–1958 pandemic (H2N2 virus) etc., but their media coverage and impact did not (for various reasons) reach the scale of the current COVID-19.
[3] https://www.unaids.org/en/resources/fact-sheet. Last accessed 16 June 2022.
[4] https://www.cdc.gov/flu/pandemic-resources/1918-pandemic-h1n1.html. As of 15 June 2022 the cumulative death toll of COVID-19 is according to WHO Coronavirus (COVID-19) Dashboard (https://covid19.who.int/) 6,3 million. Last accessed 16 June 2022.

and newspapers report that the flu claimed "many victims" between 1918 and 1920 in this country. It has been estimated that more people may have died of influenza in Estonia at that time than in the War of Estonian Independence.[5] In the 1920s, newspapers also discussed how to prevent the disease. These articles mentioned the need for quarantine, advised people not to share food or utensils with sick people and to wash their hands, etc. The tone of the articles has a certain parallel with today, because although the mechanisms of coronavirus infection are generally known, there was initially a lot of uncertainty about the spread of the disease – there were debates about whether or not wearing masks was an effective means of protecting oneself, it was unclear how great the chances of contracting the disease from surfaces exposed to the carrier of the disease were, and about how many metres away one had to stand to safely communicate with an infected person.

Another similarity is that quarantine has been the most effective measure against the spread of disease in the past and still is today. Restricting the movement of people during periods of contagious disease is a tried and tested practice. Already in the Old Testament, for example, certain requirements are laid down for dealing with potentially infectious persons (cf. Lev 13): it is stipulated that "the priest is to isolate the affected person for seven days", then to re-examine him and declare him either unsafe or safe. The quarantine was also used during the Justinian plague in the sixth century, which can be considered one of the first pandemics, given the size of the Roman Empire and the spread of the disease in Europe, Africa and Asia. Similarly, the quarantine was readily used during the plague epidemics of the fourteenth century Italy, and the quarantine as a practice gets its name from Italian language (Venetian dialect): *quarantena / quaranta giorni*, meaning forty days. Why exactly a forty days period was chosen is not entirely clear, but modern scholars generally agree that the number has a more or less religious background, reflecting the symbolism often found in the Bible (Kilwein 1995). This is attested also in the most general guidance to avoid the plague by the early modern English physician John Allen (c. 1660–1741): "most certain Prophylactick or Preservative from the Plague is to fly from it, trusting in the Lord" (Allen 1733, 88).

The understanding of illness as a medical problem on the one hand and a theological problem on the other was quite common in medieval and early modern thought: in medical manuals one can find prescriptions for the sick both to take medical remedies and to confess their sins. Sin was not only of narrow

---

5 Based on the figure of 6.45 deaths per 1,000 people in the Estonian population for Spanish influenza given in the Estonian Ministry of Social Affairs' "Pandemic Influenza Preparedness Plan", Estonia is estimated to have suffered about 7,000 influenza deaths during that period. See also http://rahvatervis.ut.ee/bitstream/1/161/1/Sotsiaalministeerium2004_3.pdf. Last accessed 16 June 2022.

theological concern. According to scientific theories of the time various bodily fluid movements were also associated with mortal sins – lust, avarice, greed, sloth, anger, envy and pride. For example, envy and sadness were associated with cold and dry melancholic humour (black bile), an excess of which could make a person susceptible to plague. Such a link is not arbitrary, as even today it has been shown that depression (which could be considered a counterpart of medieval melancholy or sadness) contributes to disease (Andersson et al. 2016). Early modern plague physicians were careful to ensure that neither their patients nor they themselves fell into melancholia. The English physician John Allen describes how, when visiting the sick, he made sure that he did not develop fear or anxiety, anger or sadness. If, however, he sensed any such movements of the soul within himself, he would treat them with a few glasses of wine (Allen 1733, 91). At the same time, caution and restraint were needed in the self-treatment with alcohol for, as Allen points out, heavy drinkers generally died easily of the plague, while moderate drinkers escaped illness (Allen 1733, 89). Consequently, cardinal virtues such as prudence, justice, temperance and fortitude, and theological virtues such as faith, hope and charity were important components in the prevention of disease and the cure of ills. These four cardinal virtues helped to balance the movements of the soul, and theological virtues contributed – it was often pointed out that if a person lost faith and hope that he could be healed, "death was inevitable" (Palmer 1982, 92).

In other words, the disease was approached as a holistic problem, including not only the medical but also the social, religious and psychological dimensions. There are many parallels with our situation today, in which the COVID-19 pandemic has provided an opportunity for different disciplines to look at this outbreak from their own perspectives. Medical, social, cultural, economic, biological and religious perspectives are being used to identify the causes and cure of the pandemic. From a medical point of view, we are interested e.g. in the mechanism of disease transmission and the long-term effects of the disease; from a psychological point of view, we are interested in how to cope with quarantine and the measurable increases in anxiety and depression; from a social and cultural point of view, we are interested in the movement of people, various reactions towards vaccination, spread of conspiracy theories etc. Economically, we are interested in how the rapid spread of the disease has affected the global economy, and biologically, how such pandemic diseases arise as an evolutionary mechanism due to the over-success of one species. Several of these points relate to religion – social constraints affect the activities of congregations, the Eucharist could be considered as a possible vector for the spread of disease, and there are theological implications to vaccination etc. There is no shortage of discussions about how the management of the coronavirus epidemic has demonstrated "the triumph of secularism over religion" (Kunnus 2020).

In short, we are looking for causes and coping mechanisms and anticipating effects. Similar sentiments can be seen in historical texts discussing the causes of the plague. Usually, the discussion begins with how the plague started in a particular region in the first place. Is it divine punishment? Does it come from another land? Is it brought on by a comet? Does it have something to do with the weather? Does it have something to do with our behaviour? Medieval and early modern medical textbooks emphasize: to know the causes is to know the thing itself! But where do we start to look for the causes of disease? This is, of course, based on the worldview of the author. The cause of disease must correspond to the way we see the world, and in a sense the cause we find for a disease reflects and explains the way we see the world. Whereas in the Middle Ages the theological dimension was very important, today some biologists have begun to speak of epidemics as an evolutionary mechanism that inevitably emerges when a species has become too numerous (as Juhan Javoiš does, for example, in the Estonian newspaper *Postimees* of 25 April 2020).

In other words, we are being called to account for some larger law against which humans are relatively powerless to act, and which limits and punishes our species because we have become too successful. Such debates are powerfully reminiscent of the story of the Tower of Babel in the Bible (Gn 11). There, in response to over-ambition, the tongues of the nations were mixed so that people would not be too successful. In other words, past perceptions coincide in some ways with modern understanding and both state that we – as a species, as a group, collectively – are to blame for our own maladies.

There is no doubt that epidemics are complex phenomena, linked to a wide range of social, economic and ecological factors. Early modern authors who discuss these issues fully appreciate the complexity of the phenomenon. As is the case sometimes today, these texts often list in turn everything that some philosopher or medical theorist has said about the disease but refrain from giving a definitive and clear assessment. The main problem for both historical medical theorists and modern scientists is that there is simply too much information that needs to be absorbed to reach some understanding. But understanding is important – what we do not know we cannot fight – and to get a better picture, early modern authors combed through all the earlier literature in the hope that, perhaps by piecing together the available information, they could get a clearer view and put a limit to the epidemic. Early modern medical literature relied on the one hand on ancient authors and on the other on contemporary medicine, which had introduced many new theories compared to the Middle Ages. Each of these authors added to the data they had collected with observations from their own experience, as Europe was hit by several plague epidemics in the sixteenth and seventeenth centuries, and those who had not practised as plague doctors themselves had at least heard stories from people who had lived through or been exposed to the plague. The discussion that follows draws heavily on the work of Austrian physician and writer Adam von Lebenwaldt (1624–1696) who summarizes and systematizes the views of many previous medical practitioners (Lebenwaldt 1695).

First of all, the question in early modern disease manuals is: what are diseases and where do they come from? Where does the cause of the illness lie: in the heavens, among the stars, or on earth, in other words in the spiritual, astral or elemental world? The first is the world inhabited by God, spirits, angels and demons; the second is the world of fixed stars and moving planets; the third is the sublunar sphere, where all things are composed of the four elements (fire, air, water and earth) and which can be further subdivided into the animal, vegetable and mineral kingdoms (Lebenwaldt 1695, 141). Authors generally agree that all three worlds contribute to the spread of disease, but to different degrees and in different ways.

In his nearly 800-page book on the plague Adam von Lebenwaldt asks if Hippocrates was right to call the plague a divine thing? In other words, does the plague come from the spiritual sphere? He goes on to give many examples of how ancient paganism regarded the plague as a punishment of the gods, and how they hoped to ward off the disease with theatrical plays and circus performances dedicated to the gods, or by the ritualistic hammering of a nail into the wall (*clavum figere*) in the temple of Jupiter to subdue the plague. He also mentions ironically the ancient miracle-worker Appolonius of Tyana, who in Ephesus called a man Plague and then had a crowd stone him to death. Lebenwaldt stresses that such superstition is certainly not the way to fight the plague. He argues that, although early Christian writers do not deny that the plague may be a divine punishment, it is generally held that the plague is something that has been present in the world since time immemorial, and thus is not something specific sent by God at certain times. The plague may indeed be seen as a punishment, but one that is generally part of the postlapsarian human condition, after Adam and Eve's expulsion from the Garden of Eden. At the same time, Lebenwaldt stresses that the plague should not be treated indifferently, as if it were somehow divinely predestined and nothing could be done about it, but rather that it is a matter of our free will and that we can avoid it and even cure it. A similar view can be found in the texts of other authors, who state that the trials of our postlapsarian world are there to be overcome (Slack 1988, 438–439).

Lebenwaldt continues to give examples of how the Cabalists (i.e. the Christian Cabalism that spread in Europe after the fifteenth century) believe that all illnesses are ultimately caused by God, but that God uses intermediaries such as angels, demons and other spiritual beings, who abound in the world and who arrange all things for him. According to the Cabalists, every plant, animal and activity has certain spirits associated with it, and so the cure for illness would also be to control and direct the activity of these spirits. Lebenwaldt mentions that these same qualities are also called occult and are thought to be the cause of many diseases. He maintains that in certain cases it is possible that these qualities are somehow influenced in an unfavourable way by demons or Satan himself, but that the cure of diseases caused in this way must always be natural and that one should not turn to demons or Satan for treatment or enter into any kind of contract with them to prevent trouble, as some people have done (Lebenwaldt 1695, 192).

Although the language of this discussion may seem strange and irrational to us today, such a view is not very different from the way we describe our world and our diseases today. The "occult" in the early modern period often meant nothing more than "invisible to the eye", and to call a disease agent occult was to say that it could not be seen or in any way perceived. Today as well disease agents are invisible and imperceptible, and only very specialized equipment can detect them. Due to its invisibility, there are people who doubt the existence of the coronavirus itself or postulate that the most diverse carriers (for instance 5G towers) spread and control it. Similarly, in the early modern period, diseases were thought to be caused by various hidden forces.

It was agreed that if we cannot see the disease with our eyes, it is possible to learn about it through other signs. Invisible pathogens can be detected naturally after infection, for example by fever or cough or other signs. But it was assumed that signs of disease could be found even earlier, when the disease had yet not developed. Early texts pay a lot of attention to this. Astrology became a controversial issue and was considered by some to be an unscientific discipline already in antiquity, while others stressed that "a doctor without astrology is like an eye without light" (Lebenwaldt 1695, 145). In certain respects early astrology should not be taken as an unscientific discipline in the way it is today, but rather as a search for universal laws. The authors point out that everyone knows about the moon's obvious influence on earthly things (e.g. tides of the ocean, but also lunar eclipses), but it is not clear how they are it accomplished. This effect of the moon was also called occult and was thought to be similar to the way a magnet affects iron (Magirus 1624, 374, 378). We see here how the moon's effect on oceans leads to the conclusion that also other bodies that have water as their constitutive component (including humans) must be somehow affected. On the basis of such observations, an attempt was made to determine whether stars and planets might be somehow involved in influencing human temperament and the spread of the disease. The attitude of many authors of the time is perhaps best summed up by

Robert Boyle in his book "Tracts containing suspicions about some hidden qualities of the air", in which he encourages researchers – despite the considerable misgivings he has about astrology as a science – still to experiment with "exotic Effluviums [. . .] because even a seemingly slight discovery in a thing of this nature may be of no small use" (Boyle 1674, 53–54). By exotic effluviums he means all kinds of occult (i.e. invisible) forces.

It was assumed that, in an occult or hidden way, disease is present all around us all the time, and that under certain favourable circumstances it becomes active. In addition to astrological observations, it was assumed that other unusual events could trigger or signal the arrival of the disease. For example, rotting fish carcasses washed up on the seashore could be a harbinger of an epidemic, or an unusually large number of insects being observed in some areas could predict a plague outbreak. Similarly, epidemics have been linked to wars and famines, and it has been suggested that corpses dumped in rivers after a war might somehow cause the disease.

Although the plague spreads invisibly to the eye, it was generally thought to be moving through the air (as opposed to, for example, food or water, which carried some other diseases). The disease can only spread if the air is contaminated in some way. The circumstances under which air pollution occurs may vary from case to case, and the capacity of the air to absorb and transmit toxic qualities does not arise immediately but over a period of time – so that a plague epidemic is often preceded by a number of other warning diseases, either in humans or in livestock. It is somewhat remarkable that air pollution has been linked with increased mortality from COVID-19. Due to lockdowns there was also a measurable decrease of air pollution: in Venice, the air and water cleared up, because there was no shipping traffic, the smog disappeared in Manila, air pollution levels in industrial areas of China and Korea were unusually low (Ravindra et al. 2022; Braga et al. 2020).

In general, early modern manuals emphasize the importance of the element of air in many natural processes. The theory of the four elements corresponded to the four main humours in medicine, and even at the end of the seventeenth and the beginning of the eighteenth century, when physics had generally abandoned the theory of the elements, humoural principles were still followed in medicine. According to Galen, a medical philosopher of the first century who became very influential in later centuries, the four humours (fluids) in the human body corresponded to elements, and the balance of these humours was the basis of a person's health or illness. Just as in physics it was (in principle) possible to manipulate the four elements in any substance and change it into a different form, the idea in medicine was to manipulate the balance of the four humours in the human body. If the manipulation of the elements that make up the metals was to achieve perfect balance, resulting in the perfect metal – gold – then in the same way, the aim of medicine was to achieve the balance of the humours, which of course expressed itself in health. In this way, the air was not just a substance that surrounded us, but in a sense was a part of us, and the processes that took place in the air directly affected our physiology. According to Lebenwaldt, the air contains a vitalizing salt that can be called the "hidden food of life" (Lebenwaldt 1695, 193) and we should take care not to destabilize or corrupt it.

Polluted air can poison a person and cause disease similarly to spoiled food. For example, air pollution can be triggered by an earthquake, which causes the release of dead bodies or underground vapours or other such gases into the atmosphere, or by floods, which can move things out of their natural place, flush out pollution and cause infectious diseases (Kircher 1659, 19). The seventeenth-century Jesuit universalist Athanasius Kircher even claimed that plague was brought about by "small wormlets invisible to the eye", which were carried by polluted air, entered the human body through respiration and caused putrefactive processes (Kircher 1659, 69, 81–82). He had arrived at these conclusions by observing the various putrefaction processes with his "smicroscopus" [sic!] and noting that, in the course of the process, wormlets often appear which may be so small that they cannot be seen with the naked eye. Although his views resemble to some extent the description of bacteria, Kircher cannot be regarded as the discoverer of plague bacteria, because at the same time he believed that these wormlets emerge spontaneously during the decay process and have no specific nature other than to reproduce the decay process.

In conclusion, if one tries to look at past perceptions of the plague with an open mind, one may infer that the differences from today may not be as great as they seem. Of course, there were many theories around at the time that tried to explain the nature of plague and disease, and some of these theories are more in line with our current understanding and others less so. If I have put forward theories here that in some ways fit in with today's understanding, it is primarily to show that the ability to look at disease as a complex phenomenon is not something that is unique to our time, and in some ways early thinkers took into account more possible factors than we tend to consider today. It is important to realize that the main aim was to understand the disease and to provide relief for the sick. The close contact with epidemics also provided a large number of observations on their spread and causes of diseases, and doctors, philosophers and theologians attempted to piece together a holistic picture of the diseases, taking into account a wide range of factors. Similarly, it is important today to try to understand the disease as a whole, how it relates to medical, psychological, social, philosophical, theological and economic aspects. Inspiration for the quest for such a holistic picture can be found perfectly in medieval and early modern texts, which were based on the assumption that everything is connected, spirit, soul and body.

References

Allen, John. *Synopsis Medicinæ: Or, a Summary View of the Whole Practice of Physick . . . By J. Allen . . . Translated by Himself from the Last Edition of His Latin Synopsis, with Very Large Improvements.* London: John Pemberton, 1733.

Andersson, Niklas W., Renee D. Goodwin, Niels Okkels, Lea N. Gustafsson, Farah Taha, Steve W. Cole, and Povl Munk-Jørgensen. "Depression and the Risk of Severe Infections: Prospective Analyses on a Nationwide Representative Sample." *International Journal of Epidemiology* 45.1 (2016): 131–139. https://doi.org/10.1093/ije/dyv333.

Boyle, Robert. *Tracts Containing I. Suspicions about Some Hidden Qualities of the Air: With an Appendix Touching Celestial Magnets and Some Other Particulars: II. Animadversions upon Mr. Hobbes's Problemata de Vacuo: III. a Discourse of the Cause of Attraction by Suction / by the Honourable Robert Boyle Esq. . . .* 1674. http://name.umdl.umich.edu/A29052.0001.001.

Braga, Federica, Gian Marco Scarpa, Vittorio Ernesto Brando, Giorgia Manfè, and Luca Zaggia. "COVID-19 Lockdown Measures Reveal Human Impact on Water Transparency in the Venice Lagoon." *Science of The Total Environment* 736.September (2020): 139612. https://doi.org/10.1016/j.scitotenv.2020.139612.

Ell, Stephen R. "Interhuman Transmission of Medieval Plague." *Bulletin of the History of Medicine* 54.4 (1980): 497–510.

Hufthammer, Anne Karin, and Lars Walløe. "Rats Cannot Have Been Intermediate Hosts for Yersinia Pestis during Medieval Plague Epidemics in Northern Europe." *Journal of Archaeological Science* 40.4 (2013): 1752–1759. https://doi.org/10.1016/j.jas.2012.12.007.

Javoiš, Juhan. "Darwini koll tuleb kapist välja. Elusolendi kolm stsenaariumit." *Postimees*. 25 April 2020. https://leht.postimees.ee/6956445/juhan-javois-darwini-koll-tuleb-kapist-valja-elusolendi-kolm-stsenaariumit.

Jedwab, Remi, Amjad M. Khan, Jason Russ, and Esha D. Zaveri. 2021. 'Epidemics, Pandemics, and Social Conflict: Lessons from the Past and Possible Scenarios for COVID-19'. *World Development* 147 (November): 105629. https://doi.org/10.1016/j.worlddev.2021.105629.

Kilwein, J. H. 1995. "Some Historical Comments on Quarantine: Part One." *Journal of Clinical Pharmacy and Therapeutics* 20.4 (1995): 185–187. https://doi.org/10.1111/j.1365-2710.1995.tb00647.x.

Kircher, Athanasius. *Scrutinium physico-medicum contagiosae luis, quae dicitur pestis*. Schürer & Götzii, 1659.

Kunnus, Mihkel. "Palve ja pangakonto." *Postimees*. 14 April 2020. https://leht.postimees.ee/6949746/mihkel-kunnus-palve-ja-pangakonto.

Lebenwaldt, Adam. *Land- Stadt- Und Hauß-Artzney-Buch: In welchem angezeigt und erwiesen wird/ wie man denjenigen Krannckheiten/ welche ein gantzes Land oder mehr Oerther anstecken/ so dann durch Contagion und Anklebung anderweitig fortgepflanztt und ausgebreitet werden/ Als da seyn: Die Pest/ Pestilenzial- und Petechialische Fieber/ Ungarische Kranckheit/ rothe Ruhr/ Kinds-Blattern . . . Samt einer Chronick Aller denckwürdigen Pesten . . . Dabey eine Fünff-fache Cur zu finden . . . Samt einer Anweisung Die Häuser und Mobilien zu reinigen . . .* Nürnberg: Lochner, 1695.

Magirus, Johann. *Johannis Magiri Physiologiae peripateticae libri sex, cum commentariis, in quibus praecepta illius perspicue, eruditeque explicantur*. Francofurti: impensis Johannis Berneri, 1624.

Palmer, Richard. "The Church, Leprosy and Plague in Medieval and Early Modern Europe." *Studies in Church History* 19 (1982): 79–99. https://doi.org/10.1017/S0424208400009311.

Ravindra, Khaiwal, Tanbir Singh, Shikha Vardhan, Aakash Shrivastava, Sujeet Singh, Prashant Kumar, and Suman Mor. 2022. "COVID-19 Pandemic: What Can We Learn for Better Air Quality and

Human Health?" *Journal of Infection and Public Health* 15.2 (2022): 187–198. https://doi.org/10.1016/j.jiph.2021.12.001.

Rigby, Emma, Melissa Symonds, and Derek Ward-Thompson. "A Comet Impact in AD 536?" *Astronomy & Geophysics* 45.1 (2004): 1.23–1.26. https://doi.org/10.1046/j.1468-4004.2003.45123.x.

Rooste, Jürgen. "Kuidas katkuepideemiad on maailma mõjutanud." *Postimees*. 6 May 2020. https://leht.postimees.ee/6967149/kuidas-katkuepideemiad-on-maailma-mojutanud.

Russell, Jeffrey Burton. *Witchcraft in the Middle Ages*. Ithaca, N.Y: Cornell University Press, 1972.

Slack, Paul. "Responses to Plague in Early Modern Europe: The Implications of Public Health." *Social Research* 55.3 (1988): 433–453.

Tsiamis, Costas, Effie Poulakou-Rebelakou, and Spyros Marketos. "Earthquakes and Plague during Byzantine Times: Can Lessons from the Past Improve Epidemic Preparedness." *Acta Medico-Historica Adriatica: AMHA* 11.1 (2013): 55–64.

Watson, John T., Michelle Gayer, and Maire A. Connolly. "Epidemics after Natural Disasters." *Emerging Infectious Diseases* 13.1 (2007): 1–5. https://doi.org/10.3201/eid1301.060779.

Yang, Ruifu, and Andrey Anisimov, eds. *Yersinia Pestis: Retrospective and Perspective*. Advances in Experimental Medicine and Biology 918. New York: Springer, 2016.

Thomas Crew
"Civilization is Sterilization": Utopia, Biopolitics and the Total Society in Horkheimer and Adorno's *Dialectic of Enlightenment* and Aldous Huxley's *Brave New World*

Abstract: It is increasingly well documented that Aldous Huxley's *Brave New World* exerted a tremendous influence not just on Theodor W. Adorno, who wrote an essay on the famous English dystopia, but on the Frankfurt School more broadly. Adorno's formal concern with Huxley's novel was triggered by a conference held at the Institute for Social Research in Los Angeles in 1942 – the same year that work began on the *Dialectic of Enlightenment*. Although this chapter contributes to this scholarship, it does so by positioning both books in the context of biopolitics. Adorno and Huxley may not have been operating with the concept in mind, but their respective works belonged and responded to an age that displayed many early and decisive biopolitical trends – from the birth of progressivism at the *fin de siècle* to the social hygiene, eugenics, and rationalization movements. By investigating these historical trends, as well as the related boom in dystopian literature, this chapter provides an additional contextual framework to the field of biopolitics. It also implicitly makes the case for the inclusion of *Brave New World* and the *Dialectic* in the biopolitical canon, which is still being established. In many ways, both books provide the much-needed language and imagery for the kind of biopolitical control that is increasingly consequential today, yet remains often obscured by more conventional political thinking. The final part of the chapter draws the connections between the worlds that Adorno and Huxley describe and the recent pandemic experience, where reference is also made to Giorgio Agamben.

> In the early twentieth century, the vision of a future society unbelievably rich, leisured, orderly, and efficient – a glittering anti-septic world of glass and steel and snow-white concrete – was part of the consciousness of nearly every literate person
> G. Orwell, *Nineteen Eighty-Four*

1 Introduction

In February 1932, when *Brave New World* was first published, Britain was at the nadir of the economic crisis known to Aldous Huxley's compatriots as The Slump. Coal production was down by twenty per cent, exports had fallen by two-thirds, and unemployment was at nearly three million, a quarter of the workforce. Some areas faced devastation. On the Tyne and the Clyde, which exemplified the plight of much of Northern England and industrial Scotland, shipbuilding was reduced to just seven per cent of its 1914 levels, resulting in both mass impoverishment and civil unrest. Unforeseen by the nation's preeminent economists, the crisis had long become political. The collapse of the Labour administration prompted the formation of the National Government in 1931, while communists sponsored regular Hunger Marches and, inspired by Mussolini's sweeping economic reforms in Italy, Oswald Mosley founded the British Union of Fascists. Speaking on the BBC in the month before the publication of his novel, Aldous Huxley captured the mood of despair and the appetite for radicalism that defined the times: "Our civilization is menaced with total collapse. Dictatorship and scientific propaganda may provide the only means for saving humanity from the miseries of anarchy" (2001a, 153).

If the Great Depression appeared to challenge the very viability of Western liberalism, this was nowhere more evident than in Germany. Having achieved an uncharacteristic stability with the introduction of the Dawes Plan in 1924, the crisis threw the Weimar Republic back into the depths of economic and political turmoil. The three national elections that were held in less than a year from the summer of 1932 saw the National Socialists win each time. Tellingly titled the Law to Remedy the Distress of People and Reich, the Enabling Act, passed amidst an atmosphere of terror and intimidation in 1933, finally brought German democracy to an end. By 1942, when Max Horkheimer and Theodor W. Adorno were working on the *Dialectic of Enlightenment*, it seemed wholly apt to speak of the "present collapse of bourgeois civilization" (2002, xiv).[1]

Both Huxley's *Brave New World* and Horkheimer and Adorno's *Dialectic* were thus conceived in and, as we will see, form urgent responses to an era of fundamental civilizational crisis. Across the political spectrum, liberal democracy was increasingly viewed as fatally flawed and anachronistic, unable to contain economic instability and unequal to the demands of an ever more industrialized

---

[1] Throughout this chapter, I quote all German in the English translation, including the original only in those cases where no published translation exists, the translation is poor, or where there is an ambiguity in the German that is inevitably lost in translation.

society. In his own visionary manifesto from 1932, the German writer and famous Great War veteran Ernst Jünger voiced the gravity of the situation: "The deep rift threatening life itself now divides not only two generations, not only two centuries, but heralds the end of a thousand-year-old configuration" (2017, 127). Civilization appeared to be at an unprecedented crossroads. Offering diagnoses and proposing potential routes forward was a task to which many contemporary intellectuals set themselves.

The biographies of Horkheimer and Adorno were intimately entwined with the unfolding crisis. On account of their neo-Marxist politics and their Jewish heritage, both philosophers fled Germany, along with the rest of the Institute for Social Research, upon the Nazi seizure of power. Eventually setting up their new headquarters in California, which becomes *the* central reference point for all three of the protagonists of this chapter, Horkheimer initially fled to Columbia University in New York, while Adorno escaped to Merton College, Oxford. It was here, so Angela Holzer suggests, that Adorno became familiar with *Brave New World* (2008, 120). While the flurry of letters he exchanged with Walter Benjamin in the mid 1930s demonstrates that Adorno was already an admirer of Huxley's work, the famous English dystopia made a profound and lasting impression on him. Holzer, for one, rightly speaks of an "immense" influence (2008, 120).[2]

The impact is immediately apparent in the preface to the *Dialectic*, in which Huxley is referenced, along with Karl Jaspers and José Ortega y Gasset, as one of the "critics of civilization" (2002, xvii). It was at this same time, Christmas 1943, that Adorno sent a copy of *Brave New World* to his parents (Adorno 2003, 227). The strength of the influence, and indeed the chronology, is confirmed by Adorno's lengthy essay, "Aldous Huxley and Utopia", which, although first published in 1951, was actually written in 1942 – the time that work began on the *Dialectic*.[3] In the essay, Adorno recognizes in Huxley a fellow intellectual émigré to the USA and credits his novel with prophetic qualities: "The more than thirty years since the book's publication have provided more than sufficient verification" (1997a, 97).[4] Contemporary "aptitude tests" reminded him of Huxley's cynically stratified society, while the very worst aspects of the Holocaust seemed to be anticipated by the novel's "rational utilization of corpses" (1997a, 97).

---

2 The other main source of scholarship on the Huxley-Adorno connection is Baker (1995).
3 In the back notes to *Prisms* (1955), where it was later published, Adorno explains that the essay emerged in the context of a seminar at the Institute for Social Research in Los Angeles, 1942. At that same seminar, Adorno adds, Herbert Marcuse gave a paper on *Brave New World* (Adorno 1969b, 343).
4 In the original German, Adorno speaks of 25, not 30 years. See 1969a, 114.

Despite the increasingly critical tone, in which Adorno ultimately accuses the novel of a "reactionary character" (1997a, 111), in the following years he continued to cite it. As late as 1964, in the preparatory lectures for his masterpiece *Negative Dialectics* (1966), Adorno invoked Bernard Marx, Huxley's protagonist. Lamenting the fact that, in modern societies, people are "reduced more and more to the status of functions", Adorno writes:

> Even captains of industry spend their time working through mountains of documents and shifting them from one side of their desk to the other, instead of ignoring office hours and reflecting in freedom [. . .]. If you were to sit down, reflect, and make decisions, you would soon fall behind and become an eccentric, like the weirdo [Einzelgänger] in Huxley's *Brave New World*. (2008, 6)[5]

On closer inspection, the figure of Bernard Marx seems to reappear throughout the *Dialectic*. Having first referenced the "eccentric loner" (2002, 106; Eigenbrötler, 2016, 140), Adorno twice invokes the "outsider", both times using the English word.[6] Such correspondences did not go unnoticed at the time. With the *Dialectic* finished in 1944, Horkheimer approached Leo Löwenthal about finding someone famous to endorse it. In English, the latter replied: "Huxley, as far as I know, does not read German, and Joyce is dead" (Horkheimer 1996, 571). For all their differences, the *Dialectic* and *Brave New World* shared a fundamental spiritual kinship.

Even the style of the two works bears conspicuous resemblances. Explaining the provocative and hyperbolic style that characterizes much of his work in 1959, Adorno writes:

> I have exaggerated the somber side, following the maxim that only exaggeration per se today can be the medium of truth. [. . .] My intention was to delineate a tendency concealed behind the smooth façade of everyday life before it overflows the institutional dams that, for the time being, are erected against it. (1998, 99)

Such exaggeration or extrapolation, especially with the intent of warning about hidden yet decisive cultural tendencies, might be regarded as the quintessential dystopian method. Musing on the future of the world in 1927, Huxley gives a similarly programmatic insight into his own working: "Prophecies of the future, if they are to be intelligent, not merely fantastic, must be based on a study of the

---

5 Here, I follow Holzer's slightly amended translation, which renders the German word *Einzelgänger* as weirdo. Although customarily translated as outsider, loner, or maverick, Rodney Livingstone's translates *Einzelgänger* as "Savage". This is a significant departure from the original not just technically, but also in terms of meaning. After all, it is Bernard Marx, not the Savage, who neglects his duties to reflect on the nature of his existence.

6 The two references can be found, in the German (2016), on pp. 143 and 159. For the English translation (2002), see pp. 107 and 121.

present. The future is the present projected" (2001b, 185).[7] In one way or another, both authors were working in the dystopian tradition, which, as I show in the following section, was flourishing at the beginning of the century.

The question is: what were the underlying cultural tendencies that so animated and distressed Huxley, Adorno, and the writers of the Frankfurt School? What accounted for the increasingly obvious "monstrous nature" of contemporary society? The answer in each case has to do with a world that was responding to the phenomena of industrialization, mass society, and economic and political instability with totalitarianism – whether in communism, fascism, or indeed liberalism. The solution to the widely perceived sense of chaos – whether within social structures or amidst the unruly, restive population – was organization, regulation, and what Horkheimer and Adorno term "administration" (2002, 65; Verwaltung, 2016, 91). As Huxley said in the same BBC broadcast cited above: "Everyone admits in principle that human activities must be regulated scientifically" (2001a, 149). The desire to apply the methods of science to public life – that is, social engineering – was widespread. The implications of this apparently progressive undertaking were of central concern to the thinkers of this chapter.[8]

It is in this context of the scientific regulation of the population that *Brave New World* and the *Dialectic of Enlightenment* can be seen as biopolitical works. In 1978, the German political scientist Dietrich Gunst defined biopolitics as "anything to do with health policy and the regulation of the population, together with environmental protection and questions concerning the future of humanity" (cited in Lemke 2011, 24).[9] The vagueness and comprehensiveness of this definition is informative. On the one hand, it points towards the scale of ambition inherent to biopolitics – towards an underlying utopianism, which necessarily aims at the restructuring of society. On the other, it indicates the still formative nature of the field itself: "it is only today", Timothy Campbell and Adam Sitze (2013, 1) suggest, "that a codification of the biopolitical is underway". The most fundamental questions – questions of the subject and object of biopolitics, as well as the wider cannon – are still being established.

---

[7] Adorno clearly recognized this dystopian dynamic in *Brave New World*: "Huxley projects observations of the present state of civilization along the lines of its own teleology to the point where its monstrous nature becomes immediately evident" (1997a, 98).
[8] In his foreword to the novel from 1946, Huxley makes this clear: "The theme of *Brave New World* is not the advancement of science as such; it is the advancement of science as it affects human individuals" (2007b, xliv).
[9] Gunst's book, *Biopolitik zwischen Macht und Recht*, deals with typically biopolitical concerns: the social and political consequences of an increasing global population, malnutrition and starvation, and the consumption and depletion of energy resources.

In this chapter, I contribute to this debate by offering an additional contextual framework to the study of biopolitics, heeding Campbell and Sitze's suggestion that the vagueness of the concept might be taken "as an invitation to be creative" (2013: 2). Although the likes of Huxley and Adorno belonged to an age unfamiliar with the term, the early twentieth century can be seen as an important incubator of biopolitical thought.[10] From the birth of progressive politics at the *fin de siècle* to the eugenics, social hygiene, and rationalization movements, the era developed novel theories of man and society that are central to the biopolitical today. The ubiquitous and unapologetic assertion of biopolitics in contemporary society – together with the state of exception that, for Giorgio Agamben (2021, 8), is its distinctive characteristic – makes reflection on its meaning essential for our age.

This chapter begins with a closer look at the USA, as both the common starting point of the *Dialectic* and *Brave New World* and, as I show, the quintessential dystopian topos. In this section, I attempt to ground both works historically and, in so doing, to offer an important contextual background to biopolitics. I then consider the nature of the utopian dream that, our two main works suggest, is the implicit aim of modernity. The penultimate section examines the enormous price of paradise, in keeping with the central claim of the *Dialectic* that the "curse of irresistible progress is irresistible regression" (2002, 28). Finally, I make the connection back to today's world, in which the rise of biopolitics once again goes hand-in-hand with a disaffection with democracy. For many of today's intellectuals, the populace seems too unstable, the politicians too conservative for contemporary problems to be effectively addressed. But whether a kind of supranational technocracy, the de facto alternative, is in any way desirable remains a point of considerable contention.

2 Americanization, or the Trend of the Twentieth Century

At the beginning of the twentieth century, the USA was everywhere seen as the source of important clues about the future of civilization. Writing for *Harper's Magazine* after his first trip to the United States in 1926, Huxley declared: "The future of America is the future of the world" (2001b, 185). The reasons for this association were less to do with America's liberal traditions than its industrial

---

10 Although biopolitics was coined as early as 1917 by the Swedish political scientist Rudolf Kjellén (*The State as Living Organism*), it was not until Foucault's use of the term in the 1970s that it began to gain currency. See the introduction to this volume, especially pp. 11–14 and 23–25, for a detailed outline of Foucault's understanding of the concept.

might. By 1913, the country was producing a third of the world's goods; with the opening of Henry Ford's Highland Park factory in 1910, which by 1924 was producing a fully assembled car every ten seconds (Baker 1990, 84), the USA was reshaping not just capitalism, but the very values of the age. As Huxley was told in California: "Business is religion" (2001b, 191). Not for nothing does Ford's *My Life and Work*, a worldwide bestseller on its publication in 1922, replace the Bible as the holy book in *Brave New World*.[11]

The strength of American industry meant that, one way or another, the American style – its economic model and social structures, as well as the attendant ethics and aesthetic – was destined to conquer the world. The rise of the USA was inexorable:

> Material circumstances are driving all nations along the path in which America is going. Living in the contemporary environment, which is everywhere becoming more and more American, men feel a psychological compulsion to go the American way. Fate acts within and without; there is no resisting. (Huxley, 2001b, 185)

This process of "reverse colonization" was identified as early as 1902 by the renowned British journalist W. T. Stead, whose book *The Americanization of the World, or the Trend of the Twentieth Century* was indicative of what was fast becoming a European fascination with the New World. Countless intellectuals crossed the Atlantic to see the feted place first hand.

In Germany, perhaps the most consequential trips were taken in 1904 by two of the country's most celebrated intellectuals – Werner Sombart and Max Weber.[12] Returning to Europe after nearly three months, Weber published *The Protestant Work Ethic*, in which he famously suggested that modern life increasingly resembled an "iron cage" (2001, 123; stahlhartes Gehäuse, 1978, 204). Far from a source of utopian hope, the United States – the land of progress and beacon of modernity – presented a decidedly more sobering sight. For all the excitement it generated, it was ultimately a sense of fear and foreboding that the USA evoked in the European imagination. This explains why so many dystopian authors either visited America or made it a principal point of reference in their stories. H. G. Wells, for example, travelled to the country no less than six times, publishing his experiences in the

---

11 Huxley discovered Ford's autobiography in the library of a ship destined for the USA in 1926. By his own admission, he was "fascinated": "In those seas [between Indonesia and Malaysia] and to one fresh from India and Indian 'spirituality', Indian dirt and religion, Ford seems a greater man than Buddha" (2000, 525–526). In the USA, Ford's autobiography sold 200,000 copies by the end of the 1920s. It was translated into German in 1923, when it was read, from his prison cell, by Adolf Hitler. As Mary Nolan notes, Ford's work was "essential reading if one wanted to participate at any level in the debate about economic rationalization and Americanism" (1994, 34).
12 For a comprehensive account of Weber's trip and its significance, see Scaff (2011).

eloquently titled book *The Future in America* (1906). Fritz Lang, meanwhile, credited his trip to New York in 1924 for the inspiration behind the cityscape in *Metropolis* (1927).[13] Two other early German dystopias – Alfred Kubin's *The Other Side* (1909) and Bernhard Kellermann's *The Tunnel* (1913) – are similarly disposed. Kubin's antagonist is the American tycoon and "king of corned beef" (Pökelfleischkönig, 2014, 159), Hercules Bell, while Kellermann's novel, one of the best selling of the time, revolves around the audacious projects of the American engineer, Mac Allan.[14]

Indeed, the era's most famous dystopia – considered paradigmatic for the genre to this day – takes not Henry Ford, but the American engineer and founder of "scientific management" F. W. Taylor as its central point of departure. In *We*, completed in 1921 and first published in 1924, Yevgeni Zamyatin writes: "No doubt about it, that Taylor was *the* genius of antiquity". "[H]ow could they write whole libraries about someone like Kant and hardly even notice Taylor – that prophet who could see ten centuries ahead?" (1993, 34). Overshadowed today by Ford, perhaps because of the success of *Brave New World*, Taylor's theory of management had a tremendous impact on contemporary Europe, influencing not just industrial practices, but also academia, art, literature, and architecture.[15] For the German engineer and war-time technocrat, Wichard von Moellendorf, Taylorism was nothing short of a "Germanic doctrine from America" (germanische Lehre aus Amerika, cited in Rohkrämer 1999, 249).

What these dystopias have in common is the depiction of an often united world – the World State in Huxley, OneState in Zamyatin – under the rule of, or centrally inspired by, an American billionaire or engineer. Not democracies, with their parliaments and presidents, but technocrats, with their impersonal models and impartial experts, rule the day. Ideas concerning the steady consolidation of political power and its simultaneous evolution towards something technocratic were prominent at the time. In his highly influential book *Zur Kritik der Zeit* (1912), famous for identifying the "mechanization of the world" ("Mechanisierung der Welt"), the German industrialist Walther Rathenau had forecast a future of a

---

13 Later describing his first sight of New York, from the deck of his approaching ship, Lang commented "I looked into the streets – the glaring lights and the tall buildings – and there I conceived *Metropolis*" (cited in Bogdanovich 1967, 124).

14 Like Huxley, Kellermann also travelled to America via the Pacific, arriving at San Francisco in 1909. He also shared Huxley's central assumption, writing in the *Tunnel*: "Europe will become a suburb of America" ("Europa wird ein Vorort Amerikas werden", 2016, 52). For more on Kellermann's novel, see Göktürk (1989) and, in the dystopian context, Crew (2022).

15 As Charles S. Maier notes: "Before 1914 Taylorism had already been picked up in Europe as one of the most provocative aspects of America's formidable economic expansion" (1970, 29). For more on Taylor's wide-ranging impact, see Olsen (2015).

"hundredfold overpopulated earth" ("hundertfach übervölkerter Erdball"), "country-sized cities" ("ländergroße Städte"), "eternal peace" ("ewiger Friede"), and an "international state of states" ("internationaler Staat der Staaten", 2008, 153). Industrial progress seemed to be bringing about a "mechanistic utopia" ("mechanistische Utopie", 1917, 12) defined by "unprecedented comforts" ("unerhörte Bequemlichkeiten") and featuring "senility as sole form of death" ("Altersschwäche als alleinige Todesart", 2008, 153).

Reflecting on the faith in progress that defined much of the nineteenth century, Gerhart Hauptmann also reports that the utopian vision of a future free of war, crime, and disease was widespread: "One day the last crime along with the last criminal would have died out, like certain epidemics as a result of hygiene and other preventative measures of medical science" ("Eines Tages würde das letzte Verbrechen mit dem letzen Verbrecher ausgesorben sein wie gewisse Epidemien infolge der Hygiene und sonstiger Prophylaxe der medizinischen Wissenschaft"). For Hauptmann, "This optimism was simply reality" ("Dieser Optimismus war schlechthin Wirklichkeit", 1937, 432–433). Faith in the socially redemptive powers of science reached to the very top of German society. Granting Germany's technical universities the power to grant doctorates in 1899, for example, Kaiser Wilhelm II explained: "I wanted to promote the technical colleges because they have great problems to solve, not just technical problems, but also great social ones" ("Ich wollte die technischen Hochschulen in den Vordergrund bringen, denn sie haben große Aufgaben zu lösen, nicht bloß technische, sondern auch große soziale", cited in König 1981, 252). The engineers trained at such institutions would go on to shape not just industry, but increasing spheres of public life. They were the original social engineers, who, at the beginning of the twentieth century, increasingly regarded themselves as the natural leaders of the industrial age.[16]

The vision of a technocratic world state was, however, nowhere more energetically promoted than in interwar Britain, especially on what Joanne Woiak calls the "scientific Left" (2007, 110). The renowned biologist and close friend of Huxley, J. B. S. Haldane, for example, was a campaigner for "rational" world government and, much like Bertrand Russell and Huxley's brother, Julian, championed the application of science to social affairs. In *Science and Human Life* (1933), Haldane writes: "It is foolish to think that the outlook which has already revolutionized

---

[16] In 1917, for example, the head of the Association of German Engineers, Anton von Rieppel, proclaimed: "We have to get to the stage in Germany where, as naturally as the officer and the lawyer today, the engineer is seen as a leader of the people" ("Es muß in Deutschland dahin kommen, daß mit der gleichen Selbstverständlichkeit, mit der heute Militär und Jurist maßgebend sind, der Ingenieur als Führer des Volkes gilt", 1917, 990). For more on the German technocracy movement in the interwar period, see Stefan Willecke (1996).

industry, agriculture, war, and medicine, will prove useless when applied to the family, the nation, or the human race" (1933, 1).[17] Where religion, politics, and capitalism had long failed, science promised to succeed.

The social utility of science was most consistently promoted by Wells, in both his hugely successful utopias, such as *Men Like Gods* (1923) and *A Modern Utopia* (1905), and in his more direct political campaigning. In his manifesto *The Open Conspiracy: Blue Prints for a World Revolution* (1928), Wells advanced the cause of a "scientific world commonweal" governed by a "common world directorate" (1933, 34, 48). Such a body would represent the "intelligent and active oligarchies" (2001b, 192) that Aldous Huxley was himself promoting at the time. In 1927, for example, Huxley suggested that the "ideal state is one in which there is material democracy controlled by an aristocracy of intellect". Italian fascism, Russian communism, and Chinese Nationalism (under the Kuomintang), Huxley maintained, formed the "still inadequate precursors" to this ideal (2001b, 192).

For many in interwar Britain, the future belonged to what Adorno and Horkheimer wryly termed "the engineers of world history" (2002, 30). Indeed, the *Dialectic* is also based on these developments, although without any of the enthusiasm shown by the likes of Wells and Huxley. Having evolved from the "slave-owner" to the "free entrepreneur", Adorno and Horkheimer regard the "administrator" as the contemporary incarnation of the bourgeoisie (2002, 65). The traditional capitalist had been disposed or made obsolete by what the American political theorist James Burnham, only three years before, called the Managerial Revolution (1941).[18]

As we have seen, the motivation for such Wellsian "conspiracies" was the chaos and permanent instability that blighted the age. Searching for more promising political endeavours, many contemporary intellectuals followed Huxley's lead and looked towards Soviet Russia and fascist Italy. In Germany, the Working Group for the Study of the Planned Soviet Economy was established in 1932. Financed by the Russian embassy, its members included such disparate thinkers as the National Bolshevist Ernst Niekisch, the Marxist Georg Lukács, and the Conser-

---

[17] Both Haldane and Russell sketched out the potential future development of science and society in ways that closely resemble *Brave New World*. See *Daedalus; or, Science and the Future* (1924) and *The Scientific Outlook* (1931), especially the final section on "The Scientific Society", respectively. For more on the affinities between these men, see Woiak (2007) and Clayton (2016).

[18] In George Orwell's reading, who was influenced by *The Managerial Revolution*, Burnham describes the irresistible emergence of "a new kind of planned, centralized society", which is neither capitalist nor socialist, but run by the "technicians, bureaucrats, and soldiers" that Burnham collectively terms "managers". Such societies, Orwell continues, "will be hierarchical, with an aristocracy of talent at the top and a mass of semi-slaves at the bottom" (2021, i).

vative Revolutionary Ernst Jünger.[19] In Britain, two similar organizations had been founded the year before: the Next Five Years' Group, inspired by the first of Stalin's Five-Year Plans, launched in 1928, and the more radical outfit, Political and Economic Planning (PEP). In July 1932, PEP put out the following, highly programmatic statement: "The plan will aim at replacing the disorderly existing political and economic system by a reconstituted machine based on the application of science to social and political affairs" (cited in Jones 1986, 113). This statement counts as one of the most concise formulations of the technocratic mission as such. It is in many ways a reformulation of Taylor's "scientific management", which had stressed, as early as 1911, the necessity of applying efficiency principles "to all social activities" (2014: xiv).

Two of the most prominent members of PEP were Julian and, at least briefly, Aldous Huxley. In an article of 1934, the former revealed the revolutionary ambition at the heart of such initiatives. Urban planning, industrial rationalization, and the attempt "to guard against exaggerated slumps and booms in the domain of finance", Julian Huxley argued, did not go far enough. Ultimately, "biological and social engineering" had to go one step further:

> In the long run, it is equally important to plan for education, for health, for self-development in adult life, for the intelligent use of the steadily increasing amount of leisure which will be available in a planned society, for quantity of population, for racial improvement. (1934, 45)

Planning, rationalization, social engineering and indeed eugenics were thus the watchwords of this burgeoning technocratic movement, which, as Julian Huxley's comments make clear, implicated almost every aspect of human life. Under the name of "social hygiene", the bodily functions and private lives of citizens became objects of government policy. Infant and child care, domestic and personal cleanliness, diet and nutrition were deemed areas of legitimate state interest by what Greta Jones calls the "social hygienist" (1986, 8). The desire for health therefore went hand-in-hand with a need for population management. As Horkheimer and Adorno put it, life itself was increasingly becoming the object of regulative control: "Being is apprehended in terms of manipulation and administration. Everything – including the individual human being, not to mention the animal – becomes a repeatable, replaceable process, a mere example of the conceptual models of the system" (2002, 65). As Taylor himself had advocated thirty years

---

19 The group, known in German as "Arplan", short for *Arbeitsgemeinschaft zum Studium der sowjetrussischen Planwirtschaft*, was shut down by the Nazis in 1933. Jünger's *Worker* (1932), a dark vision of a machine-like future, clearly bears the marks of this engagement with the USSR.

earlier: "In the past the man has been first; in the future the system must be first" (2014, xiv).

The inherent connection between the planning and efficiency movements with matters of health and leisure – that is, the inherent connection between technocracy and biopolitics – is exemplified by the case of the British businessman, Alfred Mond. As one of Britain's foremost advocates for industrial "rationalization", Mond, an avowed admirer of Mussolini, eventually became chairman of the Board at the London School of Hygiene and Tropical Medicine and, in 1921, Minister of Health. A clear source of influence for Huxley's World Controller, Mustapha Mond, in *Brave New World*, Mond was every bit as committed to the sweeping "scientific" restructuring of civilization as his more left-wing contemporaries. In *Industry and Politics* (1927), Mond declares:

> The welfare [. . .] of the human race depends on the efficiency of its scientists in every field. [. . .] Rightly or wrongly, we must pin our faith to the scientists of this and future generations. [. . .] Research and more and more research must clear the only feasible path for the forward progress of mankind (1927, 169–170).

The point is that, regardless of their ostensible political persuasion, such figures were advancing a very similar social project, underpinned by a very similar philosophy. Whether communist, liberal, or fascist, such thinkers were united by what James Sexton calls "uncritical veneration of rationalization" (1996, 89). As Huxley writes in his earlier novel, *Point Counter Point* (1928):

> The destination's the same in either case. [. . .] They all believe in industrialism in one form or another, they all believe in Americanization. Think of the Bolshevist ideal. America but much more so. [. . .] Machinery and government officials there. Machinery and Alfred Mond or Henry Ford here. [. . .] They're all equally in a hurry. In the name of science, progress and human happiness! (1928, 414–415).

Precisely this point is also implied by the seemingly random assortment of names in *Brave New World*. To give just a sample: Bernard Marx, Polly Trotsky, and Lenina Crowne; Dr Wells and Dr Shaw; Jim Bokanovsky and Benito Hoover. The first group refers to history's most prominent communists; the second invokes H. G. Wells and George Bernard Shaw, both members of the reformist Fabian Society, which advocated for such progressive policies as eugenics; while the last group suggests Maurice Bokanowski, the French politician and advocate for industrial rationalization (Sexton 1989), and both Benito Mussolini and Herbert Hoover, the latter of whom was known, on account of his work during the First World War, as "The Great Engineer". By no means part of the same political tradition, such men were nevertheless united by a common desire for the "rational" reorganization of society.

The surprising affinity between the apparently competing political ideologies need not be merely inferred. In his first major *Pravda* article as leader of the

Soviet Union, for example, Lenin invoked Taylorism as a crucial part of the nascent Soviet economy.[20] Leon Trotsky went one step further, almost wholly eliding the differences between the capitalist West and the communist East: "Americanized Bolshevism will triumph and smash imperialist Americanism" (cited in Rogger 1981, 385). For Trotsky, communism was in some way a fundamentally American undertaking. Nor was Huxley the only one to discern these similarities at the time. A range of contemporary German thinkers, from the anarchist Gustav Landauer to the conservative Ernst Jünger, saw capitalism and socialism as merely different expressions of the same mechanical spirit.[21] In 1939, Jünger's brother, Friedrich Georg, summed up the general idea: "Social thinking today means nothing other than upholding the belief in technology and organization. It is the deferential bow that man takes before the ideology of technological progress" (Sozial denken heißt heute nichts anderes, als den Glauben an Apparatur und Organisation hochhalten. Es ist der Kotau, den der Mensch vor der Ideologie des technischen Fortschritts vollführt, 1949, 190).[22]

The unfolding "mechanization of the world" and the attendant rationalization of all aspects of life might thus be seen as the quintessential modern project. As the place where this "progress" was seemingly most advanced, this project became associated with the USA, which in turn formed a widely recognized symbol of modernity as such. This, at least in part, explains why Horkheimer and Adorno take not Stalin's Russia or Hitler's Germany, where the crisis of modernity was most severe, as their starting point, but America, where they were exiled: "our book demonstrates tendencies which turn cultural progress into its opposite. We attempted to do this on the basis of social phenomena of the 1930s and 1940s in

---

[20] In 1917, Lenin wrote: "We must organize in Russia the study and teaching of the Taylor system and systematically try it out and adapt it to our purposes" (cited in Maier, 1970).

[21] Indicating the industrial heart of conventional socialism, Landauer asserts: "The father of Marxism is steam" ("Der Vater des Marxismus ist der Dampf"), before concluding: "this sort of socialism grows out of the undisturbed development of capitalism!" ("diese Sorte Sozialismus erwächst aus der ungestörten Weiterentwicklung des Kapitalismus!", 1967, 98–100). In *Total Mobilization* (1930), meanwhile, Jünger writes: "In Fascism, Bolshevism, Americanism, Zionism, in the movements of coloured peoples, progress has made advances that until recently would have seemed unthinkable. [. . .] Socialism and nationalism in particular are the two great millstones between which progress pulverizes what is left of the old world, and eventually itself" (1993, 137–138).

[22] F. G. Jünger's book *The Perfection of Technology* (*Die Perfektion der Technik*), which, although first published in 1946 was originally completed in 1939, contains one of the earliest references to technocracy in German thought. It was translated into English in 1956 as *The Failure of Technology*.

America" (2002, xiii). American society provided the keys to the most pressing problems of modernity.

While for many contemporary intellectuals this modern project was inherently progressive or even outright utopian, for Horkheimer and Adorno something was severely amiss: "While individuals as such are vanishing before the apparatus they serve, they are provided for by that apparatus and better than ever before" (2002, xvii). Progress was defined by a fundamental "dialectic". Although, as we have seen, Huxley repeatedly took the very technocratic position to which his dystopia seems so opposed, even at his most utopian, his writing is littered with criticisms of naïve progressive thinking, repeatedly lamenting the "Prophets of Utopia" (2001e, 125) and the "apostles of progress" (2001d, 220). By his own admission, it was the "horror of the Wellsian utopia"[23] that prompted him to write *Brave New World* in the first place. As the next section shows, rational, scientific thinking was leading to a sterile, regimented, and meaningless world that made all talk of progress empty. For Huxley, Adorno, and Horkheimer, the future utopia was hardly better than the Dark Ages against which it so proudly defined itself.

3 The Modern Utopia, or the New Eden

The opening scene of *Brave New World* immediately indicates that Huxley's utopian future represents a monument to progress. At the Central London Hatchery and Conditioning Centre, a building of "only thirty-four storeys",[24] the institution's director outlines the process by which future humans are born, or rather grown. As though following an assembly line at a Ford factory, we are taken on a journey first to the "Fertilizing Room" (1) and then to the "Bottling Room" (6), the "Social Pre-Destination Room" (7) and, finally, to the "Decanting Room" (14), where Huxley's New Man is "born". The process of conception, gestation, and birth has been brought wholly under human control, eliminating the need for sex, pregnancy, and labour. Indeed, the "glass and nickel and bleakly shining porcelain" (1) of the laboratories are a far cry from the flesh and bodily fluids that accompany the natural process of the all-too-human past. "Progress" (4), as the Director succinctly puts it.

---

[23] In a letter to Mrs. Kethevan Roberts, 18 May 1931. See Huxley (1969, 348).
[24] Huxley 2007, 1. All subsequent references to *Brave New World* refer to this edition, which I cite by adding the respective page number in brackets.

This vast effort, however, has not been made in the name of comfort or convenience. Instead, the idea is to apply the precise and systematic principles of science to nature. The intention, in other words, is to bring order and predictability to an otherwise chaotic world – to eliminate not pain, but chance. The technique described as "Bokanovsky's Process" (3) is a case in point. By artificially inducing the division of embryos, so that ninety-six babies can be cultivated from a single human egg, Huxley's World Controllers are furnished with a steady supply of homogenized labourers: "Ninety-six identical twins working ninety-six identical machines!" (5). Together with intensive infant conditioning, the result is a highly efficient economy and exemplary social cohesion: "We hardly ever have any trouble with our workers" (139), we later hear. In the pursuit of order, efficiency, and stability – described by Mond as the "primal and ultimate need" (36) – the machine is taken as the supreme model: "Standard men and women; in uniform batches. [. . .] The principle of mass production at last applied to biology" (5). The interwar aim of PEP – of creating a machine-like society based on systematic biological and social engineering – has been realized.

The scientific-technological domination of nature characterizes Huxley's New World at every turn. Old age has been conquered (46–47), infectious diseases have been all but wiped out, and even flies and mosquitoes have been eliminated: "We got rid of them all centuries ago" (210), Mond says matter-of-factly. Any remaining inner conflict or social unease is cured, moreover, with the ubiquitous synthetic drug, soma: "half a gramme for a half-holiday, a gramme for a weekend, two grammes for a trip to the gorgeous East, three for a dark eternity to the moon" (47). Not just productive and cohesive, Huxley's population is therefore also a model of health, on account of permanent youth, and widespread satisfaction. As Lenina says: "Everybody's happy nowadays" (79). The personal helicopters and soaring skyscrapers that dominate the cityscape underscore the impression that Huxley's world is saturated by the achievements of science. Even the harsh, barren landscape of the North Pole has become a routine holiday destination, complete with a hotel and "twenty-five Escalator Squash Courts" (75).

With the entrance into the story of "his fordship" (28), Mustapha Mond, it becomes clear that we are dealing with nothing less than a fully realized utopia – a vision of paradise. Introduced in chapter three, Mond finds himself in the garden of the Conditioning Centre: "Naked in the warm June sunshine, six or seven hundred little boys and girls were running with shrill yells over the lawns, or playing ball games, or squatting silently in twos and threes among the flowering shrubs" (25). This picture of innocence, together with the idyllic garden and the presence of "Ford himself" (29) is strongly evocative of Eden in the Book of Genesis. Even the obligatory perimeter wall – an integral part of the archetypal paradise[25] – makes an appearance. From the perspective of a helicopter window, the narrator remarks on the enormous electric fence that separates Eden from the Fallen world – the boundary dividing "civilization from savagery":

> Uphill and down, across the deserts of salt or sand, through forests, into the violet depth of canyons, over crag and peak and table-topped mesa, the fence marched on and on, irresistibly the straight line, the geometrical symbol of triumphant human purpose. (90–91)

Rivalling God, Huxley's World State is defined by hubris. Indeed, for F. T. Marinetti, pioneer of the aggressively utopian Futurism movement, *"the straight line"* is "one of the characteristics of divinity" (2009, 57). Where once man was forced to yield to the inconsistencies of nature, nature is now infinitely malleable.

Throughout *Brave New World*, Huxley alludes to man's new "lordly" status. Boasting about the medical intervention into foetal development, for example, one of the scientists at the Conditioning Centre cannot help but scoff: "His laugh was knowing and triumphant" (9). In essence, the World State is premised on the notion of fixing a natural world conceived as inherently deficient. It is based not on "the mere slavish imitation of nature", as the scientist continues, but on "the much more interesting world of human invention" (10). Horkheimer and Adorno confirm the impression: "In their mastery of nature, the creative God and the ordering mind are alike. Man's likeness to God consists in sovereignty over existence, in the lordly gaze, in the command" (2002, 6). We are dealing with the attempt to engineer a "second creation" based on the systematic principles of the natural sciences.[26]

For Horkheimer and Adorno, this demiurge-like domination or manipulation of nature is the defining feature of the modern approach to the world – what they term "calculating thought" (2002, 68) or instrumental reason. In the opening chapter, we read: "What human beings seek to learn from nature is how to use it to dominate wholly both it and human beings. Nothing else counts" (2002, 2). This

---

25 Etymologically, paradise means "walled enclosure". Accordingly, this motif is typical of the utopian imagination, as exemplified by Tommaso Campenella's *City of the Sun* (1602), which is surrounded by seven circles of walls. The wall also occupies a central place in Zamyatin's *We*: "Man ceased to be a wild man only when we built the Green Wall, only when, by means of that Wall, we isolated our perfect machine world from the irrational, ugly world of trees, birds, and animals. . . . " (1993, 91).

26 In the second volume of his highly influential *The Decline of the West* (1922), Oswald Spengler makes much the same claim. Describing the modern age as "Faustian", Spengler writes: "Man has listened-in to the march of nature and made notes of its indices. He begins to imitate it by means and methods that utilize the laws of the cosmic pulse. He is emboldened to play the part of God" (1926, 500).

approach to the world is therefore naturally "patriarchal" (2002, 2) or even dictatorial: "Enlightenment stands in the same relationship to things as the dictator to human beings. He knows them to the extent that he can manipulate them" (2002, 6). This is why, for Horkheimer and Adorno, modern thinking has a distinctive "instrumental" character. Unlike religion, philosophy, or the humanistic tradition, it aims not at theoretical knowledge or the "joy of understanding" (2002, 2); it reflects the methodical, functional, utilitarian principles upheld by Ford, whose stoic "manly competence" (2002, 79) Adorno and Horkheimer also regard as characteristic of the age.

Like Huxley's *Brave New World*, instrumental reason is also motivated by the desire for comprehensive order: "Reason is the organ of calculation, of planning; it is neutral with regard to ends; its element is coordination" (2002, 69). The key point is that, for the "scientific temper" (2002, 19; szientifischen Gesinnung, 2016, 32), everything must be brought into a coherent, rational scheme. This explains why Horkheimer and Adorno make the radical claim that "Enlightenment is totalitarian" – "its ideal is the system from which everything and anything follows" (2002, 4). The implication is that the rationalist approach to the world is predicated on a hostility towards or even outright fear of the unknown. Having been plagued by this fear since the dawn of time, Horkheimer and Adorno suggest: "Humans believe themselves free of fear when there is no longer anything unknown" (2002, 11). With its maniacal quest for universal intelligibility, it therefore follows: "Enlightenment is mythical fear radicalized. [. . .] Nothing is allowed to remain outside, since the mere idea of the 'outside' is the real source of fear" (2002, 11).

For Adorno and Horkheimer, everything must become rationally accessible according to the axioms of positivism, which forms the Enlightenment's "ultimate product" (2002, 11): "For the Enlightenment, anything which cannot be resolved into numbers, and ultimately into one, is illusion" (2002, 4). In other words, the world must become a wholly measurable and quantifiable space. That which defies logical explanation and technological control – that which remains "outside" or "irrational" – must be either defeated or denied.

Although this ethic most obviously applies to the natural world, as demonstrated by the domestication of the North Pole, it also applies to the human being, as an essential expression of nature. For the modern utopia, the human individual, acting on spontaneous flights of fancy or principled calls of conscience, threatens the imperative of order. He is therefore naturally maligned, marginalized, and ultimately cast out. In the words of Adorno and Horkheimer, such a figure "is an outsider, and – with the occasional exception of the capital crime – to be an outsider is the gravest guilt" (2002, 121; Er ist ein Outsider und, von gewissen Kapitalverbrechen zuweilen abgesehen, ist es die schwerste Schuld, Outsider zu sein, 2016, 159). In *Brave New World*, such individualized, human characters are quite literally expelled – exiled to remote islands in order to limit their subversive influence.

For Max Weber, a central point of reference for the Frankfurt School, the assumption "that one can, in principle, master all things by calculation", "that principally there are no mysterious incalculable forces" (2009, 139), is the very definition of the disenchanted world. Indeed, it is precisely this principle that Adorno sees exemplified in Huxley's novel.[27] For Huxley, Adorno, and Weber, a world conceived in such positivistic terms tends naturally towards a utopia of perfect order. It tends towards a society shorn of all dissonant, obstinate, and ambiguous elements – towards a luminous, "enlightened" world of complete intelligibility. The implicit destination of progress is thus totalitarian control.

In his essay *The Worker*, Jünger describes such a destination as the "utopia of bourgeois security [Sicherheit]" (2017, 163).[28] The central problem with the progressive thought that Adorno associates with the Enlightenment is, according to Jünger, the obsessive desire for safety: "the ideal condition of security toward which progress strives consists in the universal domination of bourgeois reason, seeking not only to diminish the sources of danger, but ultimately to run them dry" (2017: 29). Everything irrational, dangerous, or "elemental", in Jünger's parlance, is therefore rejected: "the elemental [is relegated] to the realm of error, of dreams, or a necessarily evil will" (2017, 10). It is banished, like Bernard Marx in Iceland, beyond the walls of paradise.

In *Brave New World*, this denied realm – the shadow of civilization – is given direct expression by both the Savage Reservation and Mond's descriptions of the pre-utopian past: the world Before Ford. In an account that violates multiple taboos, Mond explains the nature of a family home – a concept that, in a world of universal state childcare and polyamory, is wholly foreign: "Home, home – a few small rooms, stiflingly over-inhabited by a man, by a periodically teeming woman, by a rabble of boys and girls of all ages. No air, no space; an unsterilized prison; darkness, disease, and smells" (31). A dungeon for the body, the home was equally stifling for the mind: "Psychically, it was a rabbit hole, a midden, hot with the frictions of tightly packed life, reeking with emotion" (31). The core aspects of this description are found again in the Reservation. Being shown around by Bernard,

---

[27] In "Aldous Huxley and Utopia", Adorno writes: "The novel, a fantasy of the future with a rudimentary plot, endeavours to comprehend the shocks [of American modernity] through the principle of the disenchanted world, to heighten this principle to absurdity, and to derive the idea of human dignity from the comprehension of inhumanity" (1997a, 97).

[28] Although translated throughout this passage as security, the German word *Sicherheit* also means safety.

Lenina, a perfect product of civilization, is repulsed: "The dirt, to start with, the piles of rubbish, the dust, the dogs, the flies. Her face wrinkled up into a grimace of disgust" (94). Her encounter with Linda, the long stranded and heavily traumatized former subject of the World State, is worse still: "So fat", runs Lenina's first thought:

> And all the lines in her face, the flabbiness, the wrinkles. And the sagging cheeks, with those purplish blotches. And the red veins in her nose, the bloodshot eyes. And that neck – that neck; and the blanket she wore over her head – ragged and filthy. And under the brown sack-shaped tunic those enormous breasts, the bulge of the stomach, the hips. [. . .] Ford! Ford! It was too revolting [. . .] and smelt too horrible, obviously never had a bath. (102)

Where civilization is synonymous with pristine laboratories, "eau-de-Cologne", and the "firm and sunburnt flesh" of perennially youthful bodies (30–31) – with "regulation white viscose-linen uniform[s]" (15) and "pale corpse-coloured rubber" gloves (1) – both the Reservation and the past are associated above all with dirt, disease, old age, and superstition. Along with the sense of chaos and temporality that they imply, these are the rejected aspects of Huxley's paradise, hence the disgust that they reliably evoke in the future citizens. As one of the universal truths and clichéd propaganda lines has it: "Civilization is Sterilization" (104).

Indeed, if the past and the Reservation were reduced to a single defining characteristic, it would be that of a pervasive foul odour, like that of the "smoke and cooked grease and long-worn, long-unwashed clothes" (96) of the Savage's hut. It is the odour, in other words, of human life. Reduced, in turn, to a single characteristic, the World State would be defined not by order or stability, despite Mond's claims, but to the commitment to hygiene – defined first and foremost as sterilization. The project of eradicating chaos amounts to an act of purification, based on a deep-seated fear of life. As Horkheimer and Adorno write: "For civilization, purely natural existence, both animal and vegetative, was the absolute danger" (2002, 24). The denial of nature in the human being, they add, represents "the core of all civilizing rationality" (2002, 42).

At the bottom of the attempt to rationalize nature lurks a hidden desire to wipe it out altogether. After all, sterilization implies not only the eradication of bacteria and other such microorganisms, but induced infertility: "fertility is merely a nuisance" (10), as one of the scientists says at the opening of the novel.[29] The creativity

---

29 In his little-known dystopian play, *Gats* (1924), the prolific German playwright Georg Kaiser also considers the utopian policy of sterilization, which formed a key part of contemporary progressive thought.

inherent to existence represents the core problem that Huxley's New World attempts to solve. For this reason, it is a fundamentally misanthropic undertaking.[30]

4 The Price of Paradise

By now it is clear that the biopolitical utopia imagined by Huxley and described by Adorno and Horkheimer is fundamentally dystopian. It is fuelled by a suspicion of the unpredictable, ambivalent, and forever-ambiguous nature of the human being – by a desire to iron out the imperfections of both man and nature. It is this underlying misanthropy that undermines an ostensibly desirable world of perfect health, hedonism, and blanket satisfaction. The privileging of these values in the name of stability, together with the purging of everything that threatens them, has led not to Eden, but, in Adorno's estimation, to a "giant concentration camp".[31] As the *Dialectic* famously proclaims, "instead of entering a truly human state", promised by science and progress for over a century, "[humanity] is sinking into a new kind of barbarism" (2002, xiv).

The barbaric nature of utopia is best exemplified by the fate of Huxley's New Man – the ultimate industrial commodity. A central contention of the *Dialectic* is that man's newfound place in the world comes at a price: "Human beings purchase the increase in their power with estrangement from that over which it is exerted" (2002, 6). Conceiving of the surrounding world as nothing more than a field of potential obstacles and resources, nature is reduced to "mere objectivity" (2002, 6): it becomes wholly abstract. This instrumental relation to the world is so thorough, however, that man loses more than his connection to nature:

> Not only is domination paid for with the estrangement of human beings from the dominated objects, but the relationships of human beings, including the relationship of individuals to themselves, have themselves been bewitched by the objectification of mind. (2002, 21)

---

[30] The misanthropic nature of utopia is also vividly suggested by the blockbuster film, *The Matrix* (1999), in which man is compared to "a virus". According to Agent Smith, the rogue spokesman for the new order: "Human beings are a disease, the cancer of this planet. You are a plague, and we are the cure." With uncanny similarities to *Brave New World*, Smith continues: "I hate this place, this zoo, this prison, this reality. It's the smell. I feel saturated by it. I can taste your stink. And every time I do I feel I have somehow been infected by it. It's repulsive."

[31] The full assessment from Adorno's essay on Huxley, which is inexplicably omitted from the English translation, reads: *"Brave New World* is a giant concentration camp, which, lacking its antipode, considers itself paradise" ("Die *Brave New World* ist ein einziges Konzentrationslager, das, seines Gegensatzes ledig, sich fürs Paradies hält", 1969a, 114).

Modern man therefore relates not just to the natural world, but also towards other people and indeed himself in instrumental terms: everything is reduced to a means, a tool, or an object. According to the *Dialectic*: "anything which does not conform to the standard of calculability and utility must be viewed with suspicion" (2002, 3). In *Brave New World*, this condition of total, internalized reification is emphatically expressed by society's sexual mores. Watching on as his colleagues talk about Lenina "as though she were a bit of meat [. . .] Like mutton", Bernard is forced to concede: "And what makes it worse, she thinks of herself as meat" (39–45). Institutionalized promiscuity – "Everyone belongs to everyone else" (40) – has reduced individuals to nothing but bodies. Such self-objectification is so thorough that it reaches grotesque proportions. Proudly explaining the process of "Phosphorous recovery" practiced at crematoriums, Henry Foster, the fertility scientist from the opening scene, remarks: "Fine to think we can go on being socially useful even after we're dead" (63).

This callous attitude towards death represents the logical end of what Adorno terms the "cult of the instrument" (1997a, 102). The loss of human life is no longer an event, in the philosophical sense, but a trivial fact, akin to the inevitable and inconvenient loss of battery life. This explains why Foster speaks of the mass death caused by a recent earthquake as nothing but "Unforeseen wastages" (7). Any sense of tragedy comes not from the loss of an individual person, complete with a name, life story, and accompanying cultural context, but from "the amount of overtime" (7) it creates for the scientists at the Hatchery Centre. In a very literal sense, humans have become human resources. As Jünger puts it, inspired by the sight of mechanical slaughter during the First World War: "man no longer falls in battle, rather he malfunctions" (2017, 69; "Man fällt nicht mehr, sondern man fällt aus", 2015, 115).

Picking up Agamben's term, vital to the discussion of biopolitics, Bülent Diken suggests that *homo sacer* is the central figure of *Brave New World* (2011, 158). If, in Roman law, *homo sacer* was the person officially banished from society and stripped of all civil rights, then Agamben fittingly describes *homo sacer* as nothing but naked or "bare life".[32] He is but the "passive object" (Agamben 2021, 67) of a form of politics – biopolitics – that regards man in purely instrumental terms: as nothing but a body, akin to the slave in antiquity or the Jew in the concentration camp (Agamben 2021, 97). The thoroughly instrumental nature of human relations in *Brave New World* suggests that, in Huxley's story, *homo sacer* is no longer the exceptional figure, but the norm. We are dealing with a population subject to wanton regulation and

---

32 This is the subject of Agamben's best-known work, *Homo Sacer: Sovereign Power and Bare Life* (1995).

invasive biological and social engineering. Traditional restraints, provided by such values as dignity and autonomy, have long been abandoned. Both Huxley and Adorno are therefore ultimately concerned with what Thomas Lemke describes as the systematic production of bare life (2011, 56), or, in Agamben's words, with a fundamentally "biopolitical population" (2021, 68).

The key point is that the efficient management of human life comes – necessarily – at the price of basic humanity. This is because the very value or principle of efficiency – or "rationalization", as the term was more commonly known in Germany – belongs not to the human sphere, but to that of industry. As Adorno and Horkheimer confirm: "Industrialism makes souls into things" (2002, 21; der Industrialismus versachlicht die Seelen, 2016, 34). The efficient regulation, organization, and administration of entire populations therefore entails not only the blanket and indefinite suspension of liberal laws and humanistic ideals, such as truth, creativity, and intimacy, but the fundamental re-formation – or rather mutilation – of the human being. Reflecting on the Soviet conception of the individual in 1931, for example, Huxley comes to the conclusion:

> The aim of the Communist Revolution in Russia was to [. . .] transform him into a component cell of the great "Collective Man" – that single mechanical monster who, in the Bolshevist millennium, is to take the place of the unregimented hordes of "soul encumbered" individuals who now inhabit the earth. [. . .] The condition of their entry into the Bolsheviks' Earthly Paradise is that they shall have become like machines. (2001c, 251)

The technocratic-biopolitical ethos thus rests on a radically different view of man to that of the Western tradition, as codified by the Enlightenment. Having been turned into a mere cog in the machine or "cell in the social body" (78), the individual has virtually disappeared as a conceptual category. As Horkheimer and Adorno suggest: "Everyone amounts only to those qualities by which he or she can replace everyone else: all are fungible, mere specimens. As individuals they are absolutely replaceable, pure nothingness" (2002, 116–117). This explains their subsequent claim: "The oldest fear, that of losing one's name, is being fulfilled" (2002, 24). The individual, once the foundation of Western thought, is now a nonentity.

This reversal, along with the destruction of humanity that it implies, is one of the hallmarks of dystopian literature. As with the *Dialectic*, it is frequently portrayed by the absence of human names. In Zamyatin's *We*, for example, people are designated by barcode: D-503, I-330, O-90 – vowels for females, consonants for males. Eventually compelled to undergo lobotomy, Zamyatin's characters are "Not men but some kind of tractors in human form" (1993, 182). Similarly, in the final part of Georg Kaiser's *Gas* trilogy (1917–1920), people belong to sets of Blue and Yellow Figures, identified only by number. In *Brave New World*, such dehumanization is most powerfully conveyed not by the absence of names, although even these are but nods to the system in which people are caught, but by the prominence of the insect metaphor. Having left the Reservation, the Savage's impression of Huxley's infant labourer class – the Epsilons – at his mother's hospice provides the most striking example:

> Twin after twin, twin after twin, they came – a nightmare. Their faces, their repeated face – for there was only one between the lot of them – puggishly stared, all nostrils and pale goggling eyes. [. . .] In a moment, it seemed, the ward was maggoty with them. They swarmed between the beds, clambered over, crawled under, peeped into the television boxes [. . .] the nightmare of swarming indistinguishable sameness. (177–184)

Ironically, for the unconditioned mind it is the sight of civilized perfection that is the source of revulsion. Such metaphors were commonly used to make sense of the rapidly industrializing world at the time. In 1916, the German poet Stefan George warned of the "victory of the Anglo-American standard ant" ("Sieg der anglo-amerikanischen Normalameise", 1963, 34), while, in his book on the USA, the philosopher Hermann von Keyserling suggested that the mechanical world was bringing about a universal "termite existence" ("Termitendasein", 1930, 187). For the likes of Henry Ford, Keyserling maintained, the ultimate desire was to rule over "millions of mechanized ant people" ("Millionen völlig mechanisierter Ameisen-Menschen", 1930, 208). The perfection of humanity seemed to presuppose its very abnegation.

Whether as maggots or tractors, the modern world was thus reducing humans to populations of reliable, robotic, and faceless slave labourers.[33] Worse still, such degradation was either unacknowledged or otherwise blithely accepted – like Huxley's New Man, biopolitical populations have learnt to "love their servitude" (2007b, xlviii). The end of progress therefore heralds the end of humanity as a meaningful concept. Followed through to its logical conclusion, the modern age is destined for a state of "absolute reification" (Adorno 1997a, 101), in which the "commodity relation" becomes the "supreme standard" (Adorno 1997a, 97). Such a condition represents the culmination of the technocratic worldview, for which Friedrich Georg Jünger provided the maxim: "The world is a machine, man an automaton" ("Die Welt ist eine Maschine, der Mensch ein Automat", 1949, 201).

---

33 The very word robot, derived from the Czech *robota* and coined in Karel Čapek's dystopia *R.U.R.* (1920), implies "indentured labour" (Anderson 2014, 227–228).

5 Conclusion

With its hyperbolic style and deeply misanthropic visions, the question arises whether such dystopian literature – including the *Dialectic* – can have anything to say to our contemporary world. With the defeat of Nazi Germany and the collapse of the Soviet Union – both events subsequent to the publication of the works examined here – totalitarianism is surely long in retreat. Yet both Huxley and Adorno continued to return to the central ideas of their earlier work long after the immediate crises of Wall Street and fascism had passed: *Brave New World Revisited* was published in 1958, while Adorno maintained, as late as 1951, that the world was becoming an "open-air prison" (1997b, 33). In that same essay, Adorno warns: "the semblance of freedom makes reflection upon one's own unfreedom incomparably more difficult than formerly when such reflection stood in contradiction to manifest unfreedom" (1997b, 20). Today's ostensible commitment to democracy, as well as the absence of the conventional trappings of totalitarianism – jackboots, dictators, and internment camps – provides a false sense of security.[34]

As I argued in the second part of this chapter, the conventionally sharp distinction between liberalism, on the one hand, and the various totalitarianisms, on the other, belies a concerning underlying unity. For Huxley, Adorno, and a host of other contemporary thinkers, modernity, whatever guise it takes, is bringing about an increasingly regulated society or "administered world" (Horkheimer and Adorno 2002, xi; "verwaltete Welt", 2016, ix). Ostensibly prided on the rational principles of science, this is a world in stark violation of Enlightenment values, especially dignity and freedom. The more benign face of its post-war Western manifestation displays the same basic totalitarian tendencies. For Agamben, there is an "inner solidarity between democracy and totalitarianism" (1998, 10).[35]

---

[34] Indeed, the construction of quarantine facilities or "Centres for National Resilience" in Australia, such as that at Howard Springs in the Northern Territory, evokes disturbing historical precedents. They mark a return to the internment camp not seen in the West since the mass incarceration of Japanese Americans in the Second World War. For a first-hand account, see Freddie Sayers (2021).

[35] While careful not to elide their numerous and significant historical differences, the point for Agamben is that Western democracies also, and increasingly, relate to their populations not politically, as independent legal subjects, but sociologically, as an anonymous mass of bodies. In his own words: "the link between bare life and politics [. . .] secretly governs the modern ideologies seemingly most distant from one another" (1998, 4). Following the second part of this chapter, Agamben regards this shift away from the core tenets of bourgeois democracy – that is, away from politics itself – and towards technocratic population management as "the decisive event of modernity" (1998, 4).

In the twenty-first century, the danger is perhaps less that such tendencies are not recognized, but that they are not decried. Whether because of the threat of terrorism, populism, or pathogens, freedom is increasingly regarded as a liability – a responsibility too heavy to be borne by ordinary people. Not unlike the 1930s, there is a renewed, if largely unspoken, bourgeois crisis of confidence in democracy, which, following Huxley's own inclinations around 1930, manifests itself in admiration for totalitarian systems.[36] The unspoken maxim, as suggested by the naïve modelling of the recent pandemic response on China, is that the repressive nature of such systems might be regrettable, but it is unavoidable. In an age of digital technology and advanced globalization, democracy once again appears anachronistic.

The near-global state of emergency in effect between spring 2020 and spring 2022 brought these biopolitical-totalitarian tendencies into plain view. A recent headline in the American *Foreign Policy* magazine, for example, reads: "The Pandemic Proves Only Technocrats Can Save Us".[37] Indeed, public discourse during this period was dominated not by politicians, as elected representatives, but by an omnipresent cast of largely unknown public health officials: immunologist Anthony Fauci (USA), mathematical biologist Neil Ferguson (UK), and health economist Karl Lauterbach (Germany), to name just three. Wherever politicians did appear, it was very often in conjunction with such figures.[38]

A former employee of the World Economic Forum (WEF), the author of the *Foreign Policy* article himself points towards another layer of technocratic control. Along with other transnational NGOs and UN initiatives – such as the World Health Organization and the Rockefeller and Bill and Melinda Gates Foundations –

---

[36] As noted in the introduction to this volume (p. 25), such admiration was widespread during the pandemic. In an interview with *The Times* in December 2020, for example, the British epidemiologist Neil Ferguson, whose alarmist modelling was crucial in shaping government policy, praised China's early lockdowns as an "innovative intervention" and a model for the West: "I think people's sense of what is possible in terms of control changed quite dramatically between January and March." In a remarkably candid confession, he added: "It's a communist one party state, we said. We couldn't get away with it in Europe, we thought . . . and then Italy did it. And we realised we could" (Ferguson 2020). Similarly, at a public conference in July 2020, Britain's former and longest serving health secretary, Jeremy Hunt, gushed in support for the most authoritarian aspects of the Chinese approach (see Hunt 2022).

[37] A translation of the article appeared shortly afterwards in the Munich-based newspaper, *Merkur*. See Khanna 2021a and Khanna 2021b respectively.

[38] Probably the best example of this was the routine staging of British press conferences during the pandemic. Appearing almost always as part of a triumvirate, the Prime Minister was flanked to the left by chief medical officer Chris Witty and to the right by chief scientific officer Patrick Vallance.

the WEF represents a renewed and increasingly formalized tendency towards international technocratic governance. Such global management is characterized by its structural insulation from the voting public and its insistence on representing the impartial and objective, and therefore correct and incorruptible, scientific method. This explains the ubiquitous propaganda slogan, "Follow the Science".[39] The technocratic credentials of these organizations are underlined by the fact that two of their most prominent leaders – Klaus Schwab of the WEF and Bill Gates of the eponymous Foundation – are, by training, mechanical and software engineers respectively.

Such figures represent the Wellsian planners so brilliantly parodied by Huxley. In a quite literal sense, they are *social* engineers – the modern heirs of F. W. Taylor, Maurice Bokanovski, Alfred Mond, and Henry Ford. Frequently drawn from industry, they form the pinnacle of the new managerial class once again pursuing their vision of a harmonious, healthy global population underpinned by technology. Eschewing democracy, theirs is a rule of professional administration and covert, scientific manipulation.[40] For these reasons, they are best regarded not primarily as wealthy capitalists, but as would-be architects of a new civilization. Not unlike the 1930s, the pre-eminence of such World Controllers threatens the integrity of democracy.

It is precisely because of the rich interpretive potential of *Brave New World* and the *Dialectic of Enlightenment* for our present condition that such dystopian literature is so important today. It provides the imagery and the language to help us grasp what Agamben calls "the new forms of despotism" (2021, 65) – a form of global control that largely defies the over-familiar categories of left and right, communist and fascist. In many ways, there is a close affinity between dystopian literature and the field of biopolitics: both describe the reduction of the individual to a mere nodal point in an all-encompassing administrative system.[41] In his

---

39 The invocation of science as an unarguable defence for what amounts to political decision making – common practice during the pandemic – is best exemplified by Fauci. Explaining his contradictory policy advice in June 2021, he offered: "people who then criticize me about that are actually criticizing science". In an interview with MSNBC earlier that month, he had declared: "attacks on me, quite frankly, are attacks on science". See Fauci 2021a and 2021b respectively.

40 During the pandemic in Britain, such manipulation was directed by the Behavioural Insights Team (BIT), whose work in this field is pioneering. Until last year part of the Cabinet Office, the BIT employs "Nudge Theory" to influence population behaviour. The latter term was coined by the Americans Richard Thaler (a behavioural economist) and Cass Sunstein (a legal scholar) in their tellingly titled book, *Nudge: Improving Decisions about Health, Wealth, and Happiness* (2008).

41 This affinity is also suggested by two other contributions to this volume: Marko Pajević's chapter on Juli Zeh's *The METHOD* (2009) and Betiel Wasihun's chapter on Marc-Uwe Kling's *QualityLand* (2017).

2009 essay "Identity Without the Person", for example, Agamben offers an account of the world that is both eminently dystopian and eerily prescient. A full decade before the term "lockdown" had any meaning beyond the US penal system, Agamben writes:

> The reduction of man to a naked life is today such a fait accompli that it is by now the basis of the identity that the state recognizes in its citizens. As the deportees to Auschwitz no longer had either a name or a nationality, and were by then only the numbers that had been tattooed on their arms, so the contemporary citizens, lost in an anonymous mass and reduced to the level of potential criminals, are defined by nothing other than their biometric data. (2011, 52)

Here we have the quintessential dystopian motif of the nameless individual, only now the example – the Holocaust – is no longer fictional, but historical. The most troubling thing about Agamben's description of the reified, biometric human is the extent to which it was verified by the pandemic experience. With the overturning of the cornerstones of Western political principles – from freedom of speech and assembly to parliamentary democracy and bodily autonomy – the autonomous citizen was wholly replaced by the passive object. Legal protections and political influence made way for a de facto police state, in which everything from picnics to funerals became illegal. Stripped of all responsibility and reduced to an infantile existence, the only obligation was compliance. In the words of one of Germany's most pre-eminent public intellectuals, affirming such conditions at the time: "As citizens we are obliged to more or less function" ("Als Staatsbürger haben wir halbwegs zu funktionieren").[42]

In the UK, the proscription of everything deemed "non-essential" confirmed the instrumental character of society that Huxley and Adorno had foreseen eighty years prior. That which did not contribute to the mere functioning of society – everything, that is, that gives life meaning and value – was banished beyond the walls of the new hygienic utopia. The omnipresence of the mask, which degrades the person much like the removal of his name, together with de facto vaccine mandates, crudely underlined the dehumanization that paradoxically accompanied the attempt to "save lives".[43] Digitally entertained though we may have been at that

---

[42] This comment was uttered by Richard David Precht on Swiss television in the autumn of 2021. See Precht 2021.

[43] Interestingly, the dehumanizing implications of the mask were recognized as early as 1932 by Ernst Jünger. For Jünger, the mask was a fitting symbol of the New Man or "worker" that was emerging in the aftermath of the First World War. Regarding himself "as a pure instrument" (2017, 69), the "worker" naturally covers his face – "be it [with] the gas mask, which we are looking to issue to whole populations; the face mask for sport and for high speeds (worn by every motorist); the protection mask in places with dangerous processes involving radiation,

time, it no longer requires a great leap of imagination to see why Agamben regards the concentration camp as the "biopolitical paradigm of the West" (1998, 181).

For Adorno, the greatest failing of *Brave New World* is its lack of solution to the problem it depicts. Faced with a choice between civilization and the Reservation village known as Malpais – in Spanish, "bad place" – humanity is trapped: "No room is left for a concept of mankind that would resist absorption into the collective coercion of the system and reduction to the status of contingent individuals" (1997a, 113). Yet it is precisely the oppressive sterility of Huxley's World State – the evident "homesickness of those enmeshed in civilization" (Horkheimer and Adorno 2002, 82) – that prompts philosophical questions about the meaning of life in the first place. The consistent reduction of man to bare life – even with the promise of utopian security – is clearly intolerable. The world it creates is barren, suffocating, and degrading. In the end, we must want something more than our mere survival. We must want meaning, intimacy, truth, beauty, and freedom. We must want all those irrational, dangerous, and chaotic things that cannot be rationally measured nor technologically controlled.

It is precisely such qualitative concerns that form the object of art, literature, and the humanistic tradition. They are the object of the Enlightenment, not in its debased positivistic incarnation, but as a genuinely philosophical endeavour. Like the dystopian tradition that they represent, both *Brave New World* and the *Dialectic of Enlightenment* are explicit attempts to overcome the "triumph of the factual mentality" (Horkheimer and Adorno 2002, 2) that characterizes modernity. They suggest that the tangible realm of fact must always be counterbalanced by the intangible realm of value, which explains Adorno and Horkheimer's conception of philosophy as the conscience of science (2002, 90). From this perspective, mantras like "Follow the Science" are an absurdity; no amount of data can tell us how to live. Yet such mantras are more than just philosophically naïve. They also indicate the dogmatic, anti-modern, and misanthropic tendencies that underpin the technocratic tradition.

---

explosives, or narcotics". Anticipating future developments such as our own, Jünger adds: "We can assume that the mask will come to take on functions that we can today hardly imagine" (2017, 75–76, translation altered).

References

Adorno, Theodor W. "Aldous Huxley und die Utopie." *Prismen. Kulturkritik und Gesellschaft*. Frankfurt am Main: Suhrkamp Verlag, 1969a [1951]. 112–143.
Adorno, Theodor W. "Drucknachweise." *Prismen. Kulturkritik und Gesellschaft*. Frankfurt am Main: Suhrkamp Verlag, 1969b [1955]. 343–344.
Adorno, Theodor W. "Aldous Huxley and Utopia." *Prisms*. Trans. Samuel and Shierry Weber. Cambridge, MA: MIT Press, 1997a. 95–117.
Adorno, Theodor W. "Cultural Criticism and Society." *Prisms*. Trans. Samuel and Shierry Weber. Cambridge, Mass.: MIT Press, 1997b. 17–34.
Adorno, Theodor W. "The Meaning of Working Through the Past." *Critical Models: Interventions and Catchwords*. Trans. Henry W. Pickford. New York: Columbia University Press, 1998. 89–103.
Adorno, Theodor W. *Briefe an die Eltern*. Eds. Henri Lonitz and Christoph Gödde. Frankfurt am Main: Suhrkamp, 2003.
Adorno, Theodor W. *History and Freedom: Lectures 1964–1965*. Ed. Rolf Tiedemann. Trans. Rodney Livingstone. Cambridge: Polity, 2008.
Agamben, Giorgio. *Homo Sacer: Sovereign Power and Bare Life*. Trans. Daniel Heller-Roazen. Stanford, CA: Stanford University Press, 1998 [1995].
Agamben, Giorgio. "Identity Without the Person." *Nudities*. Trans. David Kishik and Stefan Pedatella. Stanford, CA: Stanford University Press, 2011 [2009]. 46–54.
Agamben, Giorgio. *Where Are We Now? The Epidemic as Politics*. Trans. Valeria Dani. London: Eris, 2021.
Anderson, Nicholas. "'Only We Have Perished': Karel Čapek's R.U.R. and the Catastrophe of Humankind." *Journal of the Fantastic in the Arts* 25.2/3 (2014): 226–246.
Baker, Robert S. *Brave New World: History, Science, and Dystopia*. Boston: Twayne Publishers, 1990.
Baker, Robert S. "The Nightmare of the Frankfurt School: The Marquis de Sade and the Problem of Modernity in Aldous Huxley's Dystopian Narrative." *Now More Than Ever: Proceedings of the Aldous Huxley Centenary Symposium*. Ed. Bernfried Nugel. Frankfurt a. M.: Peter Lang, 1995. 245–260.
Bogdanovich, Peter. *Fritz Lang in America*. London: Studio Vista, 1967.
Campbell, Timothy, and Adam Sitze, eds. *Biopolitics: A Reader*. Durham, NC: Duke University Press, 2013.
Clayton, Jay. "The Modern Synthesis: Genetics and Dystopia in the Huxley Circle." *Modernism/Modernity* 23.4 (2016): 875–896.
Crew, Thomas. "'Nie hatte ein Mensch etwas Ähnliches gesehen oder erträumt!' Bernhard Kellermanns Tunnel und das Spektakel Amerikas." *Geliebtes, verfluchtes Amerika. Zu Antimerikanismus und Amerika-Verehrung im deutschen Sprachraum 1888–1933*. Eds. Karsten Dahlmann and Aneta Jachimowicz. Göttingen: Vandenhoeck & Ruprecht, 2022. 27–39.
Diken, Bülent. "Huxley's Brave New World – and Ours." *Journal for Cultural Research* 15.2 (2011): 153–172.
Fauci, Anthony. "Fauci Doubles Down on Claim that Attacks on Him Are Actually 'Criticizing Science'." *The New York Post* (21 June 2021). Available at: https://nypost.com/2021/06/21/fauci-attacks-on-him-are-actually-criticizing-science/. Last accessed 8 July 2022.
Fauci, Anthony. "'Attacks on Me Are Attacks on Science': Fauci Blasts Critics in Fiery TV Appearance." *The Independent* (9 June 2021). Available at: https://www.independent.co.uk/news/world/americas/us-politics/fauci-interview-today-science-covid-b1862899.html. Last accessed 8 July 2022.

Ferguson, Neil. "Professor Neil Ferguson: People Don't Agree with Lockdown and Try to Undermine the Scientists." *The Times* (25 December 2020). Available at: https://www.thetimes.co.uk/article/people-don-t-agree-with-lockdown-and-try-to-undermine-the-scientists-gnms7mp98. Last accessed 7 July 2022.

George, Stefan, and Edith Landmann. *Gespräche mit Stefan George*. Düsseldorf: H. Küpper (previously G. Bondi), 1963.

Göktürk, Deniz. *Cowboys, Künstler, Ingenieure: kultur- und mediengeschichtliche Studien zu deutschen Amerika-Texten 1912–1920*. Munich: Fink, 1998.

Haldance, J. B. S. *Science and Human Life*. New York: Harper and Brothers, 1933.

Hauptmann, Gerhart. *Das Abenteuer meiner Jugend in zwei Bänden*. Berlin: S. Fischer Verlag, 1937.

Holzer, Angela. "To Reflect, to Sit Down: The Hinzutretende and the Huxleyan Characters in Horkheimer's and Adorno's Philosophy." *Huxley's Brave New World: Essays*. Eds. David Garrett Izzo and Kim Kirkpatrick. Jefferson, NC: McFarland, 2008. 117–131.

Horkheimer, Max, and Adorno, Theodor W. *Dialektik der Aufklärung*. Frankfurt am Main: Fischer Taschenbuch, 2016 [1944].

Horkheimer, Max, and Theodor W. Adorno. *The Dialectic of Enlightenment*. Trans. Edmund Jephcott. Stanford, CA: Stanford University Press, 2002.

Horkheimer, Max. "Briefwechsel, 1941–1948." *Gesammelte Schriften*. Eds. Alfred Schmidt and Gunzelin Schmid Noerr. Vol. 17. Frankfurt: Fischer Taschenbuch Verlag, 1996.

Hunt, Jeremy. "We Should Be Aiming for Zero Infection." Broadcast on *GB News* in May 2022. Available at: https://www.youtube.com/watch?v=35899euglYM. Last accessed 7 July 2022.

Huxley, Aldous. *Point Counter Point*. London: Chatto and Windus, 1928.

Huxley, Aldous. *Letters of Aldous Huxley*. Ed. Grover Smith. New York: Harper and Row, 1969.

Huxley, Aldous. "Malaya." *Complete Essays*. Vol. II: 1926–1929. Eds. Robert S. Baker and James Sexton. Chicago: Ivan R. Dee, 2001a. 504–539.

Huxley, Aldous. "Science and Civilization." *Complete Essays*. Vol. III: 1930–1935. Eds. Robert S. Baker and James Sexton. Chicago: Ivan R. Dee, 2001a. 148–155.

Huxley, Aldous. "The Outlook for American Culture." *Complete Essays*. Vol. III: 1930–1935. Eds. Robert S. Baker and James Sexton. Chicago: Ivan R. Dee, 2001b. 185–194.

Huxley, Aldous. "The New Romanticism." *Complete Essays*. Vol. III: 1930–1935. Eds. Robert S. Baker and James Sexton. Chicago: Ivan R. Dee, 2001c. 250–254.

Huxley, Aldous. "Machinery, Psychology, and Politics." *Complete Essays*. Vol. III: 1930–1935. Eds. Robert S. Baker and James Sexton. Chicago: Ivan R. Dee, 2001d. 218–225.

Huxley, Aldous. "Boundaries of Utopia." *Complete Essays*. Vol. III: 1930–1935. Eds. Robert S. Baker and James Sexton. Chicago: Ivan R. Dee, 2001e. 124–129.

Huxley, Aldous. *Brave New World*. London: Vintage, 2007a [1932].

Huxley, Aldous. "Foreword." *Brave New World*. London: Vintage, 2007b [1946]. XLI–L.

Huxley, Julian. "The Applied Science of the Next Hundred Years. Biological and Social Engineering." *Life and Letters*. Vol. 2 (October 1934). 38–46.

Jones, Greta. *Social Hygiene in Twentieth-Century Britain*. London: Croom Helm, 1986.

Jünger, Ernst. "Der Arbeiter. Herrschaft und Gestalt" *Sämtliche Werke in 22 Bänden*, vol. 10. Eds. Joana van de Löcht and Helmuth Kiesel, in cooperation with Friederike Mayer-Lindenberg. Stuttgart: Klett-Cotta, 2015 [1932]. 6–317.

Jünger, Ernst. *The Worker: Dominion and Form*. Trans. Bogdan Costea and Laurence Paul Hemming. Evanston, IL: Northwestern University Press, 2017.

Jünger, Ernst. "Total Mobilization." *The Heidegger Controversy: A Critical Reader*. Ed. Richard Wolin. Trans. Joel Golb and Richard Wolin. Cambridge, MA: MIT Press, 1993. 119–139.

Jünger, Friedrich Georg. *Die Perfektion der Technik*. Frankfurt am Main: Vittoria Klostermann, 1949 [1946].
Kellermann, Bernhard. *Der Tunnel*. Cadolzburg: ars Vivendi verlag, 2016 [1913].
Keyserling, Hermann von. *Amerika: Aufgang einer neuen Welt*. Stuttgart: Deutsche Verlags-Anstalt, 1930.
Khanna, Parag. "The Pandemic Proves Only Technocrats Can Save Us." *Foreign Policy*, 2021a. Available at: https://foreignpolicy.com/2021/06/24/pandemic-technocrats-global-challenges/. Last accessed 24 June 2022.
Khanna, Parag. "Die Corona-Pandemie zeigt: unsere einzige Hoffnung sind die Technokraten." *Merkur*, 2021b. Available at: https://www.merkur.de/politik/corona-pandemie-technokraten-china-klimakrise-loesung-trump-johnson-experten-zr-90868280.html. Last accessed 24 June 2022.
König, Wolfgang. "Die Ingenieure und der VDI als Großverein in der wilhelminischen Gesellschaft 1900 bis 1918." *Technik, Ingenieure und Gesellschaft. Geschichte des Vereins deutscher Ingenieure 1856–1981*. Düsseldorf: VDI-Verlag. 235–287.
Kubin, Alfred. *Die andere Seite. Ein phantastischer Roman*. Reinbeck bei Hamburg: Rowohlt Taschenbuch Verlag, 2014 [1909].
Landauer, Gustav. *Aufruf zum Sozialismus*. Ed. Heinz-Joachim Heydorn. Frankfurt am Main: Europäische Verlagsanstalt, 1967 [1911].
Lemke, Thomas. *Biopolitics: An Advanced Introduction*. Trans. Eric Frederick Trump. New York: New York University Press, 2011.
Maier, C. S. "Between Taylorism and Technocracy: European Ideologies and the Vision of Industrial Productivity in the 1920s." *Journal of Contemporary History*. 5.2 (1970): 27–61.
Marinetti, F. T. "The New Religion-Morality of Speed." *High-Speed Society: Social Acceleration, Power, and Modernity*. Eds. Hartmut Rosa and W. E. Scheuermann. University Park, PA: Pennsylvania State University Press, 2009. 57–60.
Mond, Alfred. *Industry and Politics*. London: Macmillan, 1927.
Nolan, Mary. *Visions of Modernity: American Business and the Modernization of Germany*. New York: Oxford University Press, 1994.
Olson, Richard G. *Scientism and Technocracy in the Twentieth Century: The Legacy of Scientific Management*. Lanham, MD: Lexington Books, 2015.
Orwell, George. "Second Thoughts on James Burnham." *The Managerial Revolution: What is Happening in the World*. Ed. James Burnham. London: Lume Books, 2021 [1946]. I–XXIII.
Precht, Richard David. "Als Staatsbürger haben wir halbwegs zu funktionieren." On Swiss TV, 2021. Available at: https://www.youtube.com/watch?v=AN-1C8OSYtI. Last accessed 26 June 2022.
Rathenau, Walther. *Von kommenden Dingen*. Berlin: S. Fischer Verlag, 1917.
Rathenau, Walther. *Zur Kritik der Zeit*. New York: Georg Olms Verlag, 2008 [1912].
Rieppel, Anton von. "Ingenieur und öffentliches Leben." *Z-VDI* 61 (1917): 987–992.
Rogger, Hans. "Americanizm and the Economic Development of Russia." *Comparative Studies in Society and History* 23.3 (1981): 382–420.
Rohkrämer, Thomas. *Eine andere Moderne? Zivilisationskritik, Natur und Technik in Deutschland 1880–1933*. Vienna: Schöningh, 1999.
Sayers, Freddie. "Inside Australia's Covid Internment Camp." *UnHerd* (2 December 2021). Available at: https://unherd.com/thepost/inside-australias-covid-internment-camp/. Last accessed 8 July 2022.
Scaff, L. A. *Max Weber in America*. Woodstock: Princeton University Press, 2011.
Sexton, James. "Aldous Huxley's Bokanovsky." *Science Fiction Studies* 16.1 (1989): 85–89.

Sexton, James. "Brave New World and the Rationalization of Industry." *Critical Essays on Aldous Huxley*. Ed. Jerome Meckier. New York: G. K. Hall, 1996. 88–102.

Spengler, Oswald. *Der Untergang des Abendlandes: Umrisse einer Morphologie der Weltgeschichte*, vol. 2. Munich: C. H. Beck, 1922.

Spengler, Oswald. *The Decline of the West*. Trans. Charles Francis Atkinson. London: Allen & Unwin, 1926.

Taylor, Frederick Winslow. *The Principles of Scientific Management*. Greenwood, WI: Suzeteo Enterprises, 2014 [1911].

Weber, Max. "Die protestantische Ethik und der 'Geist' des Kapitalismus." *Gesammelte Aufsätze zur Religionssoziologie*, vol. 1. Tübingen: Mohr, 1978 [1905].

Weber, Max. *The Protestant Ethic and the Spirit of Capitalism*. Trans. Talcott Parsons. London: Routledge Classics, 2001.

Weber, Max. "Science as a Vocation." *From Max Weber: Essays in Sociology*. Eds. and trans. H. H. Gerth and C. Wright Mills. Oxford: Routledge, 2009. 129–156.

Wells, Herbert George. *The Open Conspiracy and Other Writings*. London: [s.n.], 1933.

Willecke, Stefan. "Die Technokratiebewegung zwischen den Weltkriegen und der 'Kulturfaktortechnik'." *Technische Intelligenz und 'Kulturfaktor Technik'. Kulturvorstellungen von Technikern und Ingenieurenzwischen Kaiserreich und früher Bundesrepublik Deutschland*. Eds. Burkhard Dietz, Michael Fessner, and Helmut Maier. Münster: Waxmann, 1996. 203–220.

Woiak, Joanne. "Designing a Brave New World: Eugenics, Politics, and Fiction." *The Public Historian* 29.3 (2007): 105–129.

Zamyatin, Yevgeni. *We*. Trans. Clarence Brown. London: Penguin Group, 1993 [1924].

Timothy Campbell
COVID-19 as Event: Mythology and Ritual in Agamben's Pandemic Dispatches

Abstract: The following essay takes aim at a number of accounts of the COVID-19 pandemic, but especially those written by the Italian philosopher, Giorgio Agamben. In a series of short articles and essays that were first featured on the Italian publisher, Quodlibet's website, and then later collected in the volume, *Where Are We Now? The Epidemic as Politics*, Agamben objects to the political and social measures that were intended to combat the spread of the virus. Of particular interest for Agamben are those involving social distancing, the increasingly powerful voice of virologists and medical doctors in political responses to the pandemic, and the continuing role played by states of exception for governing Italy (though not only). All lead Agamben to posit that Italians have sacrificed everything for their own protection, including their religious and political convictions. Reading with and against Agamben, the essay first draws on the thought of the Italian philologist Carlo Diano and his notion of "eventic forms", to argue that many of Agamben's objections to anti-COVID measures are based on a mythologization of sacrifice that depends for its power on competing notions of what qualifies as an event. Challenging Agamben on the nature of event and its forms during the pandemic, it becomes possible to ask what eventic forms beyond bare life can be thought that do not inevitably lead either to myth or sacrifice. The essay does so by employing the thought of both René Girard and Mario Perniola as a way of reading many of the rituals associated with the COVID-19 pandemic not as ones leading to sacrifice but instead as potential examples of what Perniola terms "ritual without myth". The essay concludes with a reflection on the need to restrain linking gestures to collective or individual belief.

1 Introduction

As I write, the number of people infected by COVID-19 worldwide stands at 493,015,923. Of these more than 6 million have died, though as a recent report suggests the figure is likely closer to 15 million.[1] Yesterday, April 4, 2022, there were 19,142 new cases and 180 new deaths in the United States. The numbers are

---
1 https://www.nytimes.com/2022/04/16/health/global-covid-deaths-who-india.html. Last accessed 27 April 2022.

similar across Europe, while in India the WHO estimates that four million have died due to COVID-19.[2] In Africa nearly two-thirds of Africans may have contracted the virus.[3] In Brazil more than 660,000 have died.[4] These are staggering figures, which make SARS-CoV-2 among the worst pandemics in human history.[5]

Reminding oneself of the unprecedented nature of the COVID-19 pandemic is a necessary context for any philosophical reflection. During the pandemic millions died. Today thousands more will die. To write this means already to speak of COVID-19 as something that truly matters, as an event of life and death. Almost from the moment of contagion, this fact led thinkers as different as Bruno Latour, Catherine Malabou, Roberto Esposito, Judith Butler, and Slavoj Žižek to offer their thoughts on the pandemic by assuming precisely this: COVID-19 is an event. Yet perhaps no one more than Giorgio Agamben has employed COVID-19 negatively as an event for critiquing social distancing, mask wearing and vaccines (Agamben 2021). What is worthy of consideration is how Agamben accounts for the pandemic (which he notably first referred to as an "invention") and by so doing attempts to alter our relation to it. If we are to disagree with Agamben's account of the pandemic, the first task will be to identify the nature of the event that we are facing; to provide it with a meaning that acknowledges the coordinates used in order to make sense of it, while finding a way forward in which those same coordinates can be acknowledged as mythical. In the following essay I attempt to lay out where those coordinates might be found and in so doing challenge accounts of COVID-19 that traffic in mythology.

In discussing the globalized nature of COVID-19 as an event, I will be making two assumptions. The first is that the pandemic ought to be read as a biopolitical event that occurs for both the individual and the collective. The moment of contagion makes the pandemic an event for me and an event for society. This interaction between the individual and society provides the event with much of its biopolitical intensity, given the importance of population when defining the biopolitical (Foucault and Esposito in Campbell and Sitze 2013). The second argument revolves around describing the relation among the sacred, mythology and rituals,

---

[2] https://covid19.who.int/. Last accessed 27 April 2022.
[3] https://www.nytimes.com/live/2022/04/07/world/covid-19-mandates-cases-vaccine#nearly-two-thirds-of-africans-have-contracted-the-coronavirus-the-who-says. Last accessed 27 April 2022.
[4] https://coronavirus.jhu.edu/region/brazil. Last accessed 27 April 2022.
[5] https://www.theatlantic.com/ideas/archive/2021/08/1918-influenza-pandemic-history-coronavirus/619801. Last accessed 27 April 2022. When viewed in terms of excess mortality, the figures, according to the World Health Organization, rise to nearly 15 million in 2020 and 2021. https://www.who.int/news/item/05-05-2022-14.9-million-excess-deaths-were-associated-with-the-covid-19-pandemic-in-2020-and-2021. Last accessed 6 July 2022.

and that part of the problem with Agamben's perspective (though not only his) involves embracing a notion of the sacred and ritual that always involves sacrifice. I point to other possibilities for adopting rituals without sacrifice that allow for "the effective reality" of the pandemic to emerge.[6]

I have organized my essay into three parts. I begin with an earlier account of the biopolitical event, namely that of Michael Hardt and Antonio Negri, highlight how they underline their debt to Foucault in terms of biopower and biopolitics, and then pivot to ask if the pandemic can be described as a form of biopower. To do so I draw on the recent translation of Carlo Diano's *Form and Event* and his notion of "eventic form". In the second part I examine some of Agamben's more problematic posts over the course of the pandemic to show where the pressure points in his account of event lie. I conclude by asking what form demythologization might take today, if any, during a pandemic by reflecting on rituals in a context of genealogies of contagion and mimetic violence.

2 COVID-19 as Event / Event as COVID-19

For those interested in understanding the nature of what individuals have undergone over the last two years on account of COVID-19, a number of theories would seem decisive (Arendt 1990; 1993; Badiou 2006; Deleuze 1990; Heidegger 1989). However, no perspective on the event is more forcefully inscribed in the horizon of life and politics than the one elaborated by Michael Hardt and Antonio Negri in their book *Commonwealth*. Writing a decade ago, in the wake of a Foucauldian distinction between biopower and biopolitics, they describe the biopolitical event this way:

> The biopolitical event comes from the outside as it ruptures the continuity of history and the existing order, but it should be understood not only negatively, as rupture but also as innovation, which emerges, so to speak, from the inside (Hardt and Negri 2011, 59).

Events interest them primarily for their effects on subjects and the collective form of life that they had named "multitude" some years earlier. A biopolitical event is "an intervention in the field of subjectivity, with its accumulation of norms and modes of life, by a force of subjectification, a new production of subjectivity" (Hardt and Negri 2011, 59). The new production of subjectivity opposes global capitalism and neoliberalism as an act of resistance to biopower; it is this active

---

6 "Effective reality" as a philosophical term originates in Chapter 15 of Machiavelli's *The Prince*. For the term's relation to Italian thought, see Remo Bodei (2014, 516–528).

opposition that they characterize as an event. The biopolitical event breaks with biopower not only because it arrives from outside but also because its effects emerge from the inside, which leads to innovation and a newly produced subjectivity.

Hardt and Negri understand biopower as related not to an event but rather to an unavoidable destiny. Resistance will operate on "ontological" and "anthropological" terrains; it will be akin to "an act of freedom"; and this new subjectivity produced by the event will resist "the accumulation of norms and modes of life". Noteworthy too is the relation they see between truth and event. A subjectivity animates the event, they write, makes it possible, makes revolution possible, gives history meaning. Its ultimate meaning resides ontologically in the multitude.

By focusing on the interaction of outside and inside, Hardt and Negri clearly wish to distinguish their account of the event from others. They make this explicit:

> We also presented a biopolitical notion of the event, different from the conception that events come only "from the outside," and thus our sole political duty is to be faithful to them and their truth, to maintain discipline after the event arrives. Those who follow this notion of the event can only wait with a kind of messianic fervor for another event to come. Biopolitical events instead reside in the creative acts of the production of the common. There is indeed something mysterious about the act of creation, but it is a miracle that wells up from within the multitude every day (Hardt and Negri 2011, 176).

An ontological being held in common grounds the collective making of the common. The event does not simply begin and end with the impact on the outside but is measured in the production of a different and new subjectivity.

Certainly, after two years of the pandemic, social distancing, and mask wearing, some may feel impatient with such a theorization of the event. It does not seem clear at all that COVID-19 has led substantially to "creative acts of the production of the common" or for that matter to the appearance of an interior rupture that occurs in tandem with the outside event. Furthermore, one might ask if the biopolitical event of COVID-19 lies less in creating global resistance to capital or to the creation of a life in opposition to "the accumulation of norms" and more in having reinforced biopower, which is precisely what the biopolitical event was intended to have undercut.

As important as such a critique is, we need to move carefully. The observation that the trajectory of the pandemic does not at present confirm a creative production of subjectivity resistant to biopower does not exclude this possibility in the future. Impatience does not serve philosophical reflection, especially when the daily numbers of the contagion prove that we are still living in the time of COVID-19. To call COVID-19 an event awards it with the possibility of assembling of other events in such a way as to award it meaning for life (Burke 1984, 114). To state the obvious: what is it that makes an event in the time of COVID-19 qualify as an event? Hardt and Negri provide one clue – a biopolitical event's effects are registered in terms of freedom understood as productive of new forms of subjectivity on the inside. If some events do not arrive at the threshold of event, then what is it that distinguishes them from other events that do? What role does the relation play between an individual or more broadly a society and the event? Do "true" events share an affinity say with trauma, to the degree that "the impact of the traumatic experience lies precisely in its belatedness, in its refusal to be simply located" (Caruth 1996, 9)?

This is the context in which I want to introduce Carlo Diano's perspective on event in *Form and Event: Principles for an Interpretation of Greek Antiquity*. The book first appeared in 1952 and is Diano's attempt, framed broadly in an ontological register, to understand form and event as the two poles across which Greek antiquity can be understood. Diano's eloquent perspective on these two "categories", as he calls them, includes much more than a mere accounting of their origins in antiquity. Indeed, in Diano's existentialist view, it becomes possible to follow the play of event and form culturally and historically. To render the event meaningful for us today depends in large part on the forms that emerge as ways of "enclosing an event".

Diano's line of questioning begins with the problem of definition and here he expressly foregoes metaphysics in favour of phenomenology:

> Let's start with event. Event originates in the Latin and translates, as is often the case with Latin, the Greek word *tyche*. Event therefore is not *quicquid èvenit* [whatever happens] but rather *id quod cuique èvenit* [that which happens to each one] [. . .] The difference is crucial. If it were to rain, it is something that occurs, but that in and of itself does not make it an event. To be an event, I have to feel that such a taking place involves me [*io lo senta come un accadere per me*]. And yet, if this event appears to consciousness as an occurrence, then we know that not every occurrence is an event (Diano 2018, 89–90).

The decisive moment in Diano's analysis of event as *tyche* occurs when the ego appears in the wake of an occurrence to make the event "involve me". At first glance such a definition may seem banal. How can event function as an event if the self, the I, does not relate to the event as if the event involved, impacted, or in any way is experienced as happening to me? Obviously it cannot. Diano responds with a word dear to biopoliticians: power:

> Alright then, what power operates, what is it? What is it for me, not what is it in and of itself? How and where does it operate in the course of my life, as it marks out, even slightly an interruption or break? Choose any name you want. I am going to adopt the name that Greeks employed and say: *tyche*, an event. It is the thing that takes us by surprise, that appears to be different, that makes us see an action of a power dimly and that also underlines that a god is at work (Diano 2018, 43).

Diano points us in the direction of a fundamental definition of event: it is contingent and singular, just as the power that is represented as buttressing the event is. The phenomenological piece of Diano's readings comes to the fore here. No backward-looking fidelity to an earlier event, but instead an emphasis on interruption, not exactly Hardt and Negri's rupture of inside and outside since Diano speaks more so of the universal than the singular.

How the event becomes something for "me" depends on the nature of a particular kind of power, one that Diano will call empty as it depends for its power on the distress that one feels in its presence. It is empty because any representation of the power responsible for creating the distress or surprise experienced will not be found in a personalized narrative of who or what is responsible. According to Diano, distress and surprise do not belong to any representation of power that makes the event "involve me".[7] At its core, the event that does involve "me" does so because of the difficulty of identifying through representation the nature of the power that anchors the event.

Diano's emphasis on the impersonal and empty nature of the power should give us pause. If the subject were not free, it is difficult to see how surprise and distress would be experienced or expressed by the same subject. An important insight follows. The event is lived in the present and concerns the here and now of everyone for whom it is manifested. At the same time, it is also inscribed in the larger horizon of what takes subjects by surprise and creates distress. For Diano, the power of the event fundamentally touches on the question of why. Why now? Why me? Why is this happening right now to me? Answers will vary but no answer can ultimately be given: the nature of the event as *tyche*, as chance, as what happens when an event occurs, makes the search futile. The result is merely the personalizing of an arbitrary and ultimately empty power.

In the space that Diano opens up between event and its meaning for the self lies the possibility for freedom, which rhymes with his larger interest in Stoicism and the practice of judging those things that belong to me and those that do not, which the Stoics refer to as "externals". Thus: "Is every event therefore necessarily good? Not in and of itself but in the connection the event has with other events [. . .] Good and bad reside in judging and in the action produced by that judgment" (Diano 2018, 51). Yet, as Diano himself acknowledges in the history of *tyche* across the Hellenistic period he offers, other responses are just as likely. The name he will give to these responses to the event is "eventic form" (Diano "Appendix").

---

[7] "What holds the interest and attention of myth", Ernst Cassirer observes, is "namely the here and now of the particular case, the death of precisely this man, at this particular time" (Cassirer 1955, 49).

3 The Eventic Forms of the Pandemic

Before moving forward with the specifics of the term, it may be helpful to sketch the consequences of Diano's perspective on event for us during the time of the pandemic. What would it mean to treat COVID-19 phenomenologically, using the terms that Diano employs, to discern what is at stake during the pandemic? First, it would mean acknowledging the process by which individuals make sense of occurrences. They create narratives, they come to believe that the event is addressed to them by power that will go by different names precisely because of the empty position that it holds. Various names will be given to it: *mana* in classical anthropological terms, the virus manufactured for geopolitical aims, or God's will. Human beings narrate what happens to them, they inscribe an event in a larger series of events, and more often than not tragedy ensues. Second, the name often given to the context in which an event is made sense of – and it is a word that Diano employs – is mythology, Mythologies are written, retold, and come to be believed, precisely because the origin of the event cannot be recuperated apart from the mythology with which it is co-terminous. Pandemics are particularly fertile ground for the creation of mythologies.

Yet, and this is perhaps the most important point when considering contemporary philosophical reflections on the meaning of the pandemic, mythology always takes the form of an obscuring and covering over of the "futility" and "superfluity" of sacrifices (Horkheimer and Adorno 2002, 42). The way that individuals account for what has happened to them, by giving voice to their own subjugation, by making the event of contagion something that is theirs, makes clear the stakes of reading pandemic paradigmatically as myth. To do so means justifying the sacrificial nature of the event. The unsettling question that arises is who or what is going to be sacrificed and to what end?

Diano does not specifically answer this question but he does point us in the direction of how collective and individual forms of life arise in the wake of an event. After noting that the event breaks apart time and opens space, he observes that mankind provides "events with a structure and by enclosing them, normalizes them" (Diano 2018, 98). The process through which events are normalized by building enclosures deserves attention.

> What distinguishes human civilization as well as individual lives is the different kinds of enclosure [*chiusura*] that the *periechon's* [atmosphere, surroundings] space and time are given by them. The history of humanity (and the history of each one of us) is the history of these enclosures. Sacred moments, sacred sites, taboos, rituals and myths are nothing other than forms of enclosing (Diano 2018, 98).

Diano's history of enclosures rhymes with Heidegger's reading of dwelling and offers an inventive way of understanding COVID-19 as an event (Heidegger 1971). Event does not simply exist alone – no category does – but must be put in relation to form, enclosure in Diano's formulation. The reason for doing so, Diano answers soon after: "it is only because of form that we are able to give a structure and a direction to that incommunicable thing that is the event" (Diano 2018, 99). Since the event exceeds our ability to perceive its ultimate effects, we are invited to consider the ways through which those who are subject to the event enclose it, limit its effects, and so make the event function in terms of form. Diano is counselling us to forego an examination of the obscure origin of the pandemic, the famous "patient zero", and instead look at the ways humanity adopts a lexicon of sacrality in order to normalize the event.[8]

Social distancing in Diano's perspective would be one such eventic form of the pandemic. After more than two years, many of us know the reasons why distancing between bodies is necessary as a way of combatting the spread of the virus. The virus contained in respiratory droplets is passed more easily from one body to another the closer the bodies are to each other, hence the famous six-feet distance that has to be maintained.[9] This seems clear today but Diano's reading allows us to pose a further question. If the event of COVID-19 qualifies as an event because it "includes me"; if I risk becoming ill by not respecting the distance necessary to protect myself, then it is because the form that the event has taken cannot be separated from the event itself. There is no event as such that does not occur except through a form; they reciprocally in-form the other. On this note Diano will observe that "forms cannot be separated from events because the relation between forms and events is not about a *post* with respect to a *prius*" (Diano 2018, 99). Social distancing names one form of enclosure by which the event is limited in space and time. Importantly, the six feet of distance called social distancing would presumably have for Diano the qualities of the sacred precisely because of the inseparability of form from event.

To call a space sacred would mean for some to give it the moniker of potential sacrifice, of the place where bodies are exposed to the virus, with the potential result in contagion and ultimately death. According to one reading of the sacred, sacrifice occurs here, and as for the question of to whom the sacrifice is being offered, one answer might well be the virus itself (Di Cesare 2020). Another

---

8 On the "origins" of patient zero, see Felice Cimatti's brilliant reading from 18 March 2020, "The Metaphysics of Patient Zero, *Diacritics*, https://www.diacriticsjournal.com/the-metaphysics-of-patient-zero/. Last accessed 27 April 2022).
9 "The Science of Social Distancing." *The American Society for Microbiology*. https://asm.org/Articles/2020/April/ The-Science-of-Social-Distancing. Last accessed 27 April 2022.

answer would highlight the political and social solidarity sacrificed in favour of a communication that is merely safe; touch, contact, and intimate speech are sacrificed in the sacred site of social distance. I have more to say below about this "sacrifice" in the writings of the most famous proponent of such a perspective; clearly much is going to depend, however, on how we define the sacred.

What matters most in social distancing and the wearing of masks – aside from their efficacy in protecting those who wear them, not a small thing considering that during a pandemic it is considered a good practice to avoid contact with the sick so as not to become sick oneself – is their "eventic form". The actions adopted bring subjects into proximity of the event in order to spare them from it. The subject of the event does not want to experience the event first hand, but the fact that one has enclosed the event in such a way makes clear that the event includes one. If it did not, the subject would choose not to wear a mask and would refuse to practice social distancing. Other eventic forms could be chosen; forms do not lack in this moment of end of the world scenarios (De Martino 2019).

To be clear, Diano does not imagine a transcendent position that somehow escapes eventic forms, nor should we. This point is all too often overlooked when discussing the political and social impact of COVID-19. One follows the science and one protects oneself and one's community and family from contact with the virus. But it is also true that one adopts measures that can be both scientifically based and function as "eventic forms". Eventic forms during COVID-19 are not just modes of protection but also symbols whose function is of "a practical and not a theoretical value" (Diano 2018, 101). Social distancing, mask wearing, and the initial washing of hands do not escape the structure of the event. Instead, they are forms that give meaning to it.

We know the meaning of these eventic forms well. The eventic forms of masks and social distancing typically point to a concern for one's health but also, as so many accounts show, indicate a worry about the health of the community. They echo what Adorno and Horkheimer see as the true maxim of all Western civilization, formulated famously by Spinoza: "The endeavor of preserving oneself is the first and only basis of virtue" (Horkheimer and Adorno 2002, 22).[10] That Adorno and Horkheimer challenge Spinoza's maxim is less important than what their point allows us to put forward as a thesis. Preserving oneself, be it collectively or individually, is the most important form for enclosing the event. To say

---

[10] "Enlightenment's mythic terror springs from a horror of myth. It detects myth not only in semantically unclarified concepts and words, as linguistic criticism imagines, but in any human utterance which has no place in the functional context of self-preservation. Spinoza's proposition: 'the endeavor of preserving oneself is the first and only basis of virtue', contains the true maxim of all Western civilization" (Horkheimer and Adorno 2002, 22).

that one follows the science does not absolve mask-wearers, for instance, from acknowledging that they have also adopted an eventic form.

Can one refuse the eventic forms of the pandemic? Here I am reminded of a passage from Friedrich Kittler dear to media theorists: "A medium is a medium is a medium" (Kittler 1990, 265). For life during a pandemic, we might update Kittler's formulation this way: an event is an event is an event. The absence of masks, the failure to practice social distancing, even the refusal of vaccines – each is intended to deny that the pandemic is an event for one and for society. Yet, such a refusal does not simply remove those who do not believe in the event from engaging in eventic forms. The pandemic may not be an event for them, but that is only because other events *are* events for them. In the many justifications of those who deny COVID-19 as an event, there often appears to be a competition surrounding what qualifies as event, which begs the question whether or not such eventic forms of COVID-19 represent a threat to prior eventic forms. For many it is impossible to hold that COVID-19 is an event while simultaneously holding that another event is not. This may explain the intensity of political antagonism during the pandemic. If I do become sick, it is God's will (a phrase I heard on more than one occasion when I was visiting North Dakota during the January 2021 wave of the pandemic). To adopt the eventic forms of protection seemingly challenges a prior event to which I am subject and which is tied to sacred moments and sacred spaces.

4 Agamben's Eventic Forms

These considerations are a necessary prologue to understanding Giorgio Agamben's perspective on the pandemic over the last two years. Indeed, the impact of eventic forms on life lies at the heart of his writings and appears in one of his very first reactions, "Clarifications":

> The first thing that the wave of panic which has paralysed the country showed, was that our society believes in nothing more than bare life. It is now obvious that Italians are ready to sacrifice practically everything – their life conditions, their social relationships, their work, even their friendships, as well as their religious and political convictions – when faced with the risk of getting sick (a risk that, for now at least, is statistically not even that serious). Bare life, and the fear of losing it, is not something that unites people: rather, it blinds and separates them (Agamben 2021, 19–20).

Upon the article's publication, many immediately noted the ease with which Agamben superimposed a notion of bare life and the state of exception that he had early theorized on pandemics and emergency measures employed to combat contagion (Agamben 2017). Yet Diano's analysis of eventic forms allows further moments of criticism to be isolated, locating where precisely Agamben challenges the forms that the event has adopted. For him the eventic forms of the pandemic "have paralysed the country", have led Italians "to sacrifice practically everything", in particular "their religious and political convictions". What Agamben cannot countenance are potentially eventic forms related to the pandemic that do not belong to bare life; that would not "blind and separate" people from each other. For Agamben, eventic forms seem to lead to the unity of people, which is what separates religious and political convictions from the drift and levelling of bare life.[11]

We have now a possible answer to what is sacrificed for Agamben in the sacred moment and sacred sites that emerge in the pandemic's eventic forms. Social contact, religious and political rituals, the way that people can be together mark an event fundamentally different from previous events. The pandemic in Agamben's reading is not denied so much as it is discounted as event, in favour of some other event that has yet to take place or that has already taken place. The difference between one event and another does not lie in choice or freedom, but rather in a competing vision of whether COVID-19 qualifies as an event.

The differences between eventic forms that are truly events may be what agitates Agamben in another of his reactions. In "Medicine as Religion" he writes:

> There is a malign god or principle, namely disease, whose specific agents are bacteria and viruses, and a beneficent god or principle, which is not health, but recovery, whose cultic agents are medicines and therapy [. . .] If this cultic practice up to now was, like every liturgy, episodic and limited in time, the unexpected phenomenon that we are witnessing is that it has become permanent and all-pervasive. It is no longer a question of taking medicines or submitting when necessary to a doctor visit or surgical intervention: the whole life of human beings must become in every instant the place of an uninterrupted cultic celebration. The enemy, the virus, is always present and must be fought unceasingly and without any possible truce (Agamben 2021, 53).

According to Agamben, medicine during the pandemic extended its rituals to such a degree that the time of the event has been stretched. The event of the pandemic is not to be thought of in terms of an event that touches me directly, from which I might die, but instead is to be found in new rituals around therapy and recovery. The purposive actions that underpin cultic celebrations migrate from the distinction between science and universality to a more fundamental break –

---

[11] On the importance of the split between people and bare life, see Agamben (2000, 24–25): "One might say that modern biopolitics is supported by the principle according to which 'where there is naked life, there has to be a *People*,' as long as one adds immediately that this principle is valid also in its inverse formulation, which prescribes that 'where there is a *People*, there shall be naked life.'".

an event in Agamben's view which is the conflict among capitalism, science (medicine), and Christianity.

In order to create this break, Agamben deftly leaves most of science behind and, with a sleight of hand, shows how medicine and virology, in taking of the human body as object, blur the boundaries between science and cultic celebration. He writes that: "It is not surprising that the protagonist of this new religious war is the very branch of science whose dogmatics is less rigorous and whose pragmatic aspect is stronger: that is, medicine, whose object is the living human body" (Agamben 2021, 53). These transpositions individualize the event differently, so that doctors and virologists are seen as usurping other cultic practices that before would have been used to enclose the event symbolically.

Agamben describes these practices again in "Clarifications", where they appear as part of Christian mercy:

> The Christian religion, with its works of love and mercy and its faith to the point of martyrdom; political ideology, with the ethos of unconditional solidarity; even belief in work and money – these all seem to have taken second place as soon as bare life came under threat, albeit in the form of a risk whose statistical extent was labile and deliberately indeterminate (Agamben 2021, 31).

Perhaps the pandemic troubles Agamben because of the possibility that treating COVID-19 as an event will make it more difficult to sacrifice one's life in order to show that faith has not been relinquished; this is true regardless of whether one is speaking about Christianity or capitalism. Agamben refuses to surrender the need for sacrifice, of the acts of faith that point to a different event, one whose forms are not located in health or recovery but in the possibility that one might lose one's life because of one's faith. "Cultic forms" of medicine and virology remove the risk of losing one's life, and so forego the possibility of sacrificing for some thing or some power that would provide meaning for the event.

As both Warren Montag and Davide Tarizzo have noted, much of Agamben's recent perspective on bare life seems at odds with how he described bare life before.[12] Here it seems based less on the operation of anthropological machines and much more on belief or even ideology. The passage also throws light on why the late Jean-Luc Nancy's rejoinder to Agamben's "Invention of the Epidemic" last year remains so powerful (Nancy 2021, 28). Yes, Agamben believes in the possibility of sacrifice and sees in the eventic forms of medicine a threat to what qualifies as an event. The power of sacrifice is based on the possibility of non-recovery. It also

---

[12] Warren Montag did so in the conference, "Biopolitics & COVID-19", held on November 17, 2020. In slightly different fashion, Davide Tarizzo critiqued Agamben in a seminar he offered my students on biopolitics and COVID-19 during the fall of 2021.

indicates something else: the figure of *homo sacer* that has been the subject of so many volumes and much research on his part troubles him because it cannot potentially sacrifice itself. *Homo sacer* cannot practice eventic forms that matter most to Agamben, which are premised on the possibility and promise of dying for someone or something; of it being possible to sacrifice oneself.

Agamben's account of the pandemic depends for its force on denying that COVID-19 is an event for each of us, not simply because of its indeterminate threat but because we can recover from it. His doubling-down against the various eventic forms of mask-wearing, social distancing, and vaccine mandates make clear how much his reading of the virus and bare existence depends not simply on denying the pandemic but on denying its power as event.

5 Eventic Forms Without Sacrifice

If we are to respond to Agamben, we will need to imagine a different relation between the event of the pandemic and its forms. Although one might want to domesticate medicine and virology once again, given the fact that in my own country last year nearly a third of the population was sceptical about vaccines, the chances seem slim: the mythical thinking that has ravaged the country over the last six years both politically and culturally has created a deeply impolitical moment, in which nearly everything has fallen to a politicization of those things that do not properly belong to the political.[13] A more promising tack, following Diano's lead, might be refraining from identifying the event as an event that is happening to me. What changes if the event does not elicit an individual "why me" or a collective "why us"?

One answer may lie in how we name events. Consider Diano's final reflections near the end of *Form and Event*:

> One of the most obvious examples of enclosing an event are those that employ names [. . .] [M]yth is the figure of event which makes the archetype a ritual [. . .] There are rituals without being myths but a myth is not a myth without enjoying a relation to ritual and to the act of celebrating that ritual, in which only the myth can be lived as event (Diano 2018, 99–100).

Diano here is rehearsing an insight that has become commonplace during the last five years of populism and fake news: the power that inheres in naming reality

---

[13] "AP-NORC poll: A Third of US Adults Skeptical of COVID shots," 10 February 2021, https://apnews.com/article/ap-norc-poll-3rd-adult-skeptical-vaccine-3779574a6d45d38cfc1d8615eb176b2d. On the notion of the impolitical in relation to the philosopher Roberto Esposito, see my "Genres of the Political: The Impolitical Comedy of Conflict" (Campbell 2021, 60–82).

may be the most powerful of them all: we enclose events through the names we give them and we know the various names we have given the pandemic: Covid, COVID-19, the Delta Variant, the Omicron variant, or most recently Deltacron. Each names the mythic figure of event that is ultimately called contagion. But Diano's compact description suggests something else. Some rituals appear to descend from myths while others do not. Some myths exist in relation to an archetype while others do not. Myth is lived as event through ritual, though by the same token it seems possible to imagine living an event without myth through ritual. A ritual without myth is the one in which an event is not lived as a form; is not mythologized, since the archetype has been relinquished. Another genealogy of ritual can be conceived that does not require a myth; does not devolve sooner or later into archetype.

Diano suggests that we move carefully when deciding how to enclose events in forms since some returns to form may lead to a return to archetype. The reason is because when myth and ritual dynamically and mutually charge each other, the event is more likely to be lived as the repetition of the archetype that includes me (for Agamben the rituals surrounding bare life). The choices for a subject of the event of COVID-19 still appear to be few. In order to live the event, one chooses a ritual associated with a myth and thus with a different archetype. No position is available from which to enclose the event that is not actualized or activated according to rituals. Both positions meet at the intersection of the political and theological in a horizon of contagion and death.

This raises a question, one on which I would like to linger as my reflections come to a close. As helpful as Diano is for explicating the prison-house of eventic forms during a pandemic, he is less helpful for imagining an alternative in which an individual is able to live the event without enclosing it in a mythic form. This would be an eventic form that does not traffic in the political-theological, one that does not presume that the eventic form only takes place through rituals. Is it possible to live the event as one that does not include me or that may include me initially, but which does not set in motion those procedures that Diano describes that inevitably lead to the event that includes me?

A first step lies in thinking the sacred differently from Diano, since doing so breaks the relation between ritual and myth that lies at the heart of his notion of eventic form. René Girard in *Violence and the Sacred* offers a potential path forward:

> The sacred consists of all those forces whose dominance over man increases or seems to increase in proportion to man's effort to master them. Tempests, forest fires, and plagues, among other phenomena, may be classified as sacred. Far outranking these, however, though in a far less obvious manner, stands human violence – violence seen as something

exterior to man and henceforth as a part of all the other outside forces that threaten mankind. Violence is the heart and secret soul of the sacred (Girard 1979, 32).

From this perspective, it is not the myths that enclose the form of the event that name the sacred, but instead the forces of Nature that increase despite man's efforts to master them. In such a reading COVID-19 and its variants would seemingly be considered sacred. Note how Girard, when discussing these "other phenomena" as sacred, postpones sacrifice as the defining feature of the sacred and instead invites us to plot how the virus and its variants have been met by our attempts to evade it, contain it, or master it. He imagines what we might call a sacred *lite* though he quickly retreats to return the heart of the sacred to violence.

Let us also note how Girard examines the relation of the plague to violence in Sophocles's *Oedipus*. His perspective on the "sacrificial crisis" is of singular importance. In the Oedipus myth "the fearful transgression", he writes, "of a single individual is substituted for the universal onslaught of reciprocal violence. Oedipus is responsible for the ills that have befallen his people. He has become a prime example of the human scapegoat" (Girard 1979, 81). Two movements characterize the crisis: on the one hand, the collective character of the disaster of Oedipus is represented in the plague. On the other, the motif of patricide and incest is "presented [. . .] in highly concentrated form, but limited to a single individual" (Girard 1979, 81). Girard's analysis shows how Oedipus is blamed, allowing the Thebans to convince themselves that their miseries were due solely to the plague and not to the community itself. In such a scenario myth works to free the community from responsibility for what happened. What is required is to rid the community of the "sole malignant element", Oedipus in this case. What is required for the Thebans is an acknowledgment of a community's responsibility for contagion, as well as noticing and accounting for what goes missing when miseries are lumped together under the banner of plague and the lone scapegoat. For Girard enclosing the event as a sacred space works above all to absolve the community of responsibility.

Girard's lesson is difficult to grasp during the pandemic. Blaming those who do not wear masks or who have not been vaccinated or blaming those who support measures of social distancing – in both of these instances the community foregoes its responsibility for what has taken place. For Girard, such a responsibility will always be found in violence. Indeed, he writes of the mimetic character of violence in communities such that "each person prepares himself for the probable aggression of his neighbors and interprets his neighbor's preparations as confirmation of the latter's aggressiveness" (Girard 1979, 86). "Violence is not originary", Girard writes elsewhere. "[I]t is a by-product of mimetic rivalry. Violence is mimetic rivalry itself becoming violent as the antagonists who desire the same object, keep thwarting each other and desiring the object all the more. Violence is supremely mimetic" (Girard 2000, 11).

This may explain in part the heightened social antagonism that became more intense during COVID-19. The pandemic occurred in a context of accumulated grievance after years of greater sectarian antagonism in the United States particularly. In such a context it is natural that something like COVID-19 would lead to mimetic violence, given that eventic forms compete among themselves around whether COVID-19 or public health measures ultimately qualify as event. The power of these eventic forms depends on earlier forms of mimetic desire and violence that would in Diano's reading need to be seen against the backdrop of a power that precisely because it is empty can be given different names and hence fought over.

What ought to be the response of the community? Girard is not sanguine. If there is a struggle around scapegoating, the other name that he gives for the way by which mythical reconciliation and ritual practice are produced, then "as in the case of drugs, consumers of sacrifice tend to increase the doses when the effect becomes more difficult to achieve" (Girard 2000, 17). More victims result, which propels him to try to imagine a non-sacrificial significance to the Judeo-Christian scriptures. For my part, the gesture to let go of sacrificial dynamics for a reading of the sacred is symptomatic of what is needed and what is least visible: the sacred without sacrifice; ritual without myth; eventic forms that do not create in their wake the possibility of heightened sacrifice and mimetic violence that originate in the event having included me.

Is it possible to wear masks, maintain social distance, engage with and adopt eventic forms while understanding that these forms maintain a relation with the notion of the sacred that includes sacrifice? Is it possible to practice rituals differently? The Italian philosopher Mario Perniola, across a lifetime of research of Roman religion and rituals, speaks of "the ritual of the ritual", the ritual without myth. Of interest to him is how the Stoics proposed to live in the realm of the in-between, between the sacred and profane. He writes: "The ritual of the ritual is the ritual without myth, the demythization of myth" (Perniola 2001, 81). In an intricate and breath-taking reading, Perniola links ritual to the labyrinth, such that the former becomes "a labyrinth without entrances or exits that has value only in and of itself and not as a test to be passed or as an obstacle to be overcome" (Perniola 2001, 94). One moves between the sacred and profane, between life and death in an intermediary realm, and by overcoming obstacles, the Roman citizen "transits" between the sacred and the profane. Essentially, Perniola is arguing for the autonomy of rituals apart from mythology.

In one of his last essays, he describes "the disavowal of the autonomy of the rite" and the "prejudice of a tradition that is willing to find sense in the gesture only if this is subordinate to the word". Repetitive actions that do not find "a point of support in a genealogical story, in an individual or collective belief, are considered almost unanimously by the Western philosophical tradition as an empty behavior" (Perniola 2010, 28). Instead, he imagines repetitive actions apart from eventic forms. In a pandemic, that might mean putting on a mask or maintaining social distance not because of belief, but because these gestures exist apart from mythology.

Can one adopt measures, repeat actions, not because of a belief that the event includes one or does not and instead adopt rituals not subordinate to "ritual"? To do so would involve a practice of ritualizing without the creation of rituals, of gesturing without inscribing gestures in the horizon of a myth. Ultimately, it would be an impolitical practice, in which restraint about linking the gesture to collective or individual belief will need to be practiced.[14] The difficulty of imagining what such a practice resembles does not foreclose the significance of imagining it. For as long as eventic forms compete among themselves for dominance, we will continue to repeat gestures in ritualistic fashion whose effect is to reinforce the usual mythologies, and with them the violence that underpins the competition among eventic forms.

References

Agamben, Giorgio. *The Omnibus Homo Sacer*. Stanford: Stanford University Press, 2017.
Agamben, Giorgio. *Means without End*. Trans. Vincenzo Binetti and Cesare Casarino. Minneapolis: University of Minnesota Press, 2000.
Agamben, Giorgio. *Where Are We Now? Epidemic as Politics*. Trans. Valeria Dani. EPUB. London: Eris, 2021.
Arendt, Hannah. *On Revolution*. London: Penguin, 1990.
Arendt, Hannah. "The Concept of History: Ancient and Modern." *Between Past and Future: Eight Exercises in Political Thought*. London: Penguin, 1993. 41–90.
Badiou, Alain. *Being and Event*. Trans. Oliver Feltham. London: Continuum, 2006.
Bodei, Remo. "Italian: A Philosophy for Non-Philosophers Too." *Dictionary of Untranslatables: A Philosophical Lexicon*. Eds. Barbara Cassin, Emily Apter, Jacques Lezra, Michael Wood. Princeton: Princeton University Press, 2014. 516–528.
Burke, Kenneth. *Permanence and Change: An Anatomy of Purpose*. Berkeley: University of California Press, 1984.
Butler, Judith. "Interview: Mourning is a Political Act Amid the Pandemic and Its Disparities." *Journal of Bioethical Inquiry* 17.4 (2020): 483–487.

---

14 On the impolitical as a practice, see Campbell and Farred 2022.

Campbell, Timothy. "Genres of the Political: The Impolitical Comedy of Conflict." *Roberto Esposito: New Directions in Biophilosophy*. Eds. Tilottama Rajan and Antonio Calcagno. Edinburgh: Edinburgh University Press, 2021. 60–82.

Campbell, Timothy, and Grant Farred. *The Comic Self*. Minneapolis: The University of Minnesota Press, 2023.

Campbell, Timothy, and Adam Sitze, eds. *Biopolitics: A Reader*. Durham: Duke University Press, 2013.

Caruth, Cathy. "Trauma and Experience: Introduction." *Trauma: Explorations in Memory*. Ed. Cathy Caruth. Baltimore, MD: Johns Hopkins University Press, 1996. 3–12.

Cassirer, Ernst. *The Philosophy of Symbolic Forms, Volume 2: Mythical Thought*. Trans. Ralph Manheim. New Haven: Yale University Press, 1955.

Castrillón, Fernando, and Thomas Marchevskye, eds. *Coronavirus, Psychoanalysis, and Philosophy: Conversations on Pandemics*. London: Routledge, 2021.

Cimatti, Felice. 2022. "The Metaphysics of Patient Zero, *Diacritics*, https://www.diacriticsjournal.com/the-metaphysics-of-patient-zero/. Last accessed 27 April 2022.

Deleuze, Gilles. *The Logic of Sense*. Trans. Mark Lester and Charles Stivale. Ed. Constantin Boujndas. London: Athlone Press, 1990.

De Martino, Ernesto. *La fine del mondo: Contributo all'analisi delle apocalissi culturali*. Turin: Einaudi, 2019.

Diano, Carlo. *Form and Event: Principles for an Interpretation of the Greek World*. Trans. Timothy Campbell and Lia Turtas. New York: Fordham University Press, 2018.

Di Cesare, Donatella. *Immunodemocracy: Capitalist Asphyxia*. New York: Semiotext(e), 2021.

Di Cesare, Donatella. *Do Not Touch Me: Seeking Immunity to All Things Foreign*. Summer 2020. https://www.vision.org/interview-donatella-di-cesare-do-not-touch-me-9131. Weblog. Last accessed 27 April 2022.

Esposito, Roberto. "Cured to the Bitter End (February 28, 2020)." *Coronavirus, Psychoanalysis, and Philosophy: Conversations on Pandemics*. Eds. Fernando Castrillón and Thomas Marchevsky. London: Routledge, 2021. 28–29.

Esposito, Roberto. "The Enigma of Biopolitics." *Biopolitics: A Reader*. Eds. Timothy Campbell and Adam Sitze. Durham: Duke University Press, 2013. 317–349.

Foucault, Michel. "Right of Death and Power Over Life." *Biopolitics: A Reader*. Eds. Timothy Campbell and Adam Sitze. Durham: Duke University Press, 2013. 41–60.

Foucault, Michel."'Society Must Be Defended,' Lectures at the Collège de France, March 17, 1976." *Biopolitics: A Reader*. Eds. Timothy Campbell and Adam Sitze. Durham: Duke University Press, 2013. 61–81.

Girard, René. *Violence and the Sacred*. Trans. Patrick Gregory. Baltimore: Johns Hopkins Press, 1979.

Girard, René. *The Girard Reader*. Ed. James G. Williams. New York: The Crossroad Publishing Company, 2000.

Hardt, Michael, and Antonio Negri. *Commonwealth*. Cambridge: Harvard University Press, 2011.

Heidegger, Martin. *Poetry, Language, Thought*. Trans. A. Hofstadter. New York: HarperCollins, 1971.

Heidegger, Martin. *Contributions to Philosophy (of the Event)*. Trans. Richard Rojcewicz and Daniela Vallega-Neu. Bloomington: Indiana University Press, 1989.

Horkheimer, Max, and Theodor W. Adorno, *Dialectic of Enlightenment: Philosophical Fragments*. Trans. Edmund Jephcott. Stanford: Stanford University Press, 2002.

Kittler, Friedrich. *Discourse Networks 1800–1900*. Trans. Michael Metteer and Chris Cullins. Stanford: Stanford University Press, 1990.

Latour, Bruno. "Is This a Dress Rehearsal?" *Critical Inquiry*. https://critinq.wordpress.com/2020/03/26/is-this-a-dress-rehearsal/. Weblog. Last accessed 27 April 2022.

Malabou, Catherine. "To Quarantine from Quarantine: Rousseau, Robinson Crusoe, and 'I'." *Critical Inquiry*. https://critinq.wordpress.com/2020/03/23/to-quarantine-from-quarantine-rousseau-robinson-crusoe-and-i/. Weblog. Last accessed 27 April 2022.

Nancy, Jean-Luc. "A Viral Exception." *Coronavirus, Psychoanalysis, and Philosophy: Conversations on Pandemics*. Eds. Fernando Castrillón and Thomas Marchevsky. London: Routledge, 2021. 27.

Perniola, Mario. *Più-che sacro, più-che-profano*. E-Book. Milan: Mimesis, 2010.

Perniola, Mario. *Ritual Thinking: Sexuality, Death, World*. Trans. Massimo Verdicchio. Amherst, NY: Humanity Books, 2001.

Žižek, Slavoj. *Pandemic! COVID-19 Shakes the World*. London: Polity, 2020.

Sherryl Vint
Biopolitics, Form-of-Life, A New Use of Bodies

Abstract: This chapter draws on Giorgio Agamben's idea of the "use" [*chresis*] of bodies as a way to ground a metaphysics distinct from the structures of European modernity. Understanding the COVID-19 pandemic as a governance event that made starkly visible two ways of thinking about our taken-for-granted structures of biopolitical governance. First, it demonstrated unequivocally the uneven distribution of chances to thrive or exposure to the risk of death that structures racialized and class binaries within modernity. Second, in the decision to suspend some operations of business-as-usual capitalism to slow the spread of the pandemic, this experience revealed that it is possible to live another way, contra the prevalent ideology of austerity that insists there is no alternative to capitalism and its privileging of economic growth. Turning to a speculative fiction novel, *Ammonite* by Nicola Griffith, about a fictional plague in a colonial context, the chapter demonstrates how the themes of the novel align with Agamben's ideas about the use of bodies, and further how we might thus extrapolate from the novel to our recent pandemic context via the recognition that new structures of subjectivity are the ground from which we need to proceed to articulate new political orders of greater social justice.

1 Introduction

This chapter explores connections between the COVID-19 pandemic and biopolitics from two distinct and counterposed standpoints. First and most obviously, the experience of the pandemic has made the debilitating consequences of biopolitical governance starkly obvious to mainstream culture from the differential rates of infection and death experienced by marginalized peoples and communities, to the polarized political debates pitting the health of the citizenry against that of the economy as mask mandates and commercial lockdowns were imposed and contested. These debates turn as well on questions of the precarity and privilege, in the constitutive biopolitical question of whose lives are nurtured and protected – and at the cost of which other lives. How one experienced and thus how one theorizes the coronavirus pandemic is inescapably shaped by such matters of standpoint. As someone writing from within the United States, a country with a sparce social safety net, privatized and non-universal healthcare, and a normalized condition of extreme economic inequality, two things stand out for me. First is the

https://doi.org/10.1515/9783110799361-006

degree to which the biopolitical dialectic between protected and denigrated life become visible as the central modality of governance today: the calculus by which some lives are sustained and enabled to thrive at the expense of others was clearly visible in the daily choices made regarding access to respirators and ICU beds, transformation to hospitals (or not), and ultimately access to vaccines. How such matters map to existing racial and class inequalities also became difficult to deny in a context in which some were able to work safely from home (my personal situation), while others had to risk their health to provide services for the larger society that "must", as Foucault notes in the title of one of his lecture series, "be defended", while yet another group lost work and income entirely and were left to survive as best they could in a context where social inclusion is predicated on economic productivity. The global experience of the pandemic made plain the unequal foundations of liberal democratic orders through which biopolitical governance at the level of bodies reinscribes and at times exacerbates racialized and other existing inequalities.[1] Further, as zoonotic diseases, coronaviruses necessarily remind us of our entanglement with other species on the planet and of potential consequences that follow from the ways in which human actions destroy habitats, displace species, and create novel points of contact among them that can lead to microbial transfer. From this first perspective, the COVID-19 pandemic emblematizes all that is destructive to peoples and environments in capitalist modernity's biopolitical mode.

From my situated position, however, the second thing that stands out to me is that the pandemic also created a period during which many people, especially in the Global North, momentarily paused our business-as-usual lives, a pause that extended long enough that we were able to question whether the pre-pandemic "normal" is something toward which we should rush to return. By so conclusively

---

[1] Many of my colleagues whose work also appears in this volume, writing from other histories and embedded contexts, emphasize the massive expansion of government surveillance and restriction of civil liberties under the condition of a public health emergency. I take their point that both the state and private surveillance capitalism have enriched themselves (in wealth and power) in this context. From my own situated position, the fact that the normal rules of neoliberal accumulation were also disrupted emerges as the more urgent question. Michael Eskin's emphasis on the thanatopolitical side of US culture's normative mode, especially vis-à-vis African Americans, more closely aligns with the concerns I raise here. Yet my argument makes the case that we should not see the more humane moments of generosity such as moratoriums on evictions, the provision of free healthcare and the like as relevant only in a state of exception. As has become clear in the last two years, these kinds of measures have ended as the pandemic has been deemed over, while the expansion of surveillance and the concentration of wealth in the hands of tech entrepreneurs has only intensified. Thus in the longer perspective, these concerns are perhaps ultimately the more pressing.

making visible the gap between the ideals of democratic societies and the realities of neoliberal biopolitics, the pandemic opened a space for new political conversations about change, which range from the minor key of businesses rethinking possibilities for remote work, creating less commuter pollution and perhaps more time for non-work life, to the more radical demand that we reject and restructure a social order that inevitably produces such differential health outcomes for distinct communities due to embedded structures of discrimination. From this second point of view – while of course taking care not to overlook the losses that so many have experienced – the disaster of the pandemic might be seen as a prompt to question the foundations of the harsh biopolitical and neoliberal world order that we had come to take for granted. From this position, we can recognize that the disaster that the pandemic has been for so many represents less a disruption to pre-pandemic life than an intensification of the most damaging aspects of "normal" life in its thanatopolitical mode. Thus rather than desire a return to pre-pandemic norms, we might from this second viewpoint see the experience of the pandemic as a prompt to recognize that there can be other ways to live. Alongside Raili Marling in this volume, I am interested in how this historical experience might enable us to cultivate a relational and affirmative biopolitics.

I approach the possibilities embodied by this second way of thinking about the legacies of the coronavirus pandemic by turning to a novel about a fictional pandemic, Nicola Griffith's *Ammonite* (2002). I read the novel via Giorgio Agamben's arguments about a new ontology of the living, outlined predominantly in his *Use of Bodies*.[2] Like Agamben, Griffith calls for a new understanding of what it means to be a human and suggests that this different way of being also requires us to reimagine community and governance beyond the destructive biopolitical binaries (human/nonhuman, citizen/migrant, made-to-live/left-to-die) that structure modernity. Speculative fiction is a useful tool for this kind of imaginative political work precisely because of the genre's emphasis on worldbuilding: that is,

---

2 It is important to note here that while I draw on Agamben's philosophy to read this novel of a pandemic in the wake of the experience of COVID-19, I am drawing specifically on Agamben's rethinking of subjectivity through inoperativity. His own writings specifically about the public health restrictions enacted to combat the spread of the virus – collected in *Where Are We Now? The Epidemic as Politics* (2021) – draws on his critique of western authoritarianism via the state of exception in ways that I do not agree with. Specifically, I draw a distinction between the extension of public health measures in the context of a pandemic with a high mortality rate in the pre-vaccine stage of coronavirus and the larger critique of biopolitical governance via systems of control that Agamben theorizes as the constitutive mode of the modern state. Of course, distinctions between "real" states of exception and the normalized logic of the state of exception are themselves matters of debate; in this case, I take the pre-vaccine period of coronavirus to constitute such as "real" historical moment when unusual public health measures were necessary.

on creating a reality that functions differently than the reality its readers experience in their daily lives. Nothing can be taken for granted in a well-written work of speculative fiction, because its world's "common sense" is distinct from that structuring our quotidian world. Thus, speculative fiction can offer the radical, imaginative engagement with alterity that is required for Agamben's ambitious political critique, which asks us to rethink and remake western metaphysics as a whole.

2 Dasein, Living, *Chresis*

Use of Bodies is something of a culmination to Agamben's concern with a political tradition founded on the separation of some *Homo sapiens* (deemed human) from other life, including some members of our species (designated as sub – or non-human). According to Agamben, the foundations of human community within modernity thus rely on a structure of abjected inclusion-via-exclusion. In *Use of Bodies*, he stresses that this splitting – the becoming human of the human by its separation from animals and animalized others – is an ongoing event, precisely the reality that has been made visible by the unevenly distributed consequences of COVID-19.

In *Use of Bodies* Agamben suggests that we are living in the "shipwreck" (2015, xxi) of a Heideggerian tradition that has separated Being from living, in which the special capacity of the Dasein – its *having* of the world – covers over what life has in common. Among the problems with the Dasein is that it is not an inherent property of the species but rather a structure or orientation that *creates* the subject as the result of a task or a test: becoming human must be achieved, and the living being is "abolished and suspended so that Dasein may have a place" (Agamben 2015, 180). With the production of the Dasein, then, comes the production of bare life, because this way of theorizing humanity as a task requires that one presupposes an animal-human that comes before this human, that is, mere existence as *Homo sapiens* does not equate to the essence of the human/Dasein. Agamben focuses on this gap between what comes before the Dasein – which is not fully human by Heidegger's account – and specifically on the possibility that might be attached to the living being that exists "before or beneath it [Dasein,] a non-human human being that can or must be transformed into Dasein" (Agamben 2015, 205). According to Agamben's reading of Heidegger, then, there is no Dasein without bare life being simultaneously produced as its remainder. In his intervention, Agamben seeks to find a way outside of this binary via his interest in the kind of life that comes before this splitting into Dasein and bare life.

The limitations of this Heideggerian metaphysics of Being prompt Agamben to theorize an ontology of *living* rather than one of Being and to call continually for the suspension of what he calls the anthropogenic machine, that is, this ongoing production of Dasein from the abjection of other forms of life. In *Use of Bodies*, he suggests that living in this way requires the "destitution of the social and biological conditions into which it [life] finds itself thrown" (Agamben 2015, 277) and he seeks "to delineate the contours of a form-of-life and of a common use of bodies" (Agamben 2015, xxi) that could transform politics as well as metaphysics. Agamben articulates this as a desire for "the possibility of a relation with the self and of a form of life that never assumes the figure of a free subject" (Agamben 2015, 108): this is because the "free subject" as understood in western metaphysics can "find free political action and the work of the human being [only] by excluding – and at the same time including [via exclusion] – the use of the body and the inoperativity of the slave" (Agamben 2015, 45). The slave in this formulation, it is important to emphasise, refers to Hegel's master/slave dialectic as it pertains to the metaphysics of subjectivity in Western thought. Although the material suffering of enslaved peoples is not contemplated in this philosophical mode of talking about "the slave", it is relevant to take note of the non-contingent relation between a tradition of thought which sees intersubjectivity in terms of the struggle for dominance and the colonial political order that has structured modernity. Although Agamben himself is often insufficiently attentive to this dimension of Western culture, we should not lose sight of it as we contemplate his provocation toward a new metaphysics of subjectivity that will enable another kind of life/subject.

The slave in this context, then, becomes an important figure for Agamben's desired relation between the self and a new form-of-life. In Agamben's way of approaching this figure, the slave becomes an image of possibility rather than of deprivation, following the theorization of the slave in the Classical tradition to which Agamben responds. Aristotle theorizes the slave as a fundamentally different category of human being: the slave is a living kind of property, part of the *oikos* and someone whose *ergon* or task is different from that of the citizen. The "life of action" is the proper task of the citizen and Aristotle relates this to the unique human capacity for *logos* or reason: the human *ergon* needs to be more than just the simple fact of living and thus excludes the vegetative (nutrition and growth) and the sensitive (sense data; which animals share) aspects of our being. The slave, in contrast, is purported to have physical capacities but insufficient *logos* and thus is directed by the master, whose reason guides both his own and the slave's actions (the gender specific language is deliberate, as the master/patriarch also provides *logos* for others deemed less capable, like women and children).

Agamben objects that the gap Aristotle posits between the kind of human embodied as a slave and the fully human master/citizen has "no content other than the pure fact of the caesura as such" and further that this break means that "the concept of life will not truly be thought as long as the biopolitical machine, which has always already captured it [life] within itself [the machine] by means of a series of divisions and articulations, has not been deactivated" (Agamben 2015, 203). This "concept of life" is something that Agamben elsewhere calls a natural life, which is distinct from bare life in that natural life is not marked by lack or exclusion; that is, bare life (*zoë*) is produced as the opposite or remainder of the Dasein/citizen (*bios*), but natural life exists before or beyond the operations of such categories.

Natural life is thus not informed by the binaries that structure Western thought, binaries that, in Agamben's analysis, separate the act of *living* from an abstract notion of *life as such*.

> Just as the tradition of metaphysics has always thought the human being in the form of an articulation between two elements (nature and *logos*, body and soul, animality and humanity), so also has Western political philosophy always thought politics in the figure of the relation between two figures that it is a question of linking together: bare life and power, the household and the city, violence and institutional order, anomie (anarchy) and law, multitude and people. (Agamben 2015, 272)

Rethinking Being/Dasein thus enables rethinking all of these binaries, and what interests Agamben throughout his work is a third term or a "zone of indiscernibility" between such structuring binaries. He explains this third term through an analogy to the concept of the Christian trinity: something that is distinct from the two poles which form the binary and which complicates our sense of the difference between them, in that it is both of them but not them, and at the same time something that does not collapse the poles into a unity that erases all distinction. When life and the living, bios and *zoë*, "contract into one another and fall together" (Agamben 2015, 223), the possibility of a third term emerges; as Agamben puts it, "The soul is not (only) *zoè* [sic], natural life, or (only) *bios*, politically qualified life: it is, *in them and between them*, that which, while not coinciding with them, keeps them united and inseparable and, at the same time, prevents them from coinciding with each other" (Agamben 2015, 261). Moving beyond Western binaries to this new modality of relation between the living and form-of-life is what Agamben contends will create a new kind of political community; and "use of bodies" is the phrase he uses to describe this link between "the life by means of which we live" and that which "renders life livable and gives to it a sense and a form" (Agamben 2015, 226).

The slave is a figure of promise for Agamben because, in antiquity, the slave was seen as outside the *logos* relation to human life as a task or project (*ergon*): the master's relation to the body is directed by this notion of work, but the slave has something else, the use of the body designated by the term *chresis*. This term is a specific and reflexive one that is different from our modern notion of the verb "to use" in that *chresis* does not operate on the basis of a subject/object binary. *Chresis* exists in the doing of the act, and in *chresis* there is no abstract end or purpose to the activity beyond the activity itself. Moreover, according to Aristotle, the slave's activity is disconnected from the marketplace and thus from notions of production and accumulation, aspects of this form-of-life beyond *ergon* that are particularly striking as we try to undo the damaging metaphysics that have produced capitalism and colonialism. As Agamben describes it, this "use of body" by the slave in antiquity is something different than what we would now call labour under the wage relation; rather, *chresis* denotes activities that "preserve the memory or evoke the paradigm of a human activity that is reducible neither to labor, nor to production, nor to praxis" (Agamben 2015, 20). Such activity, to live through use rather than through the directed action of the master, offers a model of being that does not partake of the Dasein's having of the world and is not invested in notions of property. In contrast to the Dasein, *chresis* reflects a capacity or quality that is held in common by all living beings.

But *chresis* as a specific capacity of use has another connotation that is key to Agamben's intervention: to use something is to "enter into a relation of use with something", which means to be affected or changed by it, that is, to "constitute myself as one who makes use of it" (Agamben 2015, 30). This reciprocity is why *chresis* cannot be described via a subject/object relation; rather, "Human being and world are, in use, in a relationship of absolute and reciprocal immanence; in the using of something, it is the very being of the one using that is first of all at stake" (Agamben 2015, 30). Use conceived in this way offers Agamben a figuration of living that is before or beyond what he frequently terms the "capture" of the living being in the biopolitical machine of modernity. The classical ideal of the slave offers an image or model of an unmediated relationship with the world/nature, contra modernity's destructive relationship with the environment that emerges from our juridical configuration of subjectivity via mastery, according to Agamben. As he explains it, "a dominion of the relation between the human being and nature is rendered possible precisely by the fact that the relation of the human being with nature is not immediate but mediated by his or her relation with other human beings" (Agamben 2015, 15). In effect, the master's use of the slave's body is an extension of the master's *ergon*, thus the slave mediates the master's relationship with nature. In living rather than Being, we do not *have* a life but we *are* that life. Use enables a different subjectivity form than that of Dasein, for which Agamben uses the term "the self". Unlike the subject, the self cannot be split, something he glosses with the term "to dwell". This self is not an abstract thing but a relation, always in use, always thus open to change; indeed, the living being is a relation of use with/of oneself: "*The self is nothing more than use-of-oneself*" (Agamben 2015, 54). But this self is use-of-oneself of a very specific type: use as *chresis*, a use that "means not pre-supposing oneself, not appropriating being to oneself in order to subjectivate oneself in a separate substance" (Agamben 2015, 55).

In this phrase, with its emphasis on splitting the self into two substances, we can see how the concept of *chresis* opens up a different metaphysics than the structures of subjectivity that pertain to the Dasein – that is, the anthropogenic machine – precisely because there is no pre-supposed "non-human human being" (Agamben 2015, 205) that is separated and subjected such that the Dasein might appear. This gets us closer to what Agamben means by "dwelling", which is a relationship to activity not in the form of labour or in the form of a project/*ergon* – not in the form of "a potential which is realized and consumed" in use (Agamben 2015, 62) – but rather as the ongoing dwelling in habit, a state of immanence and a kind of work: "the work is that in which potential and habit are still present, still in use; it is the dwelling of habit, which does not stop appearing [. . .] ceaselessly reopening it [the work] to a new, possible use" (Agamben 2015, 62). Habitual use is a modality of living rather than Being, and this sense of untapped new, possible uses of our bodies/capacities is why Agamben argues that a new metaphysics of subjectivity (of the self) is key to new social and political orders.

3 Dwelling Outside the Human Project

It may seem that we have moved very far indeed from the opening frame of this paper, namely the biopolitical order under the shadow of the COVID-19 pandemic, but these seemingly abstract questions about subjectivity and selfhood are crucial to helping us recognize that living through the pandemic has illuminated the political consequences of Western metaphysics to such a degree that it now becomes easier to imagine how theorizing subjectivity otherwise can lead to new politics and new ethics. Following Agamben, I want to suggest that in order to address the disparities and debilitations entrenched within our structures of biopolitical governance, we need to think not merely in terms of shifting policies but also more capaciously – to recognize that a flawed metaphysics lies at the heart of our political systems. This concerns both relations between humanity and other species *and* our way of conceptualizing the human, which necessarily produces some people as its subhuman remainder. Thinking about the metaphysics of the "use of bodies" in the context of the COVID-19 pandemic, then, reminds us that these philosophical frameworks are not merely abstract ponderings: rather, they have material effects, even if we do not immediately think of metaphysics when seeking to address such political issues.

Agamben does not condone Aristotle's rationalization of slavery, but instead he engages in a *détournement* of the conceptual (and hierarchical) framework of master/slave to suggest that there is something valuable in the slave's status outside humanity-as-project. He contends that "the master/slave relation as we know it represents the capture in the juridical order of the use of bodies as an originary prejuridical relation" (Agamben 2015, 36). Finding a way to escape the damage of this juridical order and recover this originary, prejuridical capacity for use is his overall aim. Although mainly concerned with the master/slave as a dialectic of subjectivity in western metaphysics, Agamben does briefly address the material lives of those enslaved during antiquity in his suggestion that property rights over persons via slavery may be the foundation of modernity's juridical order, "could in fact be the originary form of property, the capture (the *ex-ceptio*) of the use of bodies in the juridical order" (Agamben 2015, 36). Thus, among the better possibilities figured in the slave for Agamben is a return to a notion of the commons of the species, before or beyond the dividing practices of modernity, which include notions of property. Through use-as-*chresis*, we constitute ourselves through the world via interaction with it; we do not simply exist apart as "transcendent title holders of a capacity to act or make" (Agamben 2015, 62). Use is thus the expressive embodiment of a capacity of one's body, something that exists in the doing of it, not an abstract ability or skill one "owns" in oneself. Thus, contra the Classical tradition in which a person's capacity for virtue or goodness (*aretè;* the excellence of living well) is realized in connection with a task or function, Agamben strives to "think for the body of the slave an *aretè* that knows neither *ergon* nor *energeia* and nevertheless is always in use. Perhaps one of the limits of Western ethics has been precisely the incapacity to think an *aretè* of life in all its aspects" (Agamben 2015, 22).

In modernity, however, such use/*chresis* has been captured within the juridical machine, so the project of rendering it inoperative is at the root of all of Agamben's philosophy: stopping the anthropogenic machine is what we must do in order to make use-as-*chresis* of our bodies available once more for something different. Agamben conceives of this as use "emancipated" from any predetermined end: "the simple relation of the living thing with its own body" (Agamben 2015, 51). Thus, restoring a capacity for use is closely related to Agamben's concept of inoperativity, of stalling or stopping the anthropogenic machine that has captured our species' qualities and directed them toward the project of the human, the Being of the Dasein. An important aspect of inoperativity in this context is the idea that use is not a "thing" or capacity that we engage at times or leave dormant at others, nor is it a reservoir that we can "use up" by our actions: use is a continuous dwelling in habit, and thus potential or capacity are always still in use. But under our current metaphysics, this capacity can only be understood as being without *aretè*, that is, without excellence: being without a project or *ergon* can be conceived of only as a failure or lack, rendering this mode or style of living (associated with the slave) as denigrated *bare* life rather than as *natural* life. Inoperativity is about deactivating this juridical order to make something new possible: "the capacity to deactivate something and render it inoperative – a power, a function, a human operation – without simply destroying it but by liberating the potentials that have remained inactive in it in order to allow a different use of them" (Agamben 2015, 273). This passage is key, for here we see that inoperativity must deactivate without extinguishing the capacities now freed for other uses; yet, at the same time, this liberation cannot be for a predetermined end, because use-as-*chresis* is not part of presupposed categories of given tasks.

Inoperativity has something of what Ernst Bloch describes as the utopian or of what Walter Benjamin figures as the messianic:[3] within our material world exists a fragment or shard of another possible world, an alterity that is immanent within the world-as-given by the juridical order. Agamben argues that language is itself the original *logos* that primes the anthropogenic machine and reduces the vast possibility of what might be down to the narrow limits of our flawed metaphysics. He argues that "once we have recognized the presuppositional power of the *logos* – which transforms the reality that thought must reach into the given referents of a name or a definition" we need to recognize and eliminate "the presupposed hypothesis" by "making use of language in a non-presuppositional, which is to say non-referential way" (Agamben 2015, 130). It is difficult to grasp what non-referential language might be, but here I want to suggest not only that art overall is one pathway toward trying to access this realm, but also that speculative fiction does so in particular, by using language concretely to represent and refer to an invented, estranging world.[4]

---

[3] Ernst Bloch outlines his theory of the utopian as a trace of immanent possibility that can be activated from its potentiality in the material world in his three-volume *The Principle of Hope*. Walter Benjamin offers a messianic theory of history and political change in a number of essays, most influentially "Toward a Critique of Violence" and "On the Concept of History".

[4] Here it is relevant to note that the idea of estrangement that is so central to science fiction scholarship emerges in part from critical engagement with Bloch's work, and that Bloch and Benjamin were both associated with the Frankfurt School of German philosophers displaced by

Inoperativity is closely related to another concept that Agamben develops in the final section of *Use of Bodies*: destituent potential. He talks about destituent potential in contrast to a revolutionary power that might displace a particular version of the existing order, but which then quickly seeks to constitute something else and thus "captures and neutralizes" the potentiality it has just liberated. He associates destituent potential with the third term or the point of contact that he elsewhere explains as the trinity: it is a possibility that exists between terms that (in the current juridical order) function as binaries, a point of contact that is neither an opposition nor the collapse into sameness. Destituent potential undoes or pauses the existing order, but "does not aim to found a new law" (Agamben 2015, 268): it is about liberating things for the modality of use, about refusing the Western metaphysical modality of work or task (*ergon*) that currently captures and directs these capacities. Destituent potential does not simply destroy the existing juridical/metaphysical order, but rather proceeds "by liberating the potentials that have remained inactive in it in order to allow a different use of them" (Agamben 2015, 273). And destituent potential makes possible living as form-of-life, the modality that Agamben offers in place of Heideggerian Being. As he articulates the project in his earlier book *The Highest Poverty*, his project is about "how to think a form-of-life, a human life entirely removed from the grasp of the law and a use of bodies and of the world that would never be substantiated into an appropriation. That is to say again: to think life as that which is never given as property but only as a common use" (Agamben 2013, xiii). Thus, thinking human life outside of its capture by the juridical order, by the anthropogenic machine, results in a use of bodies (a form-of-life) that remains in the realm of the common, that is never given over to the order of "having" implied by the Dasein.

He elaborates the precise parameters of what he means by form-of-life in *Use of Bodies*, in a section that is worth citing at length:

> All living beings are in a form of life, but not all are (or not all are always) a form-of-life. [. . .] It is only in living a life that it constitutes itself as a form-of-life, as the inoperativity immanent in every life. The constitution of a form-of-life fully coincides, that is to say, with the destitution of the social and biological conditions into which it finds itself thrown. [. . .] It is not a question of thinking a better or more authentic form of life, a superior principle, or an elsewhere that suddenly arrives at forms of life and factical vocations to revoke them and render them inoperative. Inoperativity is not another work that suddenly arrives and works to reactivate and depose them: it coincides completely and constitutively with their destitution, with living a life. (Agamben 2015, 277)

Nazism. The critical study of the genre is grounded by Darko Suvin's influential *Metamorphoses of Science Fiction*, first published in 1977, which drew on Bloch to argue that science fiction is the literature of cognitive estrangement.

That the metaphysics of form-of-life are specifically contra Heideggerian metaphysics is clear from Agamben's language: form-of-life is not "thrown" (*Geworfenheit*) into the world as with Dasein, or rather form-of-life does not concede to the inevitability of the conditions into which life is thrown, but sees the world as open, recognizing that the current configurations of the juridical-metaphysical order might by otherwise. But crucially, the idea of use-as-*chresis* also refuses to substitute another *ergon* – "it is not a question of thinking of a better or more authentic form of life" – but instead is a matter of "living a life that constitutes itself as a form-of-life". Form-of-life can be grasped only in the ongoing action of living it and living it specifically as an immanent inoperativity that refuses or refutes the anthropogenic machine with the same persistence as characterizes this machine's operation.

Inoperativity, destituent potential, the new metaphysics, living rather than Being: all these are intertwined in the new politics, the new community that Agamben envisions. Form-of-life does not allow us to isolate or separate something within it in the mode of bare life, out of which will come the human/Dasein. The form-of-life Agamben imagines, he admits, "does not yet exist in its fullness" within the limitations of the prism of existing Western metaphysics; form-of-life "can be attested only in places that, under present circumstances, necessarily appear unedifying" (Agamben 2015, 227). It is with this in mind that I want to suggest that we take seriously the possibilities of being human in a radically different mode that are offered within speculative fiction, a genre that many people perhaps think of as inherently unedifying, but which I suggest offer us a laboratory for thinking outside the constraints of the presupposed world and its metaphysics.

4 *Ammonite*, Form-of-Life, Community

Griffith's *Ammonite* offers a new kind of humanity that shares many characteristics with Agamben's form-of-life. Moreover, this new mode is made possible by a virus Griffith invents for her fictional world: the changes this virus makes to the biology of residents on a planetary colony demands that a new social order be invented in turn. This close relationship between bodies and polities speaks to the entangled sociobiological challenges of biopolitical governance – that is, the reality we have seen so starkly during the COVID-19 pandemic that biopolitical governance during a health crisis can reinforce inequalities, but also the opportunity to reimagine our juridical order and to live otherwise that the pandemic has equally made evident. The novel is set on the planet called Jeep, which derives from the acronym GP for Grenchstom's Planet, one of many worlds colonized by humanity in this future. Jeep also becomes the name for the virus. Colonization efforts are led by a mining corporation, Durallium Company, and profit is the priority. In the years before the novel opens, Jeep lost contact with Earth for about 300 years and has only recently been rediscovered: as the Company tries to retake control, it causes massive environmental damage due to its failure to understand planetary ecosystems, and most personnel contract a virus that is fatal to all of the men and about 25% of the women, putting their colonial extractivism on hold.

The plot concerns interactions between an anthropologist sent to test a vaccine, Marghe, and the descendent of the original colonists, whose biology has been transformed by their ancestors' survival after infection hundreds of years before. Because the entire population of the planet is female, the Company also wants to investigate what enabled them to reproduce. The novel sets up a binary contrast between Company forces – whose ethos is ultimately alienating, even toward those who serve it – and the lifestyle on the planet, characterized by values other than acquisition. The Company is thanatopolitical in orientation not only toward the settlers whom it deems irrelevant but also toward its own personnel: a military ship, aptly named the *Kurst* (cursed), circles the planet with orders to destroy the Company's base and its satellite in orbit should the containment of the virus fail. While it wants the value it believes it can extract from Jeep, the Company wishes even more strongly to prevent the virus from spreading to its other colonial holdings: the disruption the virus represents to extractivist business-as-usual is far more dire a threat than the loss of a single holding.

Although Marghe and the others are told about an extensive decontamination protocol that involves replacing all their bodily fluids, they swiftly realize the economic purpose of the colony makes this unlikely. Thus, although they are told that they can be exposed to Jeep and later treated so that they can return if the vaccine trial fails, Marghe quickly realizes that this is unlikely as she contemplates "months of full pay for personnel who did nothing but sit around in decontamination, and added to that the cost of such a facility; [and] weighed all that against Company's control of public opinion through the media" (91).[5] Marghe's calculations here might help us to recontextualize the COVID-19 controversy over lockdowns and masking mandates, which similarly required governments to balance between protection of human life from exposure vs. protection of profitability that would be risked if businesses were forced to shut down. Those opposing mask mandates and lockdowns often point out that human lives are equally lost

---

5 All page numbers in this section are from *Ammonite* and, for the sake of economy, the name of the author and the date of publication will not be repeated.

to economic hardships caused by the quarantine measures, but as with the Company this needs to be placed in a larger context which questions the priority that biopolitical governance gives to economic metrics: thus we can recognize the loss of life due to a slowed-down economy as a contingent political choice consistent with a neoliberal ideology that sees no alternative to capitalist business-as-usual. As Foucault turned from theorizing modernity in terms of biopower and began to theorize instead the emergence of biopolitical governance as a tactic of power, one of his first questions was to ask about the relationship between sovereignty and economics. In *Society Must Be Defended* he asks, "Is power always secondary to the economy? Are its finality and function always determined by the economy? Is power's raison d'être and purpose essentially to serve the economy? Is it designed to establish, solidify, perpetuate, and reproduce relations that are characteristic of the economy and essential to its working?" (14). In his lecture series *The Birth of Biopolitics*, Foucault concentrates even more on the rise of neoliberal reason and the transformation of subjects into human capital from the point of view of the states, entrepreneurs of themselves. Thus a central aspect of biopolitical governance is that the fostering of life, its optimization (or relegation to neglect) is assessed via a rationality that is structured by economic considerations above all else.

While Marghe and the Company personnel need the vaccine to survive on the planet, the descendants of the original colonists do not and, moreover, we eventually learn that the changes the virus enacted in their bodies is what enables them to reproduce without male gametes. The success of the vaccine project, then, emblematizes the future of Jeep overall: will it end the way of life of the descendants, who have developed an entire metaphysical tradition based on their relationship to this planet? The return to what the Company understands as normal life if the Jeep virus is eradicated, then, can be understood as a way of ensuring that the future unfolds according to the culture of the Company, its metaphysics and its desire for profit, rather than following those of the descendants. The virus changes those who survive the infection in two ways. First, it embeds new DNA sequences into the human genome, biological material from indigenous humanoids on the planet called the goth. Second, it reactivates parts of the human genome perhaps long dormant, giving the descendants connection to past cultures on Earth that they never personally experienced. The goth remain mainly in the background of the novel, but are symbolically significant because the original colonists refused to recognize them as sentient species. Whether the goth are kin or another species, something to be hunted, is one of the issues that divides the planetary population into rival political factions. Marghe eventually aligns herself with those open to forming a community with the goth, an option that emerges within their political factions when they are able to confirm via genetic memories that some of the goth still survive, contrary to their belief that they were either a legend or a species wiped out by the first generation of colonists. This openness to a future that includes even non-*Homo sapiens* within its ethical community is one of the ways that the novel offers a version of metaphysics that renders inoperative the Heideggerian Dasein: the goth offer an image of subjects who are made the remainder of the anthropogenic machine, but on Jeep they can be imagined as natural life just as the non-Dasein humans are natural life.

By the time Marghe encounters the planetary society, the goth exist only as memories, perhaps only as legend, but the insights the virus gives her into the past convince her of their materiality, and the novel ends with Marghe and others planning to travel to northern regions where they might encounter the goth and integrate them into the shifting social order of planetary communities. She can access memories that she concludes belong to the goth because the virus also intensifies and enhances conscious control over cellular and chemical bodily responses, a capacity that can – through trained meditation – give access to collective biological memory via a process called deepsearch. Deepsearch is a ritual trance connected in part to puberty and taking on an adult role in the Jeep community, and also connected to the exchange between partners that enables parthenogenic, but not cloned, reproduction on Jeep: two women who share deepsearch can control not only their own bodies, but one another's bodies, to stimulate an ovum to divide and to re-sequence its genome before it becomes a zygote, an extension of the electrochemical signals regularly exchanged among all bodies, here imagined as a capacity one can become conscious of and direct. As Marghe theorizes what she observes, she posits that "this ovular stimulation by another somehow encourages genetic information that is recessive to become dominant" (125), and ultimately we learn that the virus is a retrovirus that works via RNA and thus transforms the genetic material of those it infects.

Figuratively, then, the virus signifies an embodied change in the descendants that is biological as much as it is social: their way of being human puts into operation different bodily capacities than the default way of being human represented by the Company personnel. Griffith describes this in ways that suggest the option for a third term between the binaries of subject/object, and that render inoperative the metaphysics that separates humanity from all other life; that is, the version of humanity imagined for Jeep has strong parallels to the ideal of *chresis* that lie at the heart of Agamben's philosophy. Once outside the sterile Company compound, Marghe is infected by the virus (despite her vaccination), but she is one of those able to survive, mainly due to the fact that she studied philosophical traditions related to controlling bodily responses to stimuli in her past while healing from an injury. Marghe's relationship to her body changes as she recovers from her fever, and she undergoes a transformation not dissimilar to the deepsearch that the planetary inhabitants undertake at puberty. She comes to understand what it means to be human – or perhaps better put, *how to be* human – in a different way as she recovers:

> They were connected: the world, her body, her face. Perhaps she should not be asking who she was but, rather, of what she was a part. The world was telling her: her blood, the tides in her cells, and the fluctuations in her nerves already beat to its rhythm, just as they had once resonated to the electromagnetic surges of Earth. Her body rang with this world. (198)

Marghe's description of this experience of revelation once she is changed by the virus might be read through an analogy to parallel the recognition enabled by COVID-19 that many of our ways of living according to the demands of capitalist work schedules did not result in the kinds of lives we wished to pursue, sometimes prompting a revaluation of priorities. And more compellingly, we might also push this idea of revelation of the possibility of living differently further to note policies such as moratoria on evictions, enhanced protections related to loss of work, and debt forgiveness related to student loans – things that seemed impossible before the pandemic, but made briefly possible during it – to signify larger ways that the experience of the pandemic enabled a moment in which economic deprivations that are often described as inevitable proved to be otherwise. To what extent we might preserve some of these changes as the immediate threat of infection and illness recedes remains an open question, but one that is quickly closing as rhetoric asserting that the needs of the economy trump those of people are once more taken to voice so-called common sense.

Although *Ammonite* offers this symbolic representation of a virus in a positive light, the novel does not minimize the degree of suffering and death that infection caused for the first settlers. Some of the collective memories give voice to the senses of grief and the fear which structured the lives of these first generations. At the same time, however, *Ammonite* suggests that while change is difficult and painful, it can also lead to better ways of living if negotiated thoughtfully and collectively: the key is to find a way forward toward what life can be on Jeep rather than seek to restore a version of what life had been like on Earth. Life on Jeep is difficult and requires cooperation among the various communities because of the scarcity of resources and the harshness of the climate. These myriad peoples not only have distinct ways of living on the planet, but even observe different calendars and have distinct theological systems, a fact that reinforces the idea that there are multiple ways to be human and they need not be arranged in a hierarchy. In this way, the multiple cultures that human descendants enact on Jeep create a vision of a global social order that is not homogenous, but nor does it repeat the colonialist history of Western modernity and its subjugation of other cultures and peoples. Instead, the women on Jeep are bound together by a network of trade they call trata, which is more than mere economic exchange. Trata is "trade as the first step on a journey whose outcome was uncertain – an opening gambit in a game that might continue for generations. Trata could be between two people, between two or more kiths [community/profession/family groupings], or between several communities. Frequently it was all three, each exchange resonating with another in the web" (54). When most of the Company personnel on the planetary station ultimately decide they prefer life on Jeep to what is offered by their own culture, the first step they must take in belonging to the world is to form bonds of trata. Thus reciprocity, a notion of being in relation to one another and to the world – rather than owners of it – is at the centre of Jeep society.

The main plotline of the novel is about Marghe's transformation by Jeep as she moves from the abstract and distanced view of an anthropologist, to being infected by the virus, and finally to this new sensibility described above, through which she sees herself as part of this world. Marghe's transformation is analogous to a shift from being-at-work (living according to a predetermined task or project, *ergon*), the proper orientation of the citizen/master that Agamben critiques, to living in use (*chresis*). Recall that Agamben talks about use as a mode of being in relation, being affected by the world one uses and constituting oneself as a subject in the light of this relation, a mode of use that does not separate the world and self into object and subject. In his words, "human being and world are, in use, in a relationship of absolute and reciprocal immanence" (Agamben 2015, 30). This could equally be a description of Marghe on Jeep, a version of herself that she comes to prefer to her anthropologist self.

The connection between this embodied capacity to shape biological processes in the novel and its narrative about collective or genetic memory finds its parallel in Agamben's project of transitioning from Being into living. He suggests that *chresis* conveys something akin to a memory or a paradigm of a possible way of being human that precedes the capture of our capacities by the juridical order. For Agamben this concept is not precisely a memory from a specific historical state of our species in the past, but rather an intimation that is perhaps best conveyed by its contrast with Heideggerian thought. In the metaphysical order of Being that Heidegger theorizes, life finds itself thrown into conditions/expectations that always come before it. But Agamben suggests that there is another and earlier "before", a moment before this thrownness during which life is not-yet directed by the human *ergon*. We retain knowledge of this capacity to be otherwise on some level, something we might describe as memory, and this potentiality is imagined more concretely as genetic memory in the speculative world Griffith invents. *Ammonite*'s collective memories, accessible through meditation and directed dreaming, draw on the affordances of speculative fiction to offer concrete referents for abstract concepts through the genre's technique of alternative worldbuilding. The memories that planetary dwellers on Jeep learn to access connect them to an ancestral past that offers a possibility for living a less alienated life, an image that is very close to what Agamben philosophically suggests with the concepts discussed above: *chresis*, inoperativity, dwelling.

Agamben's sense of this alternative form-of-life, moreover, is articulated in contrast to the Dasein's "having" of the world and to the concepts of property as a mode of interrelation overall. The novel further seems to imply that it critiques racial capitalism and colonialism specifically in the way that it links this ancestral connection through memory to Earth's history as much as to the history of Jeep, a relationship that is conveyed through language. When Marghe and other representatives of the Company reencounter the descendants after many generations of isolation, they discover that the women on Jeep use names and words that come from languages such as Welsh, Gaelic and Zapotec, that is, cultures all-but-destroyed by modernity and its transformation of world into property. The planetary community explain this via a legend about a spirit world to which the virus gives them access, which links them to "languages and customs already dead a thousand years before they left Earth [. . .] which contains all the peoples and monsters there ever were" (110). This spirit world contains something of Agamben's inoperativity, the idea of alterity immanent within the given order, the always open door to another existence that takes on the qualities of a form-of-life instead of a project. It is crucial to note that Griffith depicts this connection to the past not as a static reiteration, but as needing to emerge from a balance between the past and the new, just as their parthenogenic reproduction is not cloning but involves novel genetic expression. One community loses this capacity for change, resulting in an ever-narrowing gene pool and a death-obsessed cult, because "All their memories interlock and look down the same path to the same places. Each memory reflects another, repeats, reinforces, until the known becomes the only" (200). This is an unhealthy relationship to the past, in contrast to what Marghe discovers once she is infected and finds "ancient Greek words and Zapotec words and phrases from Gaelic, languages dead for hundreds of years. The words just came, and they fitted" (274) – these words come from long-dead traditions and carry something of the qualities of this past, but they also must fit and engage with the uniqueness of life on a planet that is not earth.

Ultimately what we find in Marghe is a version of a new relation to her body and to the world, a form-of-life that offers a glimpse of living in the mode of use/ *chresis*. By choosing to "go native" – a term that, Marghe notes, "tasted of scorn. And fear" (58) although there is no rational reason for this response – the women formerly of the Company suspend its colonial metaphysics and create a space where their capacities, now freed from that mode, can be directed toward something else. For Marghe in particular, who has trained herself to develop a strong capacity for conscious control of the autonomic nervous system, the new capacities freed by the virus enable her to become attuned to the bodies of others as much as she is to her own body. Thus we see in her a model for intersubjective metaphysics that has no relation to the master/slave dialectic and its struggle for recognition, but instead offers an experience of self that is enriched rather than threatened by mutuality and interdependence. As she embraces her new life on Jeep, Marghe is training to be a viajera, a term that literally translates as traveller, but in this social order means someone who combines elements of sage, poet, and shaman. Viajera do not stay with one community but move among all, another emblem of reciprocity and mutual entanglement, like trata. Viajera are also healers, an activity that they accomplish by attuning themselves with the electromagnetic frequencies of their patients' bodies, finding ways to resonate with and shift these vibrations to heal others.

Yet it is crucial to recognize as well that these new capacities are not a new *ergon* or capture Marghe's human capacities toward the end of a specific new juridical order. While meditation allows for elements of the autonomic bodily systems to be brought under conscious direction, the default mode is to allow oneself to be in relation with others, with the planet, and with the ecosystem overall and to let this relation guide the act of living/use. Thus, it is less about conscious control over the autonomic nervous system and more about a new state of perception in which one allows the autonomic to extend to more bodily systems, while at the same time maintaining a consciousness of these systems that does not exist for the Dasein's way of being in the world. When Marghe is fully attuned to her new subjectivity – what I am suggesting is an image of her using her body (*chresis*; form-of-life) rather than existing in a mode of having a world (Being; Dasein) – she discovers that she can sense when things are amiss with herself, with other humans and non-human life, with planetary ecosystems:

> When the plants were wrongly ordered, it felt on some dim level as though someone were screeching metal down metal, setting her teeth on edge. When she moved the plants, the discomfort stopped. At first she had been disturbed by the fact that she was behaving without identifiable empiric reason, and had tried not to do so. But the feeling became unpleasant. Now she allowed herself to act automatically and tried not to worry about it. (237)

This default to the autonomic creates the ground for form-of-life to anchor a new ethical orientation, precisely as Agamben suggests it should function. That is, once the current juridical/metaphysical order is paused or rendered inoperative, the next move is not to install a substitute order but simply to dwell in use. So attuned, Marghe feels wrong when the ecosystem is misaligned, when human activity disrupts rather than integrates with the larger living world. Thus those who remain on Jeep cannot possibly continue the project of extractive capitalism, and their new biology, their metaphysics of *chresis*, inevitable create new politics and ethics.

In *Ammonite*, then, we see a glimpse of how we might use critiques of biopolitical governance not merely to understand the vast disparities in life outcomes made evident as the pandemic unfolded, but also to engage the larger project of transforming our politics and our metaphysics that is necessary adequately to respond to the world in which we find ourselves in the pandemic's aftermath. Agamben's work helps us to understand the connection between specific modes of biopolitical governance which unevenly distributes resources and thus chances for vitality with more fundamental questions of metaphysics, with the project of what it means to be a human subject. The concrete if fictional situation offered by the speculative narrative in *Ammonite* helps us to conceive of ways that such a metaphysics might be possible, how understanding the self differently grounds a different kind of relationship to the world and to other life, and why this new metaphysics of subjectivity would enable new priorities for daily life and thereby new modes of governance to emerge.

In terms of the experience of the COVID-19 pandemic as it refracts with Griffiths' fictional world, this novel helps us to understand what the pandemic has revealed about the shortcomings of twenty-first century modernity in a more capacious way, by providing a way to reframe our understanding of biopolitical governance and the continuation of neoliberal capitalism as the only alternative. While the shutdowns and other quarantine measures protected people from the virus, the development of the vaccine and its distribution were accomplished in a way that once again privileged wealthy countries over impoverished ones, and even distribution within the Global North prioritized returning workers to jobs deemed essential above all else. At the same time, however, the recognition of certain emergency measures that were necessary for Western nations to take to spare people (at least temporarily) from the consequences of economic hardship (moratoria on evictions, debt forgiveness, low interest loans to small businesses, extensions of unemployment and sick-pay benefits, stipends to the poorest citizens) opened a door to at least recognizing some need to protect individuals from the vagaries of market forces, contra the usual austerity politics that dominate in especially the US context. Such measures were always framed as temporary, of course, and from the vantage point of 2022 it is clear that economic protections are being allowed to subside as anxiety over inflation and the "health" of the economy takes centre stage. Yet as the example of those Company personnel who "go native" on Jeep illustrates – and as the radical edge of Agamben's notion of inoperativity advocates – there remain more radical choices to refuse to return to so-called normal. And perhaps they are closer to be activated and materialized in some contexts, now that those temporarily offered a respite from the capitalist grind have experienced another form-of-life and discovered that the goal of capitalist accumulation is not as rewarding as it might once have seemed. The period of lockdown and a different way of living were not a pause in the anthropogenic machine, but it did offer a glimpse of what pausing neoliberal governance could feel like and, in speculative mode, could function as an emblem for the possibility of a pause in our metaphysics as well.

References

Agamben, Giorgio. *Where Are We Now? The Epidemic as Politics*. Trans. Valeria Dani. Lanham: Rowman & Littlefield, 2021.
Agamben, Giorgio. *The Use of Bodies*. Trans. Adam Kotsko. Stanford: Stanford University Press, 2015.
Agamben, Giorgio. *The Highest Poverty: Monastic Rules and Form-of-Life*. Trans. Adam Kotsko. Stanford: Stanford University Press, 2013.
Benjamin, Walter. "Thesis on the Philosophy of History." *Illuminations*. Ed. Hannah Arendt. Trans. Harry Zohn. New York: Schocken Books, 1968. 253–264.
Benjamin, Walter. "Toward the Critique of Violence." *Toward the Critique of Violence: A Critical Edition*. Eds. Peter Fenves and Julia Ng. Stanford: Stanford University Press, 2021. 39–61.
Bloch, Ernst. *The Principle of Hope*. 3 Vol. Trans. Neville Placie, Stephen Placie, and Paul Knight. Cambridge: MIT Press, 1986.
Foucault, Michel. *Society Must Be Defended*. Ed. Mauro Bertani and Alessandro Fontana. Trns. David Macey, Picador, 2003.
Foucault, Michel, *The Birth of Biopolitics*. Ed. Michel Senallart. Trans. Graham Burchell. Palgrave MacMillan, 2008.
Griffith, Nicola. *Ammonite*. New York: Ballantine Books, 2002.
Heidegger, Martin. *Being and Time*. 1927. Trans. John MacQuarrie and Edward Robinson. New York: Harper & Row, 1962.
Suvin, Darko. *Metamorphoses of Science Fiction: On the Poetics and History of a Literary Genre*. Ed. Gerry Canavan. Ralahine Classics. Bern: Peter Lang, 2016.

Raili Marling
The Relationality and Representability of Biopolitical Crises

Abstract: The present chapter proposes the expansion of the discussion on biopolitics by going beyond the traditional readings of Michel Foucault and Giorgio Agamben. Instead, building on the generative opacities of Foucault's thought, as well as on feminist thinkers like Judith Butler and Rosi Braidotti, it reflects on lived life as a potential source of political response and perhaps even resistance to power. It develops its discussion not as antagonistic criticism, but in tune with Eve Kosofsky Sedgwick's notion of *beside* (Sedgwick 2003, 8).

This re-interpretation of biopolitics folds in Lauren Berlant's (2011, 2016) analysis of the affective production of the "present". In a present in which crises are overwhelming, we need to (re)discover biopolitical relationality and to grasp shared vulnerabilities as a potential source of political agency. Instead of the more habitual dystopian narratives, this chapter tackles novels that represent the slow violence and ordinariness of the crisis during the pandemic: Gary Shteyngart's *Our Country Friends* (2021) and Sarah Moss's *The Fell* (2021). I argue that inchoate affective effects that elude easy representation are central to the understanding of biopolitical relationality and shared vulnerabilities. We thus need to expand our biopolitical imaginations if we are to encourage new ways of attaching to the world and to each other.

1 Introduction

The COVID-19 pandemic has precipitated a crisis in public health and, more broadly, in our understanding of the public good. This crisis has generated fear, confusion and a lot of debate. In fact, the pandemic has been accompanied by what Foucault termed a "discursive explosion" (Foucault 1978, 17). The emerging discourses include health and public safety guidelines and competing discourses

Note: The research for the present chapter was funded by the Estonian Research Council grant PRG934.

of dissent. These are creating new forms and norms for dealing with the experience of our lived bodies.[1]

In their different modes, these discourses contribute to the shaping of a sense of biological citizenship (Rose and Novas 2005, 440) or perhaps even molecular citizenship (Hardt and Negri 2000, 22–24). This biological citizenship has been made manifest in the COVID-19 era, when test results and vaccination certificates have become as vital as actual passports for crossing increasingly tight national borders. The state, however, is not the only source of surveillance of our bodies. Technology corporations, building on neoliberal discourses of self-responsibilization, encourage different kinds of self-surveillance through a plethora of apps and devices for counting steps, measuring blood sugar and blood pressure, monitoring periods and ovulation (for an analysis, see Lupton 2016, 2019).[2] This data can give users invaluable input for being attentive to their embodied selves and health, but such data also exposes them to third-party exploitation for ends that are anything but transparent. The discursive explosion around the COVID-19 pandemic ultimately reveals a debate about different interpretations of biopower and biopolitics or, more precisely, different responsibilities for human health and human bodies.

On the one hand, the COVID-19 crisis seems like a textbook example of a biopolitical event, with its surveillance regimes and restrictions for the sake of public health. The crisis has intensified the discussion of "disciplinary societies" (Foucault 1977) and "societies of control" (Deleuze 1992). There have been emotional debates on surveillance, discipline and control during the COVID-19 crisis, perhaps best exemplified by Giorgio Agamben's (2021) pessimistic and controversial writings on the states of exception. However, the very scale of discussion about and resistance to the different public health measures indicates that we are, instead, looking at an example of biopolitical failure (cf. Arminjon and Marion-Veyron 2021, 2). The dream of biopolitical control has proven to be impossible even with the plentiful tools of surveillance capitalism. The biopolitical failures we have seen during the COVID-19 crisis and the unimpressive handling by both

---

[1] The idea of the lived body is here used in contrast to the Cartesian view of the body as an object separate from the mind. The idea of the lived body can be taken back to Husserl (his notion of *Leib*, as distinct from the physical body (*Körper*) (Husserl 1989; Merleau-Ponty 1970).

[2] The neoliberal technologies of the self suggest that everyone has to become an "entrepreneur of oneself" (Foucault 2008, 226), to maximize oneself as human capital, denying vulnerability and social inequalities. In this interpretation, health and its care are also something that each individual should be responsible for (cf. Mayes 2017). While indeed each person can and should be responsible for their wellbeing, this does not absolve states from the responsibility of offering access to affordable health care to its citizens. Surveillance accompanying the datafied self is treated more fully in Wasihun's chapter in the present volume.

welfare states and welfare-less states suggests that the biopolitical power is – fortunately – not all-powerful.

The COVID-19 crisis, indeed, has created a disruption in the techno-optimistic discourse of biopolitics. This chapter proposes that this is due to a narrow understanding of biopolitics. To expand this understanding, it is productive to attentively re-read Foucault and to take up the generative opacities of Foucault's thought, as Campbell and Sitze (2013) and Lorenzini (2021) suggest, in particular in his last lecture series, with regard to vulnerability and relationality.

Such a discussion necessitates a reconsideration of the key terms. Thinkers like Didier Fassin (2009, 45) argue that Foucault's primary interest lay on the level of the population and that he did not give enough attention to life.[3] Veena Das (2007), too, contends that conventional discussions of biopolitics privilege form over life. But in the context of COVID-19 and other instances of biopolitical control we surely need to attend to life and lived experiences (we could use Georges Canguilhem's distinction between "the lived" (*le vécu*) and "the living" (*le vivant*) (Fassin 2009, 47)). We must turn our attention to ordinary lives and the different ways in which liveable life is available to people on the basis of gender, sexuality, race, geopolitical location, class, ability, etc.[4]

The present chapter, thus, identifies a tension within the concept of biopolitics. It stresses the first two syllables of the concept, in order to reflect on lived life as a potential source of political response and perhaps even resistance to power. It develops its discussion in the spirit of not antagonistic criticism, but with Eve Kosofsky Sedgwick's notion of *beside* that, with its "spacious agnosticism", can be a tool to overcome the problem of dualistic thinking (Sedgwick 2003, 8). In her spirit, this chapter places different theories beside each other to build potentially new kinds of connections and alliances, instead of simple black-and-white dichotomies.

This re-interpretation of biopolitics will be combined with Lauren Berlant's (2011, 2016) analysis of the affective production of the present. In the present where crises are overwhelming, we need to (re)discover biopolitical relationality and to grasp shared vulnerabilities as a potential source of political agency (cf. Butler 2022).

---

3 Tellingly, for example, the word "life" does not appear in the indexes of the published versions of the lectures on biopolitics and biopower.
4 Fassin also points out that Foucault does not address inequality in his *oeuvre*. This point is also made from a feminist perspective by Ranjana Khanna (2009).

2 Another Glance at Biopolitics and Biopower

One of the theoretical impasses of the COVID-19 discourse is its reliance on a relatively narrow interpretation of biopolitics, through the notions of discipline and control, presented in an emphatically negative register, most famously by Agamben (2021) in his pandemic-era writings. I will move away from the interpretation of biopolitics as something that happens within the polis under the sanction of the state. This aspect of biopolitics is very clear and the state retreat that had been observed throughout the early twenty-first century (Lobao et al. 2018) has stalled during the pandemic as states try to regain some of the functions that they outsourced to private companies. How biopolitically effective the state has been is up for debate. One does not need to read again examples of state controls and limitations imposed on people or examples of state failure to attend to the pandemic promptly and judiciously (most famously in the case of the USA or Brazil).

Let us, instead, return to an issue in Foucault's *oeuvre* that has found much less discussion during the pandemic: what makes biopolitics possible. When Foucault theorizes biopolitics, he writes about optimization and control, and he states that this influence is "positive" (Foucault 1978, 137). Foucault is above all observing that prohibitions shape social and human bodies, seeking to make them docile. Yet the word "positive" itself stands out in its ambiguity. Because of this eye-catching ambiguity I find opacity[5] to be a productive concept in tackling Foucault's take on biopolitics. The other's opacity creates a space for an attentive reading and reflection before rushing to a judgement. This pause is also necessary in connection with biopolitics. Timothy Campbell and Adam Sitze argue that in the first volume of *The History of Sexuality*

> the encounter between life and politics reveals itself not as *a relation* but as *a series of non-relations*. In *La volonté de savoir*, it seems to us, life and politics encounter one another mainly in and through a set of *generative aporias* – impasses that aren't merely "negative," but that in each case double as productive spaces, blind spots the very opacity of which doubles, paradoxically, as a source of insight. (Campbell and Sitze 2013, 22)

It is this generative aspect of opacity that I want to take up, to try to think beyond the often-repeated facts of control and to see if we can find a space for agency in this discussion. The moulding of subjects is indeed one generative aspect of power that tends to be viewed with alarm in the discussion of biopolitical control. However,

---

[5] For Édouard Glissant (1997, 193) the other can remain inscrutable and yet open for dialogue, one in which labels do not hinder creative sense-making. I have previously argued for the political usefulness of opacity in the context of gender, as a tool for resisting co-optation within the neoliberal regimes of visibility (Marling 2021).

Foucault in the same volume also writes about how power always creates resistance (Foucault 1978, 95). Foucault's ideas on the specificities of this resistance within the all-powerful disciplinary apparatus that aims for self-discipline and self-responsibilization remain opaque, yet in his later lectures he often comes back to issues of choice and agency available to individuals, even within repressive regimes (Ettlinger 2011). He clearly sees an opening for ethical action.

The core issue for the following discussion is what kind of resistances can be created when we think not just about power over life, but also the power of life itself, in the spirit of Canguilhem's concept of the lived. As Gilles Deleuze (1990, 77) asks, "when power becomes bio-power, resistance becomes the power of life [. . .] Is not life this capacity to resist force?"[6] This is a central question of the present chapter as well: if people are organized into a population for control, what happens to their individual capacities? I am not necessarily looking for grand revolutionary gestures, but for instances of micro-resistance, creativity or perhaps even evasion; such acts allow us to see that power is not total and that there are alternative modes of being. Sergei Prozorov (2017) shows how what could be called Foucault's "affirmative biopolitics", developed in his lectures on the Cynics and the act of *parrhesia*,[7] derived from his engagement with Eastern-European dissidents. Speaking truth to power allows one to claim power over one's life and, through that, to at least become a friction that prevents the smooth operation of biopolitical control.

Affirmative biopolitics as a notion has also been associated with the work of Roberto Esposito as well as Michael Hardt and Antonio Negri, thinkers who have sought to counter the bleak biopolitical determinism of Agamben's reading of Foucault. This has often meant attention to life and thinking beyond bare biological existence. For Michael Hardt and Antonio Negri (2000, xiii) biopolitics moves beyond the human to cover "the production of social life" that allows for the development of

---

[6] It has to be added right away that much of the discussion on biopower and its relation to control relies on gaps in the writing of both Foucault and Deleuze. For example, although Foucault writes about biopower in Volume I of *The History of Sexuality*, the word does not appear in his lectures on biopolitics. How strongly Foucault equates biopower and control has been debated by different interpreters (Nail 2016, 257, 260). Thomas Nail provides a very thorough discussion of Foucault's biopower and Foucault's control, including by reading Deleuze's lectures on Foucault from 1985–1986. Yet this attention to control still does not comprehensively address the level of the individual, the focus of attention in this chapter.

[7] Foucault develops his ideas on *parrhesia* in his lecture courses on *The Government of the Self and Others* and *The Courage of Truth* (1983–1984). These end up being his last lectures, as he dies in 1984.

intersubjectivity, as well as the ontological development of the world.[8] Hardt and Negri recur to the thinking of Spinoza, specifically the notion of "multitude", people who are not (yet) organized into a population and who thus can limit the power of the sovereign. The "multiplicity"[9] and "open set of relations" that characterize the multitude make it a creative and productive force (Hardt and Negri 2000, 103, 62). This potential, I believe, is also relevant for the present discussion.

Other thinkers want to challenge the position that biological existence is bare and impoverished. An increasingly rich literature rooted in new materialist and posthumanist thought[10] gets cited, regrettably, less often in discussions on biopolitics, although COVID-19 showed the importance of the nonhuman in precipitating the crisis and living with it.[11] The philosophical foundation of affirmation has been developed across several texts by the feminist philosopher Rosi Braidotti, who seeks to claim life from a narrow discussion of human beings within the confines of the state. She thinks not so much about the normative power that surrounds humans as about the role of life itself. For this she, like Negri, refines the terminology to overcome the limitations of dialectical thinking (Braidotti 2016, 30). Her key word is *potentia*, "experimentations with new arts of existence and ethical relations", rather than the restrictive power or *potestas* that dominate the majority of biopolitical debate (Braidotti 2016, 30).[12] For Braidotti, what Agamben sees as bare life is "dynamic and generative" (Braidotti 2016, 33). Life is teeming in and around us, even if we do not notice this richness and prefer the illusion of an insular autonomous being. Embracing its potential enables Braidotti to view

---

[8] Negri also wants to show the tension inherent within the concept of biopolitics. He (in Casarino and Negri 2004, 167) makes a distinction between two sides of biopower: *biopotere* and *biopotenza* (the two are translated as "dominion over life" and "potentiality of constituent power", respectively, in Mills [2018, 88]): in the former power creates or controls life, in the latter life creates power. The latter term creates a hope for agency by seeing life as a "multitude of singularities" (Mills 2018, 88).

[9] Although multiplicity is a notion above all associated with the work of Deleuze and Guattari, Deleuze in his work on Foucault argues that Foucault theorized multiplicity already in his *The Archaeology of Knowledge* (1969) (Deleuze 1986, 14).

[10] For more on new materialist critique of biopolitics, see, for example, Bennett (2010) or Braidotti's different books from the 2000s, for example, her revised take on nomadic theory (Braidotti 2011).

[11] An intriguing feminist new materialist analysis can be found, for example, in Sikka (2021).

[12] The parallel between Negri's *biopotenza* and Braidotti's *potentia* is clear, but Negri finds hope in the multitude still conceptualized through humans, while Braidotti envisions a distributive agency beyond the human. The latter term is derived from Jane Bennett (2010, 32) whose idea of agency is not linked to a decision-making subject, but "a swarm of vitalities". This interpretation "loosens the connections between efficacy and the moral subject, bringing efficacy closer to the idea of the power to make a difference that calls for a response" (Bennett 2010, 32).

life as a potential site of political engagement.[13] Like Deleuze, Braidotti wants us to think of our experience as a site of potential change. If we cannot imagine differently, our future will be the same as our present. Braidotti calls for "an increased awareness of the shared vulnerability of embodied subjects" caught in relations of power (Braidotti 2016, 33).

Braidotti (2016, 35) wants to create an alternative to the traditionally oppositional political and critical habits. The focus for her is not uncritical affirmation, but the need for creativity, as oppositional thinking leads us into impasses, as can also be seen in the case of the COVID-19 crisis where the opposing positions almost ritualistically clash, with no opening for dialogue or compromise. The focus on death and discipline does not create space for hope, and through that, action. Braidotti asks us to imagine possible futures, tapping into underutilized resources, to create a "network, web, or rhizome of interconnections with others" and a sort of "a constitutive intimacy with the world" (Braidotti 2016, 35). This expanded sense of the human beyond an individual shell promises a radically relational way of life that respects the multiple ecologies in which we are already inevitably entangled. The focus should be not on what we are, but rather on what we could be, as she has also stressed in the context of the COVID-19 pandemic (Braidotti 2020).

Despite its seeming political naiveté, this vision of "life itself as a relentlessly generative force" described by Braidotti (2016, 39) recognizes the complexity and constant transformation inherent in life and societies. It seems impossible to achieve within neoliberal consumer capitalism that has continued to flourish during the pandemic, after the brief initial period of shock and wonder at the reappearance of life, in the form of plants and animals in our depopulated cities. The pandemic showed the vulnerability of our bodies, because of their porousness and their unavoidable openness to the other. These made us all bare, even if many of us had enough privilege not to have to radically revise our possible futures. However, Braidotti's vision reminds us that this potentiality inherent in life itself remains available to all of us, even if the resistances it creates manifest themselves in micro-practices.

If we want to take biopolitics seriously as both a theoretical and social problem we need to look for affirmative aspects of biopower to build ways of speaking truth to power and creating ethical ways of being in the world. This, as Timothy Campbell (2011) reminds us, is a path offered by Michel Foucault as well. Populations always consist of multiplicities of individuals, and Foucault does not show us how

---

[13] Braidotti (2016, 30) distinguishes between politics (*la politique*) and the political (*le politique*), the latter of which for her embraces "transformative experimentations with the new arts of existence".

they lose their individuality or intimate communities in populations (Campbell 2011, 122). Campbell sees traces in Foucault's last interviews of a "slackened" subject (Campbell 2011, 155) who is porous and open to different practices of relationality with other beings and life itself.

Foucault's relational approach to biopolitical struggle allows us to reveal the blurring of lines between subjects and objects in the constantly shifting milieu called life. The presence of the other is vital to our survival. For example, Roberto Esposito (2011) returns to the opacities of Foucault's thought to discuss the different valences of immunity: threat is reduced by incorporating it, but only to a degree necessary to ward off further threat.[14] The immunitary paradigm, if taken to its extreme, produces societies like that of Nazi Germany. However, this horrifying example also allows us to re-think the dangers of immunity to reclaim a more affirmative notion of community, life and body (Esposito 2008, 157).

The way out might come through the work of Spinoza, Canguilhem and Deleuze, all referred to in the discussion above. For Esposito (2008, 194), "every life is a form of life and every form refers to life". Esposito is not just writing about the immunitary paradigm but also social plurality, for he views community as something "open to the constitutive difference of its members" (Esposito 2011, 132). In this vision, the self is redefined as "a construct determined by a set of dynamic factors, compatible groupings, fortuitous encounters" (Esposito 2011, 169). Tolerance, thus, allows immunity to not just close itself from the other but also to open itself to the other. In this relationality, we are not bounded subjects closed off from the world and each other, but porous and leaky, perceptually open to and being with the others.

3 Relationality, Vulnerability and Potentiality

Judith Butler has, in her recent interventions, interrogated the question of whether we actually can talk about a good life when it is unavailable to so many and when the very notion has been hijacked by consumer capitalism and depleted of ethical imperatives. She argues that the question of the good life is inevitably a question of

---

[14] For the dangers of autoimmunity to politics, see Derrida (2003). Although Derrida's comments were written specifically in the atmosphere created by the 11 September 2001 attacks and the anti-terrorist fervour of the time, they are also applicable, in intriguing ways, to the situation of COVID-19. There is no space for developing this idea at length here, but one possible avenue is suggested by Gavin Rae (2022). In this volume, Käsper takes up one facet of Esposito's take on immunity.

biopolitics. Jana Sawicki (2016) has observed a development in Butler's post-9/11 engagement with Foucault toward this set of questions resonant with Foucault's late-life ethical turn, with several distinctive themes. Butler seeks to find out "what are the mechanisms of power through which life is produced?" (Butler 2009, 6). Initially, her comments were largely associated with war and terror, and follow a relatively traditional interpretation of biopolitics in the discussion of whose lives matter. Butler, though, is increasingly interested in embodiment and "affective and moral responsiveness" (Butler 2009, 50). The "fundamental dependency on anonymous others is not a condition that I can will away. No security measures will foreclose this dependency; no violent act of sovereignty will rid the world of this fact" (Butler 2004, xii). This, she hopes, makes us not just think about how to protect ourselves, but also "who else suffers" (Butler 2004, xii). This series of questions concern the broader politics of human life.

The issue of relationality is expanded through Butler's increasing attention to vulnerability as a key element of biopolitics.[15] Butler (2015, 211) specifically makes us think about vulnerability as an "aspect of the political modality of the body" because this vulnerability dispossesses us by opening us up to others. This prompts Butler (2015, 149) to ask:

> If we can become lost in another, or if our tactile, motile, haptic, visual, olfactory or auditory capacities comport us beyond ourselves, that is because the body does not stay in its own place, and because dispossession of this kind characterizes bodily sense more generally. When being dispossessed in sociality is regarded as a constitutive function of what it means to live and persist, what difference does that make to the idea of politics itself?

This provides a different logic of biopolitics, one that does not ward off vulnerability but embraces it and uses it as a basis for creating solidarity. She has made this link even stronger in her post-pandemic reflections (Butler 2022). This is in tune with the type of radical relationality and expanded notion of life that Braidotti has been developing. As Donna Haraway (1991, 2003) has shown, we need to attend to the complex set of relations without which we cannot exist at all. We all live in networks of dependency and vulnerability. Skin is a porous membrane for all of us. We all breathe air. Thus vulnerability, as Butler also stresses, is an impetus to our responsiveness to what is happening in the world or to other bodies around us. For her, as for Deleuze, "bodies are not self-enclosed kinds of entities"

---

[15] Jemima Repo (2014), however, has argued that Butler has avoided the discussion of biopolitics. I, like Sawicki, believe that Butler has become more biopolitical since the publication of Repo's initial critique. Repo's (2017) own treatment of the biopolitics of gender is interesting but will not be covered here because of the limitations of space.

but "in some sense outside themselves" (Butler 2015, 116). This creates a radically different foundation for the political, as defined by Braidotti above.

Foucault, too, as suggested by Siisiäinen (2019, 60), believes in the need to not think about politics through the language of rights but also of "affective relationality".[16] Rights alone cannot protect what Siisiäinen (2019, 60) has called the "richness of the relational fabric" from impoverishment, for example, in the context of neoliberal identity politics. While Foucault originally develops this notion in the context of gay rights, these ideas, as Siisiäinen (2019, 60) believes, are more universal and "the affective dynamics of existential sharing and open temporality" can transform human relations more broadly.

"Affective relationality" is the notion that I want to include in our discussion of biopower, not in the spirit of co-optable affirmation, the neoliberal cruel optimism[17] so evocatively described by Lauren Berlant (2011, 1), but in the recognition of our embodiment. Butler also contends that we can create friction with the status quo by "those bodily gestures of refusal, silence, movement, refusing to move" that can be employed not to suppress or overcome interdependency or vulnerability but rather, in Butler's words, "to produce the conditions under which vulnerability and interdependency become liveable" (Butler 2015, 218). This is the radical aspect of emerging *potentia* that we need to embrace, not suppress.

This, though, is anything but easy in a time when, even before the pandemic, life was characterized by depression, unease, dissipated subjectivity and animated suspension described by Berlant (2011, 9, 195). The pandemic arrived in a world where crisis was and is ordinary, or, more specifically, where crises are so manifold and omnipresent as to be received at best with resignation by overwhelmed people just scrambling to get by in a world of constant competition where only few benefit from the efforts of the many. This exhaustion and attrition of attention prevent us from seeing beyond our own vulnerability. In short, vulnerability has not been liveable for the majority. Crisis ordinariness has prevented us from imagining this vulnerability as anything but something to overcome or to hide.

---

[16] This very productive term has also been explored by philosophers of emotion, like Jan Slaby (e.g. in Slaby and Röttger-Rössler 2018) and by critical affect theorists like Lauren Berlant across her *oeuvre* (e.g. in Berlant and Edelman 2014).

[17] Berlant (2011, 1) argues that "a relation of cruel optimism exists when something you desire is actually an obstacle to your flourishing" and she explicitly mentions fantasies of good life as one of her examples in today's world. In the present context, cruel optimism can be seen in the typical self-help literature that promises acceptance and success but also puts the responsibility for achieving this success on the shoulders of the individual, with no recognition of structural issues.

In critical literature, too, it has been imperative to show people the omnipresence of disciplinary regimes and systems of control behind the fantasies of free choice and autonomy that proliferate in neoliberal societies. Yet control is never total and even the vulnerable have not been deprived of all of their agency. There has been and continues to be non-compliance, evasion, perhaps even sabotage. Registering impassive and often imperceptible reactions to the disciplinary regimes is central to the understanding of biopolitical power failures. Biopolitical control existed before the pandemic, but was boosted to alarmingly new levels by the perceived state of exception in different forms in different countries. As the analyses of previous emergencies, like the 9/11 attacks, show, control tends to stay, even when the emergency itself ends.[18] We cannot remain in this vicious circle of re-stating the omnipresence of discipline and control. Instead, we need to expand our biopolitical imaginations, to encourage new ways of attaching to the world and to each other – and do so in the reality in which we live.

4 COVID-19 as Slow Violence

Both the pre – and post-pandemic worlds have encouraged detachment and atomization under the mantra "There is no alternative".[19] This chapter argues that this failure to imagine alternatives to the disciplinary logic of negative biopolitics is among other things due to, first, an under-appreciation of the potential of individual lives that make up populations envisioned in all writing on biopolitics, as discussed above, and, second, limited attention to imaginaries. This was evident also during the pandemic where the same narratives and images were recycled, the same experts trotted out to say similar things, usually from a technocratic or narrowly virological perspective, without attention to the individual human beings and their entanglement in complex networks of life. The representations of the crisis have emphasized danger to public health, on the one hand, and danger to individual freedoms on the other. Both representations resorted to dramatic affect, rather than showing a complex interweaving of lives and life itself.

The pandemic experience needs to be viewed within crisis ordinariness and the attendant disorganization of life that we were already inhabiting before the pandemic arrived. Human life had already been impoverished and action made

---

18 In a recent analysis, for example, Harbisher (2022) traces the resurgence of eugenicist rhetoric during the COVID-19 pandemic in the UK.
19 This Thatcherian dictum has been brought to the discussion of neoliberalism by Mark Fisher (2009).

to seem meaningless beyond consumerism. That was not a type of a story easily told. In an interview the late Lauren Berlant (Berlant and Greenwald 2012, 81) argued that "it's very hard to produce a satisfying aesthetic event about the drama of not mattering where not mattering is a general historical condition". That type of life nurtured fantasies that, however, always remained unattainable and at the same time prevented us from assessing the real conditions of our existence (Berlant 2011, 195).

This is where I find it useful to think about this loss of liveliness in life with the help of what Rob Nixon (2011) calls "slow violence". Nixon uses the term to describe different after-effects of climate change, soil erosion, deforestation, oil spills, pollution of ground water and other such processes that take place so gradually as to remain invisible. When their effects are discovered, it is usually too late to take meaningful action. We respond to what we feel strongly about, but what happens if the very nature of the processes refuses easy representation and, through that, strong feeling? We have seen this in the context of climate change: we know it is there, but because nothing is happening right now, we go on with our habitual routines that contribute to the deterioration of the climate. We mostly do nothing, as the present is tough enough without having to worry about the future. I have been extending the notion of slow violence to the different processes of attrition that characterize contemporary society in different texts over the past five years. COVID-19 has been an example of slow violence, in which action was required immediately to prevent a calamity down the road. But we had already been made passive about possible futures and scrambled to live in the present, mostly failing to find liveliness in the ordinary. Yet sensing that potential is vital to finding distinctly different futures that would differ from those we are headed towards.

The COVID-19 pandemic made it possible to discuss what life is worth living and under what conditions. It made us see that a "glitch has appeared in the reproduction of life" (Berlant 2016, 393). This glitch is an opportunity for unlearning and for creating new aspirations, not necessarily out of conflict, but out of ambivalence. Berlant (2016, 414) invites us to "hold out the prospect of a world worth attaching to that's something other than an old hope's bitter echo". We need to let go of the spectres of lost futures that haunt our present discussions.[20] We need to stop reiterating the positions that have brought us to the present "malfunctioning world" (Berlant 2016, 396).

---

[20] The concept of ghosts of past futures is derived from Jacques Derrida's *The Specters of Marx* (1993, in English in 1994).

We should imagine better and open our discussion to perspectives that expand the polis, the political and the autopoietic. If we can bring more imaginative scenarios into the discussion we might be able to account better for what Judith Butler has called our shared vulnerability and make use of the *potentia* of life itself. These alternatives are unlikely to emerge from the policy papers of our competing political forces or mega-corporations whose main interest is in locking us into an ever more addictive attention-consumption economy. This alternative needs to come from the arts. They have the ability to imagine society otherwise. To get to the futures, we, however, need a more diverse range of representations of the present.

5 Literary Pandemic Imaginaries Past and Present

The pace of fiction writing and its publication, needless to say, means that fiction is necessarily slower in responding to crises than the affectively loaded social media and the blogosphere. There are exceptions to the traditional speed of the publishing cycle, like Ali Smith's seasonal quartet that the publisher produced in an expedited manner, to create an almost contemporaneous record of the crises that hit the UK between the Brexit vote and the COVID-19 pandemic.[21] The pandemic, however, took a while to be digested, perhaps because of the slowness of its violence and the energies spent on mere survival.

Hence the early months of the pandemic sent academics and common readers back to earlier literary representations, as can also be seen in the chapters of this volume where scholars re-read texts ranging from Sophocles and Boccaccio to Huxley and Zeh, all written before 2020. Eerie parallels to the pandemic were found with books published in the 2000s, like Sigrid Nunez's *Salvation City* (2010), with its references not just to a respiratory virus, but also to school closures and hand sanitizer shortages, or Emily St. John Mandel's *Station Eleven* (2014), another story of a flu that kills 99% of the world's population. A phrase of Mandel's (2014, 247) – "I can't wait till things get back to normal" – could have been uttered at any point in the spring and summer of 2020.

---

[21] The oral history of this speed-publication experience can be found on the webpage of Smith's publisher, Penguin: https://www.penguin.co.uk/articles/2020/08/ali-smith-autumn-winter-spring-summer-seasonal-quartet-oral-history. Last accessed 10 July 2022.

The first novels and short story collections actually written during the pandemic lockdown started to appear in late 2021 in the United Kingdom and United States: Gary Shteyngart's *Our Country Friends* (2021), Sarah Hall's *Burncoat* (2021), Louise Erdrich's *The Sentence* (2021), and Sarah Moss's *The Fell* (2021), to list but a few titles. More are to follow and critics already worry about the glut of pandemic fiction.

The books, when looked at collectively, try to capture something other than the disease or even the dystopian elements of the state of emergency, unlike the earlier novels analysed in this volume, possibly because of the sporadic biopolitical control in the US and UK, in comparison with Germany. Their focus is on the banality and tedium of everyday life, but also its loneliness, depression and anxiety. The novels look for the human beings behind the masks and closed doors of their homes. I will focus on the texts that try to capture the stasis and eventlessness of the pandemic for those of us lucky to be able to do remote work or even to do nothing during what Adam Grant, in his *New York Times* opinion piece, called a "boring apocalypse".[22] This stasis and limited space of the home are a representational challenge, yet namely this limitation allows us to access the vulnerabilities of people whose lives governmental biopolitics claimed to protect. This phrase shifts the focus from mere discipline to the (potential) acts of individual agency at the everyday level of survival and the relationalities it nurtures.

To illustrate, let me juxtapose two novels, Gary Shteyngart's *Our Country Friends* and Sarah Moss's[23] *The Fell*. Both focus on lockdown and isolation in a secluded rural setting where the human perspective prevails and leaves the nonhuman as background decoration. The lives of the humans who populate the novels are represented in distinctly different keys and with different answers about the enforced relationality and shared vulnerability created in the lockdown. They represent two countries – the US and the UK, respectively – as well as two social classes, which leads to very different outcomes.

Both novels are highly aware of the challenges inherent in writing about a boring apocalypse. For example, Moss makes one of her protagonists come to the following conclusion as she hallucinates towards the end of the novel: "humanity's ending appears to be slow, lacking in cliff-hangers or indeed any satisfactory narrative shape; characterized, for the lucky, by the gradual vindication of accumulating dread"[24] (Moss 2021, 117). Moss's heroine makes references to not just the pandemic,

---

[22] https://www.nytimes.com/2021/12/10/opinion/covid-omicron-psychology-fear.html. Last accessed 10 July 2022.
[23] Moss's first novel, *Cold Earth* (2009), interestingly, was a dystopian take on a mutating virus.
[24] In the same hallucinatory passage, she also comes to the conclusion that her son needs to acquire pre-industrial skills to survive the coming environmental disaster. That is, we can see traces of broader crisis ordinariness beyond COVID-19.

but the other ever-present crises, from the threat of nuclear war to shifting magnetic fields, the sense of an ending that has been wrong this far – but need not remain so forever. While Moss captures the affective challenges, Shteyngart (2021, 220) takes an ironic swipe at the many "stranded social novelists up and down the river" who are desperately taking photos of flowers and birds while "beseeching their higher power to *help me make something out of all this stillness.*" Both authors take stillness and stasis seriously, but they arrive at different readings of the slow violence of the pandemic.

The setting of *Our Country Friends* is Hudson Valley, the country retreat of many wealthy New Yorkers during the pandemic. The novel can be described as a re-interpretation of *Decameron*,[25] as here, too, a group of moderately wealthy friends (they include a successful dating app designer, a wealthy heir, a writer and a famous actor) retreat to the countryside to ride out the pandemic. Several of the group are old friends, with years of mutual memories and disappointments. To them are added a young woman writer whose social capital is based on her poor white background and an actor with an over-sized ego whose name we never learn. They are multiracial and several have immigrant backgrounds (Russian, Korean, Indian), but they still belong to the elite, however precarious, and are contrast with the locals, suspected of being Trump supporters, who hover in the background.

The novel uses traditional omniscient narration, with access to the minds of the characters. Several reviews have noted a similarity to nineteenth-century Russian novels, a point that is also conceded in the text: "in accordance with the rules of Russian novels, each thought about another" (Shteyngart 2021, 139). The characters even stage *Uncle Vanya* and the country retreat will eventually be sold like Chekhov's cherry orchard. The Chekhovian aura, with its roundelay of relationships and musings on the characters' different kinds of failures in life, is well suited to the stasis of the pandemic for this group who do not initially directly feel the repercussions of the pandemic. The references to classic Russian literature are sandwiched together with Japanese reality shows that the characters binge-watch and satirical references to social media that they are still part of despite their isolation (one character even becomes the protagonist of a social media scandal and target of public opprobrium).

The characters enjoy nature, food, plentiful drink and different romantic entanglements, but the broader world is unavoidable and breaks their isolation, as news of George Floyd's murder and the pandemic deaths seep in. Like in many a plague narrative, here too the virus finally enters the enclave and leads to infection, and a

---

25 This is not too subtly hinted by the name of one of the characters, Dee Cameron.

perhaps too long description of delirium and eventual death. This allows Shteyngart to look into the characters' growing awareness of their privilege and their ability to pretend not to see the injustice around them. This is one of the more striking elements of the novel, but the realization does not lead to any of the characters leaving the safety of their retreat.

Shteyngart, as a skilled parodist, focuses on the absurdities of the daily tedium of isolation where city people have to come to terms with spotty Internet and poor plumbing. This is where the book is at its sharpest. The escape from the city, in which the pandemic had left "nothing but ambulance wails and possibly suicidal trips to the bodega" (Shteyngart 2021, 41), is framed less as a tragedy by the more privileged characters and more as a loss of social connections. Their sojourn in nature is that of casual tourists, who seem oblivious of the birds, the deer and the groundhog named Steve. Instead, the comedy of manners focuses on the predictable pandemic tropes, from social distancing to masks. For example, the isolating friends are described to us as being "seated in their jackets and sweaters at a healthy remove from one another, as if they were organized criminals or dignitaries at the League of Nations" (Shteyngart 2021, 45). We get farcical descriptions of sex in surgical masks, but the temptation of comedy prevents Shteyngart from capturing the true tedium of a lockdown, especially as the routines of housework and childcare remain invisible and the large set of characters creates many interpersonal tensions as well as flashbacks. The novel, thus, records the mere surface of living in the pandemic. Even the one pandemic death is treated with somewhat flippant comedy: "They sat there between the ferns and the busy bike lane, passing around plates of food, surrounded by faces that looked like their own" (Shteyngart 2021, 315).

We read of many connections and liaisons, but a deeper recognition of relationality builds only indirectly, in a connection between a tech entrepreneur and the troubled child of the two Russian immigrant characters. These interactions are perhaps most affecting, as they recreate the simple ordinariness of an everyday life that is full of connections with others, even if these happen though the learning of the alphabet or gushing about a Korean boy band. Sheyngart, though, steps away from mining this connection for intersubjective vulnerability. Yet he shows the dawning realization of all of the characters about their ordinariness and a vulnerability from which they cannot hide, even if they lack the courage to use it to build new connections.

Moss chooses a different strategy. *The Fell* explicitly focuses on isolation, as the protagonists, Kate and her teenage son Matt, have done ten of the required fourteen days of self-isolation in a home in the Peak District in the UK. Kate used to work as a waitress and may have been in contact with somebody who tested positive and thus she has to be in strict isolation. Her café is closed and thus she is also economically strained. Her son Matt skips online school to game. Kate does not approve, but she is beyond caring in her own increasingly slippery mental state. Their cancer survivor neighbour Alice has to isolate because of her compromised health and she consoles herself with baking. Kate and Matt are the only living people she meets. The three go through rituals that we all remember, like filling days with cleaning or with yoga or smelling food and experiencing joy each day about not having lost the sense of smell. Boredom is a major challenge for these truly isolated characters, unlike those in the busy social world of Shteyngart's novel.

The Fell is written in the form of a series of internal monologues, which creates a sense of claustrophobia: we spend a lot of time in memories and reflections of the characters. For most of the novel, the three characters exist in isolation: there are two scenes of in-person interaction and one face-to-face conversation. The characters seem locked in by government orders, attempting to create liveable rituals, but also manifest a "dark conviction than the appalling uncertainty of hope, the risk of letting yourself believe there might be good times again, any kind of good time again" (Moss 2021, 159–160). This buried hope allows us to see the internal tension in each, their attempts to argue out different positions to themselves. This level of interiority is very different from that offered by Shteyngart, who verbally addresses privilege but none of whose characters experience the drag of daily tedium, like the pile of clothes that is dirty, but not dirty enough to wash that clutter Kate's life in *The Fell*.

The big conflict of the novel is whether Kate, a passionate hiker, will break the isolation to go on a hike. Her son is quite happy in isolation, with a modest vision in which "he games and she does yoga in the garden and they hope neither of them starts with the fever of loss of taste and smell" (Moss 2021, 9). Kate, however, is unable to enjoy the yoga or knitting that her son proposes. She semi-ironically tells herself that "respect for authority is dangerous" as this is the basis of how "totalitarian governments work" (Moss 2021, 118). It is not that she is a pandemic-sceptic, but she annoyed by the government's lack of empathy. Thus Kate breaks the quarantine, because she is suffocating not just in the house, but even more from the socioeconomic precarity and lowered expectations that the family experienced already before the pandemic. As Kate muses:

> And I have motivation, enough motivation to get out of bed every morning and get Matt off to school and go to work and come home and do the shopping and the cooking and pay the bill, that's not nothing, that's actually a whole lot, day after day, year after year (Moss 2021, 118).

This allows Moss to discuss the complexity of deciding what is essential: the containment of infection, mental health or the delicate fabric of human connection. Kate falls during the hike and has to be found by a rescue worker who, because of that, loses the limited time he can spend with his daughter. These are not dramatic incidents, although Kate's accident leads to her hallucinatory encounter with a raven. Instead, these are manifestations of the living experiment of surviving, building relations despite government orders (Alice sees Kate break the isolation but does not report her, as her daughter instructs her to do). The isolation is, above all, shown to be a drag, especially for Alice who is truly cut off her family yet aware of the relative privilege of having a garden and a house without a mortgage. This tension is well conveyed by the stream of consciousness:

> A person can doubtless live like this indefinitely, the background murmur of dread only a little louder week by week, month by month – well, that's obvious, isn't it, people don't die of dread, not even imprisonment, or at least they do but not directly from being shut away, from lack of access to healthcare and poor diet and suicide and violence and many of the reasons that put them there in the first place, shame on her for comparing her comfy house, mortgage paid off, with her kind neighbours and her garden, to a prison. (Moss 2021, 99–100)

Despite living with her son, Kate is cut off from him. This delicate balance is what Moss excels at creating: we see the interiors of the three isolated characters who, nevertheless, are brought together by small acts of care. They do not rise up in protest against government measures but muddle through and look for a potential in the recognition of a shared vulnerability that exceeds sloganeering. Moss's novel is effective precisely because it is not hyper-politicized, because it allows us, as readers, to step inside the heads of characters who are differently vulnerable to the pandemic. We experience both their visceral suffering under the biopolitical mandates of the state and their ambivalence, in the knowledge of real deaths and real suffering by others for whom they are making their sacrifices. There is no right answer, the novel reminds us, because of the complexity of human interdependence. Moss herself has said, as reported by the Twitter feed of her publisher, Picador, that "contagion is one of the oldest stories, but our fears of each other and for each other have been remade in the last year".[26] This fear shows the depth of the recognition of our mutual vulnerability; the challenge is to overcome the fear by respecting this vulnerability but also by remaining awake to our duty to maintain relationality, despite biopolitical mandates.

---

26 https://twitter.com/picadorbooks/status/1374662419730038788.

6 Conclusion

Most literary representations of pandemics have focused on dramatic – and highly spectacular – killer viruses like the plague, AIDS or Ebola, which graphically destroy the body. One just needs to think about the blockbuster hits that were rediscovered during the early pandemic, like Wolfgang Petersen's *Outbreak* (1995) or Steven Soderbergh's *Contagion* (2011) or even Lawrence Wright's prescient bestseller *The End of October* (2020). Wright's book was published in April 2020, in the early months of the special measures, but it was completed before the pandemic, so that review copies were sent out in February, just before the pandemic hit the United States with full force.[27] Wright gets the global pandemic panic right, but he, too, focuses on a dramatic haemorrhagic fever. Effective narrative depends on dramatic representations, especially in our era of the 24/7 news cycle that feeds on events. The complex entanglement of human and non-human actants within this slow violence is hard to imagine.

Fiction, however, is one space in which we can imagine new forms of liveable conditions of vulnerability, as well as new modes of affective relationality. I am not the first to observe that although Foucault makes references to literature in most of his texts, "especially in his early and late works, it remains curiously absent from his lecture courses on biopolitics. *And yet, life, care, and the state of exception take up a prominent place in contemporary fiction*" (de Boever 2013, 3, italics in the original). Fiction is also a space in which people learn to re-relate, not necessarily in the format of the dramatic gesture of resistance but also in detachment. We tend to think of resistance in heroic terms, but this type of resistance often remains locked in a vicious circle, without challenging the core terms of what is being resisted. This could be seen during the COVID-19 pandemic as well, where the two sides clashed over everything, from social distancing to vaccination, remaining locked in a zero-sum game that precluded the possibility of seeing a between, a coming together or a being with.

We do not need another calming story of revolution but one of making trouble and making do. We need to expand our biopolitical imaginations beyond the notions of discipline and control that have been glaringly obvious during the pandemic. Part of the impasse of the pandemic derives from a failure to see alternatives to the zero-sum rhetoric. Perhaps something can emerge if we embrace the concepts of vulnerability and community. Perhaps they can encourage new ways of attaching to the world and to each other.

---

27 This is mentioned, for example, in the *New York Times* review of the novel: https://www.nytimes.com/2020/05/01/books/review/lawrence-wright-end-of-october.html.

References

Agamben, Giorgio. *Means without End: Notes on Politics*. Trans. Vincenzo Binetti and Cesare Casarino. Minneapolis: University of Minnesota Press, 2000.
Agamben, Giorgio. *Where Are We Now? The Pandemic as Politics*. London: Urtext Ltd., 2021.
Arminjon, Mathieu, and Régis Marion-Veyron. "Coronavirus Biopolitics: The Paradox of France's Foucauldian Heritage." *History and Philosophy of the Life Sciences* 43, article number 5 (2021): 1–5.
Bennett, Jane. *Vibrant Matter: A Political Ecology of Things*. Durham: Duke University Press, 2010.
Berlant, Lauren. *Cruel Optimism*. Durham: Duke University Press, 2011.
Berlant, Lauren. "The Commons: Infrastructures for Troubling Times." *Environment and Planning D: Society and Space* 34.3 (2016): 393–419.
Berlant, Lauren, and Lee Edelman. *Sex, or the Unbearable*. Durham: Duke University Press, 2014.
Berlant, Lauren, and Jordan Greenwald. "Affect in the End Times: A Conversation with Lauren Berlant." *Qui Parle: Critical Humanities and Social Sciences* 20.2 (2012): 71–89.
Boever, Arne de. *Narrative Care: Biopolitics and the Novel*. New York: Bloomsbury, 2013.
Braidotti, Rosi. *Nomadic Theory: The Portable Rosi Braidotti*. New York: Columbia University Press, 2012.
Braidotti, Rosi. "Posthuman Affirmative Politics." *Resisting Biopolitics: Philosophical, Political and Performative Strategies*. Eds. S. E. Wilmer and Audronė Žukauskaitė. New York: Routledge, 2016. 30–56.
Braidotti, Rosi. "We Are in *This* Together, But We Are Not One and the Same". *Bioethical Inquiry* 17 (2020): 465–469.
Butler, Judith. *Precarious Life: The Powers of Mourning and Violence*. London: Verso Press, 2004.
Butler, Judith. *Frames of War: When is Life Grievable?* London: Verso Press, 2009.
Butler, Judith. *Notes Towards a Performative Theory of Assembly*. Cambridge: Harvard University Press, 2015.
Butler, Judith. *What World Is This? A Pandemic Phenomenology*. New York: Columbia University Press, 2022.
Campbell, Timothy C. *Improper Life. Technology and Biopolitics from Heidegger to Agamben*. Minneapolis: University of Minnesota Press, 2011.
Campbell, Timothy, and Adam Sitze. "Biopolitics: An Encounter." *Biopolitics. A Reader*. Eds. Timothy Campbell and Adam Sitze. Durham: Duke University Press, 2013. 1–40.
Casarino, Cesare, and Antonio Negri. "It's a Powerful Life: A Conversation on Contemporary Philosophy." *Cultural Critique* 57 (2004): 151–183.
Das, Veena. *Life and Words: Violence and the Descent into the Ordinary*. Berkeley: University of California Press, 2007.
Deleuze, Gilles. *Foucault*. Trans. Sean Hand. London: Athlone, 1986.
Deleuze, Gilles. "What Can a Body Do?" *Expressionism in Philosophy: Spinoza*. Trans. Martin Joughin. New York: Zone Books, 1990. 217–289.
Deleuze, Gilles. "Postscript on the Societies of Control." *October* 59 (Winter, 1992): 3–7.
Derrida, Jacques. *Specters of Marx: The State of the Debt, the Work of Mourning and the New International*. Trans. Peggy Kamuf. New York: Routledge, 1994.
Derrida, Jacques. "Autoimmunity: Real and Symbolic Suicides – A Dialogue with Jacques Derrida." *Philosophy in a Time of Terror: Dialogues with Jürgen Habermas and Jacques Derrida*. Ed. Giovanna Borradori. Chicago: University of Chicago Press, 2003. 85–136.
Esposito, Roberto. *Bios: Biopolitics and Philosophy*. Trans. Timothy Campbell. Minneapolis: University of Minnesota Press, 2008.

Esposito, Roberto. *Immunitas: The Protection and Negation of Life*. Trans. Zakiya Hanafi. Cambridge: Polity, 2011.
Ettlinger, Nancy. "Governmentality as Epistemology." *Annals of the Association of American Geographers* 101.3 (2011): 537–560.
Fassin, Didier. "Another Politics of Life Is Possible." *Theory, Culture & Society* 26.5 (2009): 44–60.
Fisher, Mark. *Capitalist Realism. Is There No Alternative?* Winchester: O Books, 2009.
Foucault, Michel. *Discipline and Punish. The Birth of the Prison*. Trans. Alan Sheridan. New York: Vintage, 1977.
Foucault, Michel. *The History of Sexuality*, vol. I. Trans. Robert Hurley. New York: Pantheon Books, 1978.
Glissant, Édouard. *Poetics of Relation*. Trans. Betsy Wing. Ann Arbor: University of Michigan Press, 1997.
Haraway, Donna. *Simians, Cyborgs and Women: The Reinvention of Nature*. London: Free Association Books, 1991.
Haraway, Donna. *Companion Species Manifesto: Dogs, People, and Significant Otherness*. Chicago: University of Chicago Press, 2003.
Harbisher, Ben. "Biopolitics, Eugenics and the New State Racism." *Power, Media and the COVID-19 Pandemic. Framing Public Discourse*. Eds. Stuart Price and Ben Harbisher. London: Routledge, 2022. 22–54.
Hardt, Michael, and Antonio Negri. *Empire*. Cambridge: Harvard University Press, 2000.
Husserl, Edmund. *Ideas Pertaining to a Pure Phenomenology and to a Phenomenological Philosophy: Second Book*. Trans. Fred Kersten. Dordrecht: Kluwer Academic Publishers, 1989.
Khanna, Ranjana. "Disposability." *Differences* 20.1 (2009): 181–198.
Lobao, Linda, Mia Gray, Levin Cox and Michael Kitson. "The Shrinking State? Understanding the Assault on the Public Sector." *Cambridge Journal of Regions, Economy and Society* 11.3 (2018): 389–408.
Lorenzini, Daniele. "Biopolitics in the Time of Coronavirus". *Critical Inquiry* 47 (2021): S40–S45.
Lupton, Deborah. *The Quantified Self. A Sociology of Self-Tracking*. Cambridge: Polity, 2016.
Lupton, Deborah. *Data Selves*. Cambridge: Polity, 2019.
Mandel, Emily St. John. *Station Eleven*. New York: Vintage, 2014.
Marling, Raili. "Opacity as a Feminist Strategy: Postcolonial and Postsocialist Entanglements with Neoliberalism." *Postcolonial and Postsocialist Dialogues: Intersections, Opacities, Challenges in Feminist Theorizing and Practice*. Eds. Redi Koobak, Madina Tlostanova and Suruchi Thapar-Björkert. London: Routledge, 2021. 94–108.
Mayes, Christopher. *The Biopolitics of Lifestyle. Foucault, Ethics and Healthy Choices*. London and New York: Routledge, 2016.
Merleau-Ponty, Maurice. *The Phenomenology of Perception*. Trans. Donald A. Landes. London: Routledge and Kegan Paul, 1970.
Mills, Catherine. *Biopolitics*. London and New York: Routledge, 2018.
Moss, Sarah. *The Fell*. New York: Farrar, Straus and Giroux, 2021.
Nail, Thomas. "Biopower and Control." *Between Deleuze and Foucault*. Eds. Nicolae Morar, Thomas Nail and Daniel W. Smith. Edinburgh: Edinburgh University Press, 2016. 247–263.
Nixon, Rob. *Slow Violence and the Environmentalism of the Poor*. Cambridge: Harvard University Press, 2011.
Nunez, Sigrid. *Salvation City*. New York: Riverhead Books, 2010.
Prozorov, Sergei. "Foucault's Affirmative Biopolitics: Cynic Parrhesia and the Biopower of the Powerless." *Political Theory* 45.6 (2017): 801–823.

Rae, Gavin. "Derrida, Autoimmunity, and Critique." *Distinktion: Journal of Social Theory* DOI: 10.1080/1600910X.2022.2039739.

Repo, Jemima. "*Herculine Barbin* and the Omission of Biopolitics in Judith Butler's Gender Genealogy." *Feminist Theory* 15.1 (2014): 73–88.

Repo, Jemima. *The Biopolitics of Gender*. New York: Oxford University Press, 2017.

Rose, Nikolas, and Carlos Novas. "Biological Citizenship." *Global Assemblages: Technology, Politics and Ethics as Anthropological Problems*. Eds. Aihwa Ong and Stephen Collier. Malden, MA: Blackwell, 2005. 439–463.

Sawicki, Jana. "Precarious Life: Butler and Foucault on Biopolitics." *Biopower: Foucault and Beyond*. Eds. Nicolae Morar and Vernon Cisney. Chicago: University of Chicago Press, 2016. 228–242.

Sedgwick, Eve Kosofsky. *Touching Feeling: Affect, Pedagogy, Performance*. Durham: Duke University Press, 2003.

Shteyngart, Gary. *Our Country Friends*. New York: Random House, 2021.

Siisiäinen, Lauri. *Foucault, Biopolitics and Resistance*. Abingdon: Routledge, 2019.

Sikka, Tina. "Feminist Materialism and Covid-19: The Agential Activation of Everyday Objects." *NORA – Nordic Journal of Feminist and Gender Research* 29.1 (2021): 4–16.

Slaby, Jan, and Birgitt Röttger-Rössler. "Introduction: Affect in Relation." *Affect in Relation. Families, Places, Technologies*. Eds.Birgitt Röttger-Rösslerand Jan Slaby. London: Routledge. 1–28.

Marko Pajević
State Control Versus Humanity: Biopolitics and Health in Juli Zeh's *The METHOD* (*Corpus Delicti*, 2009)

Abstract: We are currently experiencing an unprecedented acceleration in the biopoliticization of society. The presentation of the COVID-19 virus by the political establishment and the media has allowed for a far-reaching transformation of our forms of life that few would have considered possible at the beginning of 2020. In July 2020, the acclaimed German writer and public intellectual Juli Zeh published an explanatory book on her highly successful novel from 2009, *The METHOD*, often touted as *the* book for the COVID-19 era. The plot is set in the mid-twenty-first century and follows a court case against a woman who begins to doubt the infallibility of the METHOD, the health system the entire state is based on. This state has eradicated disease and pain, to the almost unanimous acclaim, it seems, of the population. The biopolitical state described in the novel is nonetheless not a utopia but a dystopia. Following a discussion of what biopolitics is and implies in this context, the chapter analyses how health can become a privileged lever for judicial change. The chapter connects the novel to Zeh and Trojanow's 2009 essay *Attack on Freedom. Security delusion, surveillance state and the dismantlement of civil rights*. They examine and reject the restrictions of individual liberties in the aftermath of 9/11 and remind us that democracy is fundamentally a limitation of state power. Just like terrorism, health can be instrumentalized to undermine democratic principles. The chapter investigates different definitions of health and their consequences, as well as the judicial procedures depicted in the novel. These two aspects shed critical light on the contemporary biologically determined idea of the human and on the dangers of exaggerated health politics as evoked in the novel, as well as on the parallels to recent political and social developments. Juli Zeh's literary fiction is examined as a convincing warning and a crucial tool for raising awareness and preventing corrosion of the constitutional state.

1 Introduction

We are currently experiencing an unprecedented acceleration in the biopoliticization of liberal democratic societies. The media and political presentation of the COVID-19 virus has contributed to a far-reaching transformation of our forms of life that few would have considered possible at the beginning of 2020. Fearing for their health, the majority of people have accepted curtailments of their rights and freedoms and granted the state a level of control over their lives that would have seemed ludicrous only weeks earlier. The obligatory wearing of masks, the introduction of curfews, penalties for leaving the area within a two-, five- or fifteen-kilometre radius of one's home, mandatory vaccination for some professions and indirectly for all, a ban on meeting friends and family – these measures have become reality and have met with little resistance. In this chapter, I refer mostly to the situation in Germany to remind us of how heated the public debate was (the past tense is a sign of optimism while writing this). Even though there are many comparable features throughout the Western world, every country acted in its own fashion, depending on various political, cultural and social conditions. In many places, the restrictions were accompanied by public encouragement of denunciation of rule-breakers, and critics were often vilified, even if respected before;[1] worse, journalists, police officers and medics who publicly opposed such measures lost their jobs or licences to practise.[2] Actors who produced satires on the restrictions have experienced a violent media crackdown and have been threatened by major television production companies with the loss of current and future roles.[3] Leading politicians have spoken of "privileges" when referring to what so far have been known as basic civil rights.[4]

In July 2020, the much-acclaimed German writer and public intellectual Juli Zeh published an explanatory book about her highly successful novel from 2009, *The METHOD*, in German *Corpus Delicti* (English translation 2012).[5] At the time of

---

[1] Politicians in Germany urged the media and scientists to present the virus in dramatic terms to reach consent regarding the measures. Cf. *Die Welt*, 8 February 2021, cf. also a follow-up article on 9 February 2021. The City of Essen for example prepared an anonymous online-form for denunciation, for a discussion, cf. https://www.faz.net/aktuell/politik/inland/corona-in-essen-ruft-die-stadt-zur-denunziation-von-buergern-auf-17001551.html. On 23 December 2020, the Belgian BRF even spoke of an "epidemic of denunciation": https://brf.be/national/1443092/. Examples for formerly highly respected specialists fallen in disgrace and blocked of practically all established media are in Germany Wolfgang Wodarg and Sucharit Bhakdi.
[2] In their position, they are supposed to follow and represent the official opinion, see for example *Süddeutsche Zeitung*, 4 November 2020.
[3] See for the latter the German #allesdichtmachen, April 2021. For various reactions, cf. *Berliner Zeitung*, 30 April 2021.
[4] This includes German Chancellor Angela Merkel. Israel was the first country to offer these "privileges" only to the vaccinated, beginning on 21 March 2021, whereas the unvaccinated were not allowed to fully enjoy their civil rights. Unvaccinated Israelis could not enter bars, restaurants, or sports facilities and were practically banned from public life, measures copied then by most European countries.
[5] On 2 June 2020, Julia Encke criticised Zeh in a review for not having changed her position in view of the COVID-19 context. The journalist believed that the virus called for a limitation of

its publication critics had hailed Zeh as the German George Orwell and the novel was compared to Aldous Huxley's *Brave New World*.[6] Zeh's 2020 update is no coincidence since the novel has been touted as *the* book for the COVID-19 era. The work is set in the mid-21st century, and hinges on a court case against a woman who had begun to doubt the infallibility of the METHOD, which is the health system the entire state in the novel is based on. This state has eradicated disease and pain, to the almost unanimous acclaim, it seems, of the population. I will demonstrate in the following why the the form of biopolitics described in the novel is nonetheless not a utopia but a dystopia. To this end, I will start out by giving some key elements of how biopolitics is understood here and what it implies in this context. I will explore medical and judicial aspects of the novel, and the consequences of these for our ideas about the human, in order to elucidate what this can tell us about the way COVID-19 has been dealt with over its first two years.

2 Biopolitics

I will use Michel Foucault's influential definition of biopolitics as the basis for the following. Foucault was not the first to use the term, nor does he fully develop it or is he consistent in its use; indeed he speaks at times also of biopower. Before him, throughout the twentieth century, the term biopolitics has been used for organicistic conceptions of the state, conceiving of politics and a state as a living organism.[7] More relevant for our topic than this socio-biological approach is Foucault's definition in the context of his reflections on governance from 1978. He sees biopolitics as the way the modern state manages demographic phenomena such as health, hygiene, birth rates, life expectancy and race and points to their growing importance since the nineteenth century (Foucault 2004). Two years prior, he had mentioned the term to describe a shift in the eighteenth century from a sovereign power, directed at the human body, that "makes die and lets live" towards the processes that "make live and let die". In other words, according to Foucault, in the nineteenth century, as the new liberal economic system develops, attention is directed at the population and at methods of regulating and making use of the life of the people (Foucault 1997,

---
basic rights. Almost all reader reactions, however, congratulated Zeh on confirming her prioritization of the constitution and refuted the article as weak and naive.
6 For example, Fischer 2007; Scheck 2009. For Orwell, cf. also the review by Ings 2012.
7 Cf. for the conceptual history the introduction to this volume, co-written by Raili Marling and myself, of which I repeat some essential elements for my proposition here, as well as Thumfart 2008, Lemke 2011 (originally in German 2007); and the introduction in Campbell and Sitze 2013.

213–235). The interest is obvious: in order to prosper, the state and business need people to function well.

Foucault's concept of "disciplinary society" (as analysed in his work on the psychiatric clinic from 1961, the hospital from 1963, and the prison from 1975) implies a positive suppression, a rationally evidenced care system. In spite of its risks, as with the term *power* generally in Foucault's oeuvre, this is not bad in itself: who would want to oppose the state as a provider of health care, education and infrastructure of all kinds? Every convenience of our modern life is based on this. The benefits of a regulating state are evident, and in many societies, this has given rise to historically unprecedented social circumstances with an exceptional level of justice and wellbeing for a great majority of the population.

The question Foucault raises is how biopolitics, developed to promote and care for life, could turn into fatal and destructive processes. His argument operates with a very broad notion of racism, which, he contends, is used to fragment the continuum of humanity so that the state can, on the premises of biopower, fight what is termed as "lower life" in the interest of a healthier and purer life in general. Looking at life in such a biological manner paves the way for killing some individuals in the interest of the population as a whole: an individual deemed racially or otherwise inferior is a threat to the population and needs to be eradicated. This extreme position has been put into practice, and not only by National Socialism. Its disastrous ideology was not the result of a lack of reason or education, but one of the possible logical consequences of Enlightenment when it takes the form of instrumentalized reason.[8] Biopower and biopolitics can be used to subdue the body politic and to control the population in the interest of what we hopefully agree are inhumane goals (cf. Foucault 1976).

Giorgio Agamben builds on Foucault's work but takes a more radical position. By looking at life reductively from a biological or functional perspective, late-twentieth century politics has, in his view, become completely biopolitical, and for him that equals totalitarianism. He develops this thesis via the notion of the *homo sacer*, a figure of Roman law, which places a person outside divine and human law. A *homo sacer* can therefore be killed but not sacrificed for religious purposes. Such a being becomes, according to Agamben, "bare life". Agamben compares that with the (concentration) camps, which, in his view, have become the global biopolitical paradigm (Agamben 1998, 166). He refers to the ancient Greek difference between *zoë* and *bios*, that is, the bare fact of life as opposed to life as a form of life (Agamben 1998, 11). This latter term implies for him a life that

---

[8] Cf. Horkheimer and Adorno 1947; Bauman 1989. For a treatment of Horkheimer and Adorno's position in this context of biopolitics, cf. Thomas Crew in this volume.

is impossible to separate from its form, which is possibilities and potentialities and never simply facts (Agamben 2000).⁹ Achille Mbembe (2003) then coined the term "necropolitics", the power to dictate who may live and who must die.

Agamben has applied these ideas to the current COVID-19 crisis and to his native Italy in a collection of public interventions from February to November 2020 (Agamben 2021). Seeing that Italians are willing to sacrifice practically everything when faced with the relatively small risk of getting sick, he deplores that bare life has become the sole criterion in today's society (Agamben 2021, 17–18). Referring to Carl Schmitt's notion of the *state of exception*, Agamben (2021, 18) points out that this has become the norm in a purely biological state. Agamben (2021, 8) does not shy away from pointing out the similarities to the National Socialist state of exception that lasted for twelve years. He points to the new devices of monitoring and surveillance, security cameras and cell phones, that allow for a level of control that far exceeds any former totalitarian forms (Agamben 2021, 43).

I suggested before that biopolitics for Foucault is not a normative term. Agamben, among others, radicalizes the debate by focusing on the detrimental potential of what in Foucault is simply one form of governmentality that has its liberating as well as its oppressive options and aspects. Agamben is of course aware of this ambivalence, but he chooses to use the term to attack certain tendencies that represent a risk to an open society. This has indeed stimulated much thought across social studies, even though I would be wary of unhelpful polarization. If in this essay I use the term biopolitics for undemocratic forms of governance, I do not imply that all forms of biopolitics are necessarily undemocratic and to be condemned.

In the case of Juli Zeh, we know that she was conversant with Foucault's and Agamben's ideas while writing *The METHOD*; biopolitics was a concept that informed her work on the novel (Zeh 2020, 91). The protagonist, Mia, owns a book by Agamben, a present from her brother, although Mia claims not to have read it (Zeh 2009, 128). Zeh takes a stance: even though a work of fiction, *The METHOD* conveys a clear criticisism of what can be termed a biopolitical regime with many achievements for health care which, however, come at the cost of control and, where necessary, of suppression of opposition. The book thematizes, and represents itself as, resistance against the dangerous sides of such biopolitics. Zeh's novel stands in the context of her general concern about the growing fixation on the body in our society and she fears for humanity and solidarity when a spurious notion of health is made the main criterion (Zeh 2020, 92).

---

9 That Agamben's distinction between the two Greek terms is not precise is explained in Michael Eskin's chapter to this volume.

Along with the novel, she published a political essay on how the state creates fear of terrorism to increase biopolitical power at the expense of civil rights (Trojanow and Zeh 2009). For her, the state's task is to keep people from harming each other; the relation of one individual to oneself should be of no concern to the state. The right to do harm to oneself is an essential part of personal freedom (Zeh 2020, 93). Otherwise, our society's vision of humanity is at stake, but in her view, due to the economization of our society, we are already at a point where most people think it normal to subject human beings to criteria of efficiency and optimization (Zeh 2020, 94).

Such biopolitical phenomena are all about human enhancement, of course, but we have forgotten to ask the question *cui bono* – in whose interest? Do the people themselves profit from their enhancement, and under what criteria? Or is all of that rather a question of being more economically profitable for some other people or interest group? Or does it make people more susceptible to political control? As is now widely known, practical innovations such as using a debit or credit card, a mobile phone or a smart watch instead of cash generate big data, expose us to the depredations of data-mining and enable biopolitical surveillance and control over "the transparent citizen".

Health is the key factor in biopolitics: a healthy person is functional in the economy or in war, the health care industry itself is one of the biggest economic powers, and health – or rather fear of illness, pain and death – is a very powerful tool of manipulation. We are currently experiencing how a virus is used for the transformation of society, an economic transformation towards much greater inequality and a political transformation towards what is, in biopolitical terms, a far more controlling state, or even worse, super-powerful companies that control the state.[10] Many citizens have willingly given up their fundamental civil rights, such as freedom of movement, of assembly and to some degree of expression. Huxley's 1958 prediction of future dictatorships being based on consent, partly achieved by drugs, partly by manipulative media, is close at hand. Zeh's novel, on which this chapter will now focus, draws the reader's attention to this danger. The COVID-19 crisis, at any rate, demonstrates that only a minimum of force, or

---

10 This is not new but COVID-19 made it possible to accelerate the tendency dramatically. For the connection between COVID-19 and digitalization, see Schmitt (2021) who points to the risks involved in the digitalization of the educational system which allows for a complete digital learning biography, usable by employers, that is, their algorithms scanning the Cloud without any need for a job interview, for school performance but also for conclusions concerning the character, interests and potential threats (86–89). Also Simanowski (2021) underlines that the digitalization pushed by the virus means total datafication and thus control and the transparent citizen (56–64). He warns that the year after the virus-crisis, 2021, is the year of the crisis of democracy.

even the slightest threat of it, is sufficient to get the majority to consent. Indeed, we could observe that, out of fear of illness, many people were demanding more and tighter restrictions.[11] Time has shown, however, that, once individual rights are given up due to a state of emergency, they are hardly ever fully restored.[12]

3 The Background and Plot of Zeh's Novel

Health biopolitics in this perspective is just another aspect of this restructuring of the state towards authoritarianism, driven by instrumentalized fear. It is highly instructive to read *The METHOD* as a playing out of what can happen if we give up our right to privacy and freedom for the sake of state control. Zeh wants to reach a large audience with her story in order to influence public discourse and the way people think. She explicitly opts for political literature with this novel,[13] which is also evident in the form and history of *The METHOD*. First of all, it exists in three forms: it was originally a commissioned theatre play for the *RuhrTriennale* festival in 2007 with the theme "Middle Ages", so the starting point was a modern witch hunt (Zeh 2020, 20). The play has had a series of successful runs in various theatres. Then Zeh decided to publish it in the form of a novel in 2009 to reach a wider audience. The original theatrical form can still be perceived in the classical dramatic structure with the exposition, mounting action, climax and peripeteia, retarding moments, and finally catastrophe, as well as in the prototypical character design. In 2010, Zeh also reworked it as an audio drama, together with the band *Slut*, and toured with this rock-opera (Zeh and Slut 2010). A film

---

11 The author of another dystopian novel, *Paradise City* (2020), Zoë Beck published an article in the weekly newspaper *Der Freitag* on 14 January 2021, where she explains that the events around vaccination and a resulting two-class society would be a great science-fiction topic but too close to our present reality. However, since she regards these vaccinations as reasonable, she does not want to write about it. She sees the capitalist interests at work behind these events but seems to accept them as justified responses to the risk of the virus. Until the spring of 2022, a considerable majority of the German population were in favour of strict or even stricter measures.
12 In Germany, this can be exemplified by the measures against left-wing terrorism in the 1970s – almost all of the control mechanisms and restrictions of freedom imposed at the time, supposedly only for the duration of the crisis, are still in place. The same thing is true of post-9/11 measures; cf. the interview with Heribert Prantl, a leading German journalist (*Süddeutsche Zeitung*) on 30 January 2021, in which he states that he has never before been so concerned about basic human rights and condemns the un-constitutional practice of the executive ruling by decree since the beginning of the COVID-19 crisis, with decrees cancelling basic human rights, as well as a lack of pluralism and debate.
13 Zeh 2020, 14: "*Corpus Delicti* wollte von Anfang an ein politischer Text sein."

was also planned, but the script has not yet been realized as the filmmaker fell ill. Contrary to the novel, in the script the METHOD is limited to one city area separated from the world around it, which consists of slums. The City people become infertile – their all-around sanitization leads to degeneration – and there is organized smuggling of embryos from the slum inhabitants (Zeh 2020, 192–194), a plot development that underlines the damaging effects on health of the supposed health measures. Evidently Zeh intends to reach a wide audience, and does so: today the novel is often taught in schools, there are didactic versions of it with glossaries for non-native speakers and students and also study notes for school pupils (Zeh 2015; Leis and Rieker 2016; Mayr 2013).

Now a highly acclaimed author and the holder of many literary prizes, Zeh has, however, met with criticism for her style: aesthetically it is not very elaborate and she uses metaphors considered by some critics less than successful.[14] Yet this is probably also part of her success: she writes accessibly, building her works around socially relevant topics, thematizing complex issues in a relatively straightforward narrative and in everyday language. The result is a work of literature that provides much food for thought without overwhelming the reader. Whether one likes that or not is a matter of taste or perspective. I will accordingly pay little attention to the aesthetic side of her poetics but will focus here instead on the plot and its political and social implications. This is an example of engaged literature with a clearly recognizable message.

The METHOD is about Mia Holl, a young biologist, who lives a well-adjusted life in the mid-twenty-first century, in a country we can assume to be Germany, where health in the form of the METHOD has become the foundation of the state and, with the help of state regulation, information technologies and surveillance, illness is practically eradicated. Mia is a supporter of the METHOD, as is virtually everybody else, apart from her brother Moritz, who represents free will and the choice of an unregulated joyful life. When her brother is accused of having raped and killed a woman and found guilty due to a DNA test of the sperm, he kills himself without ever stopping to claim his innocence. Mia had loved and trusted her brother and this event throws her off track. Disregarding the health, exercise and reporting requirements, she comes into conflict with the METHOD. The conflict escalates quickly, and she becomes opposed to the system, which in her view has killed her brother. Its chief representative in the novel is leading ideologue and journalist Heinrich Kramer, who, in typically totalitarian fashion, exercises power in all fields, legislative, judicial, executive and the media, "the fourth power" in the

---

[14] She says herself that the political direction of the impact of this novel comes at the expense of its literary complexity (Zeh 2020, 132).

new system. The trial is pivotal to the novel, as the German subtitle indicates: *Ein Prozess*. This word has two meanings, a court case and a process – it thus indicates the gradual change in Mia's assessment of the METHOD. Anyone acquainted with German modernist literature could hardly miss the Kafka echo, and that while it may have been unconscious on Zeh's part,[15] the connection with an absurd, omnipresent and inescapable system is thrown into sharp relief.

Apart from the verdict condemning Mia, given in the second short chapter, following the delineation of the main ideological principles of the METHOD in chapter 1, the book's structure is chronological, with only some chapters going back in time to shed light on the relationship between Mia and Moritz, and Moritz representing life as we know it and in robust opposition to the values of the new order. The novel gains philosophical depth in Moritz and Mia's discussions of these opposing worldviews and ideas about the human.

4 The Context: the Threat of a Surveillance State

Zeh's book documents in a fictional form how health can become a privileged lever for judicial change. Zeh herself holds the position of a judge at the institutional court of the federal state of Brandenburg. She is not only one of the most successful German literary writers of our time, and a very prolific one (cf. Preusser 2010, 2), but has also published in the field of law and is well informed about the judicial context of her topics. She is a public intellectual (cf. Herminghouse 2008), who places great importance on the societal and political commitment of literature and who defends the judicial basis of liberal democracy.[16] She is certainly politically active outside her literary writings (and she notes the difference between a political writer and political literature; Zeh 2020, 129–131), writing newspaper articles, appearing on talk shows, launching debates (for instance on the biometric passport by suing the state for introducing it), and publishing political essays and open letters to politicians.[17]

---

15 Zeh makes no mention of Kafka in her explanations in 2020. But she does explain that she often encounters this phenomenon of unconscious citing and refers to parallels of her book to *Antigone*, or almost literal passages from Thomas Mann's *Zauberberg* (*The Magic Mountain*) she was not aware of (Zeh 2020, 108–111).
16 Cf. Zeh and Oswald, 2011. Zeh was invited to respond to Martin R. Dean, Thomas Hettche, Matthias Politycki, and Michael Schindhelm's question "What is the novel good for?" ("Was soll der Roman?"). Zeh's response was titled "Social relevance needs a political direction" ("Gesellschaftliche Relevanz braucht eine politische Richtung"), 2005.
17 For a collection of these often brilliant public interventions over ten years, from 2005 to 2014, cf. Zeh 2014.

In 2009, in the same year as *The METHOD* appeared, Zeh published *Angriff auf die Freiheit. Sicherheitswahn, Überwachungsstaat und der Abbau bürgerlicher Rechte* (Attack on Freedom. Security delusion, surveillance state and the dismantling of civil rights) together with another activist and committed German writer, Ilija Trojanow. The context of her commitment to civil rights and her fight against the dangers of a surveillance state cannot be stressed enough in dealing with her novel. I will therefore summarize some of the most relevant aspects that Trojanow and Zeh treat in their well-informed book-length essay.

They observe the change from the 1980s West German mass protests against a simple updating of registration data to the acceptance of biometric passports with fingerprints after 9/11. They want to reawaken awareness of the attainment of civil rights and the dangers of losing them to a surveillance state. In terms of surveillance, the worst totalitarian regimes of the past pale in comparison to the boundless possibilities new media and forms of communication offer. The authors insist, quoting John Stuart Mill, that the effects of state power have proven to be infinitely worse than the misconduct of any individual (Zeh and Trojanow 2009, 26–27). They compare the growing security (sinking crime rates and relative relaxation of tension between the major global political powers) with unjustified fearmongering in the form of media hype. They see the main turning point in 9/11 and the instrumentalizing of a fabricated fear of terrorism after the attacks. The number of victims of terrorism, they point out, particularly in Western societies, is negligible compared to people dying of heat stroke in Germany or incorrect medication in hospitals. The danger of terrorism consists mostly in our destroying our democratic freedom due to fear (Zeh and Trojanow 2009, 36–37).[18] The introduction of torture and the suspension of the rule of law by the USA in Guantánamo for those deemed "terrorists" or "enemies of the USA", according to them, perpetuates the state of exception in the sense given the term by Carl Schmitt, the leading legal thinker of the Third Reich, whose ideas, notably on sovereignty, are still highly influential, particularly amongst neo-liberals. Dragnet investigation, biometric passports, surveillance of telecommunications, online monitoring, CCTV – all these measures, Zeh and Trojanow claim based on various studies, have proven to be failures in terms of their efficacy in the fight against crime or terrorism. But an entire industry dedicated to such measures and reaping great profits at the expense of civil rights continues to prosper and expand (Zeh and Trojanow 2009, 55–62). Zeh and Trojanow (2009, 68) also attack the principle of prevention – in 2009, there were one million people on

---

[18] For the dramatic change in Western societies after 9/11, cf. Weidner (2021) who claims that Al Qaida succeeded since, following 9/11, the West has dismantled its own rights of freedom and democracy and thus lost its credibility in the world.

the list of terrorist suspects in the USA, and the list continues to grow. Prevention contradicts principles of the rule of law, such as presumption of innocence, equal treatment or interdiction of discrimination (Zeh and Trojanow 2009, 70). Guantánamo has become the symbol of the new order and in Germany too there are more and more voices calling for torture as a legal means (Zeh and Trojanow 2009, 109). Trojanow and Zeh (2009, 78) remind us that democracy's basic principle is the limitation of state power and warn us that democratic countries can destroy themselves from within when they forget this principle.

Of particular interest is their discussion of the imbrication of politics and media. The media prepare the way for the new preventive state. The authors explain this first of all with the argument that fear sells and journalists as well as politicians feed off the hype (Zeh and Trojanow 2009, 82–83). They explain the fact that almost all media are streamlined and contribute, uncritically, to the unjustified fear of terrorism by their lack of resources for genuine investigative journalism. It would demand great effort to go against the mainstream, as opposed to simply showing up for the next crisis or, indeed, manufacturing one crisis after another to survive in the absence of real journalism. But this is not what a free press should do; it is manipulation (Zeh and Trojanow 2009, 86–88). "Inner security" has become an "attention cake" ("Aufmerksamkeitskuchen"), they say, and people fight for a slice of it (Zeh and Trojanow 2009, 94). In politics too fear sells: it is a tried and tested tool of power (Zeh and Trojanow 2009, 104), even when it works against our constitution and political initiatives are regularly rebuffed by constitutional courts (Zeh and Trojanow 2009, 100).

Since all these security debates bear no rational relation to the real situation of security in Germany, which has never been better, the authors conclude that the primary objective of the debate is to direct attention away from what is really going on: the worldwide struggle for information, which equals power (Zeh and Trojanow 2009, 120 and 126). The book refers to the British House of Lords, whose Constitution Committee in 2008 analysed the situation, reaching the conclusion that delusional security measures were the greatest threat to British democracy since WWII (Zeh and Trojanow 2009, 132). Trojanow and Zeh (2009, 134) state that this control hysteria has gone beyond the "fight against terrorism" and has reached other areas, including the health system. They end with an appeal to the public at large to change its attitude and not to participate in such simplifications, which lead by default to an authoritarian state (Zeh and Trojanow 2009, 137–9).

5 Definitions of Health

Like terrorism, news about health appeals to fear, and fear calls for protection by authority. The novel merely radicalizes the already existing phenomena, as we can see at the outset: its first chapter offers a one-page extract from the preface of Heinrich Kramer's ideological bible of the METHOD, titled *Health as Principle of State Legitimation*, in its 25th edition. Its first sentence says: "Gesundheit ist ein Zustand des vollkommenen körperlichen, geistigen und sozialen Wohlbefindens – und nicht die bloße Abwesenheit von Krankheit." This is actually the WHO definition of health since 1948: "Health is a state of complete physical, mental and social well-being and not merely the absence of disease or infirmity."[19] There is no explicit reference; the link is left for the reader to make.

Caroline Welsh sees in Zeh's translation a shift from *complete* to *vollkommen*, with the German term, in Welsh's view, being closer in meaning to *absolute*, so that in Zeh the definition undergoes a fundamental change in character.[20] While *complete* may indeed be rendered appropriately as *vollkommen*, Welsh's discussion draws attention to the key issue of language and translation in law. Welsh clearly demonstrates the problems inherent in the WHO's definition of health by tracing shifts from the *human right* to health to a preventive *duty* of health. Such ideas arose as early as 1806, Friedrich August Röber for instance offering this succinct formulation: "The citizen needs to be healthy and able to work to contribute his due to the conservation of the state. If he is not, he is a burden to the state and is worse than a dead member." ("Der Bürger muß gesund und arbeitsfähig seyn, um das Seine zur Erhaltung des Ganzen beitragen zu können. Ist er dies nicht, so fällt er dem Staate zur Last und ist schlimmer, als ein todtes Mitglied.")[21] Despite such voices, the canonical German position insisted on the voluntariness of using state assistance or not: Lorenz von Stein is aware of the significance of health for general welfare but nonetheless explicitly prioritizes free self-determination (1882, 133). Welsh (2016, 227) argues that during the twentieth century, the latter shifts out of sight in favour of a duty of health and demonstrates how the WHO has, in recent years, increasingly "prioritized" the principle of prevention in a "new orientation

---

[19] Cf. the WHO, https://www.who.int/about/governance/constitution.
[20] "Mit Hilfe einer leichten, aber folgenreichen Verschiebung in der Wortwahl von einem 'bestmöglichen' und 'umfassenden' (engl. complete) 'körperlichen, geistigen und sozialen Wohlbefinden' (Ottawa-Charta) hin zu einem 'vollkommenen' (engl. absolute) 'körperlichen, geistigen und sozialen Wohlbefinden' (Corpus Delicti) verlagert der Roman das Gewicht der Gesundheitsdefinition grundlegend" (Welsh 2016, 223).
[21] Quoted in Welsh (2016, 223) who takes this citation from Frevert (1984, 32).

of the health system".²² This principle of prevention is rooted also in the financial crisis of the health system due to demographic developments; this has led to a penalty system, linking health insurance benefits to a healthy lifestyle. However, this has had little practical relevance so far, since it comes into effect only if the person insured becomes ill through a premeditated criminal act (cf. Müller-Dietz 2011, 92). Welsh argues that the WHO has progressively focused on what are considered risky lifestyles. This renders the concept of health as a duty normative, and it morally stigmatizes non-conformist behaviour (Welsh 2016, 220).

Of even greater concern is the connection between contemporary fitness culture and a financially interested health insurance system, which is already working with bonuses for good health of its members – a clear step towards a surveillance system (Welsh 2016, 222). Voluntary self-tracking mechanisms such as Apple watches and health apps are already in place and internalized, with the result that we are realizing Foucault's prediction in *Discipline and Punish. The Birth of the Prison* (cf. Bröckling 2004, 214). Preventive measures made possible by such an attitude towards health are in direct opposition to fundamental human rights.²³ The danger of the idea of prevention is the focus of Christian Geyer's (2009) comment on the novel. Geyer commends it for having demonstrated that prevention becomes the pretext for the permanent state of exception in a "dictatorship of prevention" ("Diktatur der Vorsorge"). Professor of law Heinz Müller-Dietz (2011, 94) confirms this view. Hollywood blockbusters have already pointed to the risks of prevention in criminal prosecution, such as Steven Spielberg's *Minority Report* (2002). Zeh (2020, 170–172) stresses that the METHOD is based on the idea of prevention and that this idea by itself constitutes a threat to freedom.

To this tendency Welsh opposes the *Universal Declaration of Human Rights* from 1948, in which health is defined as a component of an appropriate quality of life: "Everyone has the right to a standard of living adequate for the health and wellbeing of himself and of his family, including food, clothing, housing and medical care and necessary social services, and the right to security in the event of

---

22 World Health Organization (2013a): Health 2020: a European policy framework supporting action across government and society for health and well-being. https://apps.who.int/iris/handle/10665/131300 [18.10.2015], 10: "Dies erfordert eine Neuausrichtung der Gesundheitssysteme, so dass sie Krankheitsprävention priorisieren [. . .]", cited by Welsh (2016, 219).
23 Cf. Welsh (2016, 223): "The preventive measures necessary to ensure these rights legitimize in their turn healthpolitical measures that suspend fundamental human rights freedoms. A right to health understood this way has little in common with the human rights 'right to health'." ("Die zur Gewährleistung dieses Rechts notwendigen Präventionsmaßnahmen legitimieren ihrerseits gesundheitspolitische Maßnahmen, die grundlegende menschenrechtliche Freiheiten außer Kraft setzen. Ein so verstandenes Recht auf Gesundheit hat mit dem menschenrechtlichen 'Recht auf Gesundheit' wenig gemeinsam.").

unemployment, sickness, disability, widowhood, old age or other lack of livelihood in circumstances beyond his control."[24] In 2000, the UN confirmed this much more cautious definition of health as a right "to the enjoyment of a variety of facilities, goods, services and conditions necessary for the realization of the highest attainable standard of health."[25] There is no claim to "complete health" or even a "duty of health", which would contravene the UN guidelines, which explicitly say that the state cannot insure good health or protect from ill health. The *Declaration of Human Rights* embeds health very clearly within human rights, saying that the state has to ensure health measures are compatible with other human rights and with human dignity (cf. Welsh 2016, 230). Within this context of human rights, we need, in fact, to preserve a right to illness ("ein Recht auf Krankheit"), as Welsh concludes, which is threatened by recent developments promoted by the WHO.

The novel opens thus with a conflict between the WHO and human rights, between health institutions and political emancipation. In Zeh's novel, *Recht auf Krankheit* is the name of an organization that fights the METHOD. The suggestion is that this loose "network" (Zeh 2009, 84) does not exist (Zeh 2009, 149) but rather is an invention of the METHOD to foster the feeling of a terrorist threat, in order to better control the population. Zeh (2020, 31) explains that every system needs enemy images ("Feindbilder") to create its own identity. This "terrorist group" is referred to as R.A.K., a clear allusion to the West-German leftist terror group R.A.F. in the 1970s. It is also possible that Zeh, who lived in Croatia, knows that *rak* is the Serbo-Croatian word for cancer. This biological dimension would reinforce the sense of a symbolic threat to the system. The novel thus has Heinrich Kramer, its chief ideologue, explain: "Anti-methodism is a hostile attack to which we will react with war." ("Anti-Methodismus ist ein kriegerischer Angriff, dem wir mit Krieg begegnen werden." Zeh 2009, 89)

The extract from Kramer's work on the ideology of the METHOD starts out with this seemingly innocent WHO definition of health but quickly becomes more transparent in its totalitarian character: it first connects a healthy organism to mental qualities ("geistige Kraft und ein stabiles Seelenleben"), then qualifies health as performance ("individuelle Höchstleistung") and an expression of willpower ("Ausdruck von Willensstärke") and equates this biopolitically with social life, to qualify health as a natural goal ("natürliches Ziel"). Kramer concludes that a lack of such striving for health is already illness.

---

24 Cf. Welsh (2016, 228): *Universal Declaration of Human Rights*, Art. 25.1.
25 Cf. Welsh (2016, 229): UN Committee on Economic, Social and Cultural Rights CESCR E/C.12/2000/4, 11 August 2000, Ziff. 9.

6 Inquisition and Contemporary Totalitarian Tendencies

The book at the root of the METHOD is of course fictitious, but its author has a counterpart in history. The historical Heinrich Kramer was an inquisitor and the author of the infamous *Malleus Maleficarum* (The Witch Hammer) from 1486 (Zeh 2000), the most influential writing of the Inquisition. Correspondingly, there was a historical Maria Holl, who was accused of being a witch in 1593, and who survived 62 rounds of torture without giving a false confession before she was finally released (cf. Sporhan-Krempel 1949). Her resistance is seen as contributing to the end of the Inquisition in her town of Nördlingen. As already mentioned, the starting point for Zeh's novel was the theme of the Middle Ages. But Zeh transposes the witch hunts into our times or the near future, pointing to the enduring presence of totalitarian tendencies, as for instance in the concept of enemy penal law ("Feindstrafrecht"),[26] which fortunately has not seen a reintroduction in Germany in spite of some prominent proponents. It is, however, to some degree a reality in the USA's "War on Terror", the key example being Guantánamo, which cancels the rule of law (Zeh 2020, 38–39).

The witches of today, Zeh (2020, 31) explains, are replaced by "terrorists" for instance who lose their civil rights. She insists on the rule of law for everybody and explicitly compares those labelled "terrorists" to Agamben's *homo sacer*, as the central figure of totalitarian ideologies (Zeh 2020, 36). Despite its philanthropic appearance, Kramer's health system is totalitarian in character, and Zeh brings that to the fore.

7 Totalitarian Jurisdiction

The totalitarian character of the novel's health system is confirmed in the second chapter of *The METHOD*, the verdict against Mia Holl (Zeh 2009, 9–10), which, in its position and content, functions as an illustration of the health principles outlined in the prior chapter. The verdict is declared "In the name of the METHOD!" ("Im Namen der METHODE!"), a satirical shift from the democratic "In the name of the people" ("Im Namen des Volkes"). It is not the people who are sovereign,

---

[26] This concept was coined in 1985 by the German penal law specialist Günther Jacobs to describe a penal law that deprives certain groups of people of their civil rights, since it considers them enemies of the state or of society, cf. Jacobs 1985.

but the system itself, like the party in socialist societies or in National Socialism. Holl's crime consists of "methodenfeindliche Umtriebe", an expression in pseudo-political jargon for activities against the METHOD that calls to mind the infamous *Lèse-majesté*, infinitely flexible in its vagueness and therefore at odds with the principles of the rule of law. The terms and concepts "enemy of the state", "enemy of the people" and "public enemy" have been circulating in popular discourse for several decades now (*Enemy of the State*, Hollywood action thriller with Will Smith in 1998, the hip-hop band *Public Enemy* in the 1980s). The verdict connects Holl's activities to preparation for a terrorist war, which is equated ("sachlich zusammentreffend") to a threat to the peace of the state, to dealings with toxic substances and to a refusal to follow the compulsory examinations. This verdict does not refer to any real criminal act, only its possible preparation or non-conformist actions. It is a purely pre-emptive verdict and thus against our present judicial principles. Zeh sees these principles under threat in our times, for a good reason, as already demonstrated. The penalty for Holl is to be frozen (cryonized) for an indeterminate time. This non-determination of the penalty is also against our current principles. Finally, the accused must pay the cost of the trial, a further reminder of National Socialist practice and totalitarian procedures more generally.

The METHOD punishes unhealthy behaviour such as smoking and obliges everybody to measure and report regularly on their health, including allergic sensitivity, blood pressure, urine and blood tests, calorie consumption, sleep and exercise. Everybody has an implanted chip for self-monitoring, and any shortcomings are penalized. The system chooses sexual partners for individuals according to immunological compatibility, a reminder of *Lebensborn*, the National Socialist breeding ideology and practice. Having sex with an incompatible partner is a capital crime (Zeh 2009, 113). All of this is evidently against the *European Convention for Human Rights*, which guarantees the rights to privacy, including data protection, the right of self-determination, of the inviolability of the body, as well as of lifestyle and choice of partner. But Zeh (2020, 53) stresses that her presentation of things is not altogether a future fantasy: all phenomena mentioned are in fact technically possible and already in existence somewhere in one form or another. Her book is simply an exaggeration of already existing ways of thinking and acting (Zeh 2020, 43) and she is convinced that many people would agree to the METHOD if it were a real option: the population of the depicted state is happy with the regime, including its surveillance and punishments (Zeh 2020, 45). The often-heard argument "I have nothing to hide" is a sentence Zeh and Trojanow (2009, 37; also Zeh 2020, 46) ardently condemn. Mia explicitly mistrusts people who justify total surveillance in that way (Zeh 2009, 186). But people often confuse freedom with freedom from responsibility and enjoy the fact that the state takes charge of them. The METHOD is so successful because the people feel that experts are taking care of them and they simply have to play along in order to be well (Zeh 2020, 50).

People with such an attitude have no problem with the existence of a secret service to control the population, the "Method Guard" ("Methodenschutz"), or a health police force, the "Security Watch" ("Sicherheitswacht"). The harmonizing of institutional powers (cf. the infamous *Gleichschaltung* in National Socialism) is an equally logical consequence: Kramer, who prepared and developed the METHOD, is a journalist, but there is no real separation of powers and he interferes in the media, legislative, judicial and executive powers. That manifests itself as well in social structures, such as the "guardian houses" ("Wächterhäuser"), where the inhabitants surveil each other on behalf of the state, with incentives such as reduced bills to encourage denunciation. They have disinfection machines, a "bacteriometre" and are marked by a badge, allowing them to forego indoor mask-wearing (Zeh 2009, 21–22).

Formally, many of the judicial aspects described in the novel and the terminology and structure of the trial correspond to contemporary democratic procedures. The sanctions, however, do not. In a detailed analysis of these aspects, professor of law Heinz Müller-Dietz comes to the conclusion that the trial in *The METHOD* corresponds only formally to the rule of law. In fact, the accused has no rights whatsoever since the entire system aims at total state control and leaves no space for basic rights. The lack of personal freedom is felt all the more acutely by those suspected of criminal acts (Müller-Dietz 2011, 89). Parallels to National Socialism have been mentioned above. Zeh (2009, 68 and 52) leaves little doubt about her intentions in this regard with the abbreviation "GStPo" for "Gesundheitsprozessordnung" (Health trial regulation) (cf. Finger 2009; McCalmont and Maierhofer 2012, 385). Müller-Dietz points out parallels in the novel's position to Foucault's late lectures at the Collège de France, focusing on the notion of *parrhesia*, the public commitment to individual freedom and self-determination (Foucault 2009, cf. Müller-Dietz 2011, 91; also Gehring and Gelhard 2012).

Mia, who is initially simply mourning her brother, shows no interest in *parrhesia*, but the system does not allow her to withdraw from it for this time of mourning. Her failure to adhere to the health requirements (lack of exercise and missed reports) leads to a "clarifying conversation" ("Klärungsgespräch", Zeh 2009, 19), then to a "hearing" ("Anhörung") and a penal trial ("Strafprozess", 67) with financial penalties (69). Once her lawyer Rosentreter seeks an appeal of these penalties for his own personal reasons (he loves an immunologically incompatible woman), the system fights Mia as an enemy of the method. Kramer launches a campaign against her and she is brutally arrested (Zeh 2009, 151–152). But when Rosentreter uncovers an error in the system (Zeh 2009, 162–167) – Mia's brother Moritz had a cell transplant as a child due to leukaemia, so he shared DNA with his donor, who committed the rape for which Moritz was condemned – Mia takes up the fight against the METHOD and for freedom, including the freedom to be ill (Zeh 2009, 175). She receives support from some portions of the population in demonstrations for her release from prison, and some journalists who begin to question the infallibility of the METHOD (Zeh 2009, 178–179). Mia feels emboldened now and publicly declares her criticism of the METHOD: "I withdraw my trust from a society that consists of humans but is based on fear of the human. I withdraw my trust from a civilization that has sold out the mind to the body" ("Ich entziehe einer Gesellschaft das Vertrauen, die aus Menschen besteht und trotzdem auf der Angst vor dem Menschlichen gründet. Ich entziehe einer Zivilisation das Vertrauen, die den Geist an den Körper verraten hat." Zeh 2009, 186–187).

Mia advances her critique, accusing the system of prioritizing security over life. Her declaration leads to mass demonstrations (Zeh 2009, 196). She herself explains that she has become an integrative figure ("Integrationsfigur"), uniting all people in doubt, offering a projection screen ("Projektionsfläche", 198), and that also for the R.A.K. who, supposedly, announce terrorist attacks, even though Mia wants nothing to do with that organization (Zeh 2009, 203). This offers Kramer the opportunity to retaliate, and he announces: "infectious thoughts" will be "annihilated" (Zeh 2009, 200–201). He can now justify even stricter control, also of minds, in the fight against the staged terrorist danger. For terrorists, that is enemies of the METHOD, laws of the state of exception are in place (Zeh 2009, 206).

In the final trial, riots break out and Mia finally calls for a violent revolution (Zeh 2009, 258). We know the verdict from the book's beginning, but Mia sees herself as victorious since her resistance made her a self-determined human being. Shortly before the execution, however, she is pardoned. As Kramer explains, the METHOD is not foolish enough to make her a cult figure and martyr (Zeh 2009, 263); instead, she will be given psychological care in a re-socialization institution: "Trust-building measures. Political education. Guidance in the Method." ("Vertrauensbildende Maßnahmen. Politische Bildung. Methodenlehre." Zeh 2009, 264) Thus, the system will also try to break Mia's mind, to "psychically annihilate" her in what Zeh (2020, 55) calls a "re-education camp" ("Umerziehungslager"). The novel ends with this complete defeat; however, the reader is given no perspective on subsequent events. Zeh (2020, 57) insists that humans are free because it is the mind, not the body, that shapes identity.

8 Vision of Humanity

In overcoming her fear, Mia becomes self-determined. In the best sense of Enlightenment, she escapes her "nonage", or immaturity, but is for that very reason an intolerable danger to the system. Fear is a dictatorial instrument of power and the people are kept in fear, here through the fixation on health. The promise of security, however, increases insecurity and fear (cf. Baumann 2013). A neighbour of Mia's says at one point that she almost "became ill from fear", because her daughter sneezed in the adjacent room – because of pepper while playing doctor, as it turns out (Zeh 2009, 21). But "fear renders pliable" ("Angst macht gefügig", Trojanow and Zeh 2009, 82) by shutting down self-determination and reason. The biopolitical vision of humanity builds on this paternalistic idea of controlling humans who are incapable of leading a self-determined good life. Biopolitics tends not to trust human self-determination.

Kramer is convinced that the METHOD's idea of the human is superior to all others since it is based on the body and for him the body is what makes all humans equal, not the mind (Zeh 2009, 180). This focus on the body is dangerous, as Zeh wants to demonstrate. We have to ask, along with Volker Roelcke, whether the biomedical promise of a world without illness leads to a "substantial shift in the evaluation of the human, namely, away from unconditional respect for the integrity of human life and towards general consent to its availability, manipulability and disposability".[27] Zeh's (2020, 99) intention with the book was exactly this: to criticize the contemporary economically and biologically determined idea of the human.

In Mia's brother Moritz's philosophy – he actually studies philosophy, a humanities subject as opposed to the natural-science world of the initial Mia and the METHOD – humans need to have experiences. Mia's experience of Moritz's illness as a child taught her to believe in the METHOD since the health system saved his life, while it taught Moritz to live his life, since he experienced the possibility of losing it. Consequently, he is not content with pure existence, he wants to live his own life actively in all its dimensions – this is what he calls "love" and he opposes it to the thinking of security, which suppresses real life (Zeh 2009, 90–95).

Mia's lawyer also asks at one point, explicitly "as a human being", what kind of system denies a few weeks of withdrawal to a person whose brother it just killed (Zeh 2009, 109). Since Mia at this point refuses to think in such human

---

[27] Roelcke 2003, 123: "substantiellen Verschiebung in der Bewertung des Menschen, und zwar weg vom unbedingten Respekt vor der Integrität hin zur prinzipiellen Zustimmung zu Verfügbarkeit, Manipulierbarkeit und auch Verwertbarkeit menschlichen Lebens".

terms, he screams at her: "You are an embittered, lonely rationalist! You have no clue about happiness!" ("Du bist eine verbitterte, einsame Rationalistin! Du hast keine Ahnung von Glück!" Zeh 2009, 114). Once Mia finally takes sides and fights the system, she finishes her declaration of resistance with the remark that it is only now that she understands what it means to live (Zeh 2009, 187).

This transformed Mia thinks with her heart ("Ich kann jetzt mit dem Herzen denken", Zeh 2009, 183) and considers Kramer's moral book-keeping with contempt when he explains that personal mishaps such as the METHOD having practically killed Mia's brother should not be confused with a political problem: no system, he explains, has a lower error rate than the METHOD, and a few victims must be tolerated; dissatisfaction with the existing situation, on the other hand, causes millions of deaths once per era (Zeh 2009, 183). Mia withdraws her trust and support from such a functionalistic ideology based on surveillance and fear, and she turns openly against the METHOD (Zeh 2009, 186–187). She now asks about the goals of this sort of reason and thus sees its irrationality (cf. Zeh 2020, 97).

9 Parallels to the COVID-19 Crisis

The dangers of exaggerated health biopolitics evoked in *The METHOD* and their parallels to recent developments are evident. To conclude, I will draw attention to a few concrete points raised in Zeh's book that directly apply to the COVID-19 situation from 2020 to 2022. The first one is the consequence of big data. The narrator of *The METHOD* explains towards the end that it has become obvious that "the data trace of a person contains millions of individual pieces of information, from which any arbitrary mosaic can be formed" ("die Datenspur eines Menschen Millionen von Einzelinformationen enthält, aus denen sich jedes beliebige Mosaik zusammensetzen lässt", Zeh 2009, 226). Consequently, if one wants to see potential threats ("Gefährder"), one will see them (Zeh 2009, 226). Data are always subject to interpretation. Within the logic of biopolitics and with the help of recent developments in media technology, the potential to disgrace anyone in the public eye or to have them turned over to the authorities is readily available. Applied to the health system, it is possible to surveil an entire population, to know what they consume, where they are, whom they meet. This can help to track an infection or slow down its spread. But it definitely enables those with access to these data to control the population – and that is not only the state but also private enterprise, which provides the technical know-how and infrastructure, or any hacker.[28]

The second aspect is the internal logic of the power of the media, both in conventional and social media. It is practically impossible to resist this omnipresent system.[29] Systems, including also the free press and democratic political system, create narratives; these narratives serve interests other than truth, and systemic mechanisms keep uncomfortable truths from being publicly aired. Many who do not share the official narrative do not dare to voice their positions in public. At the height of the COVID-19 crisis, journalists, doctors, and medical staff were suspended for doing so, and politicians feared public opinion and could not afford major scandals. Even actors and artists criticizing the measures were subject to violent attacks in the media. One risked being called a conspiracy theorist even when pointing to the official numbers available to all, such as that fewer than 7% of all deaths in Germany can be associated with COVID-19 (March 2020 to May 2021) or that in 2020 only 4% of all intensive care beds were occupied by COVID-19 patients.[30] People resisting the unrelenting panic narratives were discredited as psychologically disturbed and as right-wing extremists and "cancelled", no matter how respected they were before they opposed the mainstream interpretation of events.[31]

Thirdly, in the novel Kramer himself points to another problem which – strangely – has received almost no attention from the political and media establishment so far: he says that due to the METHOD natural immunity has been destroyed, since people are not in touch with bacteria and viruses to build one. This is in fact how our immune system functions, as everybody should know but seems to have forgotten: exposure to others and their bacteria is crucial for our health. Consequently, Kramer explains, once people have lost their immune powers, the system needs to be maintained flawlessly, otherwise an epidemic

---

[28] The potential for abuse of the COVID-19 passport is already evident in China, cf. CBS news 24 June 2022: https://www.cbsnews.com/news/china-covid-government-health-app-ripe-for-abuse/.
[29] We can see this in Rosentreter's case: his beloved partner leaves him after Kramer's framing of Mia as a terrorist, since she is shocked that he is defending a terrorist. He says that he could not explain the truth to her since she leads a normal life and believes the press. He wants to protect her from the truth that her life is based on a lie (Zeh 2009, 227).
[30] Cf. the official report of the German Ministry of Health: https://www.bundesgesundheitsministerium.de/service/publikationen/details/analysen-zum-leistungsgeschehen-der-krankenhaeuser-und-zur-ausgleichspauschale-in-der-corona-krise-ergebnisse-fuer-den-zeitraum-januar-bis-mai-2021.html. Last accessed 15 May 2021.
[31] Alexander-Kenneth Nagel (51–78) has made the connection between COVID-19 and apocalyptic ideas in his book *Corona und andere Weltuntergänge. Apokalyptische Krisenhermeneutik in der modernen Gesellschaft* (2021). He discusses the apocalyptic of the conspiracy theories but also in Chancellor Angela Merkel's public speeches at the start of the crisis.

would swiftly follow (Zeh 2009, 233). We must ask whether, during the COVID-19 crisis, after a considerable time of limited human contact, less physical exercise and fresh air, a vulnerable psychological situation etc., we are not already at this point where the population's immune system has suffered enough for viruses to spread more easily and where any exit from such measures will cause a new epidemic. The trumpeted new waves of the virus, with the accompanying calls for stricter measures, would then be a self-fulfilling prophecy. If we ever want to live again without such restrictions of our freedom, we probably should not go any farther down that road. Zeh's conclusion is the following:

> But what we should have avoided is the rhetorical exploitation of fear among the population for boosting the profile of individual politicians, imposing new security laws or generating media hype).
>
> (Aber was wir hätten vermeiden müssen, ist die rhetorische Ausschlachtung von Bevölkerungsängsten zur kurzfristigen Profilierung von einzelnen Politikern, zum Durchbringen neuer Sicherheitsgesetze oder zum Generieren von medialen Aufmerksamkeits-Hypes.) (2020, 86)

Biopolitics in our times is often based on governing in the form of nudging; it understands politics as a positive manipulation of people to prompt more reasonable behaviour. Zeh (2020, 96) opposes this with her vision of politics as the creation of fair conditions for all individuals to freely determine their form of life, no matter whether or not others agree with it. The main message of *The METHOD* is that human beings are determined by their minds, not their bodies, which is why the way to self-fulfilment is not health, but education (Zeh 2020, 174).

Zeh explicitly considers right-wing criticism of the German constitutional state wrong and dangerous. In her view, this state is one of the best worldwide, and wrong-headed mistrust of democracy, politicians or the state leads to damaging right-wing populism (Fragen 91). Democratic institutions indeed need to be strengthened, not weakened.[32] However, the way in which COVID-19 was dealt with officially in Germany, and the stymieing of public and parliamentary debate on appropriate management of the situation, led to increasing numbers of people

---

[32] It is remarkable that the liberal politician Wolfgang Kubicki (FDP), the vice-president of the German parliament, saw the need to publish a book in summer 2021 in which he severely criticized the political discourse in Germany with respect to COVID-19, demonstrating very clearly how the political establishment has worked against the constitution and democratic processes, manipulating public opinion and undermining the basis of democracy. The title is telling: *Die erdrückte Freiheit. Wie ein Virus unseren Rechtsstaat aushebelt* (Stymied freedom. How a virus levers out our state of law).

losing trust in politics and the media.³³ This lost trust will not be regained by continuing to suppress opinion; democracy cannot be maintained by undemocratic means. Only open debate can foster and sustain democratic trust in democracy.³⁴ This is also the principle in academia: truth is not what one school of thought says but the result of constant debate.

The parallels of the METHOD to current events are evident, and the topicality of Zeh's book for what is happening with COVID-19 is striking. The real events have confirmed that nowadays "health" and "security" are prioritized over civil and human rights by the majority of the population, or at least by what is presented as the majority, when people are manipulated by political discourse in collaboration with the press. Most journalists have agreed, probably in good faith, to support the government in the context of the state of exception, which pursued an explicit shock strategy so that the population would follow the regulations.³⁵ The German government also procured a scientific study with a "desired shock effect" ("gewünschte Schockwirkung"), so that hard measures would be accepted. The scientists complied and, in preparation for the first lockdown in spring 2020, presented a worst-case scenario with a million people being turned away from hospitals and miserably dying at home of suffocation, a horror scenario often repeated by the media (cf. fn 1). Some virologists had predicted huge numbers of victims years earlier, for instance in connection with swine flu in 2009–2010, without any real-life proof: altogether 253 people died in Germany; many millions of vaccination doses were bought, then thrown away.³⁶ But this time, people were

---

33 The former President of the German Federal Constitutional Court, Hans-Jürgen Papier, demands on 5 October 2021 that politicians and judiciary analyse the COVID-19 policies since the people's trust in the state of law is seriously damaged. Indeed, the government commissioned experts to evaluate the handling of the situation. The results have been published on 1 July 2022: the commission harshly criticized that two years after the beginning of the pandemic there are still not sufficient data to reliably judge the situation. Thus many measures were arbitrary, with often very little positive effect but considerable – particularly psychological – damage. They state that there is generally very little connection between the measures and the incidence of the virus and admonish that an apology of the government would be necessary. Strangely enough, there was little media echo. Cf. Der FREITAG 27/2022.
34 Ingo Reuter published a book on the social dimension of the metaphor of infection and the virus: *Ansteckung. Das Fremde in viralen Zeiten* (Königshausen & Neumann: Würzburg 2021). He shows that this metaphor is used to exclude people and that constructive contact with the Other is necessary in order to cope with the challenges of the future.
35 The first internal strategy paper from March 2020 is documented in https://fragdenstaat.de/blog/2020/04/01/strategiepapier-des-innenministeriums-corona-szenarien/ and was later published by the ministry https://fragdenstaat.de/dokumente/4123-wie-wir-covid-19-unter-kontrolle-bekommen/.
36 Amongst them Christian Drosten, the German government's chief COVID-19 consultant, whose influence on the country's management of the crisis cannot be overestimated. For the number of

much more biddable due to the combined efforts of politicians, scientists and journalists.

In the long run, such manipulative procedures weaken politics, established media and science. By constantly repeating hypothetical threats and using statistics shorn of their wider context,[37] politics, media and some scientists have created fear without giving sufficient space for other qualified opinions. Politicians, journalists, medical doctors, and members of the police force who reasonably and competently argued against the fearmongering, were suspended, their postings on social media often suppressed.[38] But what they warned us about has become a reality. The obligation to be vaccinated to travel or to visit cinemas and restaurants, ruled out throughout 2020 by the German government and introduced in 2021, was in clear conflict with civil rights and not logically justifiable in the given situation. Society has been split and democratic values have suffered.[39] Many lockdown measures have been considered anti-constitutional by German courts and had to be withdrawn.[40] Many of these measures in the name of health and security restricted civil rights, while alternative scientific opinions were suppressed. The German constitution requires the principle of "commensurability" ("Verhältnismäßigkeit"), that is, a measure should not cause more problems than it prevents. Warnings that the consequences of a lockdown would

---

deaths, cf. Statista: https://de.statista.com/statistik/daten/studie/156553/umfrage/anzahl-der-todesfaelle-durch-schweinegrippe/. Last accessed 10 July 2022. ARTE, a French-German TV channel, documented in 2009 the financial interests behind the at the time unsuccessful and unnecessary vaccination campaign, "Die Profiteure der Angst", cf. https://www.youtube.com/watch?v=jdF52IFb_jk. Last accessed 10 July 2022.

37 To give one example, there has been no significant excess mortality in Germany in 2020; however, repeating death statistics without ever mentioning that in Germany the normal daily death rate is between 2500 and 3000 creates panic. Likewise, intensive care beds in Germany were needed no more than in other years. Every year sees some peak periods in which they become scarce. That is in line with the economic management of the health service. Constantly repeated predictions that COVID-19 patients will no longer be accepted if the rates continue to rise are false and simply create unfounded fear.

38 For instance the epidemiologists Wolfgang Wodarg and Sucharit Bhakdi, to name but two prominent figures in Germany. Bhakdi, together with his wife Karina Reiss, published in May 2020 a critical book on the COVID-19 pandemic measures which was a number one bestseller in Germany but hardly received any attention from the German established media.

39 Alongside other positions referred to in the preceding footnotes, cf. the survey of the Körber-foundation from October/November 2021 with the result that only 50% of the German population rather trusted democracy and 30% rather not: https://koerber-stiftung.de/site/assets/files/20354/demokratie_in_der_krise.pdf. Last accessed 17 February 2023.

40 For example the imposition of a lockdown for an entire region after a local break-out of the virus or access to open-air sports only for vaccinated or healed people, cf. *Handelsblatt* 27 January 2022.

cause incommensurable suffering, i.e., much more than the virus itself causes, and corresponding studies have not been sufficiently taken into account. It took a year for these warnings to gain some momentum, swimming against a forceful tide of fabricated media consensus.

We do not have a health dictatorship, our situation is not the METHOD, but there are many signs that public discourse is heading in this direction and needs to be re-routed to prevent further undesirable developments. Juli Zeh's literary fiction is a convincing warning and a crucial tool for raising awareness and preventing corrosion of the constitutional state.

References

Agamben, Giorgio. *Homo Sacer. Sovereign Power and Bare Life*. Trans. Daniel Heller-Roazen. Stanford: Stanford University Press, 1998.
Agamben, Giorgio. *Means without End: Notes on Politics*. Trans. Vincenzo Binetti and Cesare Casarino. Minneapolis: University of Minnesota Press, 2000.
Agamben, Giorgio. *Where Are We Now? The Pandemic as Politics*. London: Urtext Ltd., 2021.
#allesdichtmachen, April 2021.
ARTE. "Die Profiteure der Angst." https://www.youtube.com/watch?v=jdF52IFb_jk. 2009. Last accessed 10 July 2022.
Bauman, Zygmunt. *Modernity and the Holocaust*. Cambridge: Polity, 1989.
Baumann, Lukas. *Zwischen Angst und Sicherheit. Juli Zehs Konstruktion eines gespaltenen Kollektivismus in Corpus Delicti*. Norderstedt: Grin, 2013.
Beck, Zoë. "Niemand stirbt." *Der Freitag*, Nr. 2, 14 January 2021.
Berliner Zeitung, 30 April 2021. "#allesdichtmachen: ARD-Rundfunkrat fordert Konsequenzen für „Tatort"-Stars." https://www.berliner-zeitung.de/news/allesdichtmachen-ard-rundfunkrat-fordert-konsequenzen-fuer-tatort-stars-li.154742. Last accessed 10 July 2022.
Bhakdi, Sucharit, and Karina Reiss. *Corona Fehlalarm*. Berlin and Vienna: Goldegg Verlag, May 2020.
BRF Nachrichten, 23 December 2020. Roger Pint. "Coronakrise – Die Epidemie der Denunziation." https://brf.be/national/1443092/. Last accessed 10 July 2022.
Bröckling, Ulrich. "Article 'Prävention.' *Glossar der Gegenwart*." Eds. Ulrich Bröckling, Susanne Krasmann and Thomas Lemke. Frankfurt am Main: Suhrkamp, 2004. 210–215.
Campbell, Timothy, and Adam Sitze, eds. *Biopolitics: A Reader*. Durham, NC: Duke University Press, 2013.
CBS News, 24 June 2022. Elizabeth Palmer and Shuai Zhang. "Life in China is ruled by the government's COVID health app. That app is ripe for abuse." https://www.cbsnews.com/news/china-covid-government-health-app-ripe-for-abuse/. Last accessed 10 July 2022.
Der FREITAG, 7 July 2022. René Schlott. "Pandemie. Zeit für ein Sorry, mindestens. Es ist amtlich: Die Coronamaßnahmen waren zu guten Teilen aus der Luft gegriffen. Wo bleiben die Konsequenzen?" https://epaper.freitag.de/de/profiles/b7258d8ff654/editions/dece11203d34de2a1b9f/pages/page/8. Last accessed 10 July 2022.
Die Welt, 8 February 2021, Anette Dowideit and Alexander Nabert. "Wenn der Staatssekretär Wissenschaftler zu 'maximaler Kollaboration' aufruft." https://www.welt.de/politik/deutschland/

plus225868061/Corona-Politik-Wie-das-Innenministerium-Wissenschaftler-einspannte.html. Last accessed 1 July 2022.

Encke, Julia. "Bloß nicht bewegen." 2 June 2020 in *Frankfurter Allgemeine Zeitung;* https://www.faz.net/aktuell/feuilleton/buecher/rezensionen/belletristik/neues-buch-von-juli-zeh-ein-buch-ueber-die-corona-pandemie-16793883-p3.html. Last accessed 7 February 2021.

Finger, Evelyn. "Das Buch der Stunde." *Die Zeit,* 26 February 2009.

Fischer, Karin. "Moderne Hexenjagd: Juli Zehs Stück Corpus Delicti in Essen uraufgeführt." Dradio.de. *Deutschlandfunk* / Kultur heute, 16 September 2007.

Foucault, Michel. *Folie et déraison. Histoire de la folie à l'âge Classique.* Paris: Librairie Plon, 1961.

Foucault, Michel. *Naissance de la clinique. Une archéologie du regard médical.* Paris: Presses Universitaires de France, 1963.

Foucault, Michel. *Surveiller et punir. Naissance de la prison.* Paris: Gallimard, 1975.

Foucault, Michel. *Histoire de la sexualité 1. La volonté de savoir.* Paris: Gallimard, nrf, 1976.

Foucault, Michel. "*Il faut défendre la société.*" *Cours au Collège de France* (1975–1976). Paris: Gallimard/ Seuil, 1997.

Foucault, Michel. *Naissance de la biopolitique (1978–1979).* Paris: EHESS/ Gallimard/ Le Seuil, collection 'Hautes études', 2004.

Foucault, Michel. *Le Courage de la verité. Le gouvernement de soi et des autres II (cours au Collège de France, 1984).* Paris: EHESS/ Gallimard/ Seuil, 2009.

Frankfurter Allgemeine Zeitung, 15 October 2020. Niklas Zimmermann. Verstöße gegen Corona-Regeln: Ruft die Stadt Essen zur Denunziation von Bürgern auf? https://www.faz.net/aktuell/politik/inland/corona-in-essen-ruft-die-stadt-zur-denunziation-von-buergern-auf-17001551.html. Last accessed 10 July 2020.

Frevert, Ute. *Krankheit als politisches Problem 1770–1880. Soziale Unterschichten in Preußen zwischen medizinischer Polizei und staatlicher Sozialversicherung.* Göttingen: Vandenhoeck & Ruprecht, 1984.

Gehring, Petra, and Andreas Gelhard, eds. *Parrhesia. Foucault und der Mut zur Wahrheit.* Zürich: Diaphanes, 2012.

Geyer, Christian. "Geruchslos im Hygieneparadies." *Frankfurter Allgemeine Zeitung,* 28 February 2009.

Handelsblatt, 27 January 2022. Heike Anger, "Grundrechte. Zwei Jahre Pandemie: Was die Corona-Urteile der Gerichte bedeuten." https://www.handelsblatt.com/politik/deutschland/grundrechte-zwei-jahre-pandemie-was-die-corona-urteile-der-gerichte-bedeuten/28007894.html. Last accessed 10 July 2022.

Herminghouse, Patricia. "The Young Author as Public Intellectual: The Case of Juli Zeh." *German Literature in a New Century: Trends, Traditions, Transitions, Transformations.* Eds. Katharina Gerstenberger and Patricia Herminghouse. New York: Berghahn, 2008. 264–84.

House of Lords, Constitution Committee, Second Report: "Surveillance: Citizens and the State." 19 November 2008; https://publications.parliament.uk/pa/ld200809/ldselect/ldconst/18/1802.htm. Last accessed 2 February 2021.

Horkheimer, Max, and Theodor W. Adorno, *Dialektik der Aufklärung.* Amsterdam: Querido, 1947.

Huxley, Aldous. Interviewed by Mike Wallace 1958. https://www.youtube.com/watch?v=alasBxZsb40. Last accessed 11 February 2021.

Ings, Simon. *The Guardian,* April 6, 2012. "The METHOD by Juli Zeh – Review". https://www.theguardian.com/books/2012/apr/06/the-method-juli-zeh-review. Last accessed 10 July 2022.

Jakobs, Günther. "Kriminalisierung im Vorfeld einer Rechtsgutsverletzung." *Zeitschrift für die gesamte Straftrechtswissenschaft* 97 (1985): 751–785.

Körber-Stiftung. Julian Nida-Rümelin: Demokratie in der Krise. Ein Weckruf zur Erneuerung im Angesicht der Pandemie. https://koerber-stiftung.de/site/assets/files/20354/demokratie_in_der_krise.pdf. Last accessed 17 February 2023.
Kramer, Heinrich. *Der Hexenhammer: Mallus Maleficarum*. Eds. and transl. by Wolfgang Behringer, Günter Jerouschek and Werner Tschacher. Munich: dtv, 2000.
Kubicki, Wolfgang. *Die erdrückte Freiheit. Wie ein Virus unseren Rechtssaat aushebelt*. Frankfurt am Main: Westend, 2021.
Leis, Mario, and Sabine Rieker. *Juli Zeh. Corpus Delicti. Reclam Lektürschlüssel*. Stuttgart: Reclam, 2016.
Lemke, Thomas. *Biopolitik zur Einführung*. Hamburg: Junius, 2007.
Lemke, Thomas. *Biopolitics: An Advanced Introduction*. New York: New York University Press, 2011.
Mayr, Sabine. *Einfach Deutsch Unterrichtsmodelle. Juli Zeh, Corpus Delicti, Gymnasiale Oberstufe*. Paderborn: Schöningh, 2013.
Mbembe, Achille. "Necropolitics." *Public Culture*, 15.1 (2003): 11–40.
McCalmont, Virginia, and Waltraud Maierhofer, "Juli Zeh's *Corpus Delicti* (2009): Health Care, Terrorists, and the Return of the Political." *Monatshefte*, 104.3 (Fall 2012): 375–392.
Ministry of Health, Germany. https://www.bundesgesundheitsministerium.de/service/publikationen/details/analysen-zum-leistungsgeschehen-der-krankenhaeuser-und-zur-ausgleichspauschale-in-der-corona-krise-ergebnisse-fuer-den-zeitraum-januar-bis-mai-2021.html. Last accessed 15 May 2021.
Ministry of the Interior, Germany, internal strategy paper from March 2020. https://fragdenstaat.de/dokumente/4123-wie-wir-covid-19-unter-kontrolle-bekommen/ und https://fragdenstaat.de/blog/2020/04/01/strategiepapier-des-innenministeriums-corona-szenarien/. Last accessed 11 February 2021.
Minority Report. Dir. Steven Spielberg. 20th Century Fox, 2002.
Müller-Dietz, Heinz. "Zur negativen Utopie von Recht und Staat – am Beispiel des Romans *Corpus Delicti* von Juli Zeh." *JuristenZeitung* 66.2 (21 January 2011). 85–95.
Nagel, Alexander-Kenneth. *Corona und andere Weltuntergänge. Apokalyptische Krisenhermeneutik in der modernen Gesellschaft*. Bielefeld: transcript, 2021.
Papier, Hans-Jürgen. "Irrational, kopflos – Vertrauen in Handlungsfähigkeit des Staates ist erschüttert." *Die Welt*, 5 October 2021. https://www.welt.de/politik/deutschland/plus234193236/Hans-Juergen-Papier-Vertrauen-in-Handlungsfaehigkeit-des-Staates-erschuettert.html. Last accessed 10 July 2022.
Prantl, Heribert. "Ich hoffe, dass die Gesellschaft aufwacht." *Berliner Zeitung*, 30 January 2021.
Preusser, Heinz-Peter. "Juli Zeh." *Kritisches Lexikon zur deutschsprachigen Gegenwartsliteratur, KLG*. Ed. Heinz Ludwig Arnold, Munich: Edition Text und Kritik. 94. Neulieferung, März 2010.
Reuter, Ingo. *Ansteckung. Das Fremde in viralen Zeiten*. Würzburg: Königshausen & Neumann, 2021.
Röber, Friedrich August. "Von der Sorge des Staats für die Gesundheit seiner Bürger." Dresden: Gärtner, 1806.
Roelcke, Volker. "Medizin – eine Kulturwissenschaft? Wissenschaftsverständnis, Anthropologie und Wertsetzungen in der modernen Heilkunde." *Phänomen Kultur. Perspektiven und Aufgaben der Kulturwissenschaften*. Ed. Klaus E. Müller. Bielefeld: transcript, 2003. 107–130.
Scheck, Denis. "Gesundheit als höchstes Gut." Dradio.de. Deutschlandradio Kultur/ Kritik, 30 June 2009.
Schmitt, Peter. *Postdigital. Medienkritik im 21. Jahrhundert*. Hamburg: Felix Meiner Verlag, 2021.
Simanowski, Roberto. *Das Virus und das Digitale*. Vienna: Passagen, 2021.
Sporhan-Krempel, Lore. *Die Hexe von Nördlingen: Das Schicksal der Maria Holl*. Stuttgart: JKA, 1949.

Statista. "Anzahl der Todesfälle durch Influenza H1N1 ("Schweinegrippe") in Deutschland nach Alter von April 2009 bis März 2010." https://de.statista.com/statistik/daten/studie/156553/umfrage/anzahl-der-todesfaelle-durch-schweinegrippe/. Last accessed 10 July 2022.

Stein, Lorenz von. *Das Gesundheitswesen. Erstes Hauptgebiet, zweiter Teil der Inneren Verwaltungslehre*. Zweite Auflage. Gänzlich neubearbeitet und bis auf die neueste Zeit verfolgt. Stuttgart: Cotta, 1882.

Süddeutsche Zeitung, 4 November 2020. "Polizist nach Auftritten auf Corona-Demos suspendiert." https://www.sueddeutsche.de/bayern/corona-demo-polizist-suspendierung-1.5105045?reduced=true. Last accessed 10 July 2022.

Thumfart, Johannes. *Ist das Zoon Politikon ein Oxymoron? Zur Dekonstruktion des Begriffs von Biopolitik bei Giorgio Agamben auf der Grundlage einer Wiederlektüre des Aristoteles*. Saarbrücken: Verlag Dr. Müller, 2008.

Trojanow, Ilija, and Juli Zeh, *Angriff auf die Freiheit. Sicherheitswahn, Überwachungsstaat und der Abbau bürgerlicher Rechte*. Munich: Hanser, 2009.

UN Committee on Economic, Social and Cultural Rights CESCR E/C.12/2000/4, August 11, 2000, Ziff. 9. UN Committee on Economic, Social and Cultural Rights CESCR E/C.12/2000/4, 11 August 2000, Ziff. 9. https://www.refworld.org/pdfid/4538838d0.pdf. Last accessed 10 July 2022.

Weidner, Stefan. *Ground Zero: 9/11 und die Geburt der Gegenwart*. Munich: Hanser, 2021.

Welsh, Caroline. "Brauchen wir ein Recht auf Krankheit? Historische und theoretische Überlegungen im Anschluss an Juli Zehs Roman Corpus Delicti." *Das Menschenrecht auf Gesundheit. Normative Grundlagen und aktuelle Diskurse*. Eds. Andreas Frewer and Heiner Bielefeldt. Bielefeld: Transcript Verlag, 2016. 215–238.

World Health Organization (2013a). Health 2020: a European policy framework supporting action across government and society for health and well-being. https://apps.who.int/iris/handle/10665/131300 (18 October 2015).

WHO Constitution. https://www.who.int/about/governance/constitution. Last accessed 10 July 2022.

Zeh, Juli. "Gesellschaftliche Relevanz braucht eine politische Richtung." *Die Zeit*. 23 June 2005.

Zeh, Juli. *Corpus Delicti. Ein Prozess*. Frankfurt am Main: Schöffling & Co, 2009.

Zeh, Juli. *The METHOD*, transl. by Sally-Ann Spencer. London: Harvill Secker, 2012.

Zeh, Juli. *Nachts sind das Tiere. Essays*. Munich: Schöffling & Co, 2014.

Zeh, Juli. *Corpus Delicti. Ein Prozess*. Stuttgart: Ernst Klett Sprachen, 2015.

Zeh, Juli. *Fragen zu Corpus Delicti*. Munich: btb, 2020.

Zeh, Juli, and Georg M. Oswald. *Aufgedrängte Bereicherung. Tübinger Poetik-Dozentur 2010*. Künzelsau: Swiridoff Verlag, 2011.

Zeh, Juli, and Slut [Christian Neuburger et al.]. *Corpus Delicti – Eine Schallnovelle*. Strange Way Records, 2010. CD.

Betiel Wasihun
The Quantified Self: Surveillance, Biopolitics and Literary Resistance

Abstract: In this chapter, I examine the biopolitical aspects of the quantified self, shedding light on theories of subjectivity implied in the self-tracking culture with reference to Foucault's take on biopolitics/biopower and current surveillance discourses against the backdrop of COVID-19. I argue that the quantified self enables biometric surveillance and facilitates the implementation of health policies. The promise of autonomy underlying the quantified self is disavowed as deceptive, since ultimately algorithms take over and control self-trackers. In my discussion of Marc-Uwe Kling's novel *QualityLand* (2017) as an example of a critical engagement with dystopian repercussions of the quantified self in contemporary literature, I show that quantification has reached yet another level, as individuals are dispossessed of their selfhood and continuously datafied in an automated world of optimization. QualityLand is a redesigned country; in this near-future dystopian world all cities are renamed, the surnames of the inhabitants indicate the occupation of the same-sex parent at the time of conception, and payments are made by kissing a touch pad. In *QualityLand* humans deliberately give up control over their life to opaque algorithms. No area of life is left out, everything is taken over by digitalization and surveillance: physical and emotional states are tracked; children are sedated with hormones at the push of a button; a robot nanny takes care of the offspring. Self-tracking technologies, e.g., smart phones or digital assistants, are turning human life into assemblages of data (Lupton 2015). Kling's novel is a critical account of how humans have become data themselves which corporations such as Google and Facebook sell to their customers. *QualityLand* is a satirical dystopia that offers a cultural critique on how continuous quantification leads "societies towards total algorithmic control" (Couldry and Mejias).

1 Pervasive Self-Tracking

Gary Wolf, one of the founders of the Quantified Self movement,[1] observes that "our sense of self" is undergoing significant change due to the way we interact with technology. He goes on to argue that "we think of these tools as pointing outward, as windows, and I'd just like to invite you to think of them as also turning inward

---

[1] Co-founder with Kevin Kelly in 2007.

https://doi.org/10.1515/9783110799361-009

and becoming mirrors. So that when we think about using them to get some systematic improvement, we also think how they can be a source of self/improvement, self/discovery, self/awareness, self/knowledge" (Ted Talk, June 2010). Wolf concludes that the self is "our operation center, our consciousness, our moral compass" and that "if we want to act more effectively in the world, we have to get to know ourselves better". Representatives of the Quantified Self community are optimistic about the progress that technologies like self-tracking seemingly bring with them. "Self-knowledge through numbers" is how the movement defines itself, believing in self-determination and self-control for the sake of a better life. As a result, the quantified-self community consists of convinced supporters of self-tracking tools, who are actively involved in both the development and distribution of such tools. Within this community, technologies for self-quantification are understood as strategies for emancipation and self-determination.

Such self-tracking is not restricted to this community of users. Rather, it has become commonplace. We can all use social media and mobile apps to collect and store data about ourselves and share or exchange that information. The "quantified self" – just like "self-tracking" and "lifelogging" – is a heuristic umbrella term for multiple forms of self-measurement, ranging from health monitoring to attendance tracking at work places (Mämecke 2021, 21; cf. Selke 2014, 3). Selke defines lifelogging as personalized informatics in the context of big data. Lifelogging describes various forms of digital capturing, storing and analysing personal data as well as behavioural traces in real time through so-called "lifelogs". Lifelogging has its origin in the quantified self, but its innovative aspect lies in the automatic and imperceptible capturing of data (Selke 2014, 3). Unlike the quantified self, the logger no longer selects or has to pay attention to the process, because the system permanently captures (without any filters) diverse data such as biometric body data, location data, time stamps or images. Lifelogging can thus be understood as a passive form of digital self-archiving (cf. Selke 2014, 3).

The quantified self, on the other hand, is anyone who actively collects biological, behavioural, physical or any other kind of information about oneself. People can be engaged in tracking almost everything from moods, heart rates, menstrual cycle, fitness, body fat, sleeping patterns, meditation practices, and cognitive performance to coffee consumption. The important element is the implied "proactive stance toward obtaining information and acting on it" (Swan 2013, 85). The idea behind the quantified self is constant self-optimization, which resonates with Foucault's notion of improvement in his examination of biopower as a disciplinary means for the regulation of human populations. In *The Will to Knowledge* (1976), Foucault writes of a "power that exerts a positive influence on life, that endeavours to administer, optimize, and multiply it, subjecting it to precise controls and comprehensive regulations" (1976/1998, 137). In his writings on the neoliberal technologies of the self, which "are pertinent to understanding the quantified self as a particular mode of governing the self" (Lupton 2013b, 28), he shifts the attention to the individual.[2] Power does not have its disciplining effect from outside but from within the subject; individuals are formed by forming themselves (cf. Wiedemann 2016, 67).

In this chapter, I will elucidate the biopolitical aspects of the quantified self, expounding on theories of subjectivity underlying the self-tracking culture with reference to Foucault's take on biopolitics/biopower and current surveillance discourses against the backdrop of COVID-19. The last section of this chapter will then offer a reading of Marc-Uwe Kling's novel *QualityLand* (2017) as an example of a critical engagement with dystopian repercussions of the quantified self in contemporary literature, foregrounding how ubiquitous surveillance not only jeopardizes the mental health of individuals but deprives them of their selfhood altogether.

2 Self-Measurement, Pandemic and Biopower

The quantification of the individual takes place through self-tracking tools to collect biodata about the self in the broadest sense – namely biologically and biographically, for biodata is a "burgeoning field" in which "control over life processes is exercised" (Jarvis 2019, 289, cf. de Souza 2014). Of course, the idea of self-tracking, self-monitoring or self-observation is not new. Diaries, autobiographies and personal letters are long established forms of self-observation. Striving for self-knowledge has always been considered commendable, a noble philosophical endeavour. What seems novel and problematic about "digital self technologies" is that quantifiable data about the body such as the volume of lungs and heart rates is equated with self-knowledge (Wiedemann 2016, 70). Self-knowledge through digital surveillance tools is detached from the philosophical notion of self-knowledge that refers to knowledge of one's mental states, i.e., feelings, emotions, thoughts (but also knowledge of the self as such and its nature). Self-measurement has displaced philosophical self-knowledge as the first step towards improvement (cf. Selke 2014, 77).

But even if the self-quantification systems (SQS) claim to be capable of "tracking, monitoring, and quantifying health aspects including mental, emotional, physical, and social aspects in order to gain self-knowledge" (Almalki et al. 2013),

---

[2] Foucault is actually not talking about "technologies" but the "specific techniques that humans use to understand themselves" (1988, 17–18). Extending the notion of "techniques" to "technologies" is meant to express the technological shaping of the self in the increasingly digitized world.

there will be limits to accessing the "inner spaces" of the individual, and measuring inevitably remains external, i.e., superficial. To be sure, some knowledge about the individual is produced, as even the measuring of moods is, to a certain degree, possible through, for example, neuroscientific computational techniques that interpret electric signals received via intra-cranial electrodes. And yet, the results can be at most only glimpses of the inner self. As Wiedemann concludes (in accordance with phenomenological premises) physical *Körper* and sentient *Leib*, the two German words for "body" (cf. Husserl 1989, 152–153), can never be quantifiable substances, for they always have an erratic character as well (Wiedemann 2016, 90). The difficulties arising here would not have come as a surprise to Foucault, who believed that "technologies of the self" are inherently problematic, as they "permit individuals to effect by their own means, or with the help of others, a certain number of operations on their own bodies and souls, thoughts, conduct and way of being, so as to transform themselves in order to attain a certain state of happiness, purity, wisdom, perfection or immorality" (Foucault 1988, 18). In Foucault's account, the main idea of the quantified self is put in a nutshell – which is foremost the promise of happiness in self-knowledge through measuring the "Körper".

Leaving aside the fact that knowledge of the self cannot be gained through digital tracking devices as proclaimed by the Quantified Self movement, the entanglement of self-observation and regulation through monitoring corporations is dangerous from a democratic point of view. After all, users of self-tracking devices do not ultimately know what happens with their personal data. Even if they seem to have total control over their data by signing consent forms, they are often left with uncertainties as to the trustworthiness of the respective providers and the whereabouts of their data.

It is clear that at the root of self-measuring practices are questions regarding control and power. According to Wolf, "pioneering self-trackers [. . .] should defend [themselves] against the imposed generalities of official knowledge" (Wolf April 2010). The official body of knowledge that everyone accesses uncritically is questioned because its non-transparent origins are believed to be suspicious and a danger to be resisted by self-trackers. However, a contradiction appears here, too. Although the Quantified Self movement opposes corporate practices or government agencies and their administrative monopolies, it still champions similar ideas and goals (cf. Mämecke 2021, 165). The way self-tracking devices provide health insurers with biological data to reduce health care expenditure is a case in point (cf. Lupton 2013a, 28). In that respect, the birth of the "digitally engaged patient" is of high interest for "government policy and practice" (Lupton 2013b, 28). As Lupton states:

> Quantifying the self as part of top-down government and corporate enterprises moves away from the focus on "self-knowledge" undertaken for personal reasons (voluntary self-surveillance) that is central to the Quantified Self movement, to a broader use of the concept that raises issues around the involuntary or even coercive monitoring and surveillance of citizens for external purposes. (Lupton 2013b, 28)

The representation of sickness, psychological instabilities and lack of happiness or productivity as failures are part of governmental strategies to engage the citizens in self-care for the sake of a "better self" through biometric control on a seemingly voluntary basis. Lupton concludes quite rightly that "[i]n the discourse of the digitally engaged patient empowerment becomes a set of obligations" (2013b, 261). A biopower is at work here that targets the social body by advocating a health-conscious lifestyle for the individual with the help of digital technologies (Wiedemann 2016, 69). Through the development and application of individual measurement procedures, the self-trackers performatively produce what they semantically negate, namely biopolitical power (cf. Mämecke 2021, 168). The self-trackers aim at emancipation and sovereignty over their own technologies and data collection but in doing so they transmit biopolitical premises into their individual lifeworlds (Mämecke 2021, 168).

COVID-19 has clearly exacerbated these biopolitical practices. A Chinese research team observed that the mortality salience caused by the pandemic has had "a positive impact on quantified self" (Liu et al. 2021). Whether we should consider it "positive" is up for debate, but it is indeed clear that the pandemic has set off a fast and innovative response by healthcare institutions which have been increasingly engaging the patient digitally through enhanced applications and personal health trackers. Digital health start-ups that offer multidisciplinary digital solutions for personalized healthcare have immediately seized the pandemic as an opportunity to promote themselves. Advertising texts such as the following have populated the Internet since the global outbreak of the pandemic in 2020:

> When COVID pushed patients from the doctor's office to home, we saw the "quantified self" movement shift from a fringe concept to a mainstream necessity. Tracking biomarkers and other health data at home doesn't just keep patients safer during a pandemic. By giving researchers and clinicians a better view of consumer behavior, it also leads to an increase in diagnostic accuracy and improved overall outcomes. (StartUp Health 20 Oct 2020)

The above-mentioned research group further claims that the rational aspects of the quantified self – "self-knowledge more strongly based on recognizable quantitative data" – "produce a sense of security and certainty, thus compensating for control loss" (Liu et al. 2021). People's awareness and fear of death has increased with the pandemic, triggering defensive actions such as self-quantification (cf. Liu et al. 2021). What has been overlooked here again (with the same optimism of the

Quantified Self movement) is that the possibility of self-determination always risks being counteracted through third parties getting their hands on the biological data collected through self-tracking devices.

As is to be expected, Quantified Self guru Wolf advised in the early days of the pandemic how people could control the virus by "using simple analysis of [their] self-tracking data by joining Quantified Flu" – a project of the *Open Humans* Foundation "that enables individuals to connect their data with research and citizen science" (Wolf May 27, 2020). Quantified Flu was initiated by a collective of self-trackers to explore whether data from their wearables could help to predict COVID-19, the flu or the common cold. In the wake of COVID-19 the *digitally engaged patient* was upgraded to the *citizen scientist*. However, this "patient empowerment" has been viewed as controversial in critical studies of health, as "strategies of contemporary health promotion [. . .] encourage individuals to view their health as a project to be managed in a way that aligns with medical regimes, thus extending the reach of medical power" (Sharon 2017, 98). Committed self-trackers, on the other hand, believe that the pandemic is a chance for the quantified self to become a mainstream necessity and were ready for the pandemic. Indeed, the technologization of self-measurement has paved the way for biopolitical procedures in Foucault's sense: COVID-19 self-testing and medical self-tracking have enabled the health measuring and state regulation of populations. Government measures were put in place on the basis of the COVID-19 test results. The whereabouts of the collected data of self-tracking practices in other areas is often unclear but they have biopolitical potential nonetheless as monitoring governments or corporation can potentially access and use them.

3 From Discipline to Control, from *Sur*veillance to *Über*veillance

The quantification of the self has emerged as a symptom of contemporary "surveillance culture" (Lyon 2018), establishing novel forms of watching oneself. After all, surveillance has become part of our everyday lives; we move within surveilled spaces which are increasingly shaped and controlled by CCTV, biometrics, data mining and automated fusion technology.[3] It is difficult to keep track of the

---

[3] "[S]urveillance fusion" is fairly novel and "particularly significant and dangerous" as it "brings together all of the disparate data feeds and data sets to reveal our movements, our associations with our network of people, our history and even, if there's a predictive element of these systems, indicate what we might do next" (Holland Michel 2021).

technological developments as new surveillance devices are coming out every month which have "a new way of watching, listening or tracking us" (Holland Michel 2021). The ubiquity of surveillance greatly affects questions of selfhood and other aspects of being human. Situating the quantified self within the theoretical frameworks of surveillance will therefore enhance our understanding of the phenomenon's intricacies.

In what follows, it will become apparent that the idea of the quantified marks a departure from the traditional panoptic surveillance which is generally associated with Bentham and Foucault. Foucault's elaboration of Jeremy Bentham's "panopticon" as a model for the "disciplinary society" is regarded as the first theoretical framework in surveillance studies (cf. Galič et al. 2017). As the editors of this volume have explicated in the introduction, Foucault develops the concept of "panopticism" and defines it as a disciplinary means, that is "a type of power that is applied to individuals in the form of continuous individual supervision, in the form of control, punishment, and compensation, and in the form of correction, that is, the modelling and transforming of individuals in terms of certain norms" (Foucault 2002, 70). Accordingly, everybody can potentially be under surveillance. Thus, people will internalize control, morals and values in analogy to Bentham's eighteenth-century panopticon model where every action of every prisoner (for instance) could be constantly surveilled from a central tower without the inmates ever knowing when they were actually being watched.

The second conceptual scaffolding in surveillance theory proceeds from Deleuze's notion of "societies of control" (1992) which is both distinct from and a further elaboration of Foucault's "panopticism". In his succinct account of Foucault's carefully developed concept of "disciplinary societies" in *Discipline and Punish*, Deleuze creates a discursive space for various forms of surveillance societies. Deleuze mainly argues that there has been a major shift from centralized surveillance to decentralized surveillance, from institutions to networks, for now surveillance primarily takes place through digital technologies rather than institutionalized enclosures such as prisons, schools or hospitals. A "society of control" is marked by the seamless continuity of the control apparatus in its spread across the length and breadth of societal institutions. What Deleuze calls "society of control" is an omnipresent surveillance by technology, that is, continuous monitoring through algorithms and data collection where authority and power are diffused. Thus, it is important to note that contemporary surveillance is not primarily characterized by a central monitoring force like in the panopticon.[4]

---

[4] Taking into account that Deleuze's article was published in 1992, one is baffled indeed by the author's prescience.

Drawing upon Deleuze's notion of decentralized surveillance in societies of control, Shoshana Zuboff observes that humans have become "raw material" (2015, 75). She goes on to speak about the rise of "surveillance capitalism" – "a new form of information capitalism" which "aims to predict and modify human behavior as a means to produce revenue and market control" (Zuboff 2015, 75). However, unlike the "classical territorialized biopower of the nineteenth century" today there is "an electronic digitized (bio)power" exercised not alone by states but also by private companies like Google (Ceyhan 2012, 38–39). The systematic use of digital surveillance by so-called big data corporations based in Silicon Valley jeopardizes individual autonomy and democratic ideals: the Self is *datafied*, endlessly dividable – or to quote from Deleuze's "Postscript on the Societies of Control", "[t]he numerical language of control is made of codes that mark access to information or reject it. We no longer find ourselves dealing with the mass/individual pair. Individuals have become 'dividuals,' and mbs samples, data, markets, or 'banks'" (1992, 5).

Against this backdrop, the phenomenon of the quantified self emerges as the embodiment of Deleuze's dystopian vision of inescapable control by technology. Even though self-tracking culture resonates with Bentham's utilitarian ideas as well as Foucault's notion of a self-caring subject (cf. Foucault 1988a) on the one hand, the quantified self diverges from the idea of an internalized disciplinary gaze on the other. After all, tracking devices, even if implanted as chips, remain external surveillance tools. Self-trackers do not exert control and discipline over themselves through "the disciplined body, where internalized normative standards are determined top-down" but on the basis of the produced data of their (external) devices (Nafus and Sherman 2014, 1792). Self-trackers are dependent on external devices in order to exert control over their bodies; this is panoptical control from outside which may or may not become effective through the collected biodata. There is, however, also another ambiguous moment in the concept of the quantified self: "the self is made subject in the double sense of the word (as both 'subject of' and as 'subject to'), through self-objectification, but this self-objectification lays claim to more far-reaching sovereignty than Foucault's model allows" (Nafus and Sherman 2014, 1792). At least in terms of the analysis and interpretation of their collected biodata, self-trackers "gain more agency" than the algorithm and potential "big data collectors" such as Google and the like (Nafus and Sherman 2014, 1792).

But even considering the partial analogies to the disciplinary regime underlying Foucault's body of thought, the datafication of the self corresponds more straightforwardly to Deleuze's notion of the "society of control". Continuous and yet diffuse control, modulation and endless division of individuals into dataselves – "di-viduals" – evoke the many terminological subtleties of the quantified self. The citizen's voluntary provision of personal data has arguably accelerated the emergence of the contemporary "society of control". Digitized biopolitics and "data-driven modes of biopower" characterize current societies (Ajana 2017, 2).

In attempts to describe the rapidly changing notions of surveillance and the increasing decentralization it implies, scholars have come up with various *veillances* to "explore the notion of watching from a variety of perspectives" (Michael et al. 2015, 108). In 1988 Clarke developed the concept of "dataveillance" which has ever since been used to refer to the gradual departure from visual surveillance. As opposed to surveillance, dataveillance does not aim "to 'see' a specific behavior so much as to continuously track for emergent patterns" (Ruckenstein and Schüll 2017, 264). Traditional forms of surveillance, for example in the context of East Germany's secret police, focus on specific details of individuals and their network of people; novel forms of surveillance, on the other hand, are more interested in recurring patterns and categories through social sorting. The term "dataveillance" is therefore more in line with the "liquid state" of late modernity surveillance has slipped into, producing endless flows of data beyond the visible (Bauman and Lyon 2013). Dataveillance aptly describes "today's regimes of in/visibility", "mutating surveillance agencies and the targeting and sorting of everyone" (Lyon 2010, 325).

Bringing yet another aspect into play, the concept of "überveillance" was recently introduced by M. G. Michael, echoing Nietzsche's notion of the "Übermensch", to define bodily invasive surveillance (such as implants) which goes beyond and above the possibilities of previous surveillance tools: "Überveillance fuses together all of the different gazes, providing the most pervasive kinds of information by converging the right data through the various lenses" (Michael et al. 2015, 108). In other words: the watching eyes are not *on* people but *part of them* in the form of implanted chips and other self-tracking devices – people have become "sensors" (Goodchild 2007). Überveillance is further defined as centralizing

> all forms of watching (from above and below, by collectives, and by individuals) because the sensor devices carried or embedded in the body are the lowest common denominator in tracking elements – the individual. The network infrastructure underlies the ability to collect data directly from the sensor devices worn by the individual, and big data analytics ensures an interpretation of the unique behavioral traits of the individual, implying not only predicted movement but intent and thought. (Michael et al. 2015, 108)

But even if it seems as if this kind of invasive surveillance has microscopically transplanted Bentham's panopticon into human bodies, we are – as discussed above – only talking about technological extensions of bodies. Surveillance is still external, demonstrating that there are boundaries technology cannot cross to access the individual's inner life.

To be sure, the datafication of humans is due to the careless or uncritical sharing of personal data, which has paved the way for the biopower and health politics we are globally exposed to, especially since the beginning of the COVID-19 pandemic in 2020. The quantified self enhances these power strategies that make use of people, exploiting them for political and/or economic reasons in Zuboff's sense of surveillance capitalism. Against this backdrop, the notion of self-determination advocated in the Quantified Self movement is deceptive, as through datafying themselves individuals are giving control to others.

4 Quantified World, Datafied Selves

Marc-Uwe Kling's novel *QualityLand*, published in 2017, takes quantification to yet another level as in this satirical dystopia of contemporary tracking culture everything is controlled through algorithms. *QualityLand* thematizes the dangerous repercussions of the quantified-self movement in times of biopower through corporate surveillance. The programmatic title suggests ironically that the aim of constant "datafication" – i.e., "the conversion of qualitative aspects of life into quantified data" (Ruckenstein and Schüll 2017, 261) – is to achieve a superlative quality. Kling leaves out no area of life in his text; everything is under surveillance. Physical and emotional states are tracked; children are sedated with hormones at the push of a button; a robot nanny takes care of the offspring. The author – also a Berlin-based songwriter and cabaret artist, well known for his political satire[5] – wanted to do justice to both the optimists and the pessimists and published the same novel in two different editions: a light one for optimists and a dark one for pessimists.

This "funny dystopia" ("lustige Dystopie")[6] captures a reality that may not be far away. QualityLand is a redesigned country where humans deliberately give up control over their life to opaque algorithms which are controlled by a few dominant platforms. In this fictitious world all cities are renamed, the surnames of the inhabitants indicate the occupation of the same-sex parent at the time of conception and payments are made by kissing a touch pad. For example, "TheShop", the world's most popular mail order company (cf. Kling 2017, 212), delivers products via drones before the customers even know that they need them, and the partner search engine "QualityPartner" even suggests better partners to married couples and also immediately dissolves the existing relationship.

---

5 See especially his Kangaroo Chronicles (2009–2018).
6 This is how Kling called his novel in a press conference. https://vimeo.com/233984085. 0:20. Last accessed 29 July 2022.

In QualityLand, everyone has a *social score* – referred to as "Level" ranging from 1 to 100, and the higher people score the more privileges they get like better jobs and higher salaries (cf. Kling 2017, 38). People with one-digit levels are officially classified by the state as needy and unofficially referred to as "useless" (cf. Kling 2017, 39). The value of people is measured according to extracted data about various criteria such as flexibility, resilience, networking, age, health, place of residence, job, income, wealth, relationships and many other things (cf. Kling 2017, 37). The text even suggests that there are no "level-100-people" ("Level-100-Menschen") at all, because even "level-99-people" ("Level-99-Menschen") are supposed to believe that there is still a need for optimization and that they still have someone above them (Kling 2017, 37).

The central character of this optimized storyworld,[7] Peter "Arbeitsloser" or "Unemployed" (named after the father's last occupation), feels discomfort towards this rating system and its endless optimization processes. A "machine scraper" ("Maschinenverschrotter") by profession, he is only on level 10 and close to being identified as "useless" as are people scoring below level 10. Underperformance is socially sanctioned with deprivation of privileges, social marginalization and discrimination such as random police searches (cf. Kling 2017, 48; 40). Peter Arbeitsloser does not thrive on the optimization mania of this digitized and categorized society. On the contrary, he senses that there is something wrong with this system and tries, as we will see, to defy it.

The ideology of the Quantified Self movement is predominant in QualityLand: optimization through continuous tracking promises happiness. There is, however, a crucial difference to bear in mind as there is no "self" left in QualityLand's automated tracking system. In this dystopia, individuals have long lost decision-making rights and are left without any agency as algorithms have taken over totally, deciding on the basis of the collected biometric data of every citizen (even without their consent). As opposed to the quantified self – which falls prey to the deceptive idea of self-determination – quantification is determined by others from the onset without the slightest illusion of freedom and autonomy.

The most efficient surveillance tools in QualityLand are personal digital assistants which are small, worm-like miniature robots called "earworms" ("Ohrwürmer") (Kling 2017, 29). They are placed in the pinna of people's ear where

---

[7] The novel is complex in terms of narrative: a travelogue (explaining "QualityLand"), ads, news and comments are interspersed in the actual storyline. Furthermore, there are several subplots featuring alternating narrative perspectives of other characters such as John of Us, who is an android and candidate for the upcoming presidential election, in which he will compete against a human being, and Martyn "Vorstand" (that is, "Chairman") who is a rather insignificant member of the same political party as John of Us and unhappily married.

they dock closely to a blood vessel near the eardrum through which they are supplied with bioenergy. These "ear worms" are removable and people are not obligated to wear them but as they fear social disadvantages, they end up wearing them around the clock (Kling 2017, 29). Funnily – or rather tragically – Peter Arbeitsloser has a personal digital assistant called "Niemand" – "Nobody":

> Nobody is Peter's personal digital assistant. Peter himself chose this name because he often has the feeling that nobody is there for him. Nobody helps him. Nobody listens to him. Nobody talks to him. *Nobody is watching him.* Nobody makes decisions for him. Peter even imagines that nobody likes him. Peter is a WINNER, because Nobody is a WIN Assistant. WIN, an abbreviation for "What-I-Need", was originally a search engine, in which you had to rather awkwardly enter your questions by voice command and before that by keyboard even. At its heart, WIN is still a search engine. But you don't have to ask questions any more. *WIN knows what you want to know.* Peter doesn't have to make the effort to find relevant information.[8]

> (Niemand ist Peters persönlicher digitaler Assistent. Peter selbst hat diesen Namen gewählt, denn er hat oft das Gefühl, dass Niemand für ihn da ist. Niemand hilft ihm. Niemand hört ihm zu. Niemand spricht mit ihm. *Niemand beobachtet ihn.* Niemand trifft für ihn Entscheidungen. Peter bildet sich sogar ein, dass Niemand ihn mag. Peter ist ein WINNER, denn Niemand ist ein WIN-Assistent. WIN, ein Kürzel für „What-I-Need", war ursprünglich eine Suchmaschine, in die man umständlich per Sprachbefehl, davor sogar noch per Tastatur, seine Fragen eingeben musste. Im Herzen ist WIN immer noch eine Suchmaschine. Aber man braucht keine Fragen mehr zu stellen. *WIN weiß, was man wissen will.* Peter muss sich nicht die Mühe machen, relevante Informationen zu finden.) (Kling 2017, 12; emphasis B.W.)

Kling's protagonist starts questioning this world of superlatives. It is not by chance that Peter names his digital assistant "Niemand" ("Nobody"). Digital assistants are nobodies. An important ambiguity is evoked through this name-giving, for the idea that "Nobody is watching him" also refers to the state of decentralized surveillance in a control society, where one – although being continuously tracked – can easily get the sense of *nobody watching* due to the invisibility and elusiveness of algorithmic control.

Furthermore, the suggestiveness of the name – "because he often has the feeling that Nobody is there for him" (Kling 2017, 12) – hints at the social isolation as a result of the ubiquitous quantification through automated systems. Revealingly, the storyworld's largest social network "Everybody" – which creates profiles for all humans, fulfilling the company's slogan "Everybody is on Everybody" – offers chatbots so that people can stay in touch with their friends without having to communicate with them: "Ideally, chatbots sit at both ends of the friendship and maintain the contact autonomously" ("Im Idealfall sitzen an beiden Enden der

---

[8] All translations of *QualityLand* are by Betiel Wasihun.

Freundschaft Chatbots und halten den Kontakt autonom aufrecht", Kling 2017, 180–181). It is clear that human relations are impossible in this optimized future world.

Machines have become the main partners for isolated individuals in QualityLand. A central topic in Kling's novel – like in many contemporary novels and films such as Ian McEwan's novel *Machines Like Me* (2019) or Alex Garland's film *Ex Machina* (2014) – is the changing relationship between humans and machines, the possibilities and limitations of artificial intelligence, the accompanying processes of dehumanization and the (dystopian) threat that humans become entirely superfluous and replaced by machines, codes, and algorithms. The danger of humans being entirely displaced by algorithms is expressed in the following dialogue between Peter Arbeitsloser and a drone who,[9] without being solicited, delivers beer to cheer him up, as his collected biodata suggests that his frame of mind is low:

> "You know what strikes me?" Peter asked. "When you've had a particularly shitty day, it happens surprisingly often that a drone awaits you at home with a great product to make you happier again."
> "I'm glad you're happy with my service," said the drone. "Please rate me now."
> "An acquaintance of mine claims that these incidents are no coincidence," said Peter. "She claims that the people who write the code – maybe I should say the people who let other people write the code – want us to be happy, because frustration is unproductive. Sometimes even dangerous."
> "An acquaintance of mine", said the drone, "claims there are no more people writing the code. *There's just the code. The code that writes the code.*"

("Weißt du, was mir aufgefallen ist?", fragt Peter. „Wenn man einen besonders beschissenen Tag hat, passiert es erstaunlich oft, dass einen zu Hause eine Drohne mit einem tollen Produkt erwartet, welches einen wieder fröhlicher stimmt."
„Ich freue mich, dass du mit meinem Service zufrieden bist", sagt die Drohne. „Bitte bewerte mich jetzt."
„Eine Bekannte von mir behauptet ja, diese Vorkommnisse seien kein Zufall", sagt Peter. „Sie behauptet, dass die Leute, die den Code schreiben – vielleicht sollte ich lieber sagen: die Leute, die den Code schreiben lassen –, wollen, dass wir glücklich sind, denn Frustration ist unproduktiv. Mitunter sogar gefährlich."
„Eine Bekannte von mir", sagt die Drohne, „behauptet, es gäbe gar keine Leute mehr, die den Code schreiben. *Es gäbe nur noch den Code. Den Code, der den Code schreibt.*") (Kling 2017, 60; emphasis B.W.)

This passage reveals several important aspects of the cultural critique represented in *QualityLand*. The author's close analysis of developments and trends of

---

9 The use of the human pronoun is meant to underline the humanized nature of machines in *QualityLand*.

current society culminates in the dystopian trajectory of a world completely controlled by algorithms. It is not a coincidence that a drone suggests that codes are taking over for there is a notable twist in Kling's engagement with machines: the anthropomorphization of machines is depicted as the consequence of the dehumanizing system. Whereas humans increasingly lose the capacity to think, machines start philosophizing like the self-driving car Herbert who reflects on the "moral implications" of accidents (Kling 2017, 154). What is more, the ubiquitous "intelligent" machines in QualityLand have emotions. There is a drone with a fear of flying, a combat robot with post-traumatic stress disorder, or the android called Kalliope 7.3 who is an e-poet with writer's block (cf. Kling 2017, 81–82).

The passage quoted above makes Kling's critique of surveillance capitalism explicit. Peter's behavioural patterns are being monitored to deduce emotional states for capitalist purposes. The goal of monopolistic companies like TheShop is efficient data collection for personalized marketing or advertising of products. Measurement and evaluation are directed not only to humans but also to machines; quantification permeates everything. Machines are represented as victims, too, and as such dependent on scoring systems.

Peter, who is becoming increasingly suspicious of the system, uses his machine parts recycling business to "save the lives" of machines which would otherwise end up on the scrap heap. Recognizing the flaws of the system, but without being able to really grasp them, he wonders why he should scrap intelligent machines just because they have become human. He is also puzzled when receiving a package that neither matches his profile nor purchasing behaviour, namely a pink dolphin vibrator delivered by a drone one day. Was he not under constant surveillance and were algorithms not supposed to know better than the customers what to do or buy next, as companies want to make people believe with their use of slogans such as "We know what you want" ("Wir wissen, was du willst", Kling 2017, 18)? Together with Kiki "Unbekannt" ("Unknown", again the status of the same-sex parent) – a young critical woman with expertise in hacking who protects her full identity – and a group of machines that he saved from the scrap press, Peter turns against TheShop. However, since algorithms are considered to be infallible (cf. Kling 2017, 126–129), there is no possibility to return the dolphin vibrator. According to the algorithmic calculations, Peter must want the dolphin vibrator.

The main plot of the novel is triggered with this wrong product delivery by a drone. Peter's attempts to return the vibrator becomes the novel's central concern: "But I don't want the fucking thing." "Yes, you do", says the woman. "You want it." "What makes you think you know what I want?" exclaims Peter. "I don't know that. But the system knows" ("'Ich will das Scheißding aber nicht.' 'Doch', sagt die Frau. 'Sie wollen es.' 'Wie kommen Sie darauf, dass Sie wissen, was ich will?', ruft Peter. 'Ich weiß das nicht. Aber das System weiß es'" Kling 2017, 148–149). Although Peter's efforts to return the vibrator fail, they can be read as acts of resistance; he senses that this seemingly perfect world is imperfect and its operating modes ethically questionable, as people are being deprived of their rights.

Tellingly, the relationship between the state and its citizen is described as "Transparent individuals in a non-transparent system" ("Transparente Individuen im intransparenten System", Kling 2017, 23). The surveillance systems function in a completely opaque and non-transparent manner. Top-down government surveillance fades into the background; and the real task of QualityLand's rather passive two-party government – which is to become a grand coalition because everyone wants only one thing, namely "the best" – seems to lie in maximizing the profits of the corporations, for example, through measures such as the "consumption protection laws" ("Konsumschutzgesetze", Kling 2017, 80) that prohibit the repair of machines. These highly monopolized corporations engage in constant surveillance of their customers and thus of almost all citizens of the state. Surveillance capitalism becomes effective with the official approval of the state.

In the light of this, the dating agency "QualityPartner" that promised to find the perfect partners reveals undemocratic methods underlying the land of superlatives:

> Many people think [that the reason for the success] is due to the user profiles being generated automatically from personal data [. . .]. But more crucial, I think, was that we did not allow our users to change these profiles from the beginning;
>
> (Viele Leute meinen, [der Erfolg] liege daran, dass die Benutzerprofile aus personenbezogenen Daten automatisch generiert werden [. . .]. Entscheidender aber war, so glaube ich, dass wir unseren Usern von Anfang an nicht erlaubt haben, diese Profile zu ändern) (Kling 2017, 43).

This passage demonstrates how surveillance capitalism takes place in secret, curtailing people's right to make their own decisions (see also Huber 2020, 77).

The core problem of digital society is described in a nutshell as "Peter's Problem" which was triggered with the unsolicited vibrator delivery (Kling 2017, 200–201). Peter seeks advice from the old wise man who has locked himself in an armoured glass box in his house to protect himself from a biological terrorist attack somewhere in QualityLand. His actual identity is never revealed but there are hints that it is the author who most likely takes a cameo role in his fictional work to offer solutions to the cultural crisis his central character senses but struggles to grasp. The old man tries to explain that Peter's problem is bigger than the pink dolphin vibrator, that it is "symptomatic of bigger social issues, against which Peter rebels via its catalyst" (Küppel 2022, 235). He explains that the Internet does not adapt to the individual but to its data doubles – which resonates with Deleuze's notion of "dividuals" – that is, to the individual's images and profiles. Peter begins to understand that if these profiles are wrong, his personalized world in QualityLand is wrong, too (cf. Kling 2017, 203–204). Kling's anti-hero embarks on an unsuccessful odyssey and neither manages to return the vibrator nor correct his profile. The supposedly happy ending reveals that even if Peter received the right delivery (a drone awaits him at home with a package), nothing has changed. The notion of "Peter's problem" has become a leitmotif and refers to the curtailing repercussions of algorithmic control.

At another point in the text, Peter Arbeitsloser reflects about the profile that was assigned to him by mistake:

> My possibilities are like a fan, which they close more and more with each of my clicks, until I can only go in one direction. They deprive my personality of all edges and corners! They take away the bifurcations in my road of life!
>
> (Meine Möglichkeiten gleichen einem Fächer, den sie mit jedem meiner Klicks immer weiter zuklappen, bis ich nur noch in eine Richtung gehen kann. Sie rauben meiner Persönlichkeit alle Ecken und Kanten! Sie nehmen meinem Lebensweg die Abzweigungen!) (Kling 2017, 297)

This quote demonstrates how datafication of human life gradually leads to personality theft; the individual gets stuck in a deadlock. Kling's novel offers a critical account of how tracking technologies turn human life into "data assemblages" (Lupton 2015, 102) and associated processes of alienation and dehumanization. Through lifelogging via digital assistants – who have lodged themselves in peoples' bodies – humans become datafied selves, and more so, calculable objects.

QualityLand creates a clear parallel to the notion of "data colonialism" – a term Couldry and Mejias developed to describe a new phase in the relationship between colonialism and capitalism. With reference to the "business cliché that data is 'the new oil'", they claim that data is "a 'raw material' with natural value" (2019a, 340). Unlike oil, however, data has to be constructed and appropriated through a process they call "data relations": "new types of human relations which enable the extraction of data for commodification" (Couldry and Mejias 2019a, 337), including "the rituals of routine self-tracking on platforms where we count our followers or likes" (Couldry and Mejias 2019a, 344). Whereas the old colonialism seizes land, the new one takes ownership of us, that is our social lives through the medium of data. Taking into account the great differences between both forms of colonialism such us the scale of violence, Couldry and Mejias draw analogies between colonialism and capitalism which helps them to create a theoretical framework that captures our data-driven world and offers analytical tools. The most significant similarity, they contend, is the historical function, as both forms of colonialism *dispossess*:

The expansion of data colonialism is a problem for all human subjects, indeed for human development as such. *A continuously trackable life is a dispossessed life, no matter how one looks at it.* Recognizing this dispossession is the start of resistance to data colonialism. [. . .] And it is exactly this alternative vision that resistance to data colonialism must affirm. (2019a: 345; emphasis B.W.)

Recalling the quoted passage above from *QualityLand* – "They deprive my personality of all edges and corners! They take away the bifurcations of my road of life!" – it becomes clear how much Kling's conceptual premise resonates with the idea of data colonialism. Sensing a real threat in continuous data extraction in contemporary societies, Couldry and Mejias argue that "data is colonizing human life and appropriating it for capitalism" (2019b: xi). Following Zuboff's concept of "surveillance capitalism", which depicts a new stage of capitalism, they define "data colonialism" as a "new form of colonialism distinctive of the 21st century" with a precarious "vision of totality":

These new types of social relations implicate human beings in processes of data extraction, but in ways that do not prima facie seem extractive. That is the key point: the audacious yet largely disguised corporate attempt to incorporate all of life, whether or not conceived by those doing it as "production," into an expanded process for the generation of surplus value. The extraction of data from bodies, things and systems creates new possibilities for managing everything. This is the new and distinctive role of platforms and other environments of routine data extraction. If successful, this transformation will leave no discernable "outside" to capitalist production: everyday life will have become directly incorporated into the capitalist process of production. (Couldry and Mejias 2019a, 343)

"Data colonialism", they argue, is not to be understood as a metaphor but an emerging reality; it is not "an echo or simple continuation of historic forms of territorial colonialism" but refers "to a new form of colonialism distinctive of the twenty-first century" (Couldry and Mejias 2019a: 336f.), "an emerging order for the appropriation of human life so that data can be continuously extracted from it for profit" (Couldry and Mejias 2019b: xiii).

Couldry and Mejias do not merely offer a theory to analyse and grasp the current era of big data and its novel notions of societal control but they spur us into action. On the basis of the term "data colonialism" they draw attention to sites of resistance. They call for "decolonizing data" (2019b: 187–211) by resisting the central problem of big data, that is, "its vision of totality" (cf. 2019a: 346). Building on Peruvian sociologist Aníbal Quijano's work on historic colonialism (2007), in which he pleads for an "epistemological decolonization" through the renunciation of "absolute universality" underlying European modernity, Couldry and Mejias call for an "alternative vision of order and totality that datafication denies" (2019a: 346).

An important step towards decolonizing data is then to reject the universal rationality of data collection or extraction. It is important to recognize that the data ecosystem rests upon (false) ideologies such as the assumption that data as a natural resource is ownerless and must be reappropriated by tech companies for profit and in the name of the community's wellbeing, facilitating sharing through digital connections. In order to resist data colonialism, Couldry and Mejias argue, its underlying ideologies must be counteracted. Programmes are needed to enhance our understanding of digital systems as well as the enforcement of legal regulations to contain uncontrolled data tracking. The idea that continuous and all-encompassing datafication is a justifiable and rational way of living must be dismissed.

However, individual decisions like opting out of platforms, revising codes or refraining from social quantification altogether or using alternative platforms would not suffice. Instead, data processes must be grounded in social processes that are fair, accurate and transparent. Although acknowledging that their proposal may be challenging, Couldry and Mejias demand reimagining forms of collectivity, finding new ways of appropriating technologies, novel ideas about knowledge and solidarity. Couldry and Mejias have also possible solutions in mind and argue that redesigning data sharing systems so as to be based on consent could be the way forward.

As we have seen, this criticism of data colonialism is put into literary practice in *QualityLand*. At one point the old man explains to Peter that it was the Internet that had enabled the emergence of corporate monopolies due to the devilish network effect (cf. Kling 2017, 257), resonating with the scepticism towards the Internet in Couldry's and Mejias' book title *The Costs of Connection*. What is more, *QualityLand* offers aspects of undermining the totality of big data. For example, in the chapter "Peter's Problem", ignorance about digital systems is identified as part of Peter's problem: a stand-in for the general problem people are facing in contemporary societies of control. The old man behind an armoured glass panel, who rebels against the system, protects his DNA from biohacking, because in QualityLand it is not only possible to construct a virus that specifically attacks whole populations or perhaps even all humans, but also to construct a virus that attacks only a single strand of DNA (Kling 2017, 201). Peter, who had not even heard about biological terror attacks, reproaches the old man for being paranoid and the old man, in turn, indirectly asks him to be better informed in order to resist control. These implications remind us of Couldry and Mejias's call for a better comprehension of our datafied world. Early in the COVID-19 pandemic, two years after Couldry and Mejias had first published on data colonialism,[10] the authors asked once again for "resistance to the new data colonialism" in an *Al Jazeera* article (April 2020). This time their postulation is even more urgent, as they were rightly concerned that the COVID-19 crisis would aggravate data colonialism

QualityLand appeared in 2017 and the publication of the sequel *Qualityland 2.0. Kikis Geheimnis* coincided with the outbreak of the pandemic in 2020. Thus, there is no direct reference to COVID-19 in these narratives. Indirectly, however, both novels deal critically with what has facilitated intensified control through biopower in the course of the pandemic in the first place, that is, digital (self-) tracking technologies. As discussed in the first part of this chapter, the promise of autonomy underlying the quantified self is deceptive as ultimately algorithms take over and control self-trackers. Kling's novel, however, goes beyond the notion of the quantified self as individuals are completely dispossessed of their selfhood and no longer exhibit even the slightest hint of a seemingly freedom of voluntary self-tracking. QualityLand is populated by datafied selves who are deprived of agency and autonomy. Quantification through algorithmic control takes place by default in order to profit corporate monopolies; surveillance capitalism is at its best in QualityLand. Kling's satirical dystopia expresses resistance to corporate surveillance and biopower, criticizing the drift of societies towards digital totalitarianism or "total algorithmic control" (Couldry and Mejias 2019a, 346).

Peter Arbeitsloser is reminiscient of traditional characters in dystopian fiction as he epitomizes the small man who tries to stand up against an overpowering system but ultimately fails to achieve any changes. And yet, his act of resistance is no less significant because his attempts to return the wrongly delivered vibrator can be read as a rebellion against the diffuse power of digital corporate monopolies. Even if he does not manage to return the product and change his profile, he still chalks up a success, as he reveals the imperfections of a supposedly perfect system: quantification through total algorithmic control is not infallible after all. Peter Arbeitsloser represents the hope that there is space for resisting digital totalitarianism for the sake of a mentally healthy society, allowing for a less bleak outlook than in a classic dystopia. *QualityLand* calls for resistance through thought-provoking near-future visions of contemporary society, not least making use of satire as an effective form of criticism.

---

10 Couldry and Mejias first published their ideas on data colonialism online in 2018. In 2019, a print version appeared, as well as their book *The Costs of Connection: How Data is Colonizing Human Life and Appropriating it for Capitalism* which includes their main arguments from the previously published articles.

References

Ajana, Btihaj. "Digital Health and the Biopolitics of the Quantified Self." *Digital Health* 3 (2017): 1–18.
Almalki, Manal, Kathleen Gray, and Fernando Martin-Sanchez. "The Use of Self Quantification Systems for Personal Health Information: Big Data Management Activities and Prospects." *Health Information Science and Systems* 3.1 (2015). https://doi.org/10.1186/2047-2501-3-S1-S1. Last accessed 19 August 2022.
Bauman, Zygmunt, and David Lyon. *Liquid Surveillance. A Conversation*. Cambridge: Polity, 2013.
Ceyhan, Ayse. "Surveillance as Biopower." *Routledge Handbook of Surveillance Studies*. Eds. Kirstie Ball, Kevin Haggerty and David Lyon. Abingdon: Routledge, 2012. 38–45. 27 March 2012. https://www.routledgehandbooks.com/doi/10.4324/9780203814949.ch1_1_c. Last accessed 28 July 2022.
Clarke, Roger. "Information, Technology and Dataveillance." *Communications of the ACM* 31.5 (1988): 498–512.
Couldry, Nick, and Ulises A. Mejias. "Data Colonialism. Rethinking Big Data's Relation to the Contemporary Subject." *Television & New Media* 20.4 (2019a): 336–349.
Couldry, Nick, and Ulises A. Mejias. *The Costs of Connection: How Data is Colonizing Human Life and Appropriating it for Capitalism*. Redwood City: Stanford University Press, 2019b.
Couldry, Nick, and Ulises A. Mejias. "Resistance to the new data colonialism must start now." *Al-Jazeera*. April 2020. https://www.aljazeera.com/opinions/2020/4/28/resistance-to-the-new-data-colonialism-must-start-now. Last accessed 28 July 2022.
de Souza, Poppy. "Self-Tracking and Body Hacking: The Biopolitics of the Quantified Self in the Age of Neoliberalism." https://www.poppydesouza.com/occasional/2015/6/5/self-tracking-and-body-hacking-the-biopolitics-of-the-quantified-self-in-the-age-of-neoliberalism. Last accessed 14 May 2022.
Deleuze, Gilles. "Postscript on the Societies of Control." *October*, 59 (1992): 3–7.
Fong, Cherize. "Open Source Body: Small Data, Self-Research, Open Humans." 29 June 2020. https://www.makery.info/en/2020/06/29/open-source-body-small-data-self-research-open-humans/. Last accessed 14 May 2022.
Foucault, Michel. *The History of Sexuality*. Volume 3: *The Care of the Self*. Trans. Robert Hurley. New York: Vintage Books, 1988.
Foucault, Michel. "Technologies of the Self." *Technologies of the Self: A Seminar with Michel Foucault*. Eds. L.H. Mating, H. Gutman, and P. H. Hutton. Cambridge, MA: The University of Massachusetts Press, 1988. 26–49.
Foucault, Michel. *Discipline and Punish: The Birth of the Prison*. Trans. Alan Sheridan, Penguin, 1991.
Foucault, Michel. *Die Geburt der Biopolitik. Geschichte der Gouvernementalität II: Vorlesungen am Collège de France 1978/1979*. Frankfurt am Main: Suhrkamp, 2004.
Foucault, Michel. *The History of Sexuality*. Volume 1: *The Will to Knowledge*. Trans. R. Hurley. New York: Pantheon, 1998.
Foucault, Michel (2002). *Power: Essential Works of Foucault 1954–1984*, Volume 3. Ed. J.D. Faubion. London: Penguin Books, 2002.
Galič, Maša, Tjerk Timan and Bert-Jaap Koops. "Bentham, Deleuze and Beyond: An Overview of Surveillance Theories from the Panopticon to Participation." *Philosophy & Technology* 30.1 (2017): 9–37.
Goodchild, Michael F. "Citizens as Sensors: The World of Volunteered Geography." *GeoJournal* 69. 4 (August 2007): 211–221.

Holland Michel, Arthur. "'How You Are, or Are Not, Being Watched'." *Democracy in Exile* (1 November 2021) https://dawnmena.org/how-you-are-or-are-not-being-watched-arthur-holland-michel-on-surveillance-tech/. Last accessed 24 July 2022.

Huber, Sabrina. "Literarische Narrative der Überwachung – Alte und neue Spielformen der dystopischen Warnung." *Narrative der Überwachung. Typen, mediale Formen und Entwicklungen*. Eds. Kilian Hauptmann, Martin Hennig, Hans Krah. Berlin: Peter Lang, 2020. 49–86.

Husserl, Edmund. *Ideas Pertaining to a Pure Phenomenology and to a Phenomenological Philosophy, Second Book. Studies in the Phenomenology of Constitution. Collected Works of Edmund Husserl, vol. 3*. Trans. R. Rojcewicz and A. Schuwer. Dordrecht: Springer, 1989.

Jarvis, Brian. "Surveillance and Spectacle Inside *The Circle*." *Surveillance, Architecture and Control. Discourses on Spatial Culture*. Eds. Susan Flynn and Antonia Mackay. London: Palgrave Macmillan, 2019. 275–294.

Kling, Marc-Uwe. *QualityLand*. Berlin: Ullstein, 2017.

Klüppel, Joscha. "Marc-Uwe Kling's QualityLand: 'Funny Dystopia' as Social and Political Commentary." *New Perspectives on Contemporary German Science Fiction*. Eds. Lars Schmeink and Ingo Cornils. Palgrave Macmillan Cham: London. 231–246. https://doi.org/10.1007/978-3-030-95963-0. Last accessed 20 March 2023.

Liu, Yue, Xingyang Lv, and Ziyan Tang. "The Impact of Mortality Salience on Quantified Self Behavior during the COVID-19 Pandemic." *Personality and Individual Differences* 180 (October 2021). https://doi.org/10.1016/j.paid.2021.110972. Last accessed 29 July 2022.

Lyon, David. *The Culture of Surveillance: Watching as a Way of Life*. Cambridge: Polity, 2018.

Lyon, David. "Liquid Surveillance: The Contribution of Zygmunt Bauman to Surveillance Studies." *International Political Sociology* 4 (2010): 325–338.

Lupton, Deborah. "Quantifying the Body: Monitoring and Measuring Health in the Age of Health Technologies." *Critical Public Health* 23.4 (2013a): 393–403.

Lupton, Deborah. "Understanding the Human Machine." *IEEE Technology and Society Magazine* 32.4 (2013b): 25–30.

Lupton, Deborah. *Digital Sociology*. London: Routledge, 2015.

Mämecke, Thorben. *Das quantifizierte Selbst. Zur Genealogie des Self-Trackings*. Bielefeld: transcript, 2021.

Michael, M. G., Katina Michael, and Christine Perakslis, "Überveillance, the Web of Things, and People: What Is the Culmination of All This Surveillance?" *IEEE Consumer Electronics Magazine* 4.2 (13 April 2015): 107–113.

Nafus, Dawn, and Jamie Sherman. "This One Does Not Go Up to 11: The Quantified Self Movement as an Alternative Big Data Practice." *International Journal of Communication* 8 (2014): 1784–1794.

Rose, Nikolas. *The Politics of Life Itself: Biomedicine, Power, and Subjectivity in the Twenty-First Century*. Princeton: Princeton University Press, 2007.

Ruckenstein, Minna, and Natasha Dow Schüll. "The Datafication of Health." *Annual Review of Anthropology* 46.1 (2017): 261–278.

Selke, Stefan. *Lifelogging. Wie die digitale Selbstvermessung unsere Gesellschaft verändert*. Berlin: Ullstein, 2014.

Sharon, Tamar. "Self-Tracking for Health and the Quantified Self: Re-Articulating Autonomy, Solidarity, and Authenticity in an Age of Personalized Healthcare." *Philosophy & Technology* 30 (2017): 93–121.

StartUp Health, 20 October 2020. https://healthtransformer.co/empowering-the-quantified-self-in-a-covid-world-a-health-transformer-showcase-recap-bcf1745f7447. Last accessed 1 May 2022.

Swan, Melanie. "The Quantified Self: Fundamental Disruption in Big Data Science and Biological Discovery." *Big Data* 1.2 (June 2013): 85–99.

Wiedemann, Lisa. "Datensätze der Selbstbeobachtung – Daten verkörpern und Leibvergessen!" 16 April 2016. *Lifelogging*. Ed. S. Selke. Springer VS: Wiesbaden. https://doi.org/10.1007/978-3-658-10416-0_4. Last accessed 28 July 2022.

Wolf, Gary. „The Data-Driven Life." *New York Times*. 28 April 2010. https://www.nytimes.com/2010/05/02/magazine/02self-measurement-t.html?_r=2&ref=magazine&page-wan-ted=all. Last accessed 23 July 2022.

Wolf, Gary. "The Quantified Self." Ted Talk, June 2010. https://www.ted.com/talks/gary_wolf_the_quantified_self. Last accessed 15 May 2022.

Wolf, Gary. "Self-Tracking for COVID-19." 27 May 2020. https://quantifiedself.com/blog/self-tracking-for-covid-19/. Last accessed 22 July 2022.

Zuboff, Shoshana. "Big Other: Surveillance Capitalism and the Prospects of an Information Civilization." *Journal of Information Technology* 30 (2015): 75–89.

Frank Kraushaar

When "Total War" Joins "People's War": China's Recent Surge of Biopolitics and Its Repercussions in Internet Poetry

Abstract: In the People's Republic of China (PRC) the long denial of an epidemic threat by the authorities led to hectic actions in late January 2020. Soon after, this official political activism resulted in a biopolitical campaign under the direct leadership of the Communist Party's (henceforth Party) Central Committee. Paramount leader Xi Jinping, in domestic speeches as well as in international communication, set out a rhetoric of war, the impact of which was not only perceived in Western public discourse, but felt even more pervasively in the language of PRC mainstream media. This essay argues that lyrical Internet poetry in China, which is a popular genre of communication that vehemently responds to public incidents, takes up the new biopolitics and bioethics proclaimed by party organs and mainstream media and translates it into a more intellectual idiom. The function of lyrical Internet poetry as a contemporary social institution will be highlighted. After that, I will present and discuss five poems partly found and accessed via Chinese websites and partly received through direct communication with authors of the online-poetry scene. These texts starkly differ from each other in terms of their literary quality and, while the authors of the first two seem to be occasional writers and more or less committed to reasserting official discourse, those of the last two poems are outstanding figures in the context of internet literature as one of the PRC's officially not recognized subcultures, heavily censored under pandemic conditions.

My analysis of the language of recent poetic texts composed in response to the public mobilization for a "total war" and "people's war" will largely rely on translation methods developed over the years in previous works on classical premodern as well as on modern and contemporary classicist Chinese poetry. I will demonstrate both the vulnerability and the subversive potential of poetic language in coping with authoritarian biopolitics.

1 Political Messiness and Ideological Metaphors or Warfare in the Name of Mankind's Destiny

In the second half of March 2020, just two months after China belatedly acknowledged its COVID-19 epidemic as a "major health crisis", imposed country-wide heavy restrictions on everyday life, and isolated the whole nation from international traffic, Central Party Committee and General Secretary *cum* State President Xi Jinping took part in a tele-conference of G20 leaders. This was the moment when European governments, shocked by the devastating outbreak of COVID-19 in Northern Italy, one after another imposed similar measures and the word "lockdown" went global. During the meeting, Xi, according to domestic media, delivered an "important speech" (*chongyao jianghua*) under the headline "Working Together to Fight the Epidemic" (*xi shou kang yi gong ke shijian*). According to deputy foreign minister Ma Zhaoxu, Xi's speech succeeded in sharing "China's experience", set forth "China's proposition", put forward a "Chinese initiative" and outlined pledges for "China's contribution" (Qian 2020). Notably, the official exegesis of the party-state-leader's words stressed that "adhering to the concept of a community of common destiny for mankind" China would be "playing an important guiding role for strengthening international cooperation on epidemic control and stabilizing the global economy" (Qian 2020). The formula "common destiny of mankind" (*renlei mingyun gongtongti*) had been promoted by Chinese diplomats at the United Nations since 2017 as a guideline for global governance, but it had failed to overcome the resistance of other nations. It is evident, however, that the moment of anxiety captured in public discourses and an ensuing unsettledness that could be observed in political and societal bodies around the globe could only appear as self-affirmation from the perspective of a party-state determined to downplay its own systemic failure to take timely preventive measures and, instead, to propagate its overwhelming capacity in mobilizing resources and regaining complete control over the situation as soon as possible.

In his comparatively brief speech, Xi also employed other well-known communist-party catchwords to demonstrate his self-confidence in this ideological context. The most notorious one was the Maoist concept of "people's war", which Xi intends as a powerful metaphor of all-over mobilization – instigated and guided by the party – within a new biopolitical framework of self-empowerment in face of a fateful threat to humanity:

> Faced with the sudden rise of the novel coronavirus epidemic, the Chinese government and the Chinese people did not shrink from adversity, but placed people's lives and health above all. With firm resolution, mutual aid, scientific prevention and precise policies, we undertook a people's war against the epidemic through national mobilization, joint prevention and control, and openness and transparency (Qian 2020).

Indeed, this was not the first time a "people's war" had been declared under Xi, and what to the Western ears sounds like an ideological phrase dismissed long ago is in contemporary China considered a "political category".[1] Already in a speech of May 2014 at the Second Central Xinjiang Work Forum, Xi had declared a "People's War on Terror", and, pointing directly to the nation's militaristic policymaking and implementation capacity, he exclaimed that "we Communists should be naturals at fighting a people's war, we are the best at organizing for a task" (Zenz 2022, 88).

However, the wording chosen by Xi's speechwriters for the international stage differs from that of previous speeches for domestic audiences after 20 January 2020, the day COVID-19 was officially recognized as a "high-level emergency" in China. During a public inspection tour on 10 February in Beijing, Xi used no less than three keywords to frame the party leadership's vision of how state and society must combat the invisible foe of mankind. These terms are "people's war" (*renmin zhanzheng*), "defensive battle" (*zujizhan*) and "total war" (*zongti zhan*). The investigative journalist and media critic Qian Gang was astonished at this obvious fusion of what, according to the traditional nomenclature of the CCP, should be qualified as either "red discourse" (*hongse ciyu* = "people's war") or "black discourse" (*heise ciyu* = "total war"), meaning politically correct versus ideologically adverse language. But Qian also saw a general tendency during the "New Era" under Xi Jinping to blur the lines of ideological distinctions between proper and improper public language. He may have a point in supposing that the "functionaries in charge of penning speeches and official documents are not as sensitive as they once were to the CCP's own history, much less to world history" (Qian 2020).

But undeniably the party under Xi regards its unique capacity of "mobilizing the masses" as a pillar of its own legitimacy, especially in times of an acute crisis. In communist China, mass mobilization is also considered a reliable device to cure bureaucratic and institutional dysfunction. This correlates with Rudolf Kjellén's ideas of biopolitics and biopower that conceptualize state and society as an organicist entity on which individual wellbeing and physical health ultimately depend (Kjellén 1924).[2] Thus, Qian's preliminary attempt to partly explain the hybridization

---

[1] In an article published in December 2020, Philipp Renninger investigates the management of the COVID-19 epidemics in Wuhan in its earlier stages until summer 2020, providing evidence for the regular employment of this and related terminology ("Defense War", "frontline", "Blockade War", etc.) in official legislative documents and party committees' decisions (Renninger 2020, 31 and footnote 263).

[2] Even during its most tolerant periods, such as in the decade which followed Deng Xiaoping's call for "reform and opening" (*gaige kaifang*) from the late 1970s to the Tiananmen Massacre in 1989, the CCP "mobilized" the country's population via campaigns to curb the growth of public support for ideas of reform that were considered a threat to the party's monopoly on political power. Even more important is the fact that dynamic economic growth to restore the wealth of the nation, in the eyes of party leaders, required a repressive biopolitical agenda fully implemented between 1979 and

of political discourse by gaps in the historical education of party functionaries must be weighed against the no less hypothetical assumption that "New Era" propaganda strategists *purposefully* combine the very distinct Maoist terminology and slogans with language referring to a broader context of authoritarian mindsets and values. Most likely, "total war", *zongti zhanzheng* in the Chinese translation of the title of Erich Ludendorff's book "Der totale Krieg" (1935), would rarely appeal to the *historical* consciousness of the average Chinese audience of Xi's speeches while it does *emotionally* address a sense of collective responsibility for defeating a common enemy. This quality, however, is not very different from the one Joseph Goebbels sought for in his notorious "Sportpalastrede" after the German *Wehrmacht*'s defeat at Stalingrad in February 1943. Needless to say, the writers of Xi's speech to the G20 leaders were well aware that this historical parallel would be made by many recipients and they adjusted the terminology by deleting "total war" from the manuscript.

2 Public Intellectual Discourse at the Junction of Biopolitics and Bellicose Language

Descending from the register of high-level diplomacy and central-government/central party-committee discourse to academic discourse involving wider circles of the country's elite, political correctness has still maintained its dominant position. Leading intellectuals of China's "New Left", in their responses to the COVID-19 crisis, *translate* the wording of political leaders into a language of their own. This language complies with the political goals of the party, as the latter are constantly framed and re-framed by mainstream media, but it also refers to a wider discursive spectrum, stressing the necessity to accomplish a transition of the "revolutionary dynamics" of the twentieth century to the new tempo of the twenty-first century. Wang Hui 汪晖, currently one of China's most prominently established public intellectuals and figurehead of the

---

2016 under the name "one-child-policy" (*yi ge haizi zhengce*). Party officials argued that the restrictions were necessary to counteract an alleged threat of over-population. However, it is undeniable that, during a period of consecutive liberalization experiments and increasing influence of a fast growing private economy on social transformation the biopolitical instruments in the hands of the party helped to preserve the latter's ultimate claim to dertermine conditions of private life. As stated in the "Introduction" to this volume, the gradual loosening of restrictions for the Han Chinese population since 2016 coincides with a much more brutal implementation of these measures against so-called ethnic minorities mostly in Xinjiang and other Muslim regions, now intended to secure a "healthy" national culture.

New Left, tortuously reintegrates the apparent inconsistency of Xi's terminological trilogy with its historical origins in the twentieth century:

> In the process of fighting against the coronavirus, the Communist Party of China made a striking appeal to this tradition [of CCP-led mobilization for "people's war"], characterizing the fight against the epidemic as "a people's war, a total war, a defensive war ["defensive battle" in my translation above of *zujizhan*]." The term "defensive war" is a definition of the goal of the battle, while the "people's war" and the "total war" are characterizations of the nature of the struggle. A people's war takes the form of group defence and group control, including communities such as families and work units, individuals, and various levels of government, and a total war signals that the struggle is a comprehensive mobilization of national systems and capacities. In the 20th century, people's war was the basic means to overcome the general warfare of imperialist countries, so people's war and total war were antagonistic, but in the 21st century, when the epidemic prompted full national mobilization, political parties once again resorted to the model of people's war, creating a new type of vertical and horizontal social mobilization. (Wang 2020)

Notably, Wang does not speak of the (Communist) Party (of China) alone when he mentions the political subjects *organizing* the new "people's war", but of "political parties", suggesting that in the twenty-first century all political parties across the globe, in seeking for proper responses to the viral invasion, were left with no alternatives to the Maoist concept of "people's war". After another long-winded episode conceding the central government's unlikely transparency in communicating all emerging problems to national stakeholders as swiftly as to international institutions and Western countries like the US, and blaming "local bureaucracy" for "insensitive" misjudgements, Wang comes back to his point, the master narrative of the victorious transition of revolutionary mobilization strategies from a century of class struggle into a century of "Great Rejuvenation of the Chinese Nation" (*zhonghuaminzu weida fuxing*). Wang is certain that the present era has erased the political antagonism of socialist revolution versus capitalist reaction, not only in China, and that "people's war" is no longer the vast wave of socialist mass movements that ultimately overcomes the fanatic mobilization of fascist reactionaries usurping state institutions. Now that antagonism of "total war" and "people's war" seems resolved, opening the gates for the next step forward into the twenty-first century is envisioned in the light of a united "struggle" under the assumed conviction of a "common destiny of mankind":[3]

---

[3] A good number of leading Chinese intellectuals – not all of them figureheads of the New Left, which insists on its loyalty to the traditions of Chinese Communism in a new era of the history of socialism – are focused in their work on developing ideas born in a hybrid mental sphere between global modernism and postmodernism, Chinese traditional intellectual history and the Party's ideological mainstream discourse rooted in Leninism, Maoism and "Xi Jinping Thought".

Comprehensive and effective anti-epidemic mobilization was effected under the direct intervention of the central government. Unlike the people's wars of the 20th century, the people's war against the virus was carried out within the framework of the country's total war. Its goal was to stop the virus through popular mobilization and scientific prevention and control, *and not to generate new political subjects*. Under emergency conditions, protecting people's lives and meeting people's daily needs are the first priorities, and capital appreciation and expansion retreat to a secondary position. Under such circumstances, the rarely seen energy of the people's war was rejuvenated, providing the greatest guarantee for the victory in the first stage of the campaign against the virus. Many Western critics attributed the success of China's efforts to "totalitarianism", but they failed to discern the energy of the people's war within the system of national mobilization, nor did they understand the complex relationship between people's war and total war.[4]

In a subtle response to Wang's attempt to disguise the Party's recourse to totalitarian governance under Xi behind pseudo-intellectual ruminations on a "Revolutionary Personality and the Philosophy of Victory" (hence the translation of the title of his essay quoted in Chinese in footnote 1), the independent thinker Rong Jian 榮劍 muses on "Wang's Heidegger moment" – an allusion to Martin Heidegger's appraisal and public endorsement of National Socialism and the "Führerkult" during his tenure as rector of Albert-Ludwigs-Universität Freiburg.[5]

In the language of official intellectual figureheads since early 2020, a weird junction of biopolitics and bellicose terminology dominates. It often seems to depend on the fictitious yet invisible adversary who disrupts concentration on any possible weak points, failures and responsibilities that the Party, central government or their "paramount leader" (*zuigao lingxiu*) might be held accountable for. Such discourses are indeed reminiscent of that sterile brutality which under totalitarian

---

Recently most debated among Western academics and intellectuals and made widely available via translations into most Western languages is Zhao Tingyang's work "All Under Heaven. The Tianxia System for a Possible World Order" (University of California Press 2021) which elaborates on the possibility to develop further the "failed" multilateralism of the past century into a system of distribution and execution of power led by "mankind" as the subject of world history. The system Zhao ventures to explore had already been invented in premodern China two-and-half thousand years ago to become the ideological superstructure of the imperial state. Without mentioning the CCP or Xi Jinping in his book, Zhao constructs a wordy intellectual framework to discuss on international stages Xi's "Chinese Dream" of a "Great Rejuvenation of the Chinese Nation" in the twenty-first century.

4 Published first 21 April 2020: 汪晖, "革命者人格与胜利的哲学——纪念列宁诞辰 150 周年" in *Beijing Cultural Review web feed*. I refer to the translation by David Ownby. See Wang, Hui.

5 荣剑, "革命者的胜利意味着什么？评汪晖 "革命者人格" 和 "胜利的哲学. The text has been censored on the original Chinese website, but it is accessible via this link: https://drive.google.com/file/d/1UdpUfPE53yUhMb1YwxAR–6CN6z1Ujwq/view. I refer to David Ownby's translation: "Rong Jian: What Does Wang Hui Mean". See Rong, Jian https://www.readingthechinadream.com/rong-jian-wang-huis-heidegger-moment.html. Last accessed 19 May 2022.

regimes of the previous century often reduced intellectuals to translators of ideological slogans and bureaucratese into a somewhat vitalized and emotionalized, yet often even more abstruse idiom.

3 Poetry as a Social Institution in the ChinaNet

Perhaps this was and still is most true for poetry *because* poetry seems naturally opposed to the kind of sterility that is always required to achieve instrumentality. To examine the impact of a highly ideologized biopolitical public discourse on contemporary Chinese poetry more closely, this chapter now focuses on Internet poetry. In contemporary China, the social status of lyrical poetry depends on its intermediate position between a still very widespread traditional understanding of the poet as a moral institution and of poetry as a literary activity that held the highest intellectual and ethical position in a pre-modern social hierarchy, and a revolutionary avant-garde mission rooted in the *modern* tradition of poetic language as a creative force that can articulate subjectivity at the grassroots level of society. Furthermore, traditional ("classical") poetry's cultural prestige, officially restored since Mao's self-presentation as a reinventor of classical verse in the spirit of the revolution (when modern verse had been violently reduced to public propaganda), is nowadays combined with multiple forms of modern poetry activism in a new and comprehensive space of literary performance.

In this context, the Internet as a public or semi-public space for literary performance is of enormous importance in China – even more so during the pandemic. The development of more than one new way of writing and reading verse is closely intertwined with, if not entirely dependent, on the medial turn. At the starting point of a short survey on the state of Internet literature in contemporary China, Michel Hockx, a leading scholar of that field at the time of writing, indicates that, according to a 2021 report, 45.6% of Chinese netizens visit webpages to read literature online, which means a total of more than 400 million readers. The same year, "reading literature" held the twelfth position in a list of the prevalent online activities of Chinese netizens, thus seeming more popular than, for example, booking travel online or Internet-based courses for self-education or advanced training (Hockx 2022).

Although Hockx and others stress the commercial function of the Internet and its impact on online literature and literary culture in China, this still leaves much space for non-commercial literary activities that impact public communication. In her seminal study "Verse Going Viral. Chinese New Media Scenes", Heather Inwood

(2014) outlines the diversification and reloading of poetic activities triggered by the medial turn:

> Since the late 1990s, a dizzying array of poetry groups, movements, generations, and incidents have punctuated overviews of contemporary poetry, indicating a whole-hearted return to the collectivism of the 1980s and giving the impression that history has been picking up speed rather than coming to an end, producing more styles of poetry and poetry-related incidents than those who attempt to document poetry scenes could possibly keep up with. (Inwood 2014, 37–38)

Inwood draws attention to the Internet's capacity to support new forms of socialization in a virtual environment and to contribute much to the astonishing diversity of virtual public spaces she calls "online poetry scenes":

> Learning how to interact in an appropriate way with other poets and how to produce an appropriate style of poetry through participation in the social processes of poetry writing and evaluation is a prerequisite for acquiring poetry literacy and achieving citizenship within online poetry scenes. (Inwood 2014, 53)

In China poetry holds considerable power as a virtual social institution because it requires the users to learn "how to interact in an appropriate way" with others, while society at large and public representations remain under the political control of a "revolutionary" party and its Leninist doctrine. The Internet's vital function lies in offering multifarious options to choose and to develop "an appropriate style of poetry" that would be less accessible within the tight bureaucratic controls and corrupt environment of official cultural institutions.[6] The latter, of course, maintain a strong and visible presence online and, as Maghiel van Crevel demonstrates in a field-work report from 2017, the dual distinction between "official" (*guanfang*) and "unofficial" (*feiguanfang*) cultural and literary institutions and discourses in public formats is both omnipresent and shifting dynamically. Moreover, in China "unofficial" means more than just a negation of the "official". In fact, it often emerges under designations alluding to long-standing and rich cultural traditions such as "Rivers and Lakes" (*jianghu*) or "Among the People" (*minjian*): "In contemporary poetry, *jianghu* and *minjian* are significant others of *guanfang* 官方 'official'" (van Crevel 2017, 46). This significant otherness, like those two popular terms, is deeply rooted in a cultural tradition that opposes the perspective on the human world as a peripheral and adventurous space (*jianghu*) to one determining human beings

---

6 Van Crevels provides this sobering remark in his 2008 in-depth study of China's contemporary poetry and poetry scene: "Crudely put, one can now buy the status of being an officially published poet at a price to the tune of 5000 RMB and up. It is common knowledge that this happens all the time, even though it is illegal" (van Crevel 2008, 12). This statement seems accurate to this day, though market prices, of course, may fluctuate over time.

within a frame of officially endorsed behavioural norms. Thus, to shed new light on what Michel Hockx has recently labelled "pandemic poetry" (cf. Picerini 2022, 122, note 1), I propose to shift the customary focus of Western critics from lyrical ("new-style") poetry written in colloquial language and free verse to lyrical poetry written in hybrid classical language according to prosodic rules of premodern Chinese verse. This is necessary to reconsider Xiaofei Tian's 2009 assumption that

> [. . .] to write old-style poetry in modern times, in light of the changed circumstances, is to self-consciously cultivate a separate space and, as new-style poetry establishes itself as the *official* modern Chinese poetry, to engage in an increasingly intensified private and personal undertaking that is entirely severed from the traditionally public realm. (Tian 2009, 9)

Although Tian's interpretation may successfully appeal to Western sinologists, who continue to be inclined to ignore the literary relevance of poetry in the "old style", it is also too focused on explaining a generic phenomenon of modern and contemporary Chinese poetry in terms of a somewhat schematic and detached liberal paradigm of private versus public. The subsequent discussions of this chapter will also look at the ambiguous tension between the "official" and the "unofficial" that penetrates the virtual environment of Chinese online poetry. It will become clear that "intensified private and personal undertaking" not only motivates online poetry no matter whether the authors opt for a "new style" or write in the "old style". The discussion of the first poem will show that a line of distinction exists between an intention in line with the official mainstream discourse and the one opposing it, but often seems blurred on purpose.

4 Negotiating Emotions in the Pandemic Public

In her pioneering 2009 essay "Muffled Dialect Spoken by Green Fruit. An Alternative History of Modern Chinese Poetry", which claims a proper place in literary history for contemporary and modern lyrical poetry written in the old style, Xiaofei Tian seems to suggest that the latter "is practiced largely as a gesture of withdrawing from, not participating in, the public discourse, and of resisting" (Tian 2009, 9). However, each of the following examples of this style of poetic writing will crystalize under the simultaneously disruptive and stimulating impact of the pandemic as a form of literary engagement rather than as a withdrawal, although the authors have to face extremely severe censorship under the pandemic conditions. On the other hand, the predominant representation of poetry in the old style on official websites, through public awards and through frequent references in quotidian and intellectual texts to Mao Zedong's old-style verse is deceptive. Virtual poetry scenes, by maintaining their peripheral character as public spaces, often defiantly resist the mainstream discourse controlled by official propaganda and censorship. This does not, however, mean that they completely withdraw from the public realm. Nor does it prevent unpredictable moments of single texts being widely shared and read, sometimes triggered by their linkage to a non-verbal comment on an incident (e.g., a video clip) going viral before censors hunt it down. Therefore, I use the term *engaged retreat* to characterize the attitude of communication in the online poetry scenes and related virtual public spaces. While the mainstream repeats the calm and serene master narrative of the Party and many authors respond to this with active support, others seem to negotiate their engagement, and still others challenge it by the force of their independent language. For the latter, the skill and ingenuity necessary to master the classical rules of prosody and style and to make them work naturally within the contemporary mentality seem to provide for an aesthetic sovereignty over the dynamics of the pandemic and its communication in the mainstream discourse. This may be considered the most provocative way of dismissing a master-narrative of mobilization for the "total war" and "people's war".

Only two examples of that latter sort – which remain the most interesting ones from the viewpoint of literary studies – will be presented later in this chapter. But online poetry covers a wide spectrum in China, sometimes called the "Borderless Republic of Poetry" (for example by Michel Yeh 2007). Others are more sceptical about the openness of poetry written in direct response to public incidents. For example, one literary critic, Zong Cheng, called most of pandemic poetry "frivolous laments" that suffer from a lack of artistic skill (quoted in Picerini 2022, 131).

An objective investigation of the phenomenon, however, requires us to develop at least a basic notion of the spectrum which will then enable us to better assess its more valuable parts. Therefore, I will begin with a poem written by a Shanghai physician, Li Jia, on 28 January 2020 and published online in Chinese before censors deleted the text. However, the poem was later translated into English by the author and republished in the American journal *Chest*, dedicated to respiratory and intensive care (6 May 2020). This poem is an obviously spontaneous and highly emotional reaction by an unprofessional writer, and it is composed in free verse and plain language, far from the intellectual and stylistic refinement which marks contemporary classicist verse. This lyrical text, however, aptly demonstrates how within a society captured by the master narrative of the "people's war" (and conceptualized within this political category) "poetry has transgressed its own boundaries to become an instrument of the whole people, also at the expense of formal refinement" and how this is "consistent with the wider mobilization of the arts in the service of the anti-epidemic effort" (Picerini 2022, 131). Yet, as will be explicated, the poem begins as a subjective response to the moment of crisis and contains elements critical of the authorities' role in the previous events, which made it an obvious target for the censors:

> Fighting the novel coronavirus together with you
> This winter was too long.
> Why was the cloud blocking the sun?
> This winter was too cold.
> You left your home,
> You were too hurried to say goodbye to your son,
> Worrying about something when you turned around.
> Your parents are aged,
> And your children are very young.
> You were conducting clinical trials and writing papers,
> But you have made a choice,
> To struggle for a free breath with your courage and a golden heart.
> I saw you in Fever Clinic and Isolation Ward,
> Pale, exhausted and trying so hard.
> You winked at me,
> And told me to be brave like an iron.
> Oh, my sisters and brothers,
> You are my sunshine.
> I am touched beyond words,
> I would like to share responsibility,
> For healing the wounded and rescuing the dying.
> You are Hippocratic's tag-along,
> I am here with you.
> Impressed by your sweat and strength,
> I believe love makes the world a better place.[7]

The brief introduction to the text on the *Shanghai Daily* online magazine's website provides readers with the basic information on the moment when the author got emotionally involved in the pandemic:

> According to Li, a doctor from Shanghai's Renji Hospital, she composed the poem after learning that a third medical team sent by Shanghai would head for Wuhan, the then epicenter of the epidemic, on January 28. She was moved by her colleagues and all medical professionals working on the front line and quickly wrote the poem. (Cai 2020)

---

7 I do not have access to the original poem in Chinese, but directly refer to the English translation as published on the website "chestnet": https://journal.chestnet.org/article/S0012-3692(20)30257-9/fulltext#relatedArticles (last accessed 24 May 2020). The text is also accessible on the English-language website of *Shanghai Daily*: https://www.shine.cn/news/metro/2005067566/ (last accessed May 24 2020), where a brief introduction exclusively stresses the intent to "encourage her colleagues in the frontline battle against the novel coronavirus".

Proceeding into the text from this angle suggests reading it as a quasi-confession of the author's engagement in the ongoing collective mobilization. But the initial three lines of the poem, which may appear quite obscure at a first glance to Western readers, employ metaphors that are standard in classical poetic language, and the meaning is not difficult to grasp for those familiar with the tradition. Imagining a "winter [. . .] too long. / [. . .] cloud blocking the sun." and, again, a "[. . .] winter [. . .] too cold" while the temporal setting coincides with the spring festival – the holidays most popular in China for family reunions – suggests that something has gone wrong. In classical poetry all images in this initial sequence (*winter, cloud blocking sun, cold*) allude to severe retention, if not suppression, of the *yang*-energy,[8] and thus also of the dynamic, restorative, orderly, light-building force of nature customarily associated with legitimate, constructive and *life-sustaining* governance, which during the season should be rising power. In other words, for an average Chinese reader, the image at the beginning of the poem discloses a sense of disenchantment and distrust if not anger over the government's rejection of warnings over the emerging epidemic and its initial mismanagement.

The poem continues by fusing a sense of dramatic collective coercion forcing doctors' families to separate at a time when they should be united ("You left your home, / You were too hurried to say goodbye to your son, [. . .] Your parents are aged / And your children are very young [. . .]") with the heroization of an individual and professional decision which had been made before the acute situation ("But you have made a choice, / To struggle for a free breath with your courage and a golden heart [. . .]"). The heroic pathos may well be inspired by spontaneous empathy and anticipating identification with the colleagues heading for Wuhan. This, however, does not prevent the poem's voice from rapidly attuning itself to the Party propaganda's battle cries. The following lines already read as a plain and rather insipid translation of officially broadcast news videos into free verse: "I saw you in Fever Clinic and Isolation Ward, / Pale, exhausted and trying so hard. / You winked at me, / And told me to be brave like an iron."

The poem ultimately enters its third stage, one which in retrospect reveals the author's intention to transgress the national discourse. This intention was not in the "spontaneous" beginning of the creative process, but may have provided

---

8 Traditional Chinese intellectual terminology is centred around the cosmogonic model of a dualism pervading all processes that take place in the universe and this fundamental dualism is characterized by the interchange of *yin* and *yang*. Both represent the fundamentally opposed aspects within a totality. For example, *yang* is the vital force of natural growth, *yin* the harmful energy of autumn winds and decreasing warmth that triggers decay. Or, also, *yang* is the moral energy of the authoritative person acting in proper position within the patriarchal social hierarchy of premodern China and, *yin*, the weird forces determined to undermine the former.

the inspiration to translate the text into English and to publish it on a virtual platform, where it became visible for international colleagues in the professional universe of respiratory medicine. Obviously, the call-to-arms addressed to "brothers and sisters" can easily be interpreted as an appeal to the transnational guild, very much in the sense that Mr. Xi used, as president of the People's Republic of China, in addressing international leaders about a month after the original poem had been written and about six weeks *before* the translation was published on the website of *Chest*. The ambiguity unfolding between the beginning of the poem, with its symbolism alluding to a lack of public transparency and threatening decay, and the pathetic closure could also be interpreted as a product of a quite ordinary poetic sense seeking to restore a rudimentary orientation in the midst of pandemic fuzziness. Indeed, the poem's deeper sense of balance between the "spontaneous" personal and prescribed collective subjectivity blurs the distinction between those two spheres of perception, and coincides with the Party's objective of mobilizing for a "people's war" against the virus.

5 "Cadres' Poetry" and the Sterilization of Public Discourse Online

Much of public discourse on the pandemic (not only in China) is characterized by anxiety, providing biopolitical agents with a huge psychological potential to realize strategies of mass mobilization. In this case mobilizing the masses while simultaneously paralyzing parts of communal, economic, cultural and individual life seems to be two sides of the same coin. The value of the coin, however, depends on the side one looks at, which brings us back to the nature of discourse in the context of the party state.

The texts below attempt to look closer at one side, and the last paragraph will focus on the other. My translations of poems written in versions of the old style will provide the basis for the analysis, while important, yet untranslated, features of the poems written following patterns of classical prosody and in diction that fuses the vocabulary of classical literary Chinese with modern literary and/or colloquial wording will be mentioned separately. I employ a translation method elaborated during a research project on modern and contemporary Chinese classicist Internet poetry conducted between 2017 and 2021 (Kraushaar 2022). The method relies on my decade-long experience in translating classical Chinese poetry into German, targeting – unlike much of modern and contemporary translation of classical Chinese verse – not primarily the "poetic image" but adequacy in terms of prosodic features and modelling. I will not consider aspects of this method in detail, but by taking advantage of its results, will give some attention to the hybrid character of this idiom that has been labelled by some "classical poetry online", by others as "classicism 2.0" and by myself as "neoklassizistische Cyberlyrik" (Tian 2009; Yang and Ma 2018; Kraushaar 2020/2022). This will support a basic comprehension of generic hybridity in pandemic poetry online and its aesthetic and ideological value in a virtual public space that is divided by biopolitical campaigns of mass mobilization.

These three quatrains were published online at about the same time as the poem discussed above. They are the first poetic embodiments of a basic mood of "angst" and agitated distress. As conscious poetic choices taken by the author – in this sense providing a clear comparison to Li's text – they join mainstream dispositions in terms of personal temper and intention and are not distinguished in terms of artistic skill and poetic ingenuity. In contrast to the previously cited poem, however, these quatrains belong to the poetic subgenre labelled "cadre-style" (*laogan ti*),[9] which, despite its notoriously low aesthetic reputation, has a strong presence in real and virtual public spaces. The author, Niu Suge, introduces himself as a "retired cadre of Henan (province) bank and insurance surveillance office".[10] To my knowledge there is no further public poetic activity of his. In a preface to a collection of some thirty poems composed in classical metres between 26 January and 26 February, published on 30 June 2020 on the webpage of "China Banking and Insurance News",[11] Niu makes his intention clear:

> This year we experienced an extraordinary New-Year's festival and an extraordinary spring season as well. The whole nation from up to low, locked like a fortress by a common will, resisted the plague and cursed the earlier losses suffered from that devilish "new coronavirus epidemic pneumonia"! Going through this kind of plague allowed us to understand: the mighty firmness and stability of the fatherland is superior! Peace and happiness of the people are superior! Physical health is superior! Felicity (resulting from the former) is superior! The well-being of relatives is superior! Friendship and love are superior!
>
> While sitting at home, I wished to pronounce what resounded in my heart via poetry, to make my brush a weapon of war, calling the fatherlands to arms and cheering Wuhan![12]

Obviously, the author reports on the patriotic intention at the heart of the poems. But the intention of the preface itself must be different, because it has been

---

9 An outline of cadre style, based on discussions of two exemplary texts on the background of the poetic writing of Mao Zedong – so-called Mao-style (*Mao ti*) – can be studied in Kraushaar 2022, 42–52 and 54–60. In their paper quoted above, Yang and Ma also dedicate a passage to cadre style.
10 河南銀保監局機關退休幹部 牛素鴿.
11 http://www.cbimc.cn/zt/2020-06/30/content_350819.htm. Last accessed 30 May 2022.
12 Beginning with this text, if not otherwise mentioned, all translations are my own.

written to accompany a new edition of the poems five months later, when the virus was considered "defeated" in China and the apparent victory was praised by mainstream media as evidence of the superiority of China's political (and scientific) systems over those of Western democracies. The re-contextualization of the poems suggested by the preface also must be considered in relation to the on-line location chosen for the publication of the thirty poems (one poem per day over the span). The retired bank and insurance supervisor primarily addresses his former cadres, as he speaks to other cadres using classical verse as proper vehicle for his message. Of course, even after "victory", the bank and insurance sector in China was under pressure, as were most parts of the country's economy, while many restrictions, especially those related to international traffic and trade, remained in force. Thus, despite the enemy having been repulsed, bellicose rhetoric continued to be used to present biopolitical objectives in public spaces, providing the setting for Niu's re-publication of his poems.

According to the author's commentary, the first quatrain was written after watching a news item of a physician leaving her husband at the train station on her departure for Wuhan. The referential object is basically the same as in the previous poem, including the fact that both poems respond to events as seen via TV screens:

Separation
Spirits of corona plague spread out on new-year's eve.
A couple – she, departing for Wuhan, is taking leave.
One instant and her ironman breaks into tears:
"So love you!" is the sigh his trembling voice must heave.

離別
冠狀瘟神春節橫, 夫妻別離赴江城. 霎時硬漢啼飛淚, 愛你情深震撼聲.

In incidents of national emergency Chinese television broadcasters customarily aim to present dramatic situations in a heroic guise. Here, the heroism of the woman determined to leave her husband to go to battle in the epidemic centre of Wuhan is highlighted by this "ironman's" (*yinghan*) ferocious tears and his desperate outcry. The obvious distortion of traditional gender roles – these have re-captured ground in contemporary Chinese representations of society – recalls Maoist slogans like "Times may change, men and women all remain the same" (*shidai bu tong le, nan nü dou yi yang*) that once were coined to spur revolutionary idealism. Now the viral threat, in its role of mobilizing an already achieved organic entity of state and society replaces that of the class enemy usurping state institutions in the former "people's war". As the husband and the wife – the nucleus of social stability in the traditional worldview – split up, primordial equality is restored to release the exuberant energy of an all-uniting mass movement, but not in the guise of chaos that Mao desired to unleash with his "Cultural Revolution". In the twenty-first century, chaotic energies of warfare are still needed to spur mankind's progress, but skilfully masterminded by the Party.

The texts discussed so far (Li's poem in free verse, Niu's preface and the first quatrain in classical metre) have presumably brought the expectations of literary and artistic quality to quite a low level. Here, where the art of poetry is the least relied-on element at work and for the most part communication depends on the dynamics of a media event, the redundancy of that coordinate communication displays itself in a bizarre manner, turning the poetic artefacts into sheer conveyers of a biopolitical agenda.

6 The Poetics of Engaged Retreat and Neoclassicist Cyberpoetry (*wangluo shici*)

It must be repeated that the vast majority of "pandemic poetry" should be understood as part of an immense matrix of a poetic culture in China whose vitality is rooted in the basic function of poetic forms as vehicles of public communication. This is also the source of a hybridity that leads from the de-poetized, politically instrumentalized public discourse verse forms to poetry proper, and to contemporary poetry written in classical metres. Using the old "time-honoured Chinese format" (Kowallis 1996, 41) to respond to a baleful incident only *seems* to set the author's subjectivity apart from the immediate shock. Li's poem in free verse strives to compensate for the latter by bridging a gap between deep distrust of the authorities (due to their untransparent mismanagement at the beginning of the crisis) and "whole-hearted" (*jinxin*) participation in the government-led "defence battle". To achieve her aim Li commits herself to a full mobilization of her imagination in favour of the official bellicose propaganda narrative. Niu communicates the emergency in classical quatrains of seven characters per line, but even the formal unity of his verse based on the smooth rhyme-scheme (aaxa) with a dramatic turning point in the third, not rhyming line, serves as rhetorical vehicle to communicate a political message packed with agitated sentiment. In no way does concentration on generic rules lead to the sublimation of the poetic form, which becomes obvious to the translator who may find his task easy, even vapid.

Encountering the most impertinent demands imposed by the official biopolitical agenda on an increasingly desperate population, authors like Li and Niu – and the mainstream of pandemic poetry – prove too weak to separate the emotional response to the rapid closure of public spaces from the official narrative of total mobilization for ultimate "victory". Another poem by Niu completely replaces the suffering under the lockdown with a weird political activism, erasing any possible trace of memory as a potentially *inherent* value of pandemic writing:

> Cheering-up Wuhan
> Closed doors. Cuffed hearts. Contaminated river metropole –
> O! why can't I be a skilful master in one hospital?
> My clumsy brush, with poems filled, drums battle-calls
> To cheer Wuhan, performing truth emotional!
>
> 為武漢加油
> 閉門心系江城疫, 恨我非醫妙手生。拙筆蘊詩搖戰鼓, 加油武漢獻真情。

According to the author's dating, the poem was composed on 10 February 2020. Thus the motivation would have arisen amid reverberations in social networks of mounting tension caused by government austerity measures under lockdown conditions. Within two juxtaposed couplets, the "retired cadre" (*tuixiu ganbu*) first performs his sincere "frustration" ("O! why", 恨, *hen*) for being incapable to join the fight on the front line. The word *hen* at the beginning of the second line marks a common sigh of frustration in classical love poetry, a lyrical subgenre which, according to traditional rules of interpretation, can be read as a metaphorical expression of loyal sentiment towards *the ruler*. However, in the concluding line, the author pretends to sublimate such sentiment to "true feelings" (a literal translation of 真情 *zhen qing*). This expression must be understood in a contemporary vernacular context as "kindred spirits". Thus the "subtlety" of Niu's quatrain lies in the effort to fuse "loyalty" (a core value in traditional hierarchical society) and a basic instinct of kinship, crudely estimated to be the driving force in the total mobilization, into overwhelming support for the Party's biopower. Contemplating Niu's poem at a greater distance from the turmoil of propaganda campaigns and relentless censorship during those days of chaotic struggle and depression, all that remains is a curious distortion of sentiment *weakened* by an almost total ignorance of the disrupted state of society.

The two poems presented in the following passages meet the expectations for "pandemic poetry" as a social phenomenon that "can be understood only if placed in its discursive context" because it was "engendered by a historical contingency fraught with political implications" (Picerini 2022, 129 and 125). At the same time, these texts contrast with the previous examples because each transcends political framing by *retreating* from the mainstream and getting *engaged* with the complex reality by implementing subtle poetic devices. Therefore, these texts *do* perform as "vehicles of public communication" in the wider traditional Chinese context wherein poetic language remains highly sensitive to political dissent, social conflicts and cultural diversity.

Both authors are outstanding senior figures in the scene of neoclassicist online poetry.[13] Yet in terms of nomenclature, one may hesitate to call them "professional" (meaning officially awarded and appointed) poets. Neither publishes regularly in print and both take marginal positions in the institutionalized business of filtering the vital literary activity online to take up a "representative" official profile in contemporary poetry. Both texts have been obtained through direct personal contact and exchange. The first one is from early summer 2020 and is by Zeng Shaoli, cybername Lizilizilizi, who at the time was based near Wuhan and managed to publish the poems temporarily via one of his WeChat-accounts, but later distributed them via email.[14] The second text has a similarly devious history of traveling via digital networks and through the obscurity of a semi-public virtual space for artistically sophisticated communication and performance under conditions of severe censorship during the Shanghai lockdown (March 2022 – May 2022). The author is Gui Qian, cybername Bo Hunzi, who, like Zeng, writes verse congruent with classical prosodic rules and, to a certain degree, with requirements of traditional style.[15] However, both authors display a nuanced knowledge of the classical language's rich treasure of forms and semantics. Their mastery lies in dissolving the aesthetically static character of "old-style poetry" into a fresh and fluid literary idiom, transforming the mental delusion of mainstream media into contemporary poetic justice:

> Pandemic, no. 1
> Screen-touch – snow blowing, cherry-blossoms everywhere.
> Pale houses, darkening lights, and sighs so deep and long.
> Constraints, broken alone by spring, mighty and vast –
> Speech, hoarded well, forlorn one sits by midnight, dull and strung.
> An orphaned city, poisoned prey, ails between life and death,
> Remains – burn all the books! – a place of grief and song.
> The warning written stays, although the whistling trails off:
> Rely only on daily notes, keep reading-well Fang Fang.

> 大疫 其一
> 觸屏櫻雪漫飛颺, 白屋青燈太息長. 限足全違春浩蕩, 噤言獨坐夜蒼茫. 孤城楚毒死生劫,
> 終古秦灰歌哭場. 訓誡書存哨音杳, 聊憑日記讀方方.

This poem is composed according to the rules of a seven-syllable-line poem in strict metre (*qi yan lüshi* 七言律詩), one of the most characteristic formal inventions of the poets close to aristocratic courts during the reign of the Tang dynasty (seventh–

---

13 See my comparison of Lizi's verse with other modern and contemporary classicist authors, which dedicates a subsection to Bo Hunzi (Kraushaar 2022, 93–191).
14 Zeng, Shaoli; 曾少立. Lizilizilizi; 李子梨子栗子.
15 Gui, Qian; 眭謙. Bo, Hunzi; 伯昏子.

early tenth century). Compared to the sonnet because of its density of metrical relations, which requires an utmost concentration on the development of the poetic concept's imaginative stimuli, the *lüshi* focuses on the couplet as the basic unit. The translation seeks to capture this not only by inventing an adequate scheme of (impure) rhymes, but also by the rhythmic balance of stressed and unstressed syllables, making the couplets inherently fluent and distinguishable as the formal structure of the poem. The quantity of syllables in each line varies between twelve and fourteen, approximately doubling that of the Chinese text; the quantity of *stressed* syllables, however, in the translation (6–7) approximately matches that of the poem.[16] Chinese poetry in strict metre, due to its elliptical style (as well as to the complicated tonal patterns that rarely translate into Western languages), requires slow and carefully pronounced recitation. The whole poem centres around couplets 2 and 3 which have not only the highest density of rhythmical figures, but also of even and contrasting conceptual elements.

For example "constraints" (line 3: 限足) and "prohibited speech" (line 4: 噤言) are placed in parallel positions in the couplet and thus suggest the severity of censorship under lockdown conditions – particularly in online communication – as the root-cause of the previously noted "sighs, so deep and long". These appear to be the last remaining, yet invisible, signs of human presence while staring at the "pale houses" and "darkening lights" that have become the image of metropolitan Wuhan at the time of the spring festival. A restive attempt to escape the dreary outward scenery opened up the imaginative space of the poem at its very beginning: "Screen-touch" (*chu ping* 觸屏) – the initial idiom of the poem – ingeniously plays on the common word *chumoping* (觸摸屏="touch-screen") and on the customary meaning of the character 屏 (*ping*: "folding screen") in classical love- or boudoir-poetry. The latter is a well-known poetic image of the abandoned courtesan in desperate isolation. But, unlike Niu in the second of his two poems presented above, Zeng does not drop back on the traditional poetic stereotype. Instead, the palpable parallel between the classical commonplace ("abandoned courtesan in isolation, sighing deep and long") and the acute isolation forced upon each resident of Wuhan by the abrupt decision of the Beijing government is explored with stunning nonchalance. No trace of a traditional poetic posture presents itself to the reader; the folding-turned-touch-

---

[16] This basic approach to the translation of *lüshi* comes close to my method applied in translating classical poetry to German. The prevalent style of English translation is indebted to the imagistic school associated with Poundian conceptualism and with such outstanding masters as Arthur Waley or David Hawkes. However, Jonathan Chaves, who also had followed this direction for decades, has proved with his translations of Zhang Ji's (766–830) verse *Cloud Gate Song* (2006) the compatibility of classical Chinese prosody with modern verse (compare his prologue on rhyme in translation in: Zhang Ji, 12–24).

screen is part of an electronic device indispensable to any form of communication with the outer world. But its usefulness has been confined to watching online video clips of wind-blown cherry-blossoms. The "screen-touch" (my German translation makes it a *Schirmtatsch*) is in fact a desperate knocking on the frozen surface of a world bereft of the floating life-energy that is at the core of traditional (and often modern) Chinese aesthetics and here seems captured in the idiom *chun haodang* 春浩蕩 ("spring, mighty and vast"). Taking the rhythmical space between the internal caesura of the seven syllable verse (between the fourth and the fifth syllable), this idiom matches its counterpart in the second half of the couplet, translated "midnight, dull and strung". This might appear at first sight as a generous translation of *ye cangmang* 夜蒼茫 (lit.: "midnight, vast and endless"), but the endless darkness which covers the city in silence is revealed by the translation as a momentary reflection of a depressive state of mind – the source of an enormous allusive unfolding at an unexpected intersection between the traditional poetic convention of boudoir-poetry (with strong portions of *public* eroticism) and the blow dealt by the authorities to public and private life under the biopolitical pretext.

In the second half of the poem (couplets 3 and 4) the intersection between the experience at stake and the textual references shifts away from the boudoir to other commonplaces. The poetic subject, too, seems to have left behind its initial isolation and irritation – facing only empty facades ("pale houses") and takes a more self-assertive stance. Without elaborating on details of the complicated allusive techniques, I will draw the contours of that shift: The city of Wuhan, modern metropolis at the Yangzi, capital of Hebei province and historical site of the 1911 Chinese revolution is called an "orphaned city" (*gu cheng* 孤城). This term traditionally refers to a borderland garrison in a far province of the empire, which may be seized by invading enemy forces as long as the imperial main forces remained stationed near the capital and out of reach. The following idiom, reading "poison of Chu" (*Chu du* 楚毒) has a strong whiff of local corruption, alluding to legends from the ancient southern state of Chu on whose territories Wuhan is located. The translation spares the historical name of the locality, obvious to the Chinese reader, and replaces it with the figurative paraphrase of a "poisoned prey", because this contains essential semantic elements situated beyond the historical reference, such as the capturing of the city and the poison of corruption. The translation relies on the same strategy in the second line of couplet 3 by replacing the term "ashes of Qin" (*Qin hui* 秦灰) – on parallel position – with a strong exclamation: "burn all the books!" The latter may be identified by Western readers as referring to the notorious burning of books allegedly initiated by The Arch Emperor of Qin (Qin Shi Huangdi; 259–210 BC), who first was the king of the northern state of Qin, but later went into history as the tyrannical inventor of a centralized bureaucracy which would become the backbone of the imperial state, prevailing for more than two thousand years. Chinese netizens often use Qin Shi Huangdi's name to hint at Xi Jinping as the "communist" emperor of a new China with hegemonic ambitions in this century. Within a single couplet the confluence of multiple layers of meaning, which became apparent in the previous couplet, culminates in a weird ambiguity of the total closure of public space, declared as "people's war" but perceived as the enclosure of an "orphaned city" by other enemies; there is an indignant sense of remaining the "poisoned prey" of the corrupt but almighty local government authorities and at the same time being exposed to the cynicism of a centralized censorship bureaucracy. A resistant self-consciousness defies the tyranny of biopower by insisting on Wuhan's proud local tradition as "a place of grief and song" (*ge ku chang* 歌哭場).

Only with the concluding couplet does the text openly confront and break the public taboos by including words like "whistling" (*xiaoyin* 哨音) – in the memory of Li Wenliang, the whistle-blower who first raised alarm over the emerging epidemic, but later became one of its early victims – and Fang Fang (方方), the name of a Wuhan writer whose online diary under lockdown went viral despite efforts by censors to prevent it. The power of the poem, however, is concentrated in its central couplets, building subtly elaborated contrasts of the natural and the human world and of allusions to the Chinese experience of a historic adversity, and opposing drastic claims of centralized power to the traditions and self-consciousness of local autonomy.

7 An Official Prerogative of Interpretation and the Irony of Poetic Realism

The next poem illustrates the latest state of "pandemic poetry" boosted by the Shanghai lockdown (5 April to June 2022).[17] After what had been hailed by the Chinese state media in summer 2020 as a great victory gained after months of

---

17 As part of Beijing's "zero-covid strategy", Chinese authorities dispose of graded measures of restriction of public and private life and employ them country-wide on four administrative levels (national, provincial, local and grass-root) with municipalities of huge metropoles like Wuhan or Shanghai on the same hierarchical level as provinces (Renninger 2020, 62–79). As a result, lockdowns are mostly implemented successively and in three degrees of intensity, declaring for defined areas either measures of "prevention", of "control" or of "closure". I chose 5 April to date the beginning of the 2022 Shanghai lockdown, because on that day this system of three-level control was expanded to the whole city. Measures were loosened significantly – after public opposition to them had steadily grown – at the beginning of June. Since then, however, they have also been reimposed in local areas of the city's territory.

fierce fighting and thanks to a unity of party and people, the epidemic continued to cause repeated lockdowns of city quarters, townships, villages or smaller residence areas but without directly affecting the majority of the country's populace. However, over two years after Xi's martial announcement of "total war" and "people's war" against the epidemic threat, more than twenty-five million residents of Shanghai were again subjected to severe restrictions implemented by local authorities who often were more anxious to fulfil orders by the central government than to treat individuals and their basic needs with respect. A month earlier, in March 2022, the Chinese government had decided to deny, in the prescribed terminology of official statements and media, the reality of Russia's brutal assault on Ukraine. This may well have contributed to the rarer application of war metaphors by official organs during the Shanghai lockdown. However, on 27 April 2022 the *Washington Post* reported on a surprising variety of verse critical of "sensitive" issues from lockdown measures to Russia's war on Ukraine, which had appeared during a student poetry contest hosted by Shanghai's Jiaotong University before most of them were taken off-line, probably in response to censorial intervention. On inquiries by netizens about the reasons for deleting several poems from the website of the poetry competition, the academic organizers answered: "Poetry soothes people's hearts and gives them peace. We believe that in the company of poetry, we will all go further".[18]

Highlighting the therapeutic effect of writing poetry also reflects the impact of the CCP's new but already entrenched biopolitical ideology of governance. Here, the response given by the organizers of the competition clearly counteracts the strong satirical disposition inherent to Chinese lyrical poetry, a tradition that continues from its beginnings to today.[19] In the language of poetry, irony and sarcasm often become the more pointed the less obviously they seem connected to their objects. This is not relevant for semantics and "contents" alone, but also applies to form and tonality. An online poem posted on WeChat (the Chinese equivalent of Twitter), via private blogs or by e-mail in a cryptic antique diction and metre,[20] provokes a dissonance of perception. Nevertheless, in the context of the related public incident (the Shanghai lockdown) the tradition of reading *Shijing*-texts as allegorical public criticism has been revived by cyberpoets in the earliest years of online literature in China (Yang and Ma 2018, 532–538).

---

[18] https://www.washingtonpost.com/world/2022/04/24/china-poetry-contest-covid-censor/. Last accessed 9 June 2022.
[19] Regarding neoclassicist cyberpoetry I have explored the transformation of the tradition in contemporary times in Kraushaar 2022, 113–192.
[20] Edited first over the middle of the first millennia BC and canonized during the second century BC, the poems of the collection are dated back to the eleventh to seventh centuries.

This becomes more apparent when we realize that the author of the poem writes *by reading* verse from parts of the *Shijing*, adapting their meaning at first, then minor parts of the wording, to create a timely and truthful poetic response to the repeated situation. In fact, the Chinese version of each line in the three stanzas can be traced back to an original in the *Shijing*. After presenting my translation and the text of the Chinese poem, and including a brief explanatory remark made by the author in an e-mail exchange, the intertextual strategy will be detailed. Poetic resilience to authoritarian assault is a matter of life and death for poetry, and its subtle energies are set free by recapturing the nuances of texts (territories of meaning), layer by layer:

Rabbit nets

Stern and seemly, those rabbit nets,
Deployed now on anyone's house
To coop up in myriad ways:
Our Prince has his teeth and his claws.

Such Greatness – like Lord of the Heavens!
Such Greatness – like God in the Skies!
Strong Warriors plunder like beasts,
Our Prince has his claws and his boys.

There's Cronos inside the palace.
Our words are like ropes to constrain.
Seeing people as foes and as traitors,
Our Prince has claws to cause pain.

兔罝　　睚謙 (伯昏子)
肅肅兔罝, 施于室家。牢籠萬態, 王有爪牙。胡然而天, 胡然而帝。孔武博攫, 王有爪士。
檮杌在宮, 言出如縛。視民寇讎, 王有爪物。

The sender of the e-mail that forwarded this poem, among others written by the poet Gui (alias Bo Hunzi) was Zeng Shaoli, the author of the previously discussed text. I quote one of his remarks, because this helped me to better understand the meaning of the poem: "This poem is an allegorical criticism of Shanghai [municipal authorities] for imposing physical means of coercion (like iron fences) on residents [to enforce the lockdown ordered by the central government]".[21]

"Contextualization" by commentators in the laconic spirit of Zeng's remark can be traced over the centuries back to the earliest preserved editions of the *Shijing*. The dissonance that prevails between archaic wording and the contemporary mindset fitting the former to an underlying intentionality always has been part of

---

21　這首詩是諷刺上海強行將居民住宅用物理措施 (例如鐵絲網) 封鎖的荒誕行為。[Zeng (2022)].

the poetic intertextuality. The question of the art is how to shape dissonance into charming irony.

Having received my translation via Zeng, Gui in a letter elaborates on the poetic techniques applied in this poem and on their relation to the text's intention:

> In fact, this poetry was written by composing of several original verses in The She King [*Shijing*],[22] some of which were revised based upon what I intended to express. I feel interested in this poetry because most of the original verses are praises or good metaphors in the old backgrounds but become a kind of irony after re-location and re-combining.[23]

This permits a re-reading of the poem through translation, which must proceed alongside the quotes and elucidate how this text re-locates and re-combines phrases and words from an ancient poetry collection to the distortions of reality by a controlled public discourse. Regarding prosody, we walk over much more level ground compared to the previous poem, which belongs to a highly sophisticated prosodic form. *Shijing* verse also is based on couplets of even length and the latter often remain the same through the whole poem, which applies to our case as well (the Chinese line consists of four characters versus syllables). But there is no dynamic prosodic structure proceeding through the condensation on several levels of rhythmical figures (only some of which can be captured by an adaptive translation strategy) and through even or contrasting concepts placed in parallel positions. Paired end rhymes simply enforce a repetitive scheme of three sections, which could be shorter or longer. Figuration, in essence, is repetition and this is proven here using basic formal elements.

The poet applies the metrical rules in a strictly imitative manner and the same can be said about his attitude toward diction, in which he differs from Lizi (Zeng Shaoli), who excels among the neoclassicist cyberpoets as a master of hybrid wording. Unlike Lizi's, Gui's vocabulary does not oscillate between ancient or medieval and contemporary modern literary idioms. The charm of his verse emerges from a sort of Socratic irony. As a mixture of quotations and variations of classical verse from the *Shijing* this text suggests that nothing particularly new has been said, that there is no unique moment of truth in the contemporary event that stimulates both the author and the readers he addresses. But my interpretation of the text shows that it works in the opposite manner: that there *is* such a moment of truth, which implies in conclusion that poetic justice is dispensed over biopolitical violence and as an act of engaged retreat from the communicational chaos caused by ceaseless party propaganda and state censorship.

---

22 Gui uses a transcription method that differs from the PRC's standard transcription-system Pinyin but remains familiar to *Shijing* experts.

23 Quoted from Gui's letter received as attachment to an email sent by Zeng on 20 May 2022.

The title of the poem cites the *Shijing*, part 1, chapter 1, poem 6, figuring under the headline *Tu Ju* 兔罝 or "Rabbit Nets".²⁴ The first line repeats the opening line of poem 6. Traditionally, the poem is interpreted allegorically as "praise of a rabbit-catcher" (Legge). This hunter is described by commentators as a commoner who, thanks to his professional virtue and diligent work, is worth being elevated to the highest ranks of state service. He may be a nobody, but doing the right things in a proper manner, he makes himself a pillar of communal stability. Thus, the formulation "stern and seemly" 肅肅 must be understood as the characterization of the catcher's working morale, rather than as the material quality of the nets. For anyone familiar with public communication on the management of COVID-19 outbreaks in China there can be no doubt that, in this context, the ancient appraisal of that catcher alludes to both the *official* appraisal of and the *unofficial* anger over the so-called Big Whites (*da bai* 大白) who are also described as the "Chinese government's social interface for managing the Omicron outbreak". An article on the webpage of the *India China Institute* reveals the tasks and social profile of front-line action forces cloaked in the notorious "big white" protective gear:

> Big White teams consist of medical workers, police officers, community office representatives, and volunteers who come (as the government repeatedly emphasizes) from all walks of life. In their capacity as service providers, Big Whites conduct COVID tests, deliver food to residents in locked-down buildings, and coordinate other public services within a designated area. However, Big Whites are also the public face of COVID security. They conduct building sweeps for testing holdouts, they act as gatekeepers at locked-down estates and neighbourhoods, and they patrol locked-down areas to ensure everyone else is in their homes.²⁵

This makes Lizi's explication of the poem as "criticism [. . .] for imposing physical means of coercion (like iron fences) on residents" even more plausible. By doing their gatekeeper jobs at the iron fences with utmost diligence, those commoners, in the eyes of the authorities, deserve the highest appraisal as fighters in the "people's war" proclaimed by the present "ruler".

The second line of couplet 1 produces a variation of *Shijing*, part 1, chapter 1, poem 4, titled "Peach-blossom's charm" (*tao yao* 桃夭). That reference evokes a little song on marriage customs in ancient China that is seen by the commentary tradition as appraisal of the virtuous art of rulership ancient kings practiced, supposedly by

---

24 In the following I will indicate quotations from the *Shijing* by referring to the classical nineteenth century edition and translation of that text by James Legge in his major work *The Chinese Classics*, vol. 4, *"The She King"*.
25 https://www.indiachinainstitute.org/2022/05/25/the-animated-pandemic-big-whites-on-shenzhen-social-media/. Last accessed 12 June 2022.

not interfering with the established old customs of the people, of which marriage at the season of blossoming peach-trees was considered the most important one.²⁶ Like the 2020 flare-up of the epidemic during the cherry-blossom season at Wuhan, its first hotspot, the Omicron outbreak of 2022 also struck Shanghai in spring, at the time of the peach-blossom season. The traditional poetic symbolism of the blossoming trees seems to be interpreted in both poems as indicating a good order of life in accordance with the seasonal cycle. This draws attention to the modification the author implements by changing the *Shijing* verse *yi qi jia shi* 宜其家室 ("well-ordered is the household") to *shi yu jia shi* 施于室家 ("Deployed now to anyone's house"). A minimal change in the wording of the phrase subtly distorts its original meaning (or traditional reading) so that the transfiguration of the sense perfectly adapts to the (unofficial) public anger over excessive incursions of "Big Whites" into people's daily lives.

The discussion could now be conducted through intertextual details in each line of the poem, explained as either full or modified quotations of other passages from the *Shijing*. The subjectivity of the reader restores its impartiality by savouring the nuances of these playful and at the same time cannily ambiguous crossovers in perceiving the pandemic through the lens of ancient verse.

Only the first couplet of stanza 3 alludes to further ancient classics. The Commentary Tradition of Mr. Zuo (*Zuozhuan*, 300 BC) describes *taowu* 檮杌 as a monster with a human face and as a son of the mythological god-emperor Zhuanxu, who also is the God of Polaris. In the Confucian tradition, which focuses on attributing to the ancient gods virtues and vices by which members of the state's ruling class should be measured, Taowu is described as "untalented" (*bu cai*), but his most characteristic deed was his revolt against the father, who was the legitimate universal ruler.²⁷ The couplet *taowu zai gong, yan chu ru fu* 檮杌在宮，言出如綍。 in a more literal translation reads "Taowu is in the palace, outspoken words [become dangerous] like the ropes [of pitfalls]". The second line of the couplet proves to be a modified quotation from the antique classic *Records of Rites* (*Liji*, 500 BC), which transforms the original meaning of "words outspoken [by the ruler]" to "words outspoken [by anyone *but* the ruler]", the author's strategy of quoting Confucian

---

26 The principle of "non-interference", or *wu-wei* 無為, is crucial in virtually all ancient Chinese theories of governance. It is not directly compatible with modern liberal theories, because of the absence of positive awareness of the social power and economic potential of free will. Instead, the principle requires the ruling subject to abstain from interference in people's affairs – essentially warning of *excessive mobilization of human and material resources* for warfare – and to respect a self-sustained good order of life as foundation of people's moral integrity.

27 Another passage in *Zuo Zhuan* employs the name Taowu to designate one of four "clans" (zu) in the mythical realm of Emperor Shun that remained disobedient (Legge, vol. V, 1991, 280).

classics while shifting their intended meaning from the focus on the (pre-modern) ruling elite to a focus on the modern political sovereign, the people. Therefore, readers may feel encouraged to suppose that, in contemporary times, a Taowu (the Party under Xi) has managed to topple the legitimate sovereign Zhuanxu (the people) by usurping the throne in the palace. This complete distortion of political power regulation makes it dangerous for anyone to speak out, because the ruling power (Taowu/*Cronos*) and legitimate political sovereign (*our words* = the people) have been turned into adversaries: those "frontline-fighters" in the "people's war" against the virus (the "Big Whites") are virtual "claws to cause pain".[28]

8 Conclusion

Under the conditions of the COVID-19 pandemic, whose initial outbreak and management remain closely intertwined with the PRC's authoritarian political system and the totalitarian traditions of statehood in modern China, biopower and bioethics have been turbocharged with fresh energy. While society as a whole seems to be accepting the biopolitical impositions, individuals and networking communities very often react and cope with it in their own ways. I have ventured to open up a necessarily limited perspective on how this works (or does not work) in lyrical Internet poetry, which offers a prismatic perspective into the world of online communication in the ChinaNet. With the last two texts in particular I hope to convince readers that *engaged retreat* as a strategy of autonomous writing in contemporary Chinese online poetry not only exists but also demonstrates a profound sense of poetic justice. Through reassessment of classical poetic traditions like verse metre, literary diction and citation techniques in search of a language, neoclassicist poets take their part in the production of a sophisticated memory of events cautiously suppressed by a bellicose public discourse regime under firm control of the party state.

---

28 My decision to choose *Cronos*, the name of the Titan who castrated his father Uranus in an attempt to usurp power over Cosmos, to replace Taowu is, of course, disputable. My choice, however, suggests that exploiting the treasures of mythologies can uncover common grounds for poetry and translation even despite apparent incongruence of their respective traditions.

References

Cai, Wenjun. "Doc's Poem about Coronavirus Battle Published in Medical Journal." Shanghai Daily's official online platform SHINE.cn. 6 May 2020. https://www.shine.cn/news/metro/2005067566/. Last accessed 5 July 2022.

Hockx, Michel. "Internet Literature in China." *Yi Magazin*. March 2022. https://www.goethe.de/prj/yim/de/mag/22802944.html. Last accessed 5 July 2022.

Inwood. Heather. *Verse Going Viral. Chinese New Media Scenes*. Washington: University of Washington Press, 2014.

Kjellén, Rudolf. *Der Staat als Lebensform*. Berlin: Kurt Vowinckel Verlag, 1924.

Kraushaar, Frank. *Fern von Geschichte und verheißungsvollen Tagen. Neoklassizistische Cyberlyrik im ChinaNetz und die Schreibweise des Lizilizilizi (2000–2020)*. Bochum: Projektverlag, 2022.

Legge, James. *The Chinese Classics with a Translation, Critical and Exegetical Notes, Prolegomena, and Copious Indexes. Vol. 4 "The She King"*. Taipei 1991 [London: Trübner 1872].

Legge, James. *The Chinese Classics with a Translation, Critical and Exegetical Notes, Prolegomena, and Copious Indexes. Vol. 5 "The Ch'un Ts'ew with the Tso Chuen"*. Taipei 1991 [London: Trübner 1872].

Picerini, Federico. "'Poets, What Can We Do?' Pandemic Poetry in China's Mobilization against COVID-19." *Asian Studies*, special issue: "Crisis and Danger and Hope in Asia". 10.1 (2022): 123–153.

Qian, Gang. The Trouble With "Total War". China Media Project (CMP). China New Speak. March 2020. https://chinamediaproject.org/2020/03/27/the-trouble-with-total-war/. Last accessed 1 July 2022.

Renninger, Philip. "The 'People's Total War on Covid 19': Urban Pandemic Management Through (Non-)Law in Wuhan, China." *Washington International Law Journal*. 3.1 (2020): 64–115.

Rong, Jian. "Wang Hui's Heidegger Moment." Translated and introduced by David Ownby. Blog: "Reading the China Dream." https://www.readingthechinadream.com/rong-jian-wang-huis-heidegger-moment.html. Last accessed 5 July 2022.

Tian, Xiaofei. "Muffled Dialect Spoken by Green Fruit. A New History of Modern Chinese Poetry." *MCLC Resource Center* 21.1 (2009): 1–45.

Van Crevel, Maghiel. "Walk on the Wild Side. Snapshots the Chinese Poetry Scene." *MCLC Resource Center* (2017): 1–64.

Van Crevel, Maghiel. Chinese *Poetry in Times of Mind, Mayhem and Money*. Leiden: Brill, 2008.

Von Kowallis, Jon Eugene. *The Lyrical Lu Xun. A Study of His Classical Style Verse*. Honolulu: University of Hawai-I Press, 1996.

Wang, Hui. "The 'Modern Prince' and the Revolutionary Personality. Translated and introduced by David Ownby. The translation is presented with an introduction under the headline. "Wang Hui, the 'Revolutionary Personality' and the Philosophy of Victory". Blog: *Reading the China Dream*. 2020. https://www.readingthechinadream.com/wang-hui-revolutionary-personality.html. Last accessed 5 July 2022.

Yang, Zhiyi, and Ma, Dayong. "Classicism 2.0. The Vitality of Classicist Poetry Online in Contemporary China." *Frontiers of Literary Study in China* 12.3 (2018): 526–557.

Yeh, Michelle. "Anxiety & Liberation: Notes on the Recent Chinese Poetry Scene." *World Literature Today* 81.4 (2007): 28–35.

Zenz, Adrian. "The Xinjiang Police Files: Re-Education Camp Security and Political Paranoia in the Xinjiang Uyghur Autonomous Region." *Journal of the European Association for Chinese Studies* 8 (2022). https://journals.univie.ac.at/index.php/jeacs/article/view/7336/7290. Last accessed 7 July 2022.

Zhao, Tingyang. *All Under Heaven. The Tianxia System for a Possible World Order*. Berkeley: University of California Press, 2021.

Marge Käsper

Inside in Immunity, Outside in Community? Discussing Esposito and Framing Pandemic Polemics in France

Abstract: The title of the chapter refers to the slogan coined by the French government to communicate measures taken in the context of the COVID-19 health crisis but paraphrases it in the light of Roberto Esposito's philosophical analysis of biopower in *Immunitas. Protection et négation de la vie (Immunitas. Protezione e negazione della vita)*, which was released in France almost at the same time as the slogan (March 2021). This simplistic slogan, with the original wording "*Dedans avec les miens, dehors en citoyens*" (Inside with those close to me, outside as citizens), sparked controversy and created ironic variations in social media that contrasted the "inside" and the "outside". The book analyses the mutual dependence of and tension between the concepts of immunity (a safe "inside" state) and community (outside social behaviour) in depth, framing them in terms of law, politics and biology. This chapter analyses the French reception of Esposito's book and its indirect dialogue with the government slogan. While the French reception places Esposito's work in the context of the topical COVID-19 polemic, it also highlights Esposito's bodily metaphor of pregnancy to conceptualize vaccination as the creation of a "healthy social body". This novel conception of immunity in relation to community also opens up a way to interpret the polemic around the French government's slogan in a new light.

1 Introduction

The COVID-19 pandemic has forced us to rethink our most ordinary habits and behaviours. Meeting friends, going out for a dinner and other ordinary activities became literally impossible during the lockdowns, when they were strongly regulated by the measures designed to fight the pandemic. The measures helped us to stay safe but also raised many questions about how to function as a society in these

Note: The research for the present chapter was funded by the Estonian Research Council grant PRG934.

conditions. Specifically, the title of the chapter – *inside in immunity, outside in community* – derives from a slogan coined by the French government during the pandemic in order to communicate measures taken in France to fight the health crisis. The campaign slogan, with the original wording *"Dedans avec les miens, dehors en citoyens"* (in direct translation: Inside with those close to me, outside as citizens), was meant to sum up the variety of measures in a clear, easily understandable way after several confusing messages from the government (*France Info* 22 March 2021; Goosz, *France Inter* 22 March 2021). The simplistic formula, however, sparked more polemics (Kerlouan, *Boulevard Voltaire* 23 March 2021; Ouangari, *Ouest France* 24 March 2021, etc.) and a considerable controversy in social media, where it was subjected to a series of ironic variations about what and who should be inside or outside (e.g. *"Dedans avec les mien. Dehors avec les tiens"* (Inside with those close to me. Outside with yours / Get out with yours!), addressed to the Prime Minister Jean Castex as a suggestion to resign from the government). The chapter will give some examples about this polemic, but without considering the action ironically as a mimicry of "doing something". Instead, the title is an invitation to discuss the polemic created by the slogan: to analyse the notions concerned and to see, in the end, whether this polemic could even be viewed as a kind of necessary immune response that helps to resolve the problem and to develop the public understanding that social existence as a complex ecosystem of agents cannot be reduced to polar oppositions.

The dichotomy between the individual and the collective and, more specifically, between the inside and the outside of societies, is discussed also in a book released in France nearly at the same time as the French government slogan. March 2021 saw the French translation of *Immunitas. Protezione e negazione della vita* by the Italian philosopher Roberto Esposito. The book, the French title of which is *Immunitas. Protection et négation de la vie*, discusses the contrasting and yet mutually dependent relationship between the concepts of immunity and community, key notions all governments dealt with in responding to the pandemic. The French government's slogan was basically part of the government's vaccination campaign, targeting immunity against the disease (*France Inter*, 22 March 2021; Weill, *Le Monde*, 23 March 2022) to which Esposito's analysis provides a broader context. As the government asked people to behave "as citizens", the slogan also provoked the question of what (and where) the community is. Esposito considers these questions in the context of legal and political philosophy.

Roberto Esposito published his *Immunitas. Protezione e negazione della vita* in Italian in 2002 (Biblioteca Einaudi), after the terrorist attacks of 11 September 2001 had caused a security crisis in the liberal world. The book discusses measures taken to protect people's lives, combining legal and political lexicons with those of theology, anthropology and biology. It was translated and published in English in 2011 (Polity Press). In the context of the COVID-19 health crisis, however, it offers "an extremely topical" analysis of "contemporary biopolitics", as pointed out by the French publisher Seuil in the cover blurb of the French translation[1] that appeared on 4 March 2021, almost on the first anniversary of nearly worldwide lockdowns in March 2020. I will focus on the French reception of this translation and trace a parallel between it and the campaign slogan released by the French government some weeks later (on 22 March 2021), because the questions the latter raised provide an interesting frame for Esposito's ideas.

2 The Reception Corpus and the Immunitary Lexicon in Politics

To study the French reception of Esposito's *Immunitas*, I consulted various sources in September 2021. I identified a series of articles dedicated to the book in the central daily newspaper *Le Monde* (LM), in the online participatory cultural and general newspaper *Mediapart* (MP) and in *Philosophie Magazine* (PhM).[2] In addition to these reviews, I consulted the cover blurbs and introductions by the publisher (Seuil) and of online bookshops (Amazon, Filigrane), as well as Esposito's special 2021 Preface to the translation.

Esposito's ideas had been discussed in France before the publication of *Immunitas* (e.g. Descendre 2006), including at the start of the pandemic (Samoyault 2020). The previous translations of Esposito's ideas into French include *Communitas. Origine et destin de la communauté* (PUF, 2000), *Catégories de l'impolitique* (Le Seuil, 2005) and *Communauté, immunité, biopolitique* (Les Prairies ordinaires, 2010 and Mimesis, 2019). The purpose of this situated reading of Esposito is to draw out the axes outlined in the COVID-19 context in France in spring 2021.

For the French edition of his *Immunitas*, Esposito provided a COVID-19 contextualized preface and he was also invited to introduce his book on the main French cultural radio channel, *France Culture*, on 7 April 2021, in the programme *La Grande Table des Idées*, directed by Olivia Gesbert. Then the book was introduced twice in *Philosophie Magazine*: first by Catherine Portevin as the "book of the day"

---

[1] Website of the publisher Seuil. *Immunitas. Protection et négation de la vie.* https://www.seuil.com/ouvrage/immunitas-roberto-esposito/9782021469080. Last accessed 10 May 2022.
[2] According to its website, the aim of the PhM is "to think about the news and the world through philosophy", in line with Foucault's idea that "the question of philosophy is the question of the present which is ourselves" (Foucault quoted in *A propos* of the PhM website). https://www.philomag.com/. Last accessed 10 May 2022.

on 12 March 2021 and in an insightful but concise review by the same author on 24 March. The daily newspaper *Le Monde* published an article on Esposito's book on 26 March by Nicolas Weill. The most detailed commentary on the book was published on 15 April by Joseph Confavreux on the online news site *Mediapart*.

Nearly all presentations of the book begin by quoting Esposito's Preface: "Rare is the author who happens to see what he had said in a book come true [. . .]."[3] (Esposito 2021, 7). Nicolas Weill in LM (26 March 2021) is the most explicit in creating a link between the vaccination campaign and the very present "war" metaphor used by French president Macron in his crisis speeches:

> *Immunitas*, a book on immunity as a political paradigm by the Italian philosopher Roberto Esposito (born in 1950), may have appeared in 2002 in his country, but it is extremely topical in the midst of a "war" against Covid-19, in the midst of a vaccination campaign seen as the only possible way out of a global crisis. "Rare is the author who sees what he had said in a book come true, well beyond even his forecasts", he notes, without any triumphalism, in his preface to this edition, revised in 2020. (LM 26 March 2021)[4]

We will see below what Esposito thinks about the war metaphor in describing the "fight" against the virus, but he does indeed analyse vaccination as a medical invention that is intertwined with politics. This relationship is again in *Le Monde* (26 March 2021) framed and explained for the readers in line with Michel Foucault's philosophy and his "controversial" concepts of biopolitics and biopower, as follows:

> The growing confluence of the political and biological domains, identified by Michel Foucault at the end of the 1970s and formulated in the controversial terms of "biopolitics" and "biopower", is the basis of the argumentation. Far from having been a theoretical fad, believes Esposito, it has turned into a structure for thinking about today's politics. When the primary concern of the governments revolves around public health, the administration of living things and bodies even before the economy or the environment, "life becomes, in every sense, a matter of government, just like the latter becomes above all governed by life", he sums up. (LM 26 March 2021)[5]

---

3 All citations are translated into English by the author and the original text of longer citations is provided in footnotes. Translations of slogans and of Twitter comments are provided in the text in brackets.

4 "*Immunitas*, ouvrage sur l'immunité comme paradigme du politique dû au philosophe italien Roberto Esposito (né en 1950), a beau avoir paru en 2002 dans son pays, il se révèle d'une brûlante actualité en pleine 'guerre' contre le Covid-19, au beau milieu d'une campagne de vaccination considérée comme seule issue possible à une crise planétaire. 'Rare est l'auteur auquel il arrive de voir ce qu'il avait avancé dans un livre se réaliser, bien au-delà même de ses prévisions', note-t-il, sans nul triomphalisme, dans sa préface à cette édition, refondue en 2020."

5 "La confluence croissante des domaines politique et biologique, repérée par Michel Foucault dès la fin des années 1970 et formulée dans les notions controversées de 'biopolitique' et de 'biopouvoir', porte le raisonnement. Loin d'avoir été une mode théorique, estime Esposito, elle s'est

In his extensive attention to the administration of people' lives, Esposito (2021 [2002]), is interested in showing the transfer of a certain "immunitary lexical paradigm" from the originally medical domain into legal and political, and even to everyday communication. Besides immunization checks and vaccination passports, he sees its metaphoric manifestations in his Preface even in broader health crisis regulation measures like "social" distancing and masks:

> Similarly, political representatives, national and local, are judged according to the level of immunization of their territories. There is, however, something even more general that is taking over the entire social sphere, threatening to transform it into a huge immune bubble. Closure, confinement, distancing that only a tasteless play on words can qualify as "social", when it is only desocializing, are they anything other than immune devices which, little by little, come to occupy the entire domain of individual and collective existence? And isn't the indispensable mask the very metaphor of the immunity affixed to our faces? (Esposito 2021, 8)[6]

Catherine Portevin, in PhM (24 March 2021), also begins by calling attention to this active presence of the "immunitary paradigm" in our time and points out the deeper insights Esposito gives to contemporary politics:

> [. . .] never, indeed, has the vocabulary of immunity been so familiar to us as it is today, to the point of swallowing up all politics: "the immunitary paradigm", as he says, [. . .] has become an axis of rotation around which our individual and collective experience revolves. And it is indeed the project of the Neapolitan philosopher to redefine and reveal the unthought of politics today. (PhM 24 March 2021)[7]

What Esposito redefines in his book is the notion of immunity and its social implications for the community. Among the review articles, the longest one by Joseph Confavreux in MP (15 April 2021) does the most to highlight these implications. The French government guidelines, in contrast, seem to neglect them. While the

---

transformée en structure pour penser la politique d'aujourd'hui. Quand la préoccupation première des États tourne autour de la santé publique, de l'administration du vivant et des corps avant même l'économie ou l'environnement, *'la vie devient, dans tous les sens, affaire de gouvernement, tout comme celui-ci devient avant tout gouverné par la vie'*, résume-t-il."

6 "De même, les représentants politiques, nationaux et locaux, sont jugés selon le niveau d'immunisation de leurs territoires. Il y a, cela dit, quelque chose d'encore plus général qui en vient à investir la sphère sociale tout entière, menaçant de la transformer en une énorme bulle immunitaire. Fermeture, confinement, distanciation que seul un jeu de mots de mauvais goût peut qualifier de 'sociale', quand elle n'est que désocialisante, sont-ils autre chose que des dispositifs immunitaires qui, peu à peu, en viennent à occuper l'entièreté du domaine de l'existence individuelle et collective? Et l'indispensable masque n'est-il pas la métaphore même de l'immunité apposée sur nos visages?".

7 "Et, en effet, jamais le vocabulaire de l'immunité ne nous aura été aussi familier qu'aujourd'hui, au point d'y engloutir toute la politique: '*Le paradigme immunitaire,* dit-il encore, [. . .] *est devenu l'axe de rotation autour duquel tourne notre expérience individuelle et collective'*. Et c'est bien le projet du philosophe napolitain que de redéfinir et de révéler les impensés de la politique aujourd'hui."

slogan was not really intended to complicate things, reactions to it showed the ambiguities of the "philosophy"[8] it expressed. Esposito thus reveals the complexity of the questions the slogan tried to fix in its simplified wording.

3 Immunity in Respect to Community. Tricky Etymology in Law and its Implications

As the nature of slogans is to be concise and, if possible, rhyming and symmetrical (cf. Maingueneau 2012), it was already the very nature of the formula that was perceived initially to be ridiculous, "clowny" and irritating in its "childish pedagogy, which decides whether you are behaving well or badly" (see Twitter comments below). In a country where the right to protest is sacred (cf. d'Iribarne 1989), such a pedagogy is likely to inspire revolt, not compliance. Besides Twitter, this revolt can be seen in a caricatured representation in a drawing by Zaïtchick "Sacré slogan!" (Damned slogan!),[9] where the people who stay inside "in immunity" are presented as prisoners, while the crowd outside behaves like real French revolutionary citizens and rushes "in community" towards the palace (of Elysée). A clear "intellectual revolt" is expressed by Philippe Kerlouan in *Boulevard Voltaire* (23 March 2021) as follows:

> The simplistic slogan has always been the preferred mode of expression of dictatorships, all the more insidious when they want to pass for democracies. It is the duty of all French people who refuse this infantilization, which is only a mode of enslavement, to rebel, at least intellectually and, whenever they can, at the ballot box, against these politicians who take themselves to be gods.[10] (Kerlouan, *Boulevard Voltaire*, 23 March 2021)

---

[8] As reports *l'Express* on 23 March 2021: "We can laugh at this slogan for hours, but there is a reality, reframes the LREM deputy and professor of medicine, Jean-François Eliaou. On the medical level, it is completely adapted to the situation." / "'A slogan is never perfect, the important thing is to pass on the philosophy of the measures and to explain the rules', it is said in Matignon." (Jean-Baptiste Daoulas, *l'Express* 23 March 2021). ("'On peut rigoler de ce slogan pendant des heures, mais il y a une réalité, recadre le député LREM et professeur de médecine, Jean-François Eliaou. Sur le plan médical, il est tout à fait adapté à la situation." / "Un slogan, ce n'est jamais parfait, l'important, c'est de faire passer la philosophie des mesures et d'expliquer les règles", indique-t-on à Matignon.")
[9] Drawing by Zaïtchick of 24 March 2021, referenced in *Blagues et dessins* 25 March 2021, https://www.blagues-et-dessins.com/tag/blague-dedans-avec-les-miens/. Last accessed 10 September 2021.
[10] "Le slogan simplificateur a toujours été le mode d'expression privilégié des dictatures, d'autant plus insidieux qu'elles veulent passer pour des démocrates. Il est du devoir de tous les Français qui refusent cette infantilisation, qui n'est qu'un mode d'asservissement, de se rebeller, au

Among the commentaries reacting to the government's slogan on Twitter,[11] there were different strategies and claims expressing this revolt:
- These clowns, this is no longer acceptable . . . (Mais les clowns, c'est plus possible . . .)
- LOL! The infantilizing pedagogy, which says if you are doing well or badly . . . which says how you should do . . . And our ministers do the opposite. STOP FUCKING PEOPLE! Thanks! (LOL ! La pédagogie enfantilisante, qui dit si tu fais bien ou mal . . . qui dit comment tu dois faire . . . Et nos ministres font le contraire. STOP AU FOUTAGE DE GUEULE ! Merci!)
- To what extent are these recommendations and to what extend legal obligations? (Quelle est la part des récommandations et des obligations légales?)

While the first commentary above claims its superiority by qualifying the authors of the slogan as childish "clowns", the second one stresses not only the unacceptability of the form but also the reason for the disagreement: the tweet suggests that the ministers are not following the prescriptions, behaving in manner opposite to what they ask the citizens to do. This is in line with the views expressed in *Boulevard Voltaire* (Kerlouan, 23 March 2021). The third commentary also explicitly points out the need to clarify whether the guidelines are just recommendations or legal obligations.

Thus the formula is also perceived to be unclear in its legal implications. There are certainly plenty of other aspects to consider in this corpus of more than 800 retweets and nearly 1500 quotations the government's slogan received, but putting them in the context of the reception of Esposito, we can focus on the legal aspect in relation to society.

To understand the legal implications of the isolation measures that parallel the notion of immunity, Esposito, as PhM puts it, "undertakes" an in-depth "genealogy of the notion of immunity, from Roman law to contemporary biopolitics (and even cyborgs), including theology, biology and medicine, anthropology and politics". However, instead of giving quick clear answers, first, "he shows the deep ambivalence of the notion of immunity, which both protects and threatens since it implies absorbing part of the evil, a foreign body, to guard against a greater evil" (PhM, 12 March 2022).

---

moins intellectuellement et, chaque fois qu'ils le pourront, dans les urnes, contre ces politiciens qui se prennent pour des dieux."

11 In total, the French government's slogan received 857 retweets and 1,480 quote tweets in response to its post announcing the slogan on its account on Twitter. Last accessed 10 September 2021.

The etymological link between the notions of immunity and community is the first key issue mentioned in all analysed presentations of the book, like this reference to the preceding *Communitas* (2019):

> *Immunitas* is the second part of a reflection begun with *Communitas* (PUF, 2000), where Roberto Esposito links immunity and community, which share the same etymological root: *munus*, which in Latin means both "the gift" and "obligation" (PhM, 12 March 2022).

Whereas Esposito's idea of the community in *Communitas* (PUF, 2000) is summed up as a category which is "ultimately tragic, because it is politically unrealizable", *immunitas* "is like the inverted project of *communitas*: the one who finds himself exempted and protected from community sharing is immune" (PhM, 24 March 2022).[12]

The review in MP (15 April 2021) details the individual and social categories that could be "immune" in this sense:

> The term "immunitas" has long been reserved for the legal field, going back to a Roman concept relating to the fact of being exempt from the obligations imposed on all: a privilege that can be granted to both individuals and collective entities: municipalities, convents, corporations, universities [. . .] But "immune" also designated, in Rome, soldiers based in the rear who thus avoided being exposed more directly to death.[13]

Considering this legally privileged sense of being immune and thereby protected against the evil, Esposito notes, as pointed out in the same article (MP, 15 April 2021), a Machiavellian "defensive significance, in a legal-political, but also military sense, which passes into the biological conception of immunity, once transposed from the social body to the individual body".[14] Moreover, Esposito also seems to show that liberal philosophy has created an impression that one has to have the right to isolate oneself from society. That is why the presentation on the book in PhM (12 March 2022) says that "Immunity is what 'takes back' the community project but at the same time

---

12 "*Immunitas* est le deuxième volet d'une trilogie, entamée avec *Communitas* (PUF, 2000), où Esposito redéfinit l'idée de communauté en montrant comment cette catégorie est au fond tragique, car irréalisable sur le plan politique. *Immunitas* est comme le projet inversé de la *communitas*: est immunisé celui qui se trouve comme exempté et protégé du partage communautaire." (PhM, 24 March 2022).

13 "Le terme d'*immunitas* a longtemps été réservé au domaine juridique, remontant à un concept romain relatif au fait d'être exempté des obligations imposées à tous: un privilège pouvant être accordé aussi bien à des individus qu'à des entités collectives: municipalités, couvents, corporations, universités . . . Mais *immunes* désignait aussi, à Rome, des soldats basés à l'arrière et évitant ainsi de se trouver exposés plus directement à la mort."

14 "C'est précisément, note le philosophe, 'cette signification défensive, dans une acception juridico-politique, mais aussi militaire, qui passe dans la conception biologique de l'immunité, une fois transposée du corps social au corps individuel'."

makes it exist" – being safe saves lives but individual fears and interests tend to take precedence.

In contrast, when it comes to the "social body" of society, the question arises of, whether the politicians "fighting" the crisis and taking care of it are justified in preserving community at all costs and in considering themselves immune from the rules, as well as from the rights concerning the community. Esposito indeed "brings to light the infrastructures of a 'biopolitics' on which rest our societies 'which have placed human life, and therefore the care of it, as their guiding principle, even to the extent that they are willing to sacrifice the values that are as inalienable as sociality and even freedom'" (MP, 15 April 2021).[15] According to LM (26 March 2021), however, this "systematic doubt about the liberal and democratic nature of our societies", practiced in particular by people following Giorgio Agamben's train of thought, leads to questionable implications, like the problematization of the legal system as "linked to violence" and the denunciation of the immune model as a means of escaping dangers:

> Roberto Esposito certainly defends himself from the accusation of reducing modern democracy to totalitarianism or to a state of exception adorned with the feathers of freedom – even if some aspects of the present situation appear to be water to his mill. But in the book's least convincing second chapter, he rushes into a questionable attempt to demonstrate that the nature of law is inextricably linked to violence and bloodshed. Doesn't that amount to denouncing the dangers of the immune model by depriving yourself of the means to get out of it? (LM 26 March 2021)[16]

Admitting, however, that Esposito's analysis is "fascinating even in its digressions", LM (26 March 2021) concludes: "the proposed route remains one of the deepest in finding meaning in the chaos of our present".

The conclusion in MP's (15 April 2021) review, in contrast, underlines the very constructive programme of Esposito's ideas on co-immunity, "something capable of uniting people". Nevertheless, Esposito's concern for the health of the social

---

[15] "[Esposito] met ainsi au jour les infrastructures d'une 'biopolitique' sur lesquelles reposent nos sociétés *'qui ont posé la vie humaine, et partant le soin de celle-ci, comme leur principe directeur, au point de pouvoir lui sacrifier des valeurs aussi imprescriptibles que la socialité et même la liberté'*." (MP, 15 April 2021).

[16] "Roberto Esposito se défend certes de réduire la démocratie moderne au totalitarisme ou à un état d'exception paré des plumes de la liberté – même si quelques aspects de la situation présente auraient de quoi apporter de l'eau à ce moulin-là. Mais il s'engouffre, au deuxième chapitre, le moins convaincant du livre, dans une tentative contestable de démontrer que la nature du droit est indissociablement liée à la violence et au sang versé. Cela ne revient-il pas à dénoncer les dangers du modèle immunitaire en se privant des moyens d'en sortir? Malgré cette limite, le parcours proposé reste l'un des plus profonds pour trouver un sens au chaos de notre présent."

body, as well as that of its parts, leads to a very categorical implication for the vaccination policy and individual rights in this community: no privileged "vaccination passports" for the "immunized" but a "healthy social body":

> Indeed, insofar as "no part of the world can save itself by itself, without all the others saving themselves in turn" and in a situation where "the global protection, of everything and everyone becomes more than a political opportunity, the categorical imperative of our time", immunity could no longer become a "mechanism of individual protection and social distancing" but "a co-immunity: something capable of uniting people".
>
> In other words, not a "vaccination passport" reserved for certain people, most often inhabitants of rich countries, but a profound modification of the very drawing of the borders of politics and of the definition of what constitutes a healthy social body. (MP, 15 April 2021)[17]

From these presentations we can conclude that community and immunity are very intimately linked concepts and that their polarized treatment is never more than schematic. Esposito helps to understand but would not suggest the radical opposition between "those close to me" and the others. The etymological link between the notions of immunity and of community leads him, on the contrary, to look for a "healthy social body" relating those in immunity and in community in a balanced way (see discussion below). The next section shows how he develops this vision.

4 Rewording Society's Threats

While the Foucauldian analysis of biopower highlighted the control mechanisms over human bodies in societies and Agamben's subsequent analysis inspected the dangers this implied, Esposito focuses on asking for a "healthy social body". As Dean (2000) argues, discussions of welfare policy and social justice lend themselves to the use of "bodily metaphors", inspired by an "organic analogy" between the human body as an organic system and a society that sustains itself through systematic welfare provision. For Esposito (2021 [2001]), the "health" of the "social body" depends on how we conceptualize the threatening evil:

---

[17] "En effet, dans la mesure où *'aucune partie du monde ne peut se sauver de par elle-même, sans que toutes les autres se sauvent à leur tour'* et dans une situation où *'la protection globale, de tout et de chacun, devient plus qu'une opportunité politique, l'impératif catégorique de notre temps'*, l'immunité pourrait devenir non plus un *'mécanisme de protection individuelle et de distanciation sociale'* mais *'une co-immunité: quelque chose capable d'unir les hommes'*. Autrement dit, non pas un *'passeport vaccinal'* réservé à certains, le plus souvent habitants des pays riches, mais une modification profonde du tracé même des frontières de la politique et de la définition de ce qu'est un corps social en bonne santé."

If the supreme evil is located in the threat of sedition and revolt, the health of the state will be located in an order guaranteed by the established control of the leader over all the other members of the body. If, on the contrary, what is feared is, rather, the tyranny of a despotic sovereign, the salvation of the political organism will be located in the balance between its various components. (Esposito cited in MP, 15 April 2021)[18]

The description of the book on the site of the Belgian bookshop *Filigrane* clearly sums up this tension:

Based on a reflection on the nature of vaccination, the author offers an analysis of contemporary biopolitics. The more individuals feel that they are on the verge of being infected by foreign bodies, the more they withdraw into their protective limits, forcing them to choose between a self-destructive way out and a radical alternative based on a new conception of community.[19]

According to Esposito, as explained in greater detail in MP (15 April 2021), the excessive protective practices are as self-destructive as the so-called "auto-immune" diseases are in medical practice. In their case, the immune response, which normally produces positive effects, begins to act against the host it intends to defend; and finally, with the intention of fighting its enemy, the immune response actually also damages itself. The same review in MP (15 April 2021) comments that this is "A situation which, for Esposito, constitutes a perfect parable of the situation of contemporary democracies that their security logic and their attacks on freedoms come to weaken from the inside."[20] Joseph Confavreux continues to explain Esposito's ideas in MP (15 April 2021): "it is by deepening the very notion of immunity in order to propose an 'alternative interpretation' that we can avoid this risk and provide 'a metaphorical proposal of high symbolic value for political life'. The

---

18 "'si le mal suprême est localisé dans la menace de sédition et de révolte, la santé de l'État se verra située dans un ordre garanti par le contrôle établi du chef sur tous les autres membres du corps. Si, au contraire, ce qui est craint est plutôt la tyrannie d'un souverain despotique, le salut de l'organisme politique sera situé dans l'équilibre entre ses divers composants.'"
19 "A partir d'une réflexion sur la nature de la vaccination, l'auteur propose une analyse de la biopolitique contemporaine. Plus les individus se sentent sur le point d'être infectés par des corps étrangers, plus ils se renferment dans leurs limites protectrices, les obligeant à choisir entre une issue autodestructrice et une alternative radicale fondée sur une nouvelle conception de la communauté." https://www.filigranes.be/immunitas-protection-et-negation-de-la-vie. Last accessed 10 September 2021.
20 "Une situation qui, pour Esposito, constitue une parabole parfaite de la situation des démocraties contemporaines que leur logique sécuritaire et leurs atteintes aux libertés en viennent à fragiliser de l'intérieur."

philosopher, to reverse the immune semantics 'in a community sense', then relies on organ transplants and the phenomenon of pregnancy."[21]

The figure that all reviews indeed highlight for the readers is Esposito's idea that the introduction of an evil or alien element in the body of our societies is like a biological metaphor of a woman being pregnant. In this vision, there is a little "alien" element in the body of a woman but, if the body integrates it properly, it gives birth to a new life without destroying the previous one. As LM (26 March 2021) puts it, "Against the metaphor of the fight to the death, in the mother's womb, the fight is 'for life'".[22]

Esposito arrives at this vision via the sixteenth century physician Paracelsus and other biologists. Paracelsus, even if he does not use the notion of immunity, already believed that the remedy for the evil consisted in its absorption in small doses. Further on, Esposito presents an in-depth study of the doctor and one of the main founders of the cell theory, Rudolf Virchow (1821–1902), who also participated in the Prussian democratic movement of 1848 and insisted on a "kind of dialectical circulation between political position and scientific research", as reports the review in MP (15 April 2021).

Within the framework of contemporary science, ultimately, the Italian philosopher places himself in line with Donna Haraway who seeks to "imagine the immune system differently from the rhetoric of the Cold War, which always represented it as a battlefield", as pointed out by Esposito in MP (15 April 2021) review. "Instead of invasion", the review quotes Esposito, "why not think of it in terms of shared specificities, within a semi-permeable self, able to interact with others?"[23] Joseph Confavreux explains in MP (15 April 2021) that according to Esposito, the immune system and the pathogen do not have to be in confrontation. On the one hand, "as for the political immunization, it means the immune system's response to external aggression must be proportionate to and targeted at the threat, to avoid autoimmune collateral damage". On the other hand, the interaction does not mean total assimilation: "Such a response, to be truly protective and beneficial, explains Confavreux, should therefore 'include a kind of internal regulator, an automatic brake, capable of containing it

---

[21] "[. . .] c'est en approfondissant la notion même d'immunité afin d'en proposer une *'interprétation alternative'* qu'on peut éviter ce risque et fournir *'une proposition métaphorique de haute valeur symbolique pour la vie politique'*. Le philosophe s'appuie alors pour renverser la sémantique immunitaire *'en un sens communautaire'* sur les transplantations d'organes et le phénomène de la grossesse."

[22] *"Contre la métaphore du combat à mort, dans le ventre maternel, le combat est 'à vie'."*

[23] "[. . .] dans les cadres de la science contemporaine, le philosophe italien se place dans la lignée de la chercheuse Donna Haraway qui cherchait à *'imaginer le système immunitaire différemment de la rhétorique de la guerre froide qui l'a toujours représenté comme un champ de bataille. 'Plutôt que dans les termes de l'invasion, pourquoi ne pas y penser dans les termes de spécificités partagées, au sein d'un soi semi-perméable, capable d'interagir avec les autres'."*

within the right limits, beyond which the organism can encounter serious problems'" (MP 15 April 2021).[24]

This novel perspective explains politics in terms of the metaphor of pregnancy in a more "inclusive" way:

> for Esposito, the protection that the mother grants to the "alien" within her, not in spite of, but indeed because of, its foreignness, represents a way of understanding the relationship with the other capable of modifying in an inclusive sense the very presuppositions of political action.[25] (MP 15 April 2021)

This inclusive way of thinking about the "alien" breaks away from the model in which "the foreigner is at best tolerable or 'thinkable only in the form of his prior dissolution', just as the dose of disease injected into a vaccine is bearable only as a defence and eradication of this same disease" (LM 26 March 2021).[26] Moreover, if we rethink now the powerful assertion that we are "at war" against the virus, used by Emmanuel Macron in his speeches at the beginning of the health crisis, in light of Esposito's ideas, this metaphor appears as "an obsolete vision of the immunity paradigm that misunderstands its real and actual functioning," as argued in MP's review (15 April 2021).[27]

What about the campaign slogan that Macron's Prime Minister, Jean Castex, launched to manage the health crisis? Following Esposito, we could say the protests against the simplistic guidelines represent, in a way, a kind of "automatic brake" against a totalitarian control of the crisis. As such, a message that calls people not to a total closure in their domestic "immunity", but to behave outside as citizens in the "community" are supposed to do, actually already represents a philosophy that moves towards learning to live with the virus. The most popular pun among the variations of the slogan even created an indirect link between the

---

24 "'Comme dans l'immunisation politique, la réponse du système immunitaire à l'agression extérieure doit être proportionnelle à la menace et ciblée sur celle-ci, pour éviter les dommages collatéraux auto-immuns'. Une telle réponse, pour être vraiment protectrice et bénéfique, devrait donc 'comporter une sorte de régulateur interne, de frein automatique, capable de la contenir dans de justes limites, au-delà desquelles l'organisme peut rencontrer de sérieux problèmes'."
25 "[P]our Esposito, 'la protection que la mère accorde à "l'étranger" en son sein, non pas en dépit mais bien en raison de son extranéité, représente une façon de comprendre les rapports avec l'autre en mesure de modifier en un sens inclusif les présupposés mêmes de l'action politique'."
26 "[. . .] les modèles de repli ou de rejet de l'*autre que soi*, dès lors que ce dernier prend la forme d'un virus mortifère. Comme si l'étranger n'était au mieux tolérable ou *'pensable que sous forme de sa dissolution préalable'*, de même que la dose de maladie injectée dans un vaccin n'est supportable qu'à titre de défense et d'éradication de cette même maladie."
27 "L'affirmation que nous serions *'en guerre'* contre le virus, formulée par Emmanuel Macron il y a un peu plus d'un an, ne serait ainsi, finalement, qu'une vision obsolète du paradigme de l'immunité saisissant mal son fonctionnement réel et actuel."

name of Prime Minister Jean Castex and the metaphor of pregnancy, albeit in a lightly hedonistic sense: "*Dedans avec Durex, dehors avec Castex*" (Inside with Durex, outside with Castex, Gerbe, *oh!mymag*, 23 March 2021). This variation of the slogan is in line with the ideas developed by Esposito: the condom (Durex) is basically a device to control the carnal relationship with the other while letting the other in, thus providing immunity without depriving oneself of the pleasure provided by the community. However, the option to be outside with the rigid protection provided "with Castex", on the contrary, seems to present a rather depressing and hopeless perspective for the people used to draconic governmental protection measures, with no intercourse, no communication nor pleasure, and thus no community as such.

According to Esposito "community" indeed also means "the risk involved in any sharing". In this respect, however, the action of the government could be interpreted as voluntarily risky yet salutary for the community. Remembering that

> Roberto Esposito links immunity and community, which share the same etymological root: *munus*, which in Latin means both gift and duty. The community is thus bound by the law of gift and debt, but also by the risk involved in any sharing.[28] (PhM, 12 March 2021)

In community, although citizens are meant to act respectfully towards each other, there is always also the risk of being affected by a different Other. As "slogans are made to be hijacked" (cf. *Ouest France below*), in the case of the slogan analysed here, the mocking commentaries present the risk that was obvious. Nevertheless, in the very need to take action for the community, the government's idea of the slogan can finally be interpreted not so much as mimicry of just "doing something" but also as a rather positive attempt to call attention to the problems that need to be resolved, as one specialist in political communication points out in *Ouest France* the 24 March 2021:

> However, if the slogan makes people react, it is also positive. "It is the nature of a slogan to be hijacked. Slogans are made to be hijacked, to be mocked", recalls Gaspard Gantzer. "It's almost a good sign because a slogan provokes reactions, it means that it has hit the mark somewhere. The worst thing for a slogan is to arouse indifference". It remains to be seen whether, behind all the reactions, the message will ultimately be heard.[29] (Ouangari, *Ouest France*, 24 March 2021)

---

28 "Roberto Esposito lie l'immunité et la communauté, qui partagent la même racine étymologique: *munus*, qui signifie en latin à la fois le don et le devoir. La communauté est ainsi liée par la loi du don et de la dette, mais aussi par le risque que comporte tout partage."

29 "Toutefois, si le slogan fait réagir, c'est aussi positif. 'C'est le propre d'un slogan d'être détourné. Les slogans sont faits pour être détournés, pour être moqués', rappelle Gaspard Gantzer. 'C'est presque bon signe parce qu'un slogan suscite des réactions, ça veut dire qu'il a touché juste

Alongside 857 retweets and 1,489 quotation tweets, the government's slogan also received 2,106 likes on Twitter, so the polemic represents perhaps a balanced reception of the slogan: healthy criticism can revert and thereby avoid the acceptance of those measures that are disproportionate while the problem is being discussed and dealt with within the community. As PhM puts it (12 March 2021), summing up Esposito's ideas: "Immunity is what 'takes back' the community project but at the same time makes it exist. There is no community without some type of immune system."[30]

5 Conclusion

This chapter discussed the reactions to a slogan coined by the French government to communicate measures taken in the context of the COVID-19 health crisis in light of the reception of Roberto Esposito's *Immunitas. Protection et négation de la vie (Immunitas. Protezione e negazione della vita)*, which was released in France almost exactly at the time as the slogan, in March 2021. While the book originally published already twenty years earlier was welcomed in France as a very topical analysis of the contemporary health crisis biopolitics, the slogan designed to manage this crisis sparked a considerable controversy on social media platforms. Besides ridiculing the form of the slogan, the Twitter commentaries also raised the question of its legal implications and of the observing of the rules. Esposito, in his philosophical analysis of the notion of immunity, showed the etymological and logical link, derived from the legal lexicon, between this notion and that of community.

The discussion of the ideas of Esposito demonstrated that the opposition in which these notions stand in the didactic form of the government's slogan concerns a basic but also a very ambiguous relation. On the one hand, he shows the deep ambivalence of immunity, which both protects and threatens since it implies absorbing part of the evil, a foreign body, to guard against a greater evil. On the other hand, his main project is in fact a reflection about community, which is based on neither resemblance nor on the fear of a war of all against all, but rather proposes taking "the risk involved in any sharing". Since his analysis of the "immunitary lexicon paradigm" greatly expands its understanding, he proposes a vision based on a

---

quelque part. Le pire pour un slogan, c'est de susciter l'indifférence'. Reste à voir si, derrière toutes les réactions, le message sera au final entendu."

30 "L'immunité est ce qui *'prend à revers'* le projet communautaire mais en même temps le fait exister. *'Il n'existe pas de communauté dépourvue d'un type quelconque d'appareil immunitaire'* ."

bodily metaphor for the society facing threats: as a woman in pregnancy takes care of her health, as well of that of the "alien" element in her body, we can think of the immune response as giving birth to something new without losing our own "body".

This positive framing of the threats that society has to face and control is, according to the French philosopher Frédéric Neyrat (2019), something that even Foucault "had missed". In his preface to Esposito's *Communitas* (2019), Neyrat observes that Esposito shows not only a vital need to take into consideration the biopolitics framework but also that he performs a kind of a "process of reversal of the biopolitical into its opposite", a politics that focuses on a "politics of life", and not on what could cause death. Thus, he does not denounce the "thanatopolitics" decried by Agamben (2015), but stresses care for life. In the case of the polemics caused by the French government's slogan, his philosophy offers, ultimately, an option to consider the playful rewordings of the slogan as a necessary immune response to the exaggerated political communication, on the one hand, but also a positive, responsible reflection on the problem, on the other hand. To push this parallel, social media networks can be considered a means for people to reject everything they fear and to stay in their "immunity bubble". On the other hand, these networks nowadays make society exist, providing the opportunities not only for sharing the contested or appreciated content but also for creating novel content. In the context of COVID-19 vaccination, the parallel discussion of the ideas of Esposito and the polemics showed that community and immunity are intimately linked and that their polarized treatment is never more than schematic. The protection of lives also means a community to manage. The translation of Esposito's work will definitely contribute to further enriching discussions on these aspects in France.

References

Agamben, Giorgio. *Stasis. Civil War as a Political Paradigm (Homo Sacer II, 2)*. Trans. Nicholas Heron. Stanford: Stanford University Press, 2015.
Confavreux, Joseph. "Une philosophie de l'immunité." *Mediapart*. 4 April 2021. https://www.mediapart.fr/journal/culture-idees/150421/une-philosophie-de-l-immunite. Last accessed 10 May 2022.
Dean, Hartley. "Bodily Metaphors and Welfare Regimes." *Social Policy and the Body*. Eds. Katherin Ellis, Hartley Dean, and Jo Campling. London: Palgrave Macmillan, 2000. 83–102. https://doi.org/10.1057/9780230377530_5. Last accessed 10 May 2022.
Descendre, Romain. "Bíos. Biopolitica e filosofia. Roberto Esposito." *Laboratoire italien* 6. 2006. https://doi.org/10.4000/laboratoireitalien.254. Last accessed 10 May 2022.
Esposito, Roberto. *Immunitas. Protezione e negazione della vita*. Torino: Biblioteca Einaudi, 2002.
Esposito, Roberto. *Catégories de l'impolitique*. Paris: Seuil, 2005.

Esposito, Roberto. *Communauté, immunité, biopolitique. Repenser les termes de la politique*, 2ème édition [2010]. Préface par Fréderic Neyrat. Sesto San Giovanni: Mimesis, 2019.

Esposito, Roberto. *Communauté, immunité, biopolitique*. Trad. de l'italien par Bernard Chamayou. Amsterdam: Les Prairies ordinaires, 2010.

Esposito, Roberto. *Communitas. Origine et destin de la communauté*. Trad. de l'italien par Nadine Le Lirzin. Préface de Jean-Luc Nancy. Paris: PUF, 2000.

Esposito, Roberto. *Immunitas. Protection et négation de la vie*. Trad. de l'italien par Léo Textier. Preface: Roberto Esposito. Paris: Seuil, 2021.

Esposito, Roberto. *Immunitas. The Protection and Negation of Life*. Cambridge: Polity Press, 2011.

France Culture. Olivia Gesbert: La Grande table idées. 7 April 2021. https://www.franceculture.fr/emissions/la-grande-table-idees/une-societe-du-tout-immunise-est-elle-souhaitable. Last accessed 10 May 2022.

France Info. "'Dedans avec les miens, dehors en citoyen': la campagne de communication du gouvernement sur les gestes barrières dévoilée par Jean Castex." *France Info*. 22 March 2021. https://www.francetvinfo.fr/sante/maladie/coronavirus/confinement/dedans-avec-les-miens-dehors-en-citoyen-la-campagne-de-communication-du-gouvernement-sur-les-gestes-barrieres-devoilee-par-jean-castex_4343313.html. Last accessed 10 May 2022.

Gerbe, Inès. "Twitter: le nouveau slogan du Gouvernement ridiculisé par les internautes." *oh!mymag*. 23 March 2021. https://www.ohmymag.com/insolite/twitter-le-nouveau-slogan-du-gouvernement-ridiculise-par-les-internautes_art141552.html. Last accessed 10 May 2022.

Goosz, Yaël. "'Dedans avec les miens, dehors en citoyen': le gouvernement cherche à clarifier les mesures de freinage." *France Inter*. 22 March 2021. https://www.franceinter.fr/politique/dedans-avec-les-miens-dehors-en-citoyen-le-gouvernement-cherche-a-clarifier-les-mesures-de-freinage. Last accessed 10 May 2022.

Iribarne, Philippe d'. *La Logique de l'honneur. Gestion des entreprises et traditions nationales*. Paris: Seuil, 1989.

Kerlouan, Philippe. "'Dedans avec les miens, dehors en citoyen': un slogan débile et infantilisant." *Boulevard Voltaire*. 23 March 2021. https://www.bvoltaire.fr/dedans-avec-les-miens-dehors-en-citoyen-un-slogan-debile-et-infantilisant/. Last accessed 10 May 2022.

Maingueneau, Dominique. *Les phrases sans texte*. Paris: Colin, 2012.

Portevin, Catherine. "'Immunitas'. Une recension de Catherine Portevin." *Philosophie magazine*. 24 March 2021. https://www.philomag.com/livres/immunitas. Last accessed 10 May 2022.

Portevin, Catherine. "Le livre du jour 'Immunitas. Protection et Négation de la vie', de Roberto Esposito." *Philosophie magazine*. 12 March 2021. https://www.philomag.com/articles/immunitas-protection-et-negation-de-la-vie-de-roberto-esposito. Last accessed 10 May 2022.

Samoyault, Tiphaine. "Communauté, immunité. Ce qui nous arrive." *Journal de la littérature, des idées et des arts, En attendant Nadeau*. 20 March 2020. https://www.en-attendant-nadeau.fr/2020/03/20/communaute-immunite-esposito/. Last accessed 10 May 2022.

Weill, Nicolas. "'Immunitas', de Roberto Esposito: Covid-19 ou le triomphe du biopouvoir." *Le Monde*. 26 March 2021. https://www.lemonde.fr/livres/article/2021/03/26/immunitas-de-roberto-esposito-covid-19-ou-le-triomphe-du-biopouvoir_6074604_3260.html. Last accessed 10 May 2022.

Zaïtchick. "Sacré slogan! 'Dedans avec les miens, dehors en citoyen.'" (24 March 2021). L'actu de Zaïtchick. blagues et dessins. 25 March 2021. https://www.blagues-et-dessins.com/tag/blague-dedans-avec-les-miens/. Last accessed 10 May 2022.

Michael Eskin
Needful Facts, Big and Small: On Bodies, Equality, and Treatment

Abstract: The COVID-19 pandemic has played out quite differently depending on the given geo-political context. How a state and culture devises and implements its biopolitics amid a real-life outbreak will be determined by presuppositions and considerations exceeding the remit of public health and HR: history, values, societal antagonisms all play a role not only in the apportionment of care and life-saving resources but also in the creation and maintenance of the requisite public organization and "order" for such apportionment. In the US context – which constitutes my main focus – the official response to the pandemic (federal, state, local, the CDC's, et cetera), in its singular attention to "saving lives", has thrown into stark relief some of the abiding inadequacies of conceiving of biopolitics primarily as targeting "lives", and this means bodies – rather than persons with histories, relationships, needs and desires: some lives-and-bodies, it turns out, are "more equal" than others, even though, officially speaking, all lives ought to be "equally equal". What does equality mean from the viewpoint of official triage and treatment? Is equality – especially as a function of biopower – the meet master concept and socio-political premise-*cum*-goal in the first place? I pursue these questions by way of the works of a number of contemporary American writers – Ta-Nehesi Coates, Ross Gay, Claudia Rankine, and Terrance Hayes, among others – who have provocatively reflected on and staged the internal tensions, paradoxes, aporias and practical failures of the very concept of biopower and its application in the US specifically, insofar as it is premised on the notion of equality.

I

Mindful of this volume's overall focus on the dual question of "health and biopolitics in literature and philosophy" against the foil of the COVID-19 pandemic, I should like to begin by observing that while the entwinement of politics and specifically *human* life as we know it, loosely and most broadly understood, is at least as old as the oldest communities of *Homo sapiens* – real or imagined, that is, historically documented or figuratively posited (think, for instance, of Hobbes' and Rousseau's respective "states of nature") – our own modern discourse on this entwinement harks back to the ancient Greeks in particular, as the very etymology of the term "politics" palpably attests to.¹ The same applies, *mutatis mutandis*, to our various European or "Western" terms-*cum*-concepts for "life" – "Leben", "leven", "liv", "vie", "vita", "vida", "zhizn", "zycie", "zhivot", et cetera – which, even though some of them may not, for geo- and ethno-historical reasons, resemble their Greek forbears morphologically and etymologically, are still traceable to the Greek lexical-conceptual brace of βιος and ζωη, as evidenced, in turn, by such cross-culturally employed terms as *biology* and *zoology*.² Thus, when we speak of biopolitics today, we invariably, and ineluctably, place ourselves in the long shadow cast by the biopolitics theorized and practiced in classical antiquity – one of the most conspicuous of such practices having arguably consisted in the well-documented theorization and practice of selective infanticide and child abandonment based on eugenic criteria throughout the Greco-Roman world, whence a direct line can be drawn to our own spectrum of sanctioned "eugenic" practices, from pre-natal and genetic testing to late- or partial-term abortion.³

---

1 "At an archaeological site near the Atlantic coast, finds of skull, face and jaw bones identified as being from early members of our species have been dated to about 315,000 years ago. That indicates *H. sapiens* appeared more than 100,000 years earlier than thought: most researchers have placed the origins of our species in East Africa about 200,000 years ago" (Callaway 2017). For the original write-ups of the find, see: Hublin et al. 2017; Richter 2017. See also: Hobbes 1996 (Part I, ch. 13): "Of the Natural Condition of Mankind as concerning their Felicity and Misery"); Rousseau 1971, 158: "Les philosophes qui ont examiné les fondements de la société ont tous senti la nécessité de remonter jusqu'à l'état de nature" (The philosophers who have examined the foundations of society all felt it necessary to go back all the way to the state of nature), 162 : "en le [l'homme] considérant [. . .] tel qu'il a dû sortir des mains de la nature, je vois un animal moins fort que les uns, moins agile que les autres, mais, à tout prendre, organisé le plus avantageusement de tous" (by considering the human being as he had to have come out of the hands of nature, I see an animal less strong than some, less agile than others, but, all in all, the most advantageously organized of all). (Translations are, if not otherwise stated, by myself.)
2 Europe and "the West", more broadly, constitute my sole cultural-linguistic remit throughout this essay, which does not mean that any and all insights generated herein may not also apply to other linguistic and cultural (including non-"Western" Indo-European) communities. I simply do not know enough about, say, Sino-Tibetan, Austronesian, or Afro-Asiatic cultures and languages to be able to reliably and credibly speak about them.
3 See, for instance: Huys 1996; Garland 1995, *passim*; Boswell, 1988, *passim*; Schmidt 1983/84; Eyben 1980/81; Plato (1930, 462–463 [460c]): "but the offspring of the inferior, and any of those of the other sort who are born defective, they will properly dispose of in secret, so that no one will know what has become of them. That is the condition [. . .] of preserving the purity of the guardians' breed"; Aristotle (1932, 632–633 [1335b]): "As to exposing or rearing the children born, let there be a law that no deformed child shall be reared"; Plutarch (1914, 254–255): "the elders of the tribes examined the infant, and if it was well-built and sturdy, they ordered the father to rear it [. . .] but if it was ill-born and deformed, they sent it to the so-called Apothetae, a chasm-like place at the foot of Mount Taygetos, in the conviction that the life [ζην] of that which nature had

I only mention all of this, however – since this is neither an essay in human evolution, classical scholarship or historical linguistics – in order to forestall potential objections to my reflections based on what might be called a *"philosophus ait* attitude" toward the two "godfathers" or "patron saints" of our symposium: Michel Foucault and Giorgio Agamben, whose philosophical-historical and conceptual-archaeological work on the biopolitical has certainly determined much contemporary academic thinking on the subject. What I mean is that whatever I may have to contribute to the discussion of the biopolitical today will neither necessarily be beholden to nor authoritatively guided by the parameters staked out by Foucault and Agamben, even though I shall engage with them, and have recourse to Foucault in particular, on my own terms. Let me briefly clarify this.

As I understand those parameters, they are constituted by the following core propositions – and I start with Foucault:
1. From the classical age onwards, the West has witnessed a profound transformation of its mechanisms of power [. . .] One could say that the old right to *make* die or to *let* live has been replaced by the power to *make* live or *reject* into death.[4]
2. For millennia, man remained what he had been for Aristotle: a living animal that was also capable of a political existence; modern man, by contrast, is an animal in whose politics his very life as a living being is at stake.[5]

What this means, according to Foucault, is nothing less than the "irruption of life into history [. . .] the irruption of the phenomena specific to the life of the human species into the orders of knowledge and power."[6] Foucault pithily surmises, "Undoubtedly, for the first time in history, the biological is reflected in the political."[7] In light of this perceived momentous *transformation* and the ostensible advent of the *biological* as such, Foucault defines biopolitics as

---

not well equipped at the very beginning for health [ευεξίαν] and strength, was of no advantage either to the state or itself."
4 Foucault (1976, 179): "l'Occident a connu depuis l'âge classique une très profonde transformation de ces mécanismes du pouvoir"; Foucault (1976, 181): "On pourrait dire qu'au vieux droit de *faire* mourir ou de *laisser* vivre s'est substitué un pouvoir de *faire* vivre ou de *rejeter* dans la mort."
5 Foucault (1976, 188): "L'homme, pendant des millénaires, est resté ce qu'il était pour Aristote: un animal vivant et de plus capable d'une existence politique; l'homme moderne est un animal dans la politique duquel sa vie d'être vivant est en question."
6 Foucault (1976, 186): "ce ne fut rien de moins que l'entrée de la vie dans l'histoire [. . .] des phénomènes propres à la vie de l'espèce humaine dans l'ordre du savoir et du pouvoir."
7 Foucault (1976, 187): "Pour la première fois sans doute dans l'histoire, le biologique se réfléchit dans le politique".

the endeavour, begun in the eighteenth century, to rationalize the problems presented to governmental practice by the phenomena characteristic of a group of living human beings constituted as a population: health, sanitation, birth-rate, longevity, race [. . .] (Foucault 1994, 73)

Drawing on the work of Foucault, among others, Agamben's virtually first order of business in the construction of his own theory of biopolitics, in turn, consists in what amounts to a wholesale debunking of Foucault's entire biopolitical argument (something that Agamben's cautious and ostensibly deferential tone should not inveigle us into overlooking or glossing over): "The Foucauldian thesis will", Agamben observes toward the beginning of his 1995 magnum opus *Homo Sacer: Sovereign Power and Bare Life*,

> have to be corrected or, at least, completed, in the sense that what characterizes modern politics is not so much the inclusion of *zoē* in the *polis* – which is, in itself, absolutely ancient – nor simply the fact that life as such becomes a principal object of the projections and calculations of State power. Instead the decisive fact is that [. . .] bare life – which is originally situated at the margins of the political order – gradually begins to coincide with the political realm."[8]

Several contextually relevant things happen in this signal passage:

First, Agamben rejects Foucault's diagnosis of an epochal "transformation of the mechanisms of power" in the eighteenth century in conjunction with the "irruption of life into history" and the "orders of knowledge and power". For if the latter is "absolutely ancient", as Agamben notes, then so must be what Foucault calls "biopolitics" in its entirety, insofar as it is premised precisely on the "irruption of life" into politics. In other words, biopolitics as conceived of by Foucault has been with us all along, according to Agamben, and in no way defines the post-classical, modern world.

Second, Agamben anchors his rejection of Foucault's approach in the fundamental and categorical distinction between the already mentioned concepts of βιος and ζωη – which he adopts as the bedrock of his own, idiosyncratic biopolitical conception of "the Modern" *qua* gradual coincidence of the two – *and* implies that Foucault's epochal argument concerning the "irruption of life" into the political refers to and aims specifically at ζωη, that is, precisely, the sub-titular "bare life [la nuda vita]" of *Homo Sacer* – "natural life [. . .] as such" as opposed to βιος, understood as "form of life" or "particular way of life", including "political life" (1995, 1). At which point we enter somewhat muddy waters on a number of levels.

---

[8] Agamben (1995, 9). The other major thinkers staking out the conceptual backdrop to Agamben's *Homo Sacer* are Hannah Arendt, Walter Benjamin and Carl Schmitt.

To begin with, Agamben's reading of Aristotle in particular – mediated through Hannah Arendt and Walter Benjamin, among others – whence he most overtly derives the categorical distinction between ζωη or "bare life" and βιος or "form of life", is patently misleading, to say the least, as any reader of Aristotle will immediately recognize. To offer just two examples from *Nicomachean Ethics* (which Agamben does not cite):

1. [. . .] if we declare that the function of man is a certain form of life [ζωην τινα], and define that form of life as the exercise of the soul's faculties and activities [. . .][9]
2. [. . .] our definition accords with the description of the happy man as one who "lives well" [ευ ζην] or "does well"; for it has virtually identified happiness with a form of good life [ευζωια] or doing well.[10]

In both instances ζωη or its cognates are used where, according to Agamben, βιος ought to be expected. Thus, when Agamben claims that Aristotle "would have never used the term *zoē*" when speaking of the various "kinds of life" in the polis, he would appear to be wrong plain and simple – intentionally and strategically so, we have to assume, given his erudition in matters classical and given the fact that an even cursory perusal of Aristotle's writings will yield the above "data points".[11]

Now, the significance of this misreading lies not in its ostensible tendentiousness *per se* – analysing which shall not be my concern here – but in the fact that it cannot but entangle Agamben in self-contradiction, which, in turn, invalidates his critique of Foucault's biopolitical thinking. For in order to be able to "correc[t] or,

---

[9] Aristotle (1926, 32–33 [1098a]):"ανθρωπου δε τιθεμεν εργον ζωην τινα, ταυτην δε ψυχης ενεργειαν και πραξεις μετα λογου".

[10] Aristotle (1926, 36–39 [1098b]): "συναδει δε τω λογω και το ευ ζην και το ευ πραττειν ταν εθδαιμονα; σχεδον γαρ ευζωια τις ειρηται και ευπραχια." Incidentally, Liddell and Scott's standard Greek-English Lexicon lists "way of life" as one of the meanings of ζωη, offering two passages from Herodotus's *Histories* by way of example (4, 112): "and both lived the same sort of life, hunting and plundering [ζοεν εζωον την αυτην]"; 114: "our present way of life [ζόην τοιήνδε εχωμεν]".

[11] Agamben (1995, 1). So is, by the way – as the above-offered quotes from *Nicomachean Ethics* saliently document – Hannah Arendt, when she observes in *The Human Condition* (1958, 97): "[. . .] it is of this life, *bios* as distinguished from mere *zoe*, that Aristotle said that it 'somehow is a kind of *praxis*'." Agamben has recourse to Arendt's work throughout *Homo Sacer* – the very term "bare life" is indebted to Arendt's "mere *zoe*" and, more immediately, to Benjamin's "bloßes Leben": "This is why it is not by chance that Benjamin [. . .] concentrates on the bearer of the link between violence and law, which he calls 'bare life' (*bloßes Leben*)" (1995, 65). For an excellent critique of Agamben's *Homo Sacer*, see also Finlayson 2010.

at least, complet[e]" Foucault's transformational thesis and to prove him wrong on the question of the inclusion of "*zoē* in the polis – which is", according to Agamben and *contra* Foucault "absolutely ancient" – Agamben has to go against his own claim that βιος and ζωη are categorically distinct and that Aristotle "would have never used the term *zoē*" in connection with "kinds of life", that is, Agamben actually needs to acknowledge, *in line with Aristotle*, that βιος and ζωη, while distinct in certain respects, do in fact overlap in certain others, and that, consequently, ζωη will have been part and parcel of βιος since antiquity. At the same time, however, in order to be able to pin Foucault's putative error on his equally putative misunderstanding of the historical significance of ζωη within the polis in particular, Agamben ostensibly needs to presuppose a categorical or essential distinction between ζωη and βιος, positing – in the face of incontrovertible textual-historical evidence to the contrary and flatly contradicting himself – that "[i]n the classical world [. . .] natural life [that is, *zoē*] is excluded from the *polis*" (Agamben 1995, 2).

But does Foucault in fact mean specifically ζωη, as presumably strictly opposed to βιος, in conceiving of biopolitics as "governmental practice" targeting its population's "health" and "longevity", among other aspects, in the first place? Would it even make sense to strictly separate ζωη from βιος in the human realm? For, as already Aristotle pointed out in the context of his multiple discussions of the four "causes": "a man takes exercise for the sake of his health [. . .] because he thinks it good for his health [υγιεια]." And it is good, fundamentally, because good health is an inexorable part of a particular "form of life", namely, the good life *qua* both βιος and ευζωια.[12] It seems to me, then, that Foucault's notion of biopolitics, which is certainly also concerned with the biological, anatomical, et cetera, is equally as concerned with what Agamben reductively conceives of as βιος – after all, the health and well-being of an entire population – an entire *polis* – in and of itself implies βιος. Not to mention the fact that we would be hard pressed to come up with even a single instance of presumably "bare" human ζωη that could or would *not* have transpired as an organic part of some sort of human βιος. In other words, to live, broadly understood, always already implies living a certain "kind of life".

These preliminary remarks shall be sufficient by way of a rough outline of the conceptual matrix underlying our current discussion of the biopolitical, and, more importantly, by way of documenting that Foucault's biopolitical endeavour has in no way been invalidated by Agamben, whose own theory of "sovereign power and bare life" it inevitably continues structurally to underlie. Neither endeavour, however,

---

[12] Aristotle (1929, 128–131 [194b]). See also Aristotle (1933, 208–211 [1013a–1013b]): "fat-reducing, purging, drugs and instruments are causes of health [υγιειας]."

ought to be taken at face value given the conceptual-historical problems outlined above.

What seems to be at stake here above all, in my view, is the question of how the singular life relates to the particular life it is distinct from and to the universal life of the group it is part of – be it in terms of an alleged comprehensive gradual coincidence of life and the polis as Agamben has it, or in terms of the perceived ability of the powers that be "to make live and reject into death" as per Foucault. It is the latter in particular that I wish to begin from.

II

"On pourrait dire qu'au vieux droit de *faire* mourir ou de *laisser* vivre s'est substitué un pouvoir de *faire* vivre ou de *rejeter* dans la mort."[13] I quote the original here solely in order to demonstrate that the English translation faithfully replicates the pivotal *figure* marking Foucault's pithy dictum, whose historical truth value I do not address as such. And, by the way, the chiastic imbalance introduced by the phrase "rejeter dans la mort" (instead of the expected "laisser mourir") to me implies a kind of a cavalier or off-handed, almost random and occasional "discarding" of certain lives in contrast to the deliberate, willful and intentional "faire mourir".

Now, suffice it to note that the dictum's major transformational premise can and has been contested by at least one authoritative reader, to wit: Agamben. And, incidentally, one does indeed wonder how Foucault's entire biopolitical framework might have to be rewritten in view of a statement such as: "the era of the great depredations, such as famines and plagues [. . .] was over before the French Revolution", which subtends and informs Foucault's transformational thesis and which has conclusively been historically disproved by the COVID-19 pandemic.[14] Besides, it is worth keeping in mind that Foucault's entire archaeology of knowledge, of which his biopolitical theory is a part, may apply – within limits having to do with demography, class, socio-economics, et cetera – to cultural-political contexts such as modern England and France, while being utterly misplaced with regard to, say, the Soviet Union, under Stalin in particular, or the United States – pre-Civil War, to be sure, but also for much of its subsequent history, where slaves and many of their descendants

---
13 Foucault (1976, 181): "One could say that the old right to *make* die or to *let* live has been replaced by the power to *make* live or *reject* into death."
14 Foucault (1976, 187): "l'ère des grands ravages de la faim et de la peste [. . .] est close avant la Révolution française."

have certainly *not* benefited from the putative *"make* live" phenomenon – not to mention contemporary political systems that are not primarily concerned with *"making* live" in the first place. Thus, for me the abiding force of Foucault's dictum lies, *a fortiori*, in its make-up as a *figure of thought* characterized by a chiasmic transposition – *"make* die and *let* live" being replaced by *"make* live and *reject* into death" – whose very tropicality functions as a conceptual, interpretive handle malleably deployable in any number of contexts – such as in the United States today, which will be my main focus for the remainder of this chapter. More specifically, it seems to me that Foucault's handle allows us *metaphorically* to frame and thus creatively to make sense of our own contemporary moment – which may or may not, in turn, help us adumbrate the limits of Foucault's biopolitical thought. (A similar metaphoricity or rather metonymicity, by the way, marks Agamben's stipulation of "the [extermination] camp as biopolitical paradigm" or "'Nomos' of the Modern" *tout court* [Agamben 1995, 166–180]).

Applying Foucault's handle to the contemporary US, then, one could say that what we have been witnessing since the inception of Black Lives Matter in 2013 and, emphatically, since the onslaught of the COVID-19 pandemic coupled with Black Lives Matter and the pushback it has received from large swaths of the powers-that-be is the *concomitant*, rather than successive – as Foucault has it – unfolding of the "right to *make* die or to *let* live" vis-à-vis some and "the power to *make* live or *reject* into death" vis-à-vis others in a most blatant and palpable fashion.[15] Whereby the chiastic "make *live* and *reject* into death"-*cum*-"*make* die and *let* live" figure gets metonymically-metaphorically focalized in the most basic activity of human life, namely, *breathing* – granted as it is by "governmental practice" to some, who are *made to breathe*, while being forcibly withheld from others, who are *made to suffocate*. From the vantage point of today's US in particular, *breathing* can be said to have assumed the position of a kind of biopolitical "paradigm" or "Nomos" – previously held, according to Agamben, by "the camp."

---

15 Black Lives Matter was born as a hashtag on social media – originated by civil rights activists Alicia Garza, Patrisse Cullors, and Opal Tometi – in July 2013 in response to George Zimmerman's acquittal in the shooting death of teenager Trayvon Martin in Sanford, Florida, in February 2012. The movement achieved national recognition in the wake of the killing through asphyxiation of forty-four-year-old Eric Garner by police officer Daniel Pantaleo in New York City, as well as the fatal shooting of eighteen-year-old Michael Brown by police officer Darren Wilson in Ferguson, Missouri, in July and August 2014, respectively. Black Lives Matter dominated national headlines – together with the COVID-19 pandemic – throughout 2020 in the wake of the killing, also through asphyxiation, of George Floyd by police officer Derek Chauvin in Minneapolis, Minnesota, on 25 May 2020. "COVID-19" stands for: "Coronavirus disease 2019", which is caused by "severe acute respiratory syndrome coronavirus 2" or "SARS-CoV-2". The pandemic originated in Wuhan, China toward the end of 2019.

Analogously, Auschwitz – the *emblematic* or *symbolic* camp *par excellence* – can be said topically to have been replaced by the *figure* of George Floyd, in whom the intersection and concatenation of a certain kind of "governmental practice" with the workings of COVID-19 have assumed the tragically *metonymic, emblematic* or *symbolic* contours of someone who died of a lack of oxygen during the COVID-19 pandemic: like millions of others across the globe, to be sure, albeit *not* due to illness, like the latter, but, rather, due to a "governmental practice" that affects, *mutatis mutandis*, a sizable number of the US population and that should, according to Foucault's interpretation of history, be above all concerned with *making live* rather than *rejecting into death* – a "practice" that predominantly targets African-Americans and that manifests itself in lethal ways not necessarily restricted to asphyxiation, which can be said to be but its most agonizing face, epitomized, precisely, by George Floyd. (That the "camp", too, employed the "governmental practice" of death by asphyxiation, moreover, points up a haunting historical continuity and gives pause as far as the arguable force of Agamben's arguments, in turn, may be concerned.) Signally, "governmental practice" presumably concerned with the just application of triage amid the pandemic has equally affected black and brown people in the US in a disproportionately negative way.

Who gets to breathe and how, and who gets to suffocate and how, has emerged as the key biopolitical question of our time – a question that concerns, to quote Foucault, "health [. . .] longevity" and, above all, "race" among the population and that has recently been taken up most forcefully and poignantly by Ta-Nahesi Coates, among others, who has made it *the* "question of [his] life": "how one should live within a black body" in a society whose "governmental practice" would appear *not* to be primarily concerned with *making* black bodies breathe – least of all, ostensibly, with "making it easier / for us to breathe", to also quote the concluding lines of "A Small Needful Fact", Ross Gay's elegy for Eric Garner.[16]

Coates's and Gay's interventions in the biopolitical through the prism of the contemporary African-American experience in the US emphatically underscore that "bare life" is but a fiction at best and cannot be conceived of other than as always already transpiring as a "form of life" – an entwinement saliently expressed in Coates's emphasis on *"how* one should live" and in Gay's subtle distinction between breathing as such and a certain kind of, "easier", breathing, which is precisely what is centrally at stake for both authors above and beyond one's putatively "bare" physiology. And let me reiterate one more time that we are dealing in the

---

[16] Coates (2015, 12). Gay's 2015 poem is available at and is cited according to: https://www.split thisrock.org/poetry-database/poem/a-small-needful-fact.

figurative here – metaphorical, metonymical, symbolic and emblematic – in the sense that any and all speculations – theoretical, fictional, poetic – as here undertaken and attested to, ought perforce, as Hannah Arendt put it, *not* to presume, as a matter of course, to be able to offer concrete solutions or "answers [in] matters of practical politics" (Arendt 1998, 5). This does not mean, of course, as James Finlayson points out, that those who theorize, fictionalize, or poeticize cannot "lobby for practical change like anyone else"; it only means that they "do so not as experts" but "as individual citizens" (Finlayson 2010, 126).

III

It is to two such individual citizens that I wish to turn on this final leg of my speculative journey, both of whom have more or less concomitantly responded to the globally headline-making killing of George Floyd in Minneapolis, Minnesota, on 25 May 2020 – an event that, for many, epitomized the hard truth that while all members of the population are presumably equal, some are more equal than others, to quote George Orwell, and that the "governmental practice" of making live did and does not seem to apply to people like George Floyd, the putative "transformation in the mechanisms of power" we have arguably witnessed since the classical age notwithstanding.

Terrance Hayes's gripping elegy for George Floyd – a poetic exercise in biopolitical denunciation published on 22 June 2020, in *The New Yorker* – concludes with the verse: "Emmet till the end of time," which emblematically fuses a line from Prince's 1987 song "Adore" with the name and historical figure of Emmet Till – notoriously lynched at the age of fourteen in 1955 in Mississippi – to project a bleak future in which the black body will be made to die "till the end of time."[17] As in Gay's elegy for Eric Garner, who died as a result of an illegal chokehold applied by a police officer, the eponymous protagonist of Hayes's elegy is made metaphorically to "inhale" "dirt" and, consequently, asphyxiate – ironically, underneath the "ring of fire" of the officer's intimated Apple Watch in line 7, whose "fire ring" is correlated with physical fitness and strength rather than its opposite, as fatally experienced by George Floyd.

What Hayes stages in his canon- or round-like poem that weaves together multiple overlapping voices and citations is, fundamentally, biopolitics in painfully witnessed action: unlike Foucault's "transformation of the mechanisms of power",

---

[17] For a more detailed analysis of this poem, see Eskin (2022, 255–260). For copyright reasons, Hayes' "George Floyd" cannot be quoted in full here.

the "transformation" depicted by Hayes does not simply "reject into death" while being concerned with "making live" overall, but brings about *active* killing: "the bullet point / of transformation both kills and fires / the life of the party" (ll. 13–14) – making some die and, perversely, contributing to the heightened vivaciousness, that is, very joy of living, on the part of others – like "the man kneeling in blue" (l. 3), that notorious representative of "governmental practice" *par excellence*. George Floyd's treatment at the hands of "the man kneeling in blue", emphatically as portrayed by Hayes, starkly epitomizes a "mechanism of power" that, Hayes poetically adumbrates, has *not* been and will *not*, "till the end of time" (l. 29), be concerned with making black lives live and breathe nor even with occasionally rejecting them into death, but with willfully and intentionally making them die, pure and simple.

What is but alluded to, intimated and poetically 'scrambled' in Hayes's poem, gets articulated full-blast and propaganda-style in Claudia Rankine's "Weather" – a poetic call to arms written immediately following the killing of George Floyd and published within a day of Hayes's poem, on 21 June 2020, on the front page of the *New York Times Book Review*, and explicitly looking out to the US November elections later that year.[18] Unlike Hayes, Rankine links the "asphyxiation" (l. 12) of George Floyd to the current pandemic and denounces the biopolitical inequalities it has thrown into particularly stark relief head-on: "I mean / a form of governing that deals out death / and names it living" (ll. 23–25) – whereby the "governmental practice" here referred to concerns both the inequitable allocation and distribution of medical treatments in view of COVID-19 at the state and federal levels, as well as the inequitable meeting out of justice on the part of state, federal and local organs of governance such as the police: "Six feet / under for underlying conditions. Black. / Just us and the blues kneeling on a neck / with the full weight of a man in blue" (ll. 6–9). The "underlying conditions" being of course both the implied general state of health of black and brown people in the U.S., who are, for a number of historical and socio-economic reasons, disproportionately affected by obesity, heart disease, diabetes, asthma, et cetera (at least in certain parts of the country), *and* the socio-political conditions under which being a person of colour is, ostensibly, in and of itself, a lethal hazard, as most memorably captured in the ubiquitous quip "driving while black".

Now, the question whether Hayes's and Rankine's poetic assessments are historically valid or correct seems less important in the present context than the very fact that their interventions explicitly belie the notion of an epochal transformation

---

[18] For a more detailed analysis of this poem, see Eskin (2022, 246–247). For copyright reasons, Rankine's "Weather" cannot be quoted in full here.

of the "mechanisms of power" as stipulated by Foucault. Rankine's "a form of governing that deals out death / and names it living," in particular, gives the screw of the Foucauldian figure yet another turn – ironically, squarely against itself: nothing has changed about the primal power "to make die" or "let live", which has remained precisely that, insofar as any putative emphasis on "making live" *is* in fact its very opposite for more than some. Interestingly, it almost seems as though Rankine, who would appear to be well-versed in French postmodern theory – as evidenced by the reference to Nietzsche's famously forgotten umbrella in lines 1–2 ("On a scrap of paper in the archive is written / *I have forgotten my umbrella*"), which Jacques Derrida has made hay of in his 1978 book *Éperons: les styles de Nietzsche* – it almost seems, then, as though Rankine were replying specifically to Foucault by denouncing "a form of governing that deals out death / and names it living".

References

Agamben, Giorgio. *Homo Sacer: Sovereign Power and Bare Life*. Trans. Daniel Heller-Roazen. Stanford, CA: Stanford University Press, 1995.
Arendt, Hannah. *The Human Condition*. Chicago and London: The University of Chicago Press, 1998.
Aristotle. *Metaphysics*. Trans. Hugh Tredennick. 2 vols. Cambridge, MA, and London: Harvard University Press, 1933.
Aristotle. *Nicomachean Ethics*. Trans. Harris Rackham. Cambridge, MA, and London: Harvard University Press, 1926.
Aristotle. *Physics*. Trans. P. H. Wicksteed and F. M. Cornford. 2 vols. Cambridge, MA, and London: Harvard University Press, 1929.
Aristotle. *Politics*. Trans. Harris Rackham. Cambridge, MA, and London: Harvard University Press, 1932.
Boswell, John. *The Kindness of Strangers: The Abandonment of Children in Western Europe from Late Antiquity through the Renaissance*. Chicago and London: The University of Chicago Press, 1988.
Callaway, Ewen. "Oldest *Homo sapiens* Fossil Claim Rewrites Our Species' History." https://www.nature.com/articles/nature.2017.22114.
Coates, Ta-Nehesi. *Between the World and Me*. New York: Spiegel and Grau, 2015.
Eskin, Michael. *Descartes der Metapher: Neun Tauchgänge ins Dichterdasein Durs Grünbeins*. Göttingen: Wallstein, 2022.
Derrida, Jacques. *Éperons: les styles de Nietzsche*. Paris: Flammarion, 1978.
Eyben, Emiel. "Family Planning in Graeco-Roman Antiquity." *Ancient Society*, vol. 11/12 (1980/81): 5–82.
Finlayson, James Gordon. "'Bare Life' and Politics in Agamben's Reading of Aristotle." *The Review of Politics* 72 (2010): 97–126.
Foucault, Michel. *Histoire de la Sexualité I: La volonté de savoir*. Paris: Gallimard, 1976.
Foucault, Michel. "The Birth of Biopolitics." *Ethics: Subjectivity and Truth. Essential Works of Foucault 1954–1984, vol. 1*. Trans. Robert Hurley et al. Ed. Paul Rabinow. New York: The New Press, 1994. 73–80.

Garland, Robert. *The Eye of the Beholder: Deformity and Disability in the Graeco-Roman World*. Ithaca: Cornell University Press, 1995.
Gay, Ross. "A Small Needful Fact." https://www.splitthisrock.org/poetry-database/poem/a-small-needful-fact.
Hayes, Terrance. "George Floyd." *The New Yorker* (22 June 2020): 68.
Hobbes, Thomas. *Leviathan, or The Matter, Forme, & Power of a Common-Wealth Ecclesiasticall and Civill*. Ed. J. C. A. Gaskin. Oxford: Oxford University Press, 1996.
Hublin, Jean-Jacques, et al. "New Fossils from Jebel Irhoud, Morocco and the Pan-African Origin of *Homo sapiens*." *Nature*, vol. 546, no. 7657 (8 June 2017): 289–292.
Huys, Marc. "The Spartan Practice of Selective Infanticide and Its Parallels in Ancient Utopian Tradition." *Ancient Society*, vol. 27 (1996): 47–74.
Liddell, Henry George, Robert Scott, Henry Stuart Jones, and Roderick McKenzie. *A Greek-English Lexicon*. Oxford: Clarendon Press, 1996.
Plato. *Republic*. Trans. Paul Shorey. 2 vols. Cambridge, MA, and London: Harvard University Press, 1930.
Plutarch. *Lives: Theseus and Romulus, Lycurgus and Numa, Solon and Publicola*. Trans. Bernadotte Perrin. Cambridge, MA, and London: Harvard University Press, 1914.
Rankine, Claudia. "Weather." *The New York Times Book Review* (21 June 2020): 1.
Richter, Daniel. "The Age of the Hominin Fossils from Jebel Irhoud, Morocco, and the Origins of the Middle Stone Age." *Nature*, vol. 546, no. 7657 (8 June 2017): 293–296.
Rousseau, Jean-Jacques. *Discours sur les sciences et les arts & Discours sur l'origine et les fondements de l'inégalité parmi les hommes*. Paris: Garnier-Flammarion, 1971.
Schmidt, Martin. "Hephaistos lebt: Untersuchungen zur Frage der Behandlung behinderter Kinder in der Antike." *Hephaistos* vol. 5/6 (1983/84): 133–161.

About the Authors

Timothy Campbell is Professor of Italian in the Department of Romance Studies at Cornell University. He has published extensively on Italian literature and culture with particular focus on their relation to twentieth-century media technology, with articles appearing in *Modern Language Notes* (January 2005) and *Modern Italy* (November 2006). His first monograph, *Wireless Writing in the Age of Marconi* (Minnesota, 2006), is an account of modern poetry and "heroic media" (the telegraph and radio in particular) in Italy and the United Kingdom before and immediately after the First World War. It won the Media Ecology Association's Lewis Mumford Outstanding Scholarship Award in 2007 in the category of Ecology of Technics. Soon after his interest shifted to the burgeoning field of biopolitics with his translation of two of Roberto Esposito's, most important works: *Bios: Biopolitics and Philosophy* (Minnesota, 2008) and *Communitas: The Origin and Destiny of Community* (Stanford, 2009). In 2011 Campbell's *Improper Life: Technology and Biopolitics from Heidegger to Agamben* (Minnesota, 2011) appeared, which was followed by *Biopolitics: A Reader* (Duke, 2013), co-edited with Adam Sitze. In 2017 he published another monograph on biopolitics and philosophy. Titled *The Techne of Giving: Cinema and the Generous Form of Life* (Fordham), the book won the American Association of Italian Studies (AAIS) Book Prize for Film in 2019. More recently, he co-translated with Lia Turtas *Form and Event: Principles for an Interpretation of the Greek World* (Fordham, 2020) by the Italian philologist Carlo Diano. His next monograph, *The Comic Self*, written with Grant Farred, is slated to appear in 2023 from the University of Minnesota Press. From 2009 to 2021 he edited *Commonalities* (Fordham University Press), a series dedicated to publishing works in the field of contemporary European philosophy. His current project is an examination of Italian thought and its vicissitudes during the COVID-19 pandemic.

Thomas Crew has recently gained his doctorate from the University of Cambridge, researching "Visions of Dystopia in German literature". The project is based on four works: Bernhard Kellermann's novel *The Tunnel* (1913), Georg Kaiser's *Gas* trilogy (1917–1920), and two texts by Ernst Jünger: *The Worker* (1932) and *The Glass Bees* (1957). The project traces the genesis and analyses the main features of German dystopian literature, which, until now, has been subsumed under the much broader and poorly defined utopian genre. As a result, German dystopianism has not yet been identified as a coherent body of thought. A primary aim of the project is therefore to establish the field of dystopian research in the German context. Besides novelists and playwrights, close attention is also paid to various contemporary thinkers and philosophers, with a particular emphasis on Walther Rathenau, Gustav Landauer, Friedrich Georg Jünger, and Martin Heidegger. Recent publications include journal articles on the Jungian dimensions of the plays by Ernst Barlach, the question of individuation in Hermann Hesse and Friedrich Nietzsche, and the dystopian credentials of Jünger's novel, *The Glass Bees*. A chapter on Kellermann's *Tunnel* appeared in a volume on Americanism in September 2022. Crew has also published numerous journalistic articles on the political response to the pandemic.

Michael Eskin is an author, critic, translator, philosopher, publisher and co-founder of Upper West Side Philosophers, Inc., in New York City. He has taught at Rutgers, Cambridge and Columbia Universities. His numerous books include: *Nabokovs Version von Puskins "Evgenij Onegin": eine übersetzungs- und fiktionstheoretische Untersuchung* (1994); *Ethics and Dialogue in the Works of Levinas, Bakhtin, Mandel'shtam, and Celan* (2000); *Poetic Affairs: Celan, Grünbein, Brodsky* (2008); *17 Vorurteile, die wir Deutschen gegen Amerika und die Amerikaner haben und die so nicht ganz stimmen können*

(2008); *The DNA of Prejudice: On the One and the Many* (2010; Winner of the Next Generation Book Award for Social Change); *The Wisdom of Parenthood* (2013); *Yoga for the Mind: An New Ethic for Thinking & Being* (2013; with Kathrin Stengel, Winner of the Living Now Book Award); *"Schwerer werden. Leichter sein" – Gespräche um Paul Celan. Mit Durs Grünbein, Gerhard Falkner, Aris Fioretos und Ulrike Draesner* (2020); *Descartes der Metapher: Neun Tauchgänge ins Dichterdasein Durs Grünbeins* (2022); *On Writing Philosophy: A Manifesto* (2023; forthcoming). His essays, reviews and translations have appeared in *TLS*, *World Literature Today* and *The New Yorker*. A frequent guest on talk radio, Michael Eskin lectures regularly on cultural, philosophical and literary subjects across the US and Europe.

Meelis Friedenthal studied theology at the Universities of Tartu and Heidelberg. He received his doctorate from the University of Tartu in 2008 for his thesis "Tractatus moralis de oculo of the Tallinn City Archives". The dissertation presents a transcription, translation and commentary of a fourteenth-century manuscript containing a moral allegorical treatise on vision and the eye. Between 2008 and 2013, Friedenthal worked on a project at the University of Tartu Library on the intellectual history of the Baltic provinces during periods of the Swedish and Russian empire. In addition, Friedenthal has led a project to describe the watermarks and paper of the seventeenth-century Tartu University printing house. In 2014–2015, Friedenthal was a research fellow at the Lichtenberg-Kolleg (University of Göttingen), on a project to study the concept of tolerance in early medieval German universities. From 2015–2020, Friedenthal was a researcher in the Pro Futura Scientia programme at Uppsala University (SCAS), working on early modern university disputations. Together with Robert Seidel and Hanspeter Marti, he edited a major collection of articles on the early modern disputation genre (*Early Modern Disputations and Dissertations in an Interdisciplinary and European Context*). He currently works at the University of Tartu as a researcher of early modern intellectual history. In addition to academic publications, Friedenthal has also published short stories, plays and novels. His second novel, *The Willow King*, was awarded the European Union Prize for Literature in 2013 and is translated into many languages.

Marge Käsper is Lecturer of French Language and Linguistics and Researcher in French Studies at the University of Tartu, Estonia. Her research focuses on socio-cultural discourse analysis, mainly in the framework of French Discourse Analysis methods. In her PhD thesis she developed a methodology for a contrastive discourse analysis of the academic book review genre in Estonian and French socio-cultural contexts. She has worked extensively on media discourse, publishing articles on various topics and discourse genres represented in traditional as well as in social media. Currently, she studies COVID-19 crisis discourses together with Raili Marling in the Estonian Research Council grant "Imagining Crisis Ordinariness". In this research, they have gathered a COVID-19 crisis media corpus where they have compared Estonian, French and American media representation of scientists, remote work, and other aspects of the health crisis media coverage. Käsper has also researched the use of diverse linguistic units in socio-cultural reference and social representations in discourse: the French preposition *selon* (according to) to study the health crisis information mechanisms, the interjection *hélas*! (alas) to study the emotional impact of COVID-19 crisis on people, modal verbs *devoir* (must) and *pouvoir* (can) to study the ideologies promoted in the health crisis media, etc.

Frank Kraushaar held positions as research assistant at the Institute for Sinology of LMU Munich (1999–2005), lecturer and senior research fellow of Chinese literature and history at the University of Latvia (2005–2009), as Professor of Chinese Studies at Tallinn University (2009–2015) and as professor of Chinese literature at the University of Latvia (2014–2020). Since 2018 he is editor of the *Journal of the European Association for Chinese Studies*. His research focuses on classical Chinese poetry, its reception and translation into Western modernity and on modern and contemporary Chinese poetry written following patterns of classical prosody. His most recent publication is a book in German: *Fern von Geschichte und verheißungsvollen Tagen. Neoklassizistische Cyberlyrik im ChinaNetz und der Stil des Lizilizilizi (2000 – 2020)* (Distant from History and Auspicious Days. Neoclassicist Cyberpoetry in the ChinaNet and the Poetic Diction of Lizilizilizi (2000–2020)). Bochum/Freiburg i.Br.: Projektverlag, 2022 (https://chinesestudies.eu/?p=5200)). Other recent publications include: "Diesseits der Aura: Vom Umbruch klassischer ostasiatischer Naturästhetik in der klassizistischen Cyberlyrik des Lizi." Henrieke Stahl (ed.): *Natur in der Lyrik und Philosophie des Anthropozäns: zwischen Diagnose, Widerstand und Therapie*. Münster: In Press, 2021; "Neoklassizistische Cyberlyrik im ChinaNetz – Übersetzung und Hypothese." *Hefte für Ostasiatische Literatur* (2020); (2017) "Fighting Swaying Imbalances of Powers: The Transformation of Spiritual Freedom in Tang Tales into Individual Freedom in Hou Hsiao-hsien's Film *The Assassin*." *Acta Universitatis Carolinae* (Prague, 2017).

Raili Marling is Professor of English Studies at the University of Tartu, Estonia. Her main areas of research are the politics of affect, representations of gender and neoliberalism in contemporary literature, gender and feminist theory. Marling currently leads an Estonian Research Council research project on the representations and representability of crises. Within this project, she works on contemporary literature, affect and neoliberalism, comparing them in American, French and Estonian literature and culture. Her most recent publications in different international journals and collections have tackled the representations of minor affects in contemporary American fiction by women as well as the possibility of interpersonal connection and intimacy in the context of social precarity. In parallel, she has also worked on the possibility of combing affect and discourse, most recently in the analysis of media texts in the context of the COVID-19 pandemic. In the past, Marling has also written about modernist women's writing, modernism and masculinities, masculinity crisis discourses, the travel of feminist theory and gender equality discourses. In addition to her academic work, she has collaborated with the Estonian Ministry of Social Affairs on gender equality initiatives and written literary criticism and opinion pieces in Estonian media.

Daniele Monticelli is a Professor of Semiotics and Translation Studies at Tallinn University. His wide research interests include translation history, comparative literature and contemporary critical theory with focus on the works of Agamben, Badiou and Rancière. He has published widely on these topics. More recently his work has focused on the potentialities and constraints of translation in contexts of radical cultural and social change – the construction and deconstruction of national identities in Central and Eastern Europe at the end of the nineteenth and the beginning of the twentieth centuries, censorship and dissidence under communism and the contemporary debates on world literature and translation. He has developed Juri Lotman's understanding of translation into a general framework for the study of translation and translators as agents of cultural change and seeded translation studies with concepts from poststructuralist and critical theory. He is the co-editor of the collective volumes and special issues *Between Cultures and Texts. Itineraries in Translation History* (2011), *Testo e metodo. Prospettive teoriche sulla letteratura italiana* (2011), *L'incipit et l'explicit. Perpectives interdisciplinaires* (2017), *Italianistica 2.0 Tradizione e innovazione* (2020) *Translation Under*

Communism (2022), the *Routledge Handbook of the History of Translation Studies* (forthcoming). He is currently the head of the research project "Translation in History, Estonia 1850–2010: Texts, Agents, Institutions and Practices" (2021–2025). He has authored literary translations from Estonian into Italian and regularly publishes essays in cultural journals and Estonian newspapers.

Marko Pajević took up an EU funded Professorship of German Studies at the University of Tartu in January 2018 after holding positions at the Sorbonne, Paris IV, at Queen's University Belfast as well as Royal Holloway and Queen Mary, Universities of London. He has published widely on poetics, with (co-)edited volumes on *Paul Celan Today. A Companion* (Berlin/Boston 2021), *Mehrsprachigkeit und das Politische. Interferenzen in zeitgenössischer deutschsprachiger und baltischer Literatur* (Tübingen 2020), *German and European Poetics after the Holocaust* (Rochester, NY 2012) and on *Poésie et musicalité. Liens, croisements, mutations* (Paris 2007). He wrote monographs on Paul Celan, *Zur Poetik Paul Celans. Gedicht und Mensch – Die Arbeit am Sinn* (Heidelberg 2000), and Franz Kafka, *Kafka lesen. Acht Textanalysen* (Bonn 2009). At the heart of his work stands the development of a *poetological anthropology*, as presented most prominently in the monograph *Poetisches Denken und die Frage nach dem Menschen. Grundzüge einer poetologischen Anthropologie* (Freiburg i. Br. 2012) and the essay *Poetisch denken. Jetzt* (Vienna 2022), in English translation *Poetic thinking. Now* (New York 2023). His interest in "Thinking Language" became manifest in two British Academy-funded projects on Wilhelm von Humboldt and Henri Meschonnic, resulting in Special Issues of *Forum for Modern Language Studies* (Humboldt, 2017, 53/1) and *Comparative Critical Studies* (Meschonnic, 2018, 15/3), and *The Meschonnic Reader. A Poetics of Society* (Edinburgh 2019) and finds a continuation in his edited volume *The Abyss as a Concept for Cultural Theory. A Comparative Exploration* (Leiden 2023). This is part of his overarching research project, see APT (Academia for Poetic Thinking): apt.ut.ee.

Sherryl Vint is Professor of Media and Cultural Studies, and a Professor and the Chair of English, at the University of California, Riverside, where she directs the Speculative Fictions and Cultures of Science programme. She was a founding editor of *Science Fiction Film and Television* and is currently an editor for the journal *Science Fiction Studies* and the book series *Science and Popular Culture*. She is the author of *Bodies of Tomorrow* (2007), *Animal Alterity* (2010), *The Wire* (2013), *Science Fiction: A Guide to the Perplexed* (2014); *Science Fiction: The Essential Knowledge* (2020) and *Biopolitical Futures in Twenty-First Century Speculative Fiction* (2021), as well as the co-author of *The Routledge Concise History of Science Fiction* (2011). Her co-authored book *Programming the Future: Politics, Resistance and Utopia in Speculative TV* will appear in 2022 from Columbia University Press. She has edited multiple books, including most recently *Technologies of Feminist Speculative Fiction: Gender, Artificial Life and the Politics of Reproduction* (2022), *After the Human: Culture, Theory & Criticism in the 21st Century* (2020), and *Science Fiction and Culture Theory: A Reader* (2015). A recipient of the Science Fiction Research Association's Innovative Research and its Lifetime Achievement awards, she is currently working on a research project on speculative finance and speculative fiction.

Betiel Wasihun is a Literary Scholar and a Cultural Theorist as well as a Lecturer at Arden University Berlin. She is interested in the literary and philosophical aspects of cultural phenomena such as competition, betrayal, surveillance, shame and migration in German and English literature, with a focus on the twentieth and twenty-first centuries. From 2021–2022 she was a Postdoctoral Research Fellow working on the AHRC funded project "Knowing the Secret Police: Secrecy and Knowledge in East German Society" (University of Birmingham/Newcastle University), undertaking research at the Stasi Records Archive in Berlin. Before coming to Berlin in 2017 to take up an IPODI Marie Curie Postdoctoral Fellowship at the Institute of Philosophy, History of Literature, Science and Technology at the TU Berlin, she was a Montgomery-DAAD Fellow at Lincoln College and a member of the Faculty of Medieval and Modern Languages at Oxford University. She is the author of the monograph *Gewollt – Nicht-Gewollt: Wettkampf bei Kafka. Mit Blick auf R. Walser und Beckett* (Winter 2010). Her second monograph *Resisting Surveillance: Storytelling, Fiction and Selfhood in the Digital Age* is forthcoming (transcript). Other publications include the edited volume *Narrating Surveillance – Überwachen erzählen* (Ergon 2019) and the co-edited volume *Playing False – Representations of Betrayal* (Peter Lang Oxford). She is currently co-editing a special issue for *Weimarer Beiträge* on surveillance and the constitution of the self.

Index

9/11 8, 141, 143, 155, 161, 164

Adorno, Theodor W. 7, 20, 59–64, 68–69, 71–72, 74–83, 86, 97, 99, 158
Agamben, Giorgio 5–9, 14, 20, 25–39, 41–44, 59, 64, 79–80, 82, 84–86, 91–93, 100–104, 111, 113–122, 125, 127–130, 133–134, 136–138, 158–159, 169, 241–242, 248, 253–259
Allan, John 47, 50–51
America/ American 9, 12, 21, 64–66, 68, 70–72, 76, 81–84, 112, 214, 251, 259
– Americanism 65, 71
– Americanization 64–65, 70
Anthropogenic/ the anthropogenic machine 20, 115, 118–122, 125, 131
anthropology/ anthropological/ anthropologist 94, 97, 102, 123, 127, 234, 239
app 11, 147
Arendt, Hannah 93, 254–255, 260
Aristotle 115–117, 119, 253, 255–256
Asphyxiation 258–259, 261
authoritarianism, authoritarian 3, 15, 19–20, 83, 113, 161, 165, 205, 208, 227, 231
authorities 10, 12, 14, 39, 41, 174, 205, 215, 220, 224–227, 229

Badiou, Alain 93
Bauman, Zygmunt 7, 158, 191
Benjamin, Walter 61, 120, 254–255
Bennett, Jane 138
Bergson, Henri 4
Bentham, Jeremy 6, 14, 189–191
Berlant, Lauren 133, 135, 142, 144
Bezos, Jeff 11
Bhakdi, Sucharit 156, 178
Bible/ biblical 50, 52, 65, 166
big data 9–10, 160, 174, 184, 190–191, 199–200
biodata 185, 190, 195
biology 73, 122–123, 130, 233–234, 239, 252
biometric 85, 163–164, 183–184, 187–188, 193
biopolitics/ biopolitical 1–9, 11–21, 25–29, 31–34, 37–45, 59, 63–64, 70, 78–81, 83–84, 86, 92–94, 101–102, 111–113, 116–118, 122, 124, 130, 133–141, 143, 146, 150–151, 155, 157–161, 168, 173–174, 176, 183, 185, 187–188, 191, 205–208, 210–211, 217–220, 224, 226, 228, 231, 235–236, 239, 241, 243, 247–248, 251–261
biopolitician 5, 95
biopower 6–7, 21, 26, 43–44, 93–94, 124, 134–139, 142, 157–158, 183–185, 187, 190–192, 201, 207, 221, 225, 231, 233, 236, 242, 251
bios/ bíos 8, 26–27, 116, 158, 255
biosecurity (see also security) 28, 38–44
Black Lives Matter 258
Bloch, Ernst 120–121
Bo Hunzi (see Gui Qian)
Boccaccio, Giovanni 25, 29, 34–38, 40, 42, 44, 145
Body 1, 6, 8, 26, 30, 34, 36–37, 55–56, 68, 76, 79, 98, 102, 116–117, 119, 125–126, 128–129, 134, 140–141, 151, 157, 159, 170, 172–173, 184–186, 190–191, 239–240, 243–244, 247–248, 259–260, 265
– biopolitical body 25, 27, 34
– body of the people 4, 39–40, 42–43
– body politic 7, 8, 13, 26, 37, 39, 158
– political body 30–32, 34, 38, 44
– social body 27–28, 32–34, 40–41, 43, 80, 187, 233, 240–242
– use of the body 115, 117, 129
Bokanowski, Maurice 70, 73, 84
bolshevism/ bolshevist 68, 70–72, 80
Braidotti, Rosi 20, 28, 133, 138–139, 141–142
Butler, Judith 8, 20, 28, 92, 133, 135, 140–142, 145

Campenella, Tommaso 74
Camps (concentration camp) 8–9, 35, 82, 158
Canguilhem, Georges 135, 137, 140
Čapek, Karel 33
capitalism/ capitalist (see also surveillance capitalism) 15, 65, 68, 71, 84, 93, 102, 111–112, 117, 124, 126, 128–131, 139–140, 161, 190, 196, 198–199, 201, 209
care 1, 6–7, 17–19, 33, 36, 69, 134, 150–151, 158–160, 167, 171–172, 175, 178, 186–187, 214, 241, 248, 251
– caring 149, 190

Cartesian 134
Castex, Jean 234, 245–246
Censorship 213–214, 221–223, 225, 228
Chauvin, Derek 266
China, Chinese 1–2, 4–5, 7, 15, 20, 55, 68, 83, 175, 187, 205–221, 223–231, 258
chresis 111, 114, 117–120, 122, 125, 127–130
citizen 1, 8, 9, 14, 17, 19, 35, 37–39, 44, 69, 77, 85, 106, 111, 113, 115–116, 127, 130, 134, 160, 166, 187–188, 190, 193, 197, 212, 233–234, 238–239, 245–246, 260
– transparent citizen 9, 160
– biological citizenship 2, 134
– molecular citizenship 134
civil rights 79, 155–156, 160, 164, 169, 178, 258
class struggle 209
Coates, Ta-Nehesi 251, 259
colonialism/ colonial 8, 111, 115, 117, 123, 126, 128, 198–199
– data colonialism 198–201
– post-colonial 8
commercial 18, 111, 211
communism/ communist 4, 60, 63, 68, 70–71, 80, 83–84, 205–207, 209, 225
community 8, 13, 20–21, 29–30, 37, 99, 125, 140, 151, 184, 200, 206, 229, 233–234, 237–248
confinement/ confine 14, 39, 42–43, 138, 224, 237
Confucius, Confucian 230
conspiracy 2–3, 15, 40, 51, 68, 175
constitution 121, 155, 157, 161, 165, 176–179
contagion/ contagious 29, 33, 35–38, 40–42, 50, 92–94, 97–98, 100, 104–105, 150, 151
containment/ contain 2, 38–39, 41–44, 105, 123, 149, 200, 244
control 1, 2, 5–7, 9–13, 16, 19–21, 26–28, 40, 54, 59, 68–70, 71–73, 75–76, 83–84, 86, 113, 123, 125, 129, 134–138, 143, 146, 151, 155–156, 158–161, 165, 168, 171, 173, 183–192, 194, 196, 198–200, 206, 209–210, 212, 214, 225, 228, 231, 242–3, 245–246, 248
– control society / society of control 9, 134, 189–191, 200
corona/ coronavirus 17, 49–50, 52, 54, 111–113, 206, 209, 215, 218–219, 258

COVID-19 (see also SARS-CoV-2) 1–2, 6, 8, 10–11, 13–17, 20–21, 25, 28, 35, 37–38, 41–44, 47, 49, 51, 55, 91–4, 97–106, 111–114, 118–119, 122–123, 126, 130, 133–136, 138, 140, 143–146, 151, 155–157, 159–161, 174–178, 183, 185, 187–188, 192, 200–201, 205–208, 225, 229, 231, 233, 235–236, 247–248, 251, 257–259, 261
cyberpoetry (see also internet poetry) 20, 220, 226

Dasein 114–118, 120–122, 125, 128–129
data colonialism (see under colonialism)
Defoe, Daniel 20, 25, 29, 39, 41–44
dehumanization/ dehumanizing 80, 85, 195–196, 198
Deleuze, Gilles 6–7, 9, 93, 134, 137–141, 189–190, 198
democracy/ democratic 3, 6, 8, 10, 12, 27, 60, 64, 66, 68, 82–85, 112–113, 155, 159–160, 163–165, 169, 171, 175–178, 186, 190, 197, 219, 238, 241, 243–244
Derrida, Jacques 140, 144, 262
Diano, Carlo 20, 91, 93, 95–100, 103–104, 106
dictator/ dictatorial 40–41, 75, 82, 173
– dictatorship 28, 40, 60, 160, 167, 179, 238
digitalization 9–10, 12, 17, 19, 160, 183
disciplinarization/ disciplinary 4, 14, 134, 137, 143, 184, 189–190
– disciplinary society 6, 9, 14, 134, 158, 189
discourse 15–17, 133–136, 170, 176–177, 183, 185, 187, 205, 207–210, 212–214, 216–217, 251
– public discourse 3, 15, 17, 21, 83, 161, 179, 205–206, 208, 211, 217, 220, 228, 231
– discursive 133–134, 189, 208, 221
discrimination 113, 165, 193
disease 15, 26, 31–32, 37–38, 40, 43, 47, 49–56, 67, 73, 76–78, 101, 112, 146, 155, 157, 166, 234, 243, 245, 258, 261
Drosten, Christian 16, 177
dwelling 98, 118, 120, 128
dystopia/ dystopian 11, 20, 59, 61–66, 72, 77–78, 80–82, 84–86, 133, 146, 155, 157, 161, 183, 185, 190, 192–193, 195–196, 201

ecology/ ecological 5, 52, 139
economy/ economic 6, 10–11, 14, 16–19, 51–52, 56, 60, 65–66, 68–69, 71, 73, 83, 111–112,

123–124, 126–127, 130, 145, 149, 157, 160, 168, 173, 178, 192, 206–209, 217, 219, 230, 236–237, 257, 261
– economist 2, 60, 83–84
Eggers, Dave 10
embodiment/ embodied 27, 30, 41, 113, 116, 119, 125, 127, 134, 139, 141–142, 190, 218
emergency 3, 28, 37, 40–41, 100, 112, 130, 143, 207, 210, 219–220
– state of emergency 25, 28, 30, 35, 44, 83, 146, 161
enlightenment/ enlightened 3, 7, 20, 41, 59–60, 63, 75–76, 80, 82, 84, 86, 99, 166, 173
epidemic 18, 25, 27–35, 37–44, 47–50, 52–53, 55–56, 67, 101–102, 113, 156, 175–176, 205–207, 209–210, 214–216, 218–219, 225–226, 230
equality/ equal 219, 251
– inequality 15, 19, 111, 135, 160
Erdrich, Louise 146
Esposito, Roberto 9, 13–14, 20, 92, 103, 137, 140, 233–248
Estonia/ Estonian 4, 9, 17, 47–50, 52
ethics/ ethical 2, 16, 20, 65, 75, 118–119, 125, 129–130, 137–141, 197, 205, 211, 231, 255
eventic form 20, 91, 93, 96–104, 106–107
exception, state of 8, 27–28, 32, 35–38, 43–44, 64, 100, 112–113, 143, 151, 159, 164, 167, 172, 177, 241

fascism/ fascist 60, 63, 68, 70–71, 82, 84, 209
Fang Fang 222, 225
Fassin, Didier 135
Fauci, Anthony 83–84
Ferguson, Neil 83
Fisher, Mark 143
Floyd, George 147, 258–261
Ford, Henry 65–66, 70, 81, 84
form-of-life 20, 111, 115–117, 121–122, 128–129, 131
Foucault, Michael 5–9, 13–14, 20, 25–29, 39–40, 44, 64, 92–93, 112, 124, 133–142, 151, 157–159, 167, 171, 183–186, 188–190, 235–236, 248, 253–260
France, French 1, 16, 20–21, 41, 70, 171, 178, 233–239, 246–248, 257, 262

Freedom 1–2, 6, 10, 14, 28, 36–37, 42, 62, 82–83, 85–86, 94–96, 101, 143, 155–156, 160–161, 164, 167, 170–172, 176, 193, 241, 243

Galen 55
Gates, Bill 83–84
Gay, Ross 251, 259–260
gender 1, 116, 135–136, 141, 219
George, Stefan 81
Germany/ German 2, 4–5, 12–13, 16, 18, 20, 27, 48, 60–63, 65–68, 71, 76–77, 80–83, 85, 120, 140, 146, 155–157, 161–166, 168–169, 175–178, 186, 191, 208, 217, 223–224
Glissant, Édouard 136
Goebbels, Joseph 208
governance 84, 111–113, 118, 122, 124, 130–131, 157, 159, 206, 210, 216, 226, 230, 261
government 8, 12–16, 21, 25–26, 28, 35, 40–41, 44, 60, 67, 69–70, 83, 112, 123, 137, 146, 149, 150, 167, 177–178, 186–188, 197, 206, 208–210, 216, 220–221, 223, 225–227, 229, 233–237, 239, 246–248, 254
– governmental practice 15, 186, 256, 258–261
– governmentality 5–6, 14–15, 44, 159
Gui Qian, cybername Bo Hunzi 222, 227–228
Griffith, Nicola 20, 111, 113, 122, 125, 127–128, 130

Haldane, J.B.S. 67
Hall, Sarah 146
Haraway, Donna 141, 244
Hardt, Michael 93–96, 134, 137–138
Hauptmann, Gerhart 67
Hayes, Terrance 251, 260–261
health/ healthy 1–3, 5, 7, 9, 13–18, 25–28, 35, 38–30, 42–45, 56, 70, 73, 78, 83–84, 99, 101–102, 106, 111–113, 122, 128, 130, 133–134, 143, 148–149, 155–163, 166–171, 173, 175–179, 184–188, 193, 201, 206–208, 218, 233–237, 241–243, 245, 247–248, 251, 253–254, 256, 259, 261
– healthcare 1, 7, 18, 111–112, 134, 150, 155, 158–160, 186, 188
– health policy 3, 63, 155, 167, 174, 183, 191
– health system 155, 157, 165, 167, 169, 173–174
Hegel, Georg Wilhelm Friedrich 115

Heidegger, Martin 93, 98, 114–115, 121–122, 125, 127, 210
Herodotus 255
Hippocrates/ hippocratic 35, 53, 215
Hitler, Adolf 13, 65, 71
Hobbes, Thomas 6, 36–37, 251–252
Homer 25, 30–34, 37, 44
homo sacer 7–8, 26–28, 33, 79, 103, 158, 169, 254–255
Hoover, Herbert 70
Horkheimer, Max 7, 20, 59–63, 68–69, 71–72, 74–5, 77–78, 80, 82, 86, 97, 99, 158
human rights 1, 44, 161, 167–168, 170, 177
humanism/ humanistic 75, 80, 86, 138
Husserl, Edmund 134, 186
Huxley, Aldous 20, 59–86, 145, 157, 160
Huxley, Julian 69

ideology/ ideological 7, 9, 163, 166, 206–207, 209, 210–211, 218
imperialist 71, 209
immunity/ immunitary/ immune/ Immunitas 13, 20, 49, 83, 140, 170–171, 175–176, 233–148
individuality/ individualize/ the individual 2–4, 6–7, 14, 18, 19, 35, 44–45, 63, 69, 72, 75–76, 78–80, 84–86, 92–93, 95, 97, 99, 102, 104–105, 107, 130, 134, 137, 139–140, 142–143, 158, 160, 164, 170, 176, 183, 185–193, 195, 197–198, 201, 209, 216, 226, 231, 234, 240, 243
inequality (see under equality)
infection/ infectious 3, 13, 43, 47, 49–50, 54, 56, 73, 111, 123–124, 126, 147, 149, 171–172, 174, 177
inoperativity 113, 115, 119–122, 128, 130
instrumentalization/ instrumentality/ instrumental 75, 78–79, 85, 155, 161, 164, 211, 220
– instrumental/ instrumentalized reason 7, 74–75, 158
internet poetry (see also cyberpoetry) 205, 211, 217, 231
isolation/ isolated 12, 16, 40, 43–44, 47, 50, 74, 101, 122, 128, 146–150, 194–195, 206, 215–216, 223–224, 239–240
Italy, Italian 8, 20, 28, 50, 60, 68, 83, 91, 93, 100–101, 106, 159, 206, 234, 236, 244

Jaspers, Karl 61
Jünger, Ernst 61, 69, 71, 76, 79, 81, 85–86
Jünger, Friedrich Georg 71

Kaiser, Georg 77, 80
Kant, Immanuel 66
Kellermann, Bernhard 66
Keyserling, Hermann von 81
Kircher, Athanasius 56
Kittler, Friedrich 100
Kjellén, Rudolf 12, 64, 207
Kling, Marc-Uwe 20, 84, 183, 185, 192–203
Kosofsky, Eve: see also Sedgwick, Eve 133, 135
Kubin, Alfred 66

Landauer, Gustav 71
Lang, Fritz 66
Latour, Bruno 92
Lauterbach, Karl 83
Lebenwaldt, Adam von 47, 53–54, 56
Lenin, Vladimir Illich 71
Leninism 209
Li Jia 214–215, 220
Li Wenliang 225
life
– bare life 8, 26–28, 35, 37, 44, 79–80, 82, 86, 91, 100–102, 104, 114–116, 120, 122, 138, 158–159, 254–256, 259
– philosophy of life 4
lifelogging 184, 198
Lizilizilizi (see Zeng Shaoli)
lockdown 9, 11–12, 25, 40, 43, 55, 83, 85, 111, 123, 131, 146, 148, 177–178, 206, 221–223, 225–227, 233, 235
Lucretius 35
Ludendorff, Erich 208
Lukács, Georg 68

Ma Zhaoxu 206
Machiavelli, Niccolò/ Machiavellian 93, 240
Macron, Emmanuel 1, 236, 245
Mao Zedong, Maoist, Maoism 206, 208–209, 211, 213, 218–220
Mandel, Emily St. John 145
Manzoni, Alessandro 20, 25, 29, 39–44
Marcuse, Herbert 61

Marinetti, Filippo Tommaso 74
mask 11, 16–17, 36, 50, 85–86, 92, 94, 99–100, 103, 105–107, 111, 123, 146, 148, 156, 171, 237
materialism/ materialist 138
Mbembe, Achille 8, 159
McKay, Adam 11
McLuhan, Marshal 10
measures (biopolitical) 1–3, 7, 11–17, 20, 32, 35, 37, 39–44, 50, 67, 91, 94, 99–100, 104–107, 112–123, 124, 130, 134, 141, 150–151, 156, 161–162, 164–165, 167–168, 170, 172, 175–178, 184–188, 197, 206, 208, 221, 225–226, 233–234, 237–239, 246–247
media 2–3, 10, 12, 16–17, 19–20, 25, 49, 100, 123, 155–156, 160, 162, 164–165, 171, 174–179, 205–208, 211–212, 210–220, 222, 225–226, 233
– social media 1, 3, 10–13, 15, 17, 21, 145, 175, 178, 184, 234, 247–248, 258
medicalization 9, 17, 18, 27
medicine, medical 2–3, 9, 13, 15, 17–19, 21, 27–31, 33, 35, 38, 40, 42, 47, 50, 53, 55–56, 67–68, 70, 74, 83, 91, 101–103, 156–157, 164, 167, 173, 175, 178, 188, 215, 217, 229, 236–239, 243, 261
Merkel, Angela 2, 156, 175
Merleau-Ponty, Maurice 134
Messianic 94, 120
metaphysics 95, 111, 114–120, 122, 124–125, 128–131
Mill, John Stuart 164
mimesis/ mimetic 93, 103–106, 235
mobilization/mobilize 1–32, 71, 205–207, 209–210, 214, 216–221, 230
modernism 209
modernity/ modern 1, 15, 14, 17–18, 20, 25–27, 35, 39, 43–44, 47–48, 50–56, 62, 64–65, 68, 71–72, 74–76, 79, 81–82, 84, 86, 111–115, 117, 119, 124, 126, 128, 130, 157–158, 161, 163, 175, 191, 199, 205, 209–211, 213, 216–217, 222–224, 228, 230–231, 241, 251, 253–254, 257–258, 262
Mond, Alfred 70, 73, 76–77, 84
Moss, Sarah 133, 146–150
multiplicity 138–139

multitude 31–32, 36, 40, 93–94, 116, 138
Mussolini, Benito 60, 70
myth/ mythical 20, 75, 91–92, 96–97, 99, 103–107, 230
mythology/ mythological 33, 91–92, 97, 106–107, 130, 231
mythologization/ mythologize 91, 93, 104

Nancy, Jean-Luc 9, 102
narrative 17, 19–20, 25, 28–31, 34–35, 37–41, 43–45, 96–97, 127, 130, 133, 143, 146–147, 151, 162, 175, 193, 201, 209, 214, 220
National Socialism 7–8, 60, 158–159, 170–171, 210
Nazi, Nazism 4, 35, 61, 69, 82, 121, 140
necropolitics 8, 159
Negri, Antonio 93–96, 134, 137–138
neoliberalism/ neoliberal 6, 16, 93, 112–113, 124, 130–131, 134, 136, 139, 142–143, 184
New Man, the 72, 78, 81, 85
Neyrat, Frédéric 248
Niekisch, Ernst 68
Nietzsche, Friedrich 4, 191, 262
Niu Suge 218–221, 223
Nixon, Rob 144
Nunez, Sigrid 145

Oedipus 25, 29–30, 32–34, 38, 44–45, 105
ontology/ ontological 94–95, 113, 115, 138
opacity/ opaque 10, 12, 133, 135–137, 140, 183, 185, 192, 197
open society 3, 159
organicism/ organic/ organicist 4, 157, 207, 219, 242, 256
Ortega y Gasset, José 61
Orwell, George 59, 68, 157, 260

pandemic 1–4, 6, 8–13, 15, 17, 19–20, 25, 28, 35, 37, 41–43, 47, 49–51, 59, 83–85, 91–94, 97–107, 111–113, 118–119, 122, 126, 130, 133–134, 136, 139, 141, 151, 177–178, 185, 187–188, 192, 200–201, 205, 211–215, 217–218, 220–222, 225, 230–231, 233–234, 251, 257–259, 261
Paracelsus 244
parrhesia 137, 177

paternalizing 1
people's war 205–207, 209–210, 214, 217, 219, 225–226, 229, 231
Perniola, Mario 91, 106–107
pestilence 29–31, 33–35
Petersen, Wolfgang 151
Pharma 11, 15, 18
Plague 13–14, 20, 25–45, 47–53, 55–56, 78, 104–105, 111, 147, 151, 218–219, 257
Plato 31, 252
Plutarch 252
politics/ political 1–5, 7–11, 15–16, 19–21, 25–28, 30, 33–34, 36, 49, 59–61, 63–64, 66, 68–70, 79, 82–85, 91–93, 99–104, 107, 111, 113–115, 118–120, 122, 124, 130, 133, 135–136, 139–142, 145, 155–156, 158, 160–165, 167–170, 172, 174–178, 191–193, 205–210, 212, 219–221, 231, 233–237, 239–240, 242–246, 248, 251–254, 257–258, 260–261
– political agency 28, 133
– politically correct/ political correctness 207–208
– political establishment 16, 155, 176
– politician 2–3, 16–17, 64, 70, 83, 156, 163, 165, 175–178, 237, 241
– politicization 9, 27–28, 103, 150 (see also biopolitics, the body politic, thanatopolitics and necropolitics)
posthumanism/ posthumanist 138
postmodernism 209, 262
potentiality/ potential/ *potentia* 1–2, 5–6, 8, 10, 12, 21, 28, 33, 35, 42–44, 50, 61, 68, 78, 84–85, 91, 98, 101, 103–104, 112, 118, 120–121, 127, 133, 135, 138–140, 142–146, 150, 159–160, 174–175, 188–190, 205, 217, 221, 230, 253
pragmatism 9
Precht, Richard David 85
prevention 51, 164–167, 206, 210, 225
progress/ progressive 5, 28, 37, 42, 49, 59, 63–65, 67, 70–72, 76–78, 81, 167, 184, 220
propaganda 4, 60, 77, 84, 208, 211, 214, 216, 220–221, 261
psychology/ psychological/ psychologist 2, 47, 51, 56, 65, 172, 175–177, 187, 217

quantification/ quantified 20, 75, 183–190, 192–194, 196, 200–201
– quantified self 183–193, 201
Qin Shi Huangdi 224–225

radical/ radicalism 2, 7–8, 27, 60, 69, 75, 80, 113–114, 122, 130, 139, 141–142, 158, 242–243
radicalization/ radicalize 12, 75, 159, 166
race/ racial 5, 7, 68–70, 111–112, 128, 135, 147, 157–158, 254, 259
racism 7, 158
Rankine, Claudia 251, 261–262
Rathenau, Walther 66
regulation 5, 11–12, 14–15, 17, 26, 63, 77, 79–80, 162, 171, 177, 184, 186, 188, 200, 231, 237
relationality/ relational 20, 28, 113, 133, 135, 139–142, 146, 148, 150–151
religion/ religious 8, 30–31, 50–52, 65, 68, 75, 91, 100–102, 106, 158
repressive 1, 83, 137, 207
resistance/ resist 14, 18, 21, 65, 86, 93–94, 133–139, 151, 156, 159, 169, 172, 174–175, 183, 186, 197, 199–201, 206, 213–214, 218, 225
responsibility/ responsible 10, 16–18, 32–33, 83, 85, 96, 105, 134, 137, 142, 170, 208, 210, 215, 248
restrictions 20, 112–113, 134, 155–156, 161, 176, 206, 208, 219, 225–226
revolution/ revolutionary 41, 67–69, 80, 94, 121, 137, 151, 172, 208–212, 219–220, 224, 238, 257
ritual 20, 37, 53, 91–93, 97, 101, 103–104, 106–107, 125, 139, 149, 198
Roberts, Morley 5
Rong Jian 210
Rousseau, Jean-Jacques 251–252
rule of law 26, 164–165, 169–171
Russell, Bertrand 67–68
Russia/ Russian 68, 71, 80, 147–148, 226, 266

sacred 92–93, 97–101, 104–106, 238
sacrifice/ sacrificed 8, 33, 91, 93, 97–103, 105–106, 150, 158–159, 241

safety/ safe 11, 32, 33, 41, 50, 76, 99, 111–112, 133, 148, 187, 233, 241
SARS-CoV-2 (see COVID-19) 92, 258
scapegoat/ scapegoating 33, 35, 105–106
Schmitt, Carl 8, 12, 159–160, 164, 254
Schwab, Klaus 84
science/ scientific 2–3, 5, 16, 18, 47, 48, 51, 54–55, 60, 63, 66–70, 72–74, 78, 82–84, 86, 91–102, 120–121, 173, 177–178, 186, 188, 206, 210, 219, 244
scientist 2–4, 16, 52, 63, 70, 74, 77, 79, 156, 177–178, 188
science fiction 120–121, 161
security 9, 13, 32, 76, 82, 86, 141, 155, 159, 164–165, 167, 171–173, 176–178, 187, 229, 234, 243
– biosecurity 28, 38–44
Sedgwick, Eve Kosofsky (see also Kosofsky, Eve) 133, 135
self-measurement 184–185, 188
self-monitoring 170
self-observation 185–186
Shaw, George Bernard 70
Shijing, the 226–230
Shteyngart, Gary 20, 133, 146–149
slave 30–31, 68, 79, 81, 114–117, 119–120, 129, 238, 257
slow violence 133, 143–144, 147, 151
Smith, Ali 145
socialism/ socialist 68, 71, 170, 209
social distance/ social distancing 25, 28, 35–38, 40, 42–44, 91–92, 94, 98–100, 103, 105–107, 151, 237, 242
social engineering/ social engineers 63, 67, 69, 73, 80, 84
Soderbergh, Steven 151
solidarity 1, 17, 33, 43, 82, 99, 102, 141, 159, 200
Sombart, Werner 65
Sontag, Susan 31
Sophocles 20, 25, 29, 30, 32–34, 37, 44, 105, 145
sovereignty, sovereign 5, 8, 14, 25–28, 30–40, 44–45, 74, 79, 124, 138, 141, 157, 164, 169, 187, 190, 214, 231, 343, 254, 256
Soviet Union, Soviet 4, 68, 71, 80, 82, 257
Spengler, Oswald 74

Spinoza 99, 138, 140
Stalin, Joseph 4, 69, 71, 257
stasis 30–32, 34, 42, 146–147
Stoicism/ Stoics 75, 96, 106
surveillance/ to surveil 1, 6, 9, 11–12, 14, 17, 40, 43, 112, 134, 155, 159–160, 162–164, 167, 170–171, 174, 183, 185, 187–194, 196–199, 201, 218
surveillance capitalism 9, 112, 134, 190, 192, 196–197, 199, 201

Taylor, F.W./ Taylorism 66, 69, 71, 84
technics/ technical 62, 67–68, 170, 175
technocracy/ technocratic 64, 66–67, 69–72, 80–84, 86, 143
technology/ technological 3, 5–6, 9–11, 15, 71, 73, 75, 83–84, 86, 134, 162, 174, 183–191, 198, 200–201
terror/ terrorism 8, 35, 41, 44, 60, 83, 99, 140–141, 155, 160–161, 164–166, 168–170, 172, 175, 197, 200, 207, 234
thanatopolitics 8, 27, 112–113, 123, 248
theology/ theological 50–52, 56, 104, 126, 234, 239
Third Reich 164
Thucydides 25, 29, 34–38, 40, 42, 44
totalitarianism/ totalitarian 3, 7, 9, 14–15, 26, 63, 75–76, 82–83, 149, 158–159, 162, 164, 168–170, 199–201, 210, 216, 231, 241, 245
tracking 10, 184–187, 189–193, 198, 200–201
– self-tracking 167, 183–186, 188, 190–191, 198, 201
transparency/ transparent 10, 134, 168, 186, 197, 200, 206, 209, 217, 220
transparent citizen, the 9, 160
trauma 77, 95, 196
Trotsky, Leon 70–71
Trump, Donald 11, 147

überveillance 188, 191
United Kingdom/ UK 10, 83, 85, 145–146, 148
United States / USA 4–5, 12, 15, 18, 20, 61, 64–65, 71, 81, 83, 91–92, 106, 111, 136, 146, 151, 164–165, 169, 257–258
utilitarianism/ utility 6, 9, 68, 75, 79, 190

utopia/ utopian 14, 38, 59, 61, 63–65, 67–68, 72–78, 85–86, 120, 155, 157

vaccination/ vaccinated/ vaccine 2–3, 14, 17, 51, 85, 92, 100, 103, 105, 112–113, 123–125, 130, 134, 151, 156, 161, 177–178, 233–234, 236–237, 242–243, 245
Vermes, Timur 13
violence/ violent (see also slow violence) 30–31, 93, 103–107, 116, 120, 133, 143, 145, 147, 150–151, 198, 228, 241, 255
Virchow, Rudolf 244
viral 13, 209, 211, 214, 219, 225
virus (see also coronavirus) 1–2, 10, 13, 16–17, 19, 49–50, 78, 91–92, 97–99, 101, 103, 105, 113, 122–130, 145–147, 151, 155–156, 160–161, 175–179, 188, 200, 210, 217, 219, 231, 236, 245
vulnerability 19–20, 133–135, 139–143, 145–146, 148, 150–151, 176, 205

Wang Hui 208, 210
war 1–3, 5, 18, 29–32, 34, 49, 50, 55, 61, 66–68, 70, 73, 79, 82, 85, 102, 141, 147, 160, 168–170, 205–210, 214, 217–220, 225–226, 229–231, 236, 245, 247, 257
Weber, Max 65, 76
Wells, H.G. 65, 68, 70, 72, 84
Western/ the West 1, 5, 7, 17–20, 25–26, 28, 30, 49, 60, 71, 74, 80, 82–83, 85–86, 99, 107, 113–116, 118–122, 126, 130, 156, 164, 168, 205, 207, 209–210, 213, 216, 219, 223–224, 252–253
Wodarg, Wolfgang 156, 178
Wright, Lawrence 151
Wuhan 207, 215–216, 218–219, 221–225, 230, 258

Xi Jinping 1, 205–207, 209–210, 225

Zamyatin, Yevgeny 66, 74, 80
Zeh, Juli 20, 84, 145, 155–157, 159–177, 179
Zeng Shaoli, cybername Lizilizilizi 222, 227–228
Žižek, Slavoj 15, 92
zoē (zoë/zoe/ zoé) 8, 26–27, 116, 158, 254–256
Zuboff, Shoshana 9, 190, 192, 199
Zuckerberg, Mark 10–12

www.ingramcontent.com/pod-product-compliance
Lightning Source LLC
Chambersburg PA
CBHW020224170426
43201CB00007B/310